MARKETING MISTAKES

SIXTH EDITION

MARKETING
MISTAKES

Robert F. Hartley
Cleveland State University

JOHN WILEY & SONS, INC.

New York • Chichester • Brisbane
Toronto • Singapore

ACQUISITIONS EDITOR Tim Kent
ASSISTANT EDITOR Ellen Ford
MARKETING MANAGER Debra Riegert
SENIOR PRODUCTION EDITOR Jeanine Furino
DESIGNER Ann Marie Renzi
MANUFACTURING MANAGER Susan Stetzer
ILLUSTRATION COORDINATOR Sandra Rigby
COVER DESIGN David Levy

This book was set in Palatino by V & M Graphics and printed and bound by Courier
Stoughton. The cover was printed by NEBC.

Recognizing the importance of preserving what has been written, it is a policy of John Wiley
& Sons, Inc. to have books of enduring value published in the United States printed on acid-
free paper, and we exert our best efforts to that end.

Library of Congress Cataloging in Publication Data

Hartley, Robert F., 1927–   Marketing mistakes / Robert F. Hartley.—6th ed.
        p.   cm.
    Includes bibliographical references.
    ISBN 0-471-00088-4 (pbk.)
    1. Marketing—United States—Case studies.   I. Title
    HF5415.1.H37   1992   94-33752
    658.8'00973—dc20   CIP

Printed in the United States of America

10 9 8 7 6 5 4 3 2 1

Preface

Once again, I would like to welcome back past users of *Marketing Mistakes.* I hope you will find this new edition and format, with its many new and very current cases, a worthwhile change from the earlier editions. It is always difficult to abandon interesting cases that have stimulated student discussions and provided interesting learning experiences, but newer case possibilities are ever competing for inclusion. Examples of good and bad handling of problems and opportunities are always emerging.

For new users, I hope the book will meet your full expectations and be an effective instructional tool. Although case books abound, you and your students may find this somewhat unique, very readable, and, hopefully, able to transform dry and rather remote concepts into practical reality.

NEW TO THIS EDITION

In contrast to four of the five previous editions, which examined only notable mistakes, I have also included a number of well-known successes. The hypothesis is that we can learn from mistakes, we can learn from successes, and we can learn by comparing the unsuccessful with the successful.

Additional cases, which I hope you will find particularly worthwhile, deal with the challenges but great satisfaction that can come from entrepreneurship.

Table 1   Classification of Cases by Major Marketing Topics

Topics	Most Relevant Cases
Marketing research and consumer analysis	Maytag, Euro Disney, Coca-Cola
Product	Perrier, Borden, Coca-Cola, Osborne, Chrysler, Harley, Microsoft, Southwest Airlines, Saturn, Dow Corning, Cigarettes
Distribution	Sears, Coca-Cola, Wal-Mart, OfficeMax
Promotion	Maytag, Coca-Cola,Chrysler, Harley, Southwest, Saturn, Wal-Mart, Parma P., Cigarettes

Price	IBM, Borden, Euro Disney, Osborne, Southwest, Wal-Mart, Southern Motel, OfficeMax
Total Marketing Strategy	Food Lion, IBM, Sears, Borden, Euro Disney, Adidas, Osborne, Chrysler, Harley, Microsoft, Southwest, Saturn, Wal-Mart, Parma P., Antiquarian Books, OfficeMax
International	Perrier, Maytag, Euro Disney, Harley
Non-Product/Profit	United Way, Euro Disney
Social and Ethical	Food Lion, United Way, Dow Corning, Cigarettes

A number of you have asked that I identify which cases would be most appropriate for the traditional coverage of marketing topics as organized in traditional marketing texts. With most cases it is not possible to truly compartmentalize the mistake or success strictly according to each topic. The patterns of success or failure tend to be more pervasive. Still, I think you will find the classification in Table 1 of cases by their major subject matter to be helpful. I thank those of you for this and other suggestions.

TARGETED COURSES

As a supplemental text, this book can be used in a great variety of courses, both undergraduate and graduate, ranging from principles of marketing to marketing management or strategic marketing. Even retailing, entrepreneurship, and ethics courses could well use a number of these cases and their learning insights.

TEACHING AIDS

As in the previous editions, this edition presents a number of teaching aids within and at the end of each chapter. Some of these will be common to several cases, to illustrate that certain successful and unsuccessful practices tend to cross company lines.

This edition includes more pedagogical features than previous editions did. Updated Information Boxes and Issue Boxes are included within every chapter to highlight relevant marketing concepts. Learning insights help students see how certain practices—both errors and successes—cross company lines and are prone to be either traps for the unwary or success modes. Discussion questions and role-playing exercises encourage and stimulate student involvement. Invitation to Research suggestions allow students to take the cases a step further, to learn what has happened since the case was written, thus keeping the book current and up to date. In the final chapter, the various learning insights are summarized and classified into general conclusions.

An Instructor's Manual accompanies this text to provide additional ideas for stimulating class discussion and role plays, as well as possible answers and considerations for the pedagogical material within and at the ends of chapters.

ACKNOWLEDGMENTS

A number of persons have provided encouragement, information, advice, and constructive criticism. I thank in particular Barbara Coe, University of North Texas; H. Lee Meadow, Northern Illinois; Gregory Gundlach, University of Notre Dame; Eldon Little, Indiana University; Allan Reddy, Valdosta State University; Neal Pruchansky, Keene State College; Donna Giertz, Parkland College; Richard Cooley, Cal State Chico; Don Johnson, Oregon State University; John Gottko, Hampston University; Ken Mayer, University of Nebraska; William Rice, Cal State Fresno.

Finally, I express my appreciation to Tim Kent, marketing editor at Wiley, and to Ellen Ford, assistant editor, for their kind assistance and support.

Contents

ix

CHAPTER 1

Introduction

For this sixth edition, 18 of the 22 cases are new from the fifth edition. Most of these are as recent as today's headlines. The older cases that are continued are classics, and we have brought them back by your expressed preferences.

We changed the format somewhat from the previous editions by adding some cases dealing with successful marketing efforts, including several turn-arounds, in which a firm changed its mistake into a success. Other additions are cases dealing with entrepreneurial adventures—the problems and successes of new enterprises.

We continue to seek what can be learned—from companies' experience—insights that are transferable to other firms, other times, and other situations. What key factors brought monumental failure to some firms and resounding successes for others? Through such evaluations and studies of contrasts, we may learn to improve the "batting average" in the intriguing, ever-challenging art of decision making.

We will encounter many examples of the phenomenon of organizational life cycles, in which an organization grows and prospers then fails (just as humans), but occasionally resurges. Success rarely lasts forever, but on the other hand even the most serious mistakes can be (but are not always) overcome.

A variety of firms, industries, problems, mistakes, and successes are presented. You will be familiar with most of the firms, although perhaps not with the details of their situations. Although most of the cases are very recent, a few go back several decades. For these older classics, the circumstances and lessons that can be learned are far from dated.

We chose these particular cases to bring out certain points or caveats in the art of decision making, as well as to give a balanced view of the spectrum of marketing problems. We sought to present examples that provide somewhat different learning experiences, such that at least some aspect of the mistake or success differs from the others described. Still, we see similar mistakes occurring time and again. The universality of some of these mistakes makes us wonder how much decision making has improved over the decades.

Let us then consider what learning insights we should gain, with the benefit of hindsight, from examining the mistakes and successes of well-known firms.

LEARNING INSIGHTS

Analyzing Mistakes

In looking at sick companies, or even healthy ones that have experienced failures of certain parts of their operations, the temptation is to be unduly critical. It is easy to criticize with the benefit of hindsight. Mistakes are inevitable, given the present state of the art of decision making and the dynamic environment facing the organization.

Mistakes can be categorized as errors of omission and errors of commission. *Mistakes of omission* are those in which managers take no action but instead contentedly embrace the status quo amid a changing environment. Such errors, which often characterize conservative or stodgy management, are less obvious than the other category of mistakes. They seldom involve tumultuous upheaval. Rather, the company's fortunes and competitive position slowly fade, until years later the managers suddenly realize that they have allowed mistakes of monumental impact to happen. The firm's fortunes rarely regain their former luster. Examples in the book of such mistakes include IBM, Harley Davidson, and Sears.

Mistakes of commission are more spectacular. They involve bad decisions, wrong actions, misspent or misdirected expansion, and the like. Although the costs of the erosion of competitive position coming from errors of omission are difficult to calculate precisely, the costs of errors of commission often are fully evident. The latest costs of the Maytag British subsidiary's ill-fated promotion, for example, have been calculated at $90 million, a hefty burden for a firm of $3 billion in sales.

Although they may suffer mistakes of omission or commission, organizations with alert and aggressive management are characterized by certain actions or reactions when probing their own mistakes or problem situations:

1. They quickly recognize looming problems or present mistakes.
2. They carefully determine the causes of the problem(s).

3. They evaluate alternative corrective actions in view of the organization's resources and constraints.
4. They promptly take corrective action. Sometimes this requires a ruthless axing of the product, the division, or whatever is at fault.
5. They learn from mistakes. They do not repeat the same mistakes, but instead improve their operations.

Management's slowness to recognize emerging problems leads us to think that management is lethargic and incompetent or that managers have not established controls to provide prompt feedback at strategic points. For example, a declining competitive position in one or a few geographical areas should be a red flag to management that something is amiss. To wait months before investigating or taking action may mean a permanent loss of business. Admittedly, signals sometimes get mixed, and information may not be as complete as desired, but procrastination cannot be easily defended.

Just as problems should be quickly recognized, the causes of these problems—the *why* of the unexpected results—must be determined as quickly as possible. It is premature to take action before knowing where the problems really lie. To go back to the previous example, the loss of competitive position in one or a few areas may occur because of circumstances beyond the firm's immediate control, such as the entrance of an aggressive new competitor who is drastically cutting prices to "buy sales." In such a situation, all the competing firms in that area will likely lose some market share, and companies can do little except to remain as competitive as possible with prices and servicing. However, closer investigation may disclose that the erosion of business is due to unreliable deliveries, poor quality control, or lost technological advantage. Or perhaps field personnel are not doing their job satisfactorily.

Once the cause of the problem is identified, managers should evaluate various alternatives for dealing with it and should choose corrective action as objectively and prudently as possible. This may require further research, such as obtaining feedback from customers or from field personnel. If drastic action is needed, managers should not delay: Serious problems do not go away by themselves; they tend to fester and become worse.

Finally, companies should learn from the misadventure. A vice president of one successful firm said

> I try to give my subordinates as much decision-making power as possible. Perhaps I err on the side of delegating too much. In any case, I expect some mistakes to be made, some decisions that were not for the best. I don't come down too hard usually. This is part of the learning experience. But God help them if they make the same mistake twice. There has been no learning experience, and I question their competence for higher executive positions.

Analyzing Successes and Turnarounds

Successes deserve as much analysis as mistakes, although admittedly the urgency is less than with an emerging problem that requires remedial action lest it spread. If we can uncover the magic ingredients to a success, then perhaps we may apply it to other situations.

Any analysis of success should seek answers to at least the following questions:

Why were such actions successful?

Was it due to the nature of the environment, and if so, how?

Was it due to marketing research, and if so, how?

Was it due to any particular element of the strategy—such as products or services, promotional activities, or distribution methods—and if so, how?

Was it due to the specific elements of the strategy meshing well together, and if so, how was this achieved?

Was the situation unique and unlikely to be encountered again?

If not, how can we use these successful techniques in the future or in other present operations?

ORGANIZATION OF BOOK

We have endeavored to classify the cases into the following categories: public image problems, marketing strategy mistakes, notable turnarounds, outstanding contemporary successes, entrepreneurial adventures, and ethical and social crises.

Mishandling the Public Image

Again, as in earlier editions, I have chosen to place public image miscues in the most prominent position. So many times I have found that students as well as executives gloss over the importance of an organization's public image or reputation. Yet, in studying mistakes and successes for almost three decades, I have become more and more convinced that the perception of an organization by its various publics plays a crucial role in success or failure.

Three very current cases graphically illustrate the pitfalls of a denigrated public image. Food Lion was devastated by national publicity from investigative TV reporters' reports of its food handling and labor practices. Although such practices as repackaging outdated food were unacceptable, they were not uncommon in this industry. But the media, egged on by a militant union, blew the short-sighted blunder far out of proportion. A growing company was brought to its knees.

United Way of America is a nonbusiness organization. The man who led it to prominence as the nation's largest charity came to perceive himself as virtually beyond authority. His exorbitant spending, favoritism, and conflicts of interest went uncriticized until investigative reporters for the *Washington Post* publicized the scandalous conduct. Amid the hue and cry, charitable contributions nationwide fell drastically.

Perrier, the bottled water firm, encountered adversity in the form of traces of benzene found in some of its product. Responsibly, it ordered a sweeping recall of all bottles in North America and a few days later in the rest of the world while the company sought to correct the problem. For 5 months the company kept the product off the market, thereby allowing competitors an unparalleled windfall. Worse was public recognition that the claims regarding the purity of its product were false.

Marketing Strategy Mistakes

The first case in this section concerns the behemoth IBM, the darling of investors for decades. By the early 1990s, IBM was on the ropes, reeling from a surprising lapse in ability to cope with a changed environment amid a spate of eager and hungry competitors.

Next we turn our attention to a major factor in retailing since before the turn of the century. For well over one-half a century, Sears had been the country's largest retailer, only recently supplanted by Wal-Mart and Kmart. Sears found itself in danger of losing much more than first place as it struggled to survive in a rapidly changing industry, harnessed as it was with bureaucratic bloat and outmoded policies.

Borden, with its enduring symbol, Elsie the Cow, is the country's largest producer of dairy products. In the 1980s through a host of acquisitions it became a diversified food processor and marketer, and a $7 billion company. But Borden allowed consumer acceptance of its many brands to deteriorate through unrealistic pricing and ineffective advertising.

The problems of Maytag's Hoover subsidiary in Great Britain almost defy reason and logic. The subsidiary, acting under very loose reins from corporate Maytag, planned a promotional campaign so generous that the company was overwhelmed with takers; it was unable either to supply the products or to grant the prizes. In a marketing miscue of multimillion-dollar consequences, Maytag had to foot the bill while trying to appease irate customers.

Just outside Paris, Disney opened its first theme park in Europe. It had high expectations and supreme self-confidence (critics would say this confidence bordered on arrogance). The earlier Disney parks in California,

Florida, and, more recently, Japan were all spectacular successes. But the rosy expectations soon became a delusion as a variety of marketing strategy miscues finally showed Disney that Europeans, and particularly the French, are not necessarily carbon copies of visitors elsewhere.

The miscalculations of Coca-Cola in changing the flavor of its traditional and major product shows flawed marketing decisions even with the use of extensive evaluation and research. Although the situation eventually worked out, embarrassed executives had to make a major improvization.

The rapidly growing world market for running shoes was long dominated by Adidas. Its strategy seemed unassailable. But somehow Nike, using essentially the same strategy and starting from scratch decades after Adidas had become well established, drove the old master to the sidelines.

In one of the most violent roller coaster rides in business history, the young computer firm Osborne saw its sales jump from nothing to $100 million in only 18 months, and then collapse even faster. While in the heady growth mode, the company wore blinders. In particular, Osborne failed to recognize that in a technologically dynamic industry, product uniqueness could be short lived indeed.

Notable Turnarounds

Unlike earlier editions, this edition includes two classic cases of firms' turning themselves around from monumental defeat, and even threatened viability, into great successes.

Chrysler's troubles in the late 1970s and early 1980s epitomized the dilemma facing many other U.S. firms, although the company's financial straits, brought on partly by poor management decisions in the past, made its position more precarious. Into the breach came Chrysler's great savior, Lee Iacocca. He saved the firm and gave it a growth mode. Unfortunately, Iacocca's success with Chrysler and his resulting fame diluted his concentration on the auto industry. By the late 1980s, Chrysler had lapsed into another looming disaster. An aging Iacocca once more charged to the scene to rescue his company.

Harley Davidson also turned itself around after disaster. In the early 1960s, Harley Davidson had dominated a static motorcycle industry. Suddenly Honda, a newcomer from overseas, burst onto the scene and vastly changed the industry. Harley Davidson's market share dropped from 70 percent to 5 percent in only a few years. Years of travail and mediocrity were ahead. But in the late 1980s, Harley made a comeback. It did not attempt to meet Honda and the other foreign cycle makers head on, but rather brought its traditional market for heavy motorcycles into popularity and even prestige. It succeeded in creating a mystique for its products.

Marketing Successes

The first case in this section describes the breakthrough of Microsoft with its software and its continuing innovation and aggressiveness. This spirit led it to far surpass once-mighty IBM in stock market valuation and profits. Bill Gates, its young founder, was by 1992 the richest man in America, with a net worth of over $7 billion. At that time he was 36 years old and still a bachelor.

Southwest Airlines found a strategic window of opportunity as the lowest cost and lowest price carrier between certain cities. And how it milked this opportunity! Now it is threatening major airlines in all their domestic routes.

General Motors' Saturn project may represent the new tomorrow in U.S. automaking, although this future is far from certain as we go to press. Relying on a motivated workforce, Saturn has been able to produce cars matching Japanese cars in quality, often priced lower, that feature trend-setting styling. Perhaps its greatest strength is a marketing and customer service strategy unmatched in the auto industry. But profits have mostly eluded it, and some union officials remain critical of the progressive labor-management relationship. GM management is still torn in allocating investment funds to Saturn versus the other divisions. But the promise is intriguing.

The last case in this section describes Sam Walton and his Wal-Mart empire, now the biggest retailer of all. The patterns of success are clearly evident here, and the story of one man's rise to the pinnacle in his chosen field in just a few decades is inspiring indeed. Despite his wealth and prestige, his was still the common touch.

Entrepreneurial Adventures

Part Five is a new section for this edition. We examine here small-business successes and failures. My surveys of students' career expectations today show an ever-increasing interest in entrepreneurship: for example, whereas 5 percent of students 20 years ago showed such an interest, 50 percent and more in some classes today express a strong desire for self-employment.

The first case in this section concerns a young woman who has a natural flair for public relations. She found investors for her Parma Pierogies Polish-style restaurant in a truly ingenious way. Even President Clinton was impressed, became a customer, and extolled her as an example of "Faces of Hope," Americans who have succeeded despite major obstacles.

The second case depicts two rather typical small businesses, neither very exciting nor on the threshhold of great growth. Can such small ventures successfully compete against their bigger, better endowed competitors? Surprisingly, the answer is a qualified yes. As we explore in the text, small firms often have unique advantages that larger firms cannot match. Yet they need marketing and financial expertise to be successful.

The third chapter in this section describes OfficeMax, a truly successful business that grew to $2.5 billion in sales in only a few years. The dedication and creative efforts of its founder can serve as a model for any would-be entrepreneur who aspires to make it big.

Disregard for Ethical and Social Pressures

In this last section we examine a firm and an industry that are confronting critical social scrutinies. The firm, Dow Corning, fell into its dilemma innocently enough. It did not realize the product safety problems of its silicone breast implants until late in the game. A controversy still simmers as to the desirability of such breast implants. But a host of litigation over allegedly leaking implants has caused most of the major firms, including Dow Corning, to leave the scene, scared by millions of dollars in lawsuits.

The tobacco industry is also under fire again. Its problems are intensifying, as are its critics, while its supporters on Capital Hill are fading away. Yet the tobacco industry continues to pursue its profit-maximizing strategy and to deny all harmful effects of smoking. Rather than assume a defensive stance, tobacco firms are continuing an aggressive stance. Is this wise?

GENERAL WRAP-UP

When possible, we have depicted the major people involved in these cases. Imagine yourself in their position, confronting the problems and decisions they faced at their points of crisis or just-recognized opportunities. What would you have done differently, and why? We invite you to participate in the discussion questions and role-playing episodes appearing at the ends of chapters, as well as in the discussion topics in the various boxes within chapters. We urge you to consider the pros and cons of alternative actions in your thoughts and discussions.

In so doing you may gain a feel for the challenges and excitement of decision making under conditions of uncertainty. You may even become better future executives and decision makers as a result.

QUESTIONS

1. Do you agree that it is impossible for a firm to avoid mistakes? Why or why not?
2. How can a firm speed up its awareness of emerging problems so that it can take responsive action? Be as specific as you can.

3. Large firms tend to err on the side of conservatism and are slower to take corrective action than smaller ones. Why do you suppose this is so?
4. Which do you think is likely to be more costly to a firm, errors of omission or errors of commission? Why?
5. So often we see the successful firm eventually losing its pattern of success. Why cannot success have more durability?

PART I

MISHANDLING THE PUBLIC IMAGE

CHAPTER 2

Food Lion: Bad Publicity Throttles Success

For 10 years, Food Lion, a regional supermarket giant, had seen its sales and profits steadily rise. It had a 10-year compounded growth rate of 22.5 percent. From 1983 to 1992 sales had risen from $1.172 billion to $7.196 billion. Net income had risen from $27.718 million to $178.005 million during this time. Such performance had made Food Lion the nation's fastest growing supermarket chain. Its customer appeal rested on everyday low prices.

On the night of November 5, 1992, however, an event occurred that was to seriously affect sales for the peak months of November and December and subdue the total 1992 figures. The impact of negative publicity was both immediate and profound. It was to sabotage the growth momentum of the company and test the mettle of Tom E. Smith, president and CEO.

NOVEMBER 5, 1992

On the evening of November 5, 1992, before a nationwide audience, the ABC television news program "Primetime Live" severely and graphically criticized Food Lion's sanitation and food-handling procedures in its meat and deli departments. ABC backed up the charges with hidden camera videotape of employees forced to cut corners on food safety and sanitation by the company's stringent demands for operational results. Spoiled and outdated food was shown being repackaged for sale to unsuspecting customers. Overnight, Food Lion's public image was devastated. See the following information box for a discussion of public image.

INFORMATION BOX

WHAT IS THE PUBLIC IMAGE?

The public image of an organization is its reputation, how it and its output (products, services, or both) are viewed by its various publics: customers, suppliers, employees, stockholders, financial institutions, the communities in which it dwells, and the various governments, both local and federal. And to these groups must be added the press, which is influenced by the subject's reputation and cannot always be relied upon to deliver objective and unbiased reporting.

Two other terms, *publicity* and *public relations,* are related to public image development. Publicity is communication about the firm, sometimes but not always initiated by the firm, which is disseminated by the media without charge and with little or no control by the firm. Public relations involves a broad set of planned communications about the company, including publicity releases designed to promote goodwill and a favorable image.

Publicity, then, is part of public relations when it is initiated by the firm. When it comes about through no planned efforts of the firm, it is often adverse and detrimental, as was the "Primetime Live" exposé. Such revealing of misdeeds, real or alleged, enhances audience appeal. Because public relations involves communications with stockholders, financial analysts, government officials, and other noncustomer groups, it is usually placed outside the marketing function, perhaps as a staff department or as the responsibility of an outside consultant who reports to top management.

What do you think is the effectiveness of advertising in enhancing the public image?

Immediately after the program aired, Tom Smith, Food Lion's president, called it "lies" and "fabrication." He blamed the United Food and Commercial Workers Union (UFCW) for originating the idea and working closely with ABC in developing the charges. The enmity of the union toward Food Lion was well known. The union had failed in its efforts to organize Food Lion employees and allegedly was committed to "economically damaging the company." As Smith charged in the company's annual report,

> By its own admission, the UFCW plans to continue its "corporate campaign," which is designed to eliminate the competitive pressure Food Lion has caused unionized chains because of their inefficiencies and additional costs. The stakes are high for the UFCW. It is our belief that the UFCW will go to great lengths to harass, pressure and cause trouble for the Company so that it can accomplish its stated objective of economically damaging the Company.[1]

[1] Tom E. Smith, "Letter to Shareholders," *Food Lion 1993 Annual Report,* 3.

LABOR DEPARTMENT PROBLEMS

The UFCW had been instrumental in initiating a 1991 Labor Department investigation, contending that Food Lion had saved $65 million each year by not paying employees' overtime. In its subsequent investigation, the U.S. Department of Labor charged the chain with both widespread overtime violations and child labor law violations. The charges were first aired in a Congressional hearing in September 1992.

In early August 1993, Food Lion agreed to pay a record $16.2 million to settle the charges, this being the largest settlement ever reached with a private employer over federal wage and hour violations. Tom Smith said the settlement allowed Food Lion to avoid spending "considerable resources and years in litigation," thus allowing the chain to "turn a page" and move forward. Food Lion admitted no wrongdoing in this agreement.[2]

The union was not pleased. Al Zack, assistant director for organizing, claimed the settlement fell far short of compensating workers for lost wages: "You still have the problem of . . . management physically and verbally abusing workers who ask for overtime. A supervisor will say, 'If you can't do your job, then I have 10 people out on the street who will.'"[3]

THE COMPANY

Food Lion operates a chain of retail food supermarkets in 14 states, principally in the southeast states. As of January 2, 1993, it operated 1,012 stores, with 353 located in North Carolina, 98 in South Carolina, 196 in Virginia, 69 in Tennessee, 50 in Georgia, 110 in Florida, 14 in Maryland, 6 in Delaware, 12 in Kentucky, 8 in West Virginia, 3 in Pennsylvania, 70 in Texas, 18 in Oklahoma, and 5 in Louisiana.

Ralph Ketner, together with his brother Brown Ketner and Wilson Smith, founded Food Lion in 1957. In 1967, when it had only seven stores, Food Lion lowered 3,000 items' prices. In an interview with the Salisbury, North Carolina *Post*, Ralph Ketner took credit for introducing everyday low pricing, forward buying, and centralized buying to the food industry.[4]

The company has grown vigorously. Table 2.1 shows the growth in sales for the 10 years from 1983 to 1993. Table 2.2 gives the growth in net income, and Table 2.3 shows the growth in number of stores opened during this period.

---

[2]Joanne Ramey, "Food Lion to Pay Record Labor Settlement Sum," *Supermarket News* (Aug. 9, 1993): 1.

[3]Ramey, "Food Lion to Pay Record Labor Settlement Sum," 2.

[4]"Disputes Prompt Ketner to Quit Food Lion Board," *Supermarket News* (May 3, 1993): 6.

Table 2.1   Food Lion's Sales Growth, 1983–1992

	Sales (000)	Percent Change
1983	$1,172,459	—
1984	1,469,564	25.3%
1985	1,865,632	30.0
1986	2,406,582	29.0
1987	2,953,807	22.7
1988	3,815,426	29.2
1989	4,717,066	23.6
1990	5,584,410	18.4
1991	6,438,507	15.3
1992	7,195,923	11.8

Source: Company public records.
Commentary: The company showed a strong growth pattern during these years, but the sales in later years were increasing at a decreasing rate. This, of course, reflects the difficulty of maintaining the same growth rate as a firm becomes larger.

CONSEQUENCES

In October 1992, before the "Primetime Live" broadcast, same-store sales were 1 percent higher than October 1991 sales. But for November, after broadcast, sales plummeted to 9.5 percent below the previous November's sales. Sales were slow in coming back, showing the lasting impact of the bad publicity: For the entire fourth quarter of 1992, same-store sales were down 4.6 percent compared with 1991 sales. They fell to a negative 6 percent below previous year's sales in the first quarter of 1993, climbed

Table 2.2   Food Lion's Net Income Growth, 1983–1992

	Net Income (000)	Percent Change
1983	$ 27,718	—
1984	37,305	34.6%
1985	47,585	27.6
1986	61,823	30.0
1987	85,802	38.8
1988	112,541	31.2
1989	139,775	24.2
1990	172,571	23.5
1991	205,171	18.9
1992	178,005	(13.2)

Source: Company public records.
Commentary: Note the decline in net income in 1992, reflecting the November 5 broadcast.

Table 2.3   Food Lion's Growth in Number of Stores, 1983–1992

	Number of Stores Opened	Total Number of Stores	Percentage Increase
1983	44	226	
1984	25	251	11.1%
1985	66	317	26.3
1986	71	388	22.4
1987	87	475	22.4
1988	92	567	19.4
1989	96	663	16.9
1990	115	778	17.3
1991	103	881	13.2
1992	131	1,012	14.9

Source: Company public records.

to a negative 4.8 percent in the second quarter, and moved up to a negative 4 percent by the third quarter. Earnings for the first three quarters of 1993 fell 48.7 percent, although overall sales rose 5.8 percent owing to new store openings. Food Lion's stock slipped from $18 to $6 per share between early 1992 and early 1994. Experts were quick to cast a pall over the company:

> "Food Lion won't ever go back to being the kind of growth company it once was. Like an automobile that goes in for an overhaul, it will never be the same again."

> "The company suffered a mass exodus of customers at the end of 1992, and it's working to rebuild things gradually. But there's been a permanent crack in Food Lion's fundamentals."

> "Food Lion customers have always been very loyal, but maybe some of them tried an alternative and in some cases didn't come back."[5]

The consequences of the damaged public image of Food Lion thus were more enduring than might have been expected. Part of the reason for this may have been the union. The UFCW continued its unrelenting efforts to undermine nonunion Food Lion. It refused to let the "PrimeTime Live" story die: Food Lion officials claimed it mailed more than a million brochures to consumers to remind them of the exposé.[6] And early in 1994, a labor-backed consumer coalition, of which the UFCW was a member, accused Food Lion of repeatedly selling outdated infant formula in violation of state and federal

[5] Elliot Zwiebach, "Food Lion Struggles Back," *Supermarket News* (Nov. 8, 1993).
[6] James Ketelsen, "Lionized No More," *Forbes* (January 17, 1994): 16.

regulations. The group presented its findings to the Food and Drug Administration, which planned an investigation.[7]

See the following box for a general discussion of the importance of the public image.

Food Lion reluctantly found it prudent to tone down its expansion plans. In mid-1991, before the broadcast, the company, in its role of America's fastest growing supermarket chain, had planned to open 145 to 150 stores in 1993 and as many as 165 in 1994. It continued some of its expansion after the crisis, primarily because of real estate commitments made prior to the broadcast, but the company now expected to open only about 100 new stores in 1993 and possibly 40 to 50 in 1994.[8] It was going ahead with plans to complete 60 to 70 renovations in 1994 as a partial substitute for new store openings.

In May 1993 Ralph W. Keener, one of the founders of Food Lion, resigned from the company's board. In an interview with the Salisbury, North Carolina, *Post*, Ketner said he was "in disagreement with too many decisions of the management and board." In particular, he disagreed with the company's reaction to the "PrimeTime" broadcast. In addition, he cited his disagreement with management's growth philosophy. He thought Food Lion should have "enlarged the circle" of existing stores rather than jumping over several states to expand, as the chain did in moving into Texas.[9]

DEFENSE OF FOOD LION

The company bitterly condemned the actions of ABC's "PrimeTime Live" in its attack. It filed a lawsuit charging that ABC had illegally entered Food Lion facilities and had broadcast a knowingly biased report using unreliable sources. Food Lion vice president Vince Watkins claimed ABC had chosen not to use evidence it had gathered disproving some of its allegations regarding the meat-handling practices and employee management. The company was able to obtain the complete unedited videotape, which had been taken surreptitiously by ABC's undercover reporters during the investigation. "If you look at all the raw videotape, ABC could very well have put together a show showing what a fine company Food Lion is," said Watkins.[10]

Watkins also objected that Food Lion was the only company investigated, maintaining that a more thorough look at food safety in supermarkets

[7]Frank Swoboda, "Food Lion Accused of Selling Outdated Infant Formula," *Wall Street Journal* (Feb 4, 1994): B5.

[8]Mark Tosh, "Expansion Plans Cut Back by Food Lion," *Supermarket News* (Aug. 9, 1993): 34.

[9]Reported in "Disputes Prompt Ketner to Quit Food Lion Board," *Supermarket News* (May 3, 1993): 6.

[10]Michael Garry, "The Lion Talks," *Progressive Grocer* (June 1993): 19.

INFORMATION BOX

IMPORTANCE OF THE PUBLIC IMAGE

A firm's public image plays a vital role in the attractiveness of the firm and its products. In some situations it is impossible to satisfy all the diverse publics: for example, a new, highly automated plant may meet the approval of creditors and stockholders, but it will undoubtedly find resistance from employees who see jobs threatened. On the other hand, high-quality products and service standards should bring almost complete approval and pride of association—given that operating costs are competitive—while shoddy products and false claims would be widely decried.

A firm's public image, if it is good, should be cherished and protected. It is a valuable asset built up from a long and satisfying relationship with the various publics. If a firm has developed a quality image, this image is not easily countered or imitated by competitors. Such an image may enable a firm to charge higher prices, to woo the best distributors and dealers, to attract the best employees, and to expect the most favorable creditor relationships and the lowest borrowing costs. It should enable a firm's stock to command a higher price-to-earnings ratio than other firms in the same industry that lack such a good reputation and public image. All these factors can give a competitive advantage.

Of course, as we see from the Food Lion example, a bad image hurts a firm with all the different publics with which it deals. All can turn critical and even litigious, depending on the source and extent of the bad image. At best, present and potential customers may simply seek alternative sources for goods and services and switch to competitors' products whenever possible.

How long would you estimate it normally should take for a damaged public image, such as Food Lion's, to be forgotten by the interested publics? What factors might influence this length of time?

---

would have included other companies. The company adamantly maintained a major union connection in the ABC exposé:

> We believe that UFCW officials approached ABC to do a show on Food Lion, supplied ABC with the names of disgruntled former and current employees of the Company to assist in creating a story, provided ABC's undercover reporters with phony references in order to gain employment with the Company, and even provided training to the undercover reporters. "PrimeTime Live" chose to ignore independent evidence, such as state health inspection reports and, instead, chose to rely upon the information and assistance of the UFCW—an organization with the stated purpose of economically damaging the Company.[11]

---

[11]The President's Message to Stockholders," *Food Lion 1993 Annual Report*, 3.

RECOVERY EFFORTS

The damage to the public image of Food Lion as evidenced by the diminished sales of existing stores naturally was of great concern to company executives, who sought to counter the damage and bolster the image. In the days following the broadcast, Food Lion gave store tours to shoppers, media, and members of Congress. In a rather unique attempt to allay customer concerns, it put windows in new stores so that shoppers could see inside the meat-cutting room; in renovated stores, it installed glass doors. The company changed its policy regarding the sale of meat after its expiration date. In the past, if the meat was still good, it remained on sale for one day at a reduced price. The new policy mandated that nothing could be sold after the expiration date, at any price. And management made a major commitment to clean and renovate all the stores, improve lighting, and buy new uniforms for employees.

In perhaps the most significant action, Food Lion hired Webb Technical Group of Raleigh, North Carolina, as consultants to thoroughly investigate Food Lion products and implement a quality control program. "We're going to inspect at every point, including when we get [products] from the manufacturer. We could have done a better job in the past, when it was inspected at random."[12]

The company also aired TV commercials emphasizing its efforts to improve quality control and citing the hiring of outside consultants to ensure quality. In a major departure from its strict everyday-low-pricing policy, it began offering hot promotional specials and double coupons in some markets. These efforts, in addition to the legal efforts, were, not surprisingly, a drain on profits as Food Lion committed time, money, and resources to counteract the accusations. Some analysts saw such efforts as mere window dressing, creating an illusion of better service, but others saw these as positive steps.

The United Food and Commercial Workers Union was quick to criticize Food Lion efforts: "Consumer wariness about Food Lion's denials prompted the hiring of consultants to fix a problem Food Lion said didn't exist. Shoppers shouldn't have to accept conclusions about nonexistent problems made by handpicked, paid consultants who now appear in Food Lion's paid television ads." It called for Food Lion to submit the findings of a 100-store safety survey of the Webb consultants to an independent panel of public health experts: "A review by public health experts, whose credentials and credibility speak louder than any commercial, would assure the public that this is not another public relations gimmick."[13]

---

[12] As reported in "Food Lion Hires Consulting Firm," *Supermarket News* (Oct. 18, 1993): 16.
[13] "Independent Experts Should Review Safety Survey Conducted by Food Lion's Consultants, UFCW Says," *PR Newswire* (Nov. 4, 1993): 1104.

Other Problems

Not all of Food Lion's problems could be attributed directly to the TV exposé or to UFCW machinations. Some of the company's expansion efforts had been less than noteworthy. The stores in Texas and, to a lesser degree, Florida remained significant problem areas. Although the Food Lion marketing strategy had been strong in the southeast, customers were not so quick to embrace low prices and minimum amenities elsewhere. In its marginal markets of Texas and Florida, the impact of the TV report may have been greater because the company had not been able to build up a loyal customer base. Winn-Dixie in particular posed a strong challenge. It offered prices similar to Food Lion's, but in addition it had newer, larger stores with more service departments and other amenities. With the handicap of a wounded public image and the presence of a strong and aggressive competitor in some markets, the wavering comeback of Food Lion was perhaps not surprising.

ANALYSIS

We have in this case a dilemma of sorts. Who should carry the burden of blame: Food Lion, ABC and "PrimeTime Live," the union? Was Food Lion truly guilty of the charges of blatantly and unethically cutting corners on food safety and sanitation as well as abusive employment practices? Or was it the innocent victim of a vengeful union and a TV network interested only in sensationalizing alleged wrongdoings with no desire to uncover facts that might not match the charges? Most likely, all three parties were culpable. Whether Food Lion's guilt was related to carelessness or deliberate company policy may never be fully known. Perhaps Food Lion's fault was one of corporate insistence on profit goals that in turn led to less-than-desirable conduct by some employees.

What we do know is that an attack on a firm's reputation or public image is not to be taken lightly. It can have immediate repercussions on sales and profitability. It can waylay a growth trend of years. And the damage to the public image may be enduring. Especially is this likely when aggressive competitors are given the opportunity to gain market share they could not easily have gained otherwise; this loss of market share may never be recovered.

Could Food Lion have done a better job of trying to recover its reputation? Perhaps. The founder of the company and chairman emeritus, Ralph Ketner, apparently thought more could have been done and resigned from the board in disagreement. Yet the company seemed aggressive in trying to recover and to assure consumers that problems were not widespread and that strong efforts were being made to ensure no further repetition. These efforts, however, produced no immediate positive results. The following box shows the various factors that contribute to the public image mix, as well as the outputs or consequences of such a public image.

INFORMATION BOX

THE PUBLIC IMAGE MIX

Figure 2.1 shows the major inputs in creating an image, as well as the outputs or consequences of the resulting image on the various publics. Notice that some of the factors are both inputs and outputs—employees, for example. Employees can help foster a negative or a positive image, but they are also affected by their firm's image, with better employees attracted only to the firm with a good reputation. And price can be both an input and an output, in the sense that a favorable image may enable a firm to charge higher prices than a less regarded competitor, one without the reputation for quality and service.

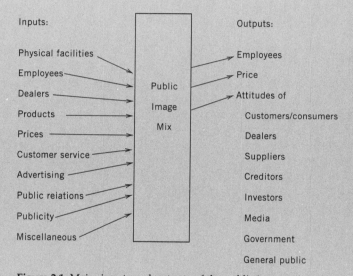

Figure 2.1. Major inputs and outputs of the public image mix.

The very negative publicity of "PrimeTime Live" of course also involved products and employees and raised concerns about health. Perhaps more damaging was the raising of doubts about the company as a responsible citizen. Could the company be trusted not to shortchange its publics in other ways? Was Food Lion's primary motivation to "[take] the bottom line as [its] guiding beacon and the low road as [its] route"?[14]

You can see that most of the inputs or factors that affect the public image are controllable to a considerable extent. A firm can determine its facilities, products,

---

[14]This is a quote of a federal judge concerning another firm and another product, the Dalkon Shield: Miles W. Lord, "A Plea for Corporate Conscience," as reprinted in *Harpers* (June 1984): 13–14.

advertising, customer service, and prices relative to competing products and can develop public relation and publicity efforts to favorably affect the image. But the firm can hardly escape blame for poor customer service, poor quality control, or the bad publicity about product safety or pollution or employee abuses. In such serious matters, public relations efforts may do little to salvage the image.

Given the bad publicity about Food Lion, do you think any public relations efforts could have erased the problem? Why or why not?

Perhaps the company was guilty of overemphasizing its growth commitment. Increasing the number of stores—adding close to 10 percent every year—dilutes top management attention from existing stores and operations; most attention has to be devoted to the planning and establishment of the new stores.

We have to wonder at the extreme adversarial position of the union. Its attempts at unionizing Food Lion failed, but such animosity seems extreme. Maybe Food Lion could have handled the situation more diplomatically, possibly more fairly, and not incurred such enmity, which was to come back to haunt the company.

WHAT CAN BE LEARNED?

The Food Lion experience should be sobering for many firms. It should raise some real concerns about the possibility of damage to the public image, damage that can be difficult to rebuild. Specifically, these are major points to be learned from this experience:

The vulnerability of the public image. A reputable image, or at least one that is neutral and not negative, can be quickly besmirched. A firm should not underestimate the danger of a looseness in the operation and a willingness to tread the thin line between scrupulously honest dealings and something less so. It must be wary of sacrificing a good reputation as it walks the edge in the quest for more profits. Once the public image has been denigrated, it is not easily or quickly recovered.

The power of a hostile media. In its quest for newsworthy items, the media—print, broadcast or both—is quick to pounce on alleged instances of misdeeds, especially by well-known organizations. No firm can anticipate that the media will be objective and unbiased in its reporting. Rather, the media tends to be eager to find a "fault object," and when this is a large and rather impersonal target, a firm, the media will likely emphasize the negatives of a particular situation far more than any positive side of the issue. And, as Food Lion found, the media may even ignore information supportive of the firm in seeking sensational and inflammatory news.

The longevity of a besmirched reputation. One would think that negative publicity would soon be forgotten in an environment in which critical disclosures are more the rule than the exception. Perhaps this may be the case in many scenarios. But when another party—in the case of Food Lion, a militant and unforgiving union denied acceptance by the company's employees—continually seeks to keep the allegations of misdeeds in the limelight, disclosure of misdeeds may not be allowed to sleep.

Public relations deficiencies. Public relations is not the answer when certain aspects of a firm's operation are the focal point of criticism. The act must be cleaned up first, but even then, public relations efforts may be negatively labeled as mere "posturing." Tom Smith tried to correct the situation and introduce highly visible measures to ensure compliance with highly ethical standards, but the critics were not appeased.

The power of a militant and hostile union. The UFCW union played a major role in initiating the bad publicity and in maintaining it. A hostile union allied with an eager media is a dangerous combination for any organization. It is easy for an organization to say that it will never leave itself vulnerable to critical public scrutiny; but probers intent on uncovering misconduct may still find something to trumpet. It is better to avoid severe confrontations with any group—be it unions, environmentalists, social activists, or another group—by either bowing to some of the demands or seeking a compromise solution.

The potential of marketing efforts to affect the public image. Marketing inputs have the greatest potential for affecting the public image, positively or negatively. A firm's marketing efforts are the most visible aspects of the operation. This visibility can be a curse sometimes, as it was with Food Lion, when marketing efforts regarding product quality and packaging were compromised in some instances in the quest for higher profits. The caveat is to consider marketing efforts part of the public image mix, one of the aspects of the operation most vulnerable to critical scrutiny, and to be guided accordingly.

CONSIDER

Do you see any other learning insights coming from this case?

QUESTIONS

1. "Good customer service doesn't do you much good, but poor customer service can kill you." Evaluate this statement.
2. Can a firm guarantee complete product safety and sanitation?

3. Give some specific examples of how a firm's public image both affects and is affected by the other components of the marketing mix (i.e., products, price, promotion, and place).
4. Discuss the pros and cons of placing the public relations function under the control of the marketing department.
5. Do you think Food Lion was unfairly picked on? Why or why not?
6. Given the exceedingly adversarial stance of the UFCW, would you recommend that Food Lion's top managers try to do anything to lessen it? If so, what? How successful do you think such efforts would likely be?
7. How could the public relations efforts of Food Lion have been used more effectively?

INVITATION TO ROLE PLAY

1. Several years have gone by since the negative "PrimeTime Live" broadcast, and same-store sales have still not achieved their pre-broadcast levels. CEO Tom Smith has asked you to design a program to restore the public image. What specifics can you suggest? How successful do you think such remedial efforts could be?
2. Sales and profits of the 70 stores in Texas are still far below expectations and are a drain on the rest of the company. The board has asked you for your recommendations about the Texas situation. Present your recommendations as persuasively as you can. (If you need to make some assumptions, keep them reasonable and specific.)

INVITATION TO RESEARCH

What is Food Lion's current situation? Has it been able to resume its growth pattern in sales and profits? Has it still been able to escape unionization? Has its lawsuit with ABC been settled yet?

CHAPTER 3

United Way:
A Not-for-Profit
Destroys Its Image:
And Girl Scout Doubts

The United Way, the preeminent charitable organization in the United States, celebrated its 100-year anniversary in 1987. It had evolved from local community chests, and its strategy for fund raising had proven highly effective: funding local charities through payroll deductions. The good it did seemed unassailable.

Abruptly in 1992, the image that United Way had created was jolted by revelations from investigative reporters of free-spending and other questionable deeds of its greatest builder and president, William Aramony. A major point of public concern was Aramony's salary and uncontrolled perks in a lifestyle that seemed inappropriate for the head of a charitable organization that depended mostly on contributions from working people.

In 1993 another paragon of not-for-profit social enhancement organizations came under fire: the venerable Girl Scouts. Multimillion-dollar profits from the marketing of Girl Scout cookies were found to be used mostly to support a sprawling bureaucracy instead of the Girl Scout troops that provided the labor in the first place.

We are left to question the callousness and lack of concern with the public image of such major charitable and not-for-profit entities. After all, unlike business firms that offer products or services to potential customers, charitable organizations depend on contributions that people give freely out of a desire to help society, with no tangible personal benefits. An image of high integrity and honest dealings without any semblance of corruption or privilege would seem essential for such organizations.

THE STATURE AND ACCOMPLISHMENTS OF THE UNITED WAY

For its 100-year anniversary, then President Ronald Reagan summed up what the United Way stood for:

December 10, 1986

United Way Centennial, 1887–1987
By The President Of The United States Of America
A Proclamation

Since earliest times, we Americans have joined together to help each other and to strengthen our communities. Our deep-roots spirit of caring, of neighbor helping neighbor, has become an American trademark—and an American way of life. Over the Years, our generous and inventive people have created an ingenious network of voluntary organizations to help give help where help is needed.

United Way gives that help very well indeed, and truly exemplifies our spirit of voluntarism. United Way has been a helping force in America right from the first community-wide fund raising campaign in Denver, Colorado, in 1887. Today, more than 2,200 local United Ways across the land raise funds for more than 37,000 voluntary groups that assist millions of people.

The United Way of caring allows volunteers from all walks of life to effectively meet critical needs and solve community problems. At the centennial of the founding of this indispensable voluntary group, it is most fitting that we Americans recognize and commend all the good United Way has done and continues to do.

The congress, by Public Law 99-612, has expressed gratitude to United Way, congratulated it, and applauded and encouraged its fine work and its goals.

NOW, THEREFORE, I, RONALD REAGAN, President of the United States of America, by virtue of the authority vested in me by the Constitution and laws of the United States, do hereby proclaim heartfelt thanks to a century of Americans who have shaped and supported United Way, and encourage the continuation of its efforts.

IN WITNESS WHEREOF, I have hereunto set my hand this tenth day of December, in the year of our lord nineteen hundred and eighty-six, and of the independence of the United States of America the two hundred and eleventh.

Ronald Reagan

135057

Organizing the United Way as the umbrella charity to fund other local charities through payroll deductions established a most effective means of fundraising. As a not-for-profit marketer, the United Way became the recipient of 90 percent of all charitable donations. Employers sometimes used extreme pressure to achieve 100 percent participation of employees, which qualified companies for organizational bonuses. Business organizations achieved further cooperation by involving their executives as leaders of annual campaigns, amid widespread publicity. It would consequently cause such an executive acute loss of face if his or her own organization did not go "over the top" in meeting campaign goals. A local United Way executive admitted that "if participation is 100 percent, it means someone has been coerced."[1]

For many years, except for some tight-lipped gripes of corporate employees, the organization moved smoothly along, generally increasing local contributions every year, although the needs for charitable contributions invariably increased all the more.

The national organization, United Way of America (UWA), is a separate corporation and has no direct control over the approximately 2100 local United Ways. But most of the locals voluntarily contributed 1 cent on the dollar of all funds they collected. In return the national organization provided training and promoted local United Way agencies through advertising and other marketing efforts.

Much of the success of the United Way movement in becoming the largest and most respected charity in the United States was due to the 22 years of William Aramony's leadership of the national organization. When he first took over, the United Ways were not operating under a common name. He built a nationwide network of agencies, all operating under the same name and all using the same logo of outstretched hands, which became nationally recognized as the symbol of charitable giving. Unfortunately, in 1992 an expose of Aramony's lavish lifestyle, as well as other questionable dealings, led to his downfall and burdened local United Ways with serious difficulties in fundraising.

WILLIAM ARAMONY

During Aramony's tenure, United Way contributions increased from $787 million in 1970 to $3 billion in 1990. He increased his headquarters budget from less than $3 million to $29 million in 1991. Of this, $24 million came

---

[1]Susan Garland, "Keeping a Sharper Eye on Those Who Pass the Hat," *Business Week* (March 16, 1992): 39.

from the local United Ways, with the rest coming from corporate grants, investment income, and consulting.[2] He built up the headquarters staff to 275 employees. Figure 3.1 shows the organizational chart as of 1987.

Aramony moved comfortably among the most influential people in our society. He attracted a prestigious board of governors, many of these top executives from America's largest corporations, with only 3 of the 37 from not-for-profit organizations. The board was chaired by John Akers, chairman and CEO of IBM. Other board members included Edward A. Brennan, CEO of Sears, James D. Robinson III, CEO of American Express, and Paul J. Tagliabue, commissioner of the National Football League. The presence on the board of such top executives brought prestige to United Way and spurred contributions from the some of the largest and most visible organizations in the United States.

Aramony was the highest paid executive in the charity field. In 1992 his compensation package was $463,000—nearly double that of the next highest paid executive in the industry, Dudley H. Hafner of the American Heart Association.[3] The board fully supported Aramony, regularly giving him 6 percent annual raises.[4]

Investigative Disclosures.

The *Washington Post* began investigating Aramony's tenure as president of United Way of America in 1991, raising questions about his high salary, travel habits, possible cronyism, and dubious relations with five spinoff companies. In February 1992 it released the following information of Aramony's expense charges:[5]

- Aramony had charged $92,265 in limousine expenses to the charity during the previous five years.
- He had charged $40,762 on airfare for the supersonic Concorde.
- He had charged more than $72,000 on international airfare, which included first class flights for himself, his wife and others.
- He had charged thousands more for personal trips, gifts, and luxuries.

---

[2]Charles E. Shepard, "Perks, Privileges and Power in a Nonprofit World," *The Washington Post* (February 16, 1992): A38.

[3]Shepard, *Perks, Privileges, and Power,* A38; and Charles E. Shepard, "United Way of America President is Urged to Resign," *The Washington Post* (February 27, 1992): Al.

[4]Joseph Finder, "Charity Case," *The New Republic* (May 4, 1992): 11.

[5]Shepard, *Perks, Privileges and Power;* Shepard, *Urged to Resign;* Kathleen Teltsch, "United Way Awaits Inquiry on its President's Practices," *New York Times* (February 24, 1992): A12 (L); Charles E. Shepard, "United Way Report Criticizes Ex-Leader's Lavish Lifestyle," *The Washington Post* (April 4, 1992): Al.

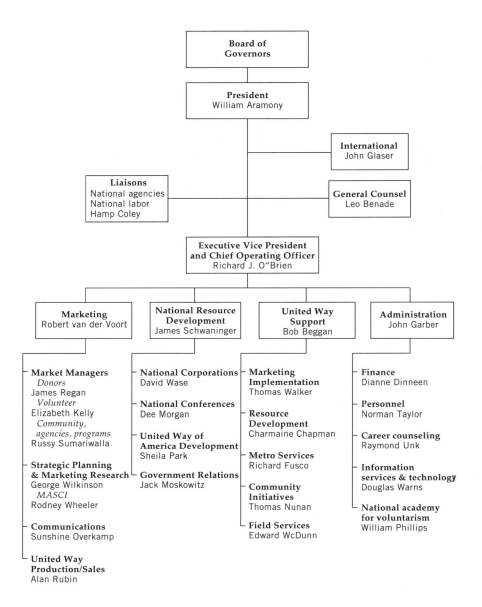

Figure 3.1. Organizational chart, United Way of America, 1987.
Source: E.L. Brilliant, "Appendix B" *United Way: Dilemmas of Organized Charity* (New York: Columbia University Press, 1990, 272).

- He had made 29 trips to Las Vegas between 1988 and 1991.
- He had expensed 49 journeys to Gainesville, Florida, the home of his daughter and a woman with whom he had had a relationship.
- He had allegedly approved a $2 million loan to a firm run by his chief financial officer.
- He had approved the diversion of donors' money to questionable spin-off organizations run by long-time aides and had provided benefits to family members as well.
- He had passed tens of thousands of dollars in consulting contracts from the UWA to friends and associates.

United Way of America's corporate policy prohibited the hiring of family members within the actual organization, but Aramony skirted the direct violation by hiring friends and relatives as consultants and within the spin-off companies. The United Way paid hundreds of thousands of dollars in consulting fees, for example, to two aides in vaguely documented and even undocumented business transactions.

The use of spin-off companies provided flexible maneuvering. One of the spin-off companies Aramony created to provide travel and bulk purchasing for United Way chapters purchased a $430,000 condominium in Manhattan and a $125,000 apartment in Coral Gables, Florida, for use by Aramony. Another of the spin-off companies hired Aramony's son, Robert Aramony, as its president. Loans and money transfers between the spin-off companies and the national organization raised questions. No records showed that the board members had been given the opportunity to approve such loans and transfers.[6]

CONSEQUENCES

When the information about Aramony's salary and expenses became public, reaction was severe. Stanley C. Gault, CEO of Goodyear Tire & Rubber Co., asked "Where was the board? The outside auditors?"[7] Robert O. Bothwell, executive director of the National Committee for Responsive Philanthropy, said, "I think it is obscene that he is making that kind of salary and asking people who are making $10,000 a year to give 5 percent of their income."[8] At this point, let us examine the issue of executive compensation: Are many executives overpaid? See the following issue box.

---

[6] Shepard, *Perks, Privileges and Power;* A38.
[7] Susan Garland, "Keeping a Sharper Eye," 39.
[8] Felicity Barringer, "United Way Head Is Forced Out In a Furor Over His Lavish Style," *New York Times* (February 28, 1992): A1.

ISSUE BOX

EXECUTIVE COMPENSATION: IS IT TOO MUCH?

A controversy is mounting over multimillion-dollar annual compensations of corporate executives. For example, in 1992 the average annual pay of CEOs was $3,842,247; the 20 highest paid ranged from over $11 million to a mind-boggling $127 million (for Thomas F. Frist, Jr., of Hospital Corporation of America).[9]

Activist shareholders, including some large mutual and pension funds, began protesting pay practices, especially for top executives of those firms that were not even doing well. New disclosure rules imposed in 1993 by the Securities & Exchange Commission (SEC) spotlighted questionable executive-pay practices. In the past complacent boards, themselves well paid and often closely aligned with the top executives of the organization, condoned liberal compensations. Now this may be changing. Still, the major argument supporting high executive compensations is that compared to some entertainers' and athletes' salaries they are modest. And are not their responsibilities far greater than those of any entertainer or athlete?

In light of the for-profit executive compensations, Aramony's salary was modest. And results were on his side: He made $369,000 in basic salary while raising $3 billion; Lee Iacocca, on the other hand, made $3 million while Chrysler lost $795 million. Where is the justice?

Undoubtedly as head of a large for-profit corporation Aramony could have earned several zeros more in compensation and perks, with no raised eyebrows. But is the situation different for a not-for-profit organization? Especially when revenues are derived from donations of millions of people of modest means? This is a real controversy. On one side, shouldn't a charity be willing to pay for the professional competence to run the organization as effectively as possible? But how do revelations of high compensation affect the public image and fund-raising marketing of such not-for-profit organizations?

What is your position regarding Aramony's compensation and perks, relative to the many times greater compensations of for-profit executives?

As a major consequence of the scandal, some United Way locals withheld their funds, at least pending a thorough investigation of the allegations. John Akers, chairman of the board, noted that by March 7, 1992, dues payments were running 20 percent behind those of the previous year, and he admitted, "I don't think this process that the United Way of America is going through, or Mr. Aramony is going through, is a process that's bestowing a lot of honor."[10]

In addition to the decrease in dues payments, UWA was in danger of having its not-for-profit status revoked by the Internal Revenue Service due to the relationship of loans made to the spin-off companies. For example, it

---

[9]John A. Byrne, "Executive Pay: The Party Ain't Over Yet," *Business Week* (April 26, 1993): 56–64.

[10]Felicity Barringer, "United Way Head Tries to Restore Trust," *New York Times* (March 7, 1992): 8L.

loaned $2 million to a spin-off corporation of which UWA's chief financial officer was a director—a violation of not-for-profit corporate law. UWA also guaranteed a bank loan taken out by one of the spin-offs, another violation of not-for-profit corporate law.[11]

The adverse publicity benefitted competing charities, such as Earth Share, an environmental group. United Way, at one time the only major organization to receive contributions through payroll deductions, now found itself losing market share to other charities able to garner contributions in the same manner. All the building that William Aramony had done for the United Way as the primary player in the American charitable industry was now in danger of disintegration owing to his uncontrolled excesses.

On February 28, amid mounting pressure from local chapters threatening to withhold their annual dues, Aramony resigned. In August 1992 the United Way board of directors hired Elaine Chao, Peace Corps director, to replace Aramony.

ELAINE CHAO

Chao's story is one of great achievement for one only 39 years old. She is the oldest of six daughters in a family that came to California from Taiwan when Elaine was 8 years old. She did not then know a word of English. Through hard work, the family prospered. "Despite the difficulties . . . we had tremendous optimism in the basic goodness of this country, that people are decent here, that we would be given a fair opportunity to demonstrate our abilities," she told an interviewer.[12] Chao's parents instilled in their six daughters the conviction that they could do anything they set their minds to, and the daughters all went to prestigious universities.

Elaine Chao earned an economics degree from Mount Holyoke in 1975, then went on for a Harvard MBA. She was a White House fellow, an international banker, chair of the Federal Maritime Commission, deputy secretary of the U.S. Transportation Department, and director of the Peace Corps before accepting the presidency of the United Way of America.

Chao's salary was $195,000, less than one-half that of Aramony. She cut budgets and staffs: no transatlantic flights on the Concorde, no limousine service, no plush condominiums. She expanded the board of governors to include more local representatives, and she established committees on ethics and finance. Still, she had no illusions about her job: "Trust and confidence once damaged will take a great deal of effort and time to heal."[13] The following box discusses the particular importance of the public image for not-for-profit agencies.

---

[11]Shepard, *Perks, Privileges and Power*, A38; Charles E. Shepard, "United Way Chief Says He Will Retire," *Washington Post* (February 28, 1992): A1.

[12]"United Way Chief Dedicated," *Cleveland Plain Dealer* (March 28, 1993): 24-A.f.

[13]"United Way Chief Dedicated," 24-A.f.

INFORMATION BOX

PUBLIC IMAGE FOR NOT-FOR-PROFIT ORGANIZATIONS

Product-oriented firms ought to be concerned and protective of their public image; even more so not-for-profit organizations such as schools, police departments, hospitals, politicians, and most of all, charitable organizations should be concerned. Let us consider here the importance of public image for representative not-for-profits.

Large city police departments often have a poor image among important segments of the population. The need to improve this image is hardly less important than for a manufacturer faced with a deteriorating brand image. A police department can develop a "marketing" campaign to win friends; examples of possible activities aimed at creating a better image are promoting tours and open houses of police stations, crime laboratories, police lineups, and cells; speaking at schools; and sponsoring recreation projects, such as a day at the ballpark for youngsters.

Public school systems, faced with taxpayers' revolts against mounting costs and image damage owing to teacher strikes, need conscious effort to improve their image in order to obtain more public support and funds.

Many nonbusiness organizations and institutions, such as hospitals, governmental bodies, even labor unions, have grown self-serving, dominated by a bureaucratic mentality so that perfunctory and callous treatment is the rule and the image is in the pits. Improvement of the image can come only through a greater emphasis on satisfying the public's needs, which in the case of not-for-profits is really the customers' needs.

Not-for-profits are particularly vulnerable to public image problems because they may depend solely on voluntary support. The need to be untainted by any scandal becomes crucial. In particular, great care should be exerted that contributions are being spent wisely and equitably, that overhead costs are kept reasonable, and that no opportunities exist for fraud and other misdeeds. The threat of investigative reporting must be feared and guarded against.

How can a not-for-profit organization be absolutely assured that moneys are not being misspent and that there are no ripoffs?

A Local United Way's Concerns

In April 1993, for the second time in a year, United Way of Greater Lorain County (Ohio) withdrew from the United Way of America. The board of the local chapter was still concerned about the financial stability and accountability of the national agency. In particular, it was concerned about the retirement settlement for Aramony. A significant "golden parachute" retirement package was being negotiated by the national board and Aramony; it was in the neighborhood of $4 million. Learning of this triggered the decision to again withdraw from UWA.

There were other reasons as well for this decision. The national agency was falling far short of its projected budget, as only 890 of the 1,400 affiliates that had paid membership dues two years before were still paying. Roy Church, president of the Lorain Agency, explained their decision: "Since February . . . it has become clear that United Way of America's financial stability and ability to assist locals has been put in question. The benefit of being a United Way of America member isn't there at this time for Lorain's United Way."[14]

Elaine Chao's task of resurrecting United Way of America would not be easy.

ANOTHER CONTROVERSY: GIRL SCOUTS AND THEIR COOKIES

The main funding source for the nation's 2.6 million girl scouts is their annual cookie sale, estimated to generate $400 million in revenue.[15] The practice goes back some 70 years, although in the 1920s the girls sold home-made cookies. Now it is big, with each regional council negotiating with one or two bakeries that produce the cookies, setting the price per box (which ranges from $2 to $3), and dividing the proceeds as it sees fit. Typically, the Girl Scout troops get 10 percent to 15 percent, the council takes over one-half, and the rest goes to the manufacturer.

Criticisms have emerged and received public attention regarding the dictatorial handling of these funds by the councils. There are 332 regional councils in the United States, each having an office and a paid staff overseen by a volunteer board; some councils have dozens of employees, with most serving mainly as policy enforcers and supervisors. At the troop level, volunteer leaders, often with daughters in the troop, guide their units in the true tradition of scouting, giving tirelessly of their time. For the cookie drives, the girls are an unpaid sales force—child labor, as critics assail—that supports a huge bureaucratic structure, with little of the cookie revenue coming back to the local troops.

The bureaucracy does not well tolerate dissent. *Wall Street Journal* cites the case of a West Haven troop leader, Beth Denton, who protested both the way the Connecticut Trails council apportioned revenue and the $1.6 million

---

[14]Karen Henderson, "Lorain Agency Cuts Ties with National United Way," *Cleveland Plain Dealer* (April 16, 1993): 7C.
[15]Ellen Graham, "Sprawling Bureaucracy Eats Up Most Profits of Girl Scout Cookies," *Wall Street Journal* (May 13, 1992): A1.

in salaries and benefits paid to 42 council employees. After she complained to the state attorney general, the council dismissed her as leader.[16]

Admittedly, the individual salaries in the bureaucracy were not high by corporate standards or even nonprofit standards. Council administrators' salaries ranged up to about $90,000.

What was perhaps more disturbing was that volunteer leaders saw no annual financial statements of their council's expenditures and activities.[17] Administrators' callousness and aloofness was destroying an image cherished for generations.

ANALYSIS

The lack of accountability to the donating public was a major contributor to UWA's problems. Such a loosely run operation, with no one to approve or halt administrators' actions, encouraged questionable practices. It also opened the way for great shock and criticism, come the revelation. The fact that voluntary donations were the principal source of revenues made the lack of accountability all the more crucial. The situation was similar for the Girl Scouts. In a for-profit organization, lack of accountability affects primarily stockholders; for a major charitable organization, it affects millions of contributors, who see their money and commitment being squandered.

Where full disclosure and a system of checks and balances is lacking, two consequences tend to prevail, neither one desirable nor totally acceptable. The worst case scenario is outright "white-collar theft," when the unscrupulous see it as an opportunity for personal gain. The absence of sufficient controls and accountability can make even normally honest persons succumb to temptation. Second, insufficient controls tend to promote a mindset of arrogance and allow people to play fast and loose with the system. Aramony seemed to fall into this mindset, with his spending extravagances, cronyism, and other conflict-of-interest activities. (At least some of the Girl Scout Councils, too, perceived themselves as aloof from the dedicated volunteer troop leaders, tolerating no criticism or questioning, dictating and enforcing all policies without consultation or participation, and allowing no scrutiny of their own operation.)

The UWA theoretically had an overseer: the board, similar to the board of directors of business corporations. But when such boards act as rubber stamps, where they are solidly in the camp of the chief executives, they are not really exercising control. This appeared to be the case with United Way

---

[16]Graham, "Sprawling Bureaucracy," A4.
[17]Graham, "Sprawling Bureaucracy," A4.

of America during the "reign" of Aramony; similarly with the regional councils of the Girl Scouts, many of the volunteer boards appear to have exercised little or no oversight.

Certainly such a situation of a board's failure to fulfill its responsibility is not unique to not-for-profits. Corporate boards have often been notorious for promoting the interests of the incumbent executives. Although this situation is changing today, it still prevails. See the following issue box for a discussion of the role of boards of directors.

ISSUE BOX

WHAT SHOULD BE THE ROLE OF THE BOARD OF DIRECTORS?

In the past, most boards of directors have tended to be rubber-stamps, closely allied with top executives and even composed mostly of corporate officials. In some organizations today this is changing, mostly in response to criticism of board tendencies always to support the status quo and to perpetuate the "establishment."

More and more, opinion is shifting to the idea that boards must assume a more activist role:

> The board can no longer play a passive role in corporate governance. Today, more than ever, the board must assume . . . a role that is protective of shareholder rights, sensitive to communities in which the company operates, responsive to the needs of company vendors and customers, and fair to its employees.[18]

Incentives for more active boards have been the increasing risks of liability for board decisions, as well as liability insurance costs. Although the board of directors has long been seen as responsible for establishing corporate objectives, developing broad policies, and selecting top executives, this is no longer viewed as sufficient. Boards must also review management's performance to ensure that the company is well run and that stockholders' interests are furthered. And, today, they must ensure that society's best interests are not disregarded. All of this translates into an active concern for the organization's public image or reputation.

But the issue remains: To whom should the board owe its greatest allegiance—the entrenched bureaucracy or the external publics? Without having board members representative of the many special interests affected by the organization, board members may be inclined to support the interests of the establishment.

Do you think a more representative and active board will prevent a similar scenario for United Way in the future? Why or why not?

---

[18]Lester B. Korn and Richard M. Ferry, *Board of Directors Thirteenth Annual Study* (New York: Korn/Ferry International, February 1986): 1–2.

WHAT CAN BE LEARNED?

Beware the arrogant mindset. A leader's mindset that he or she is so superior to subordinates—and even to concerned outsiders—that other opinions are unacceptable is a formula for disaster, both for an organization and for a society. It promotes dictatorship, intolerance of contrary opinions, and an attitude that "we need answer to no one." The consequences are such as we have seen with William Aramony: moving over the edge of what is deemed by most as acceptable and ethical conduct, assuming the role of the final judge who brooks no questions or criticisms. The absence of real or imagined controls or reviews seems to bring out the worst in humans. We seem to need periodic scrutiny to avoid the trap of arrogant decision making devoid of responsiveness to other concerns. The Girl Scout bureaucracy's dealings with its volunteers corroborates the inclination toward arrogance and dictatorship in the absence of objective oversight.

Checks and balances are even more important in not-for-profit and governmental bodies than in corporate entities. For-profit organizations have "bottom-line" performance (i.e., profit and loss statistics) as the ultimate control and standard. Not-for-profit and governmental organizations do not have this control, so they have no ultimate measure of their effectiveness.

Consequently, not-for-profit organizations should be subject to the utmost scrutiny of objective outsiders. Otherwise, abuses seem to be encouraged and perpetuated. Often these not-for-profit organizations are sheltered from competition, which protects them from demands for greater efficiency. Thus, without objective scrutiny, not-for-profits have a tendency to get out of hand, to be run as little dynasties unencumbered by the constraints that face most businesses. Fortunately, investigative reports and increased litigation by allegedly abused parties today act as the needed controls for such organizations. In view of the revelations of investigative reporters, we are left to wonder how many other abusive and reprehensible activities have not yet been detected.

Marketing of not-for-profits depends on trust and is particularly vulnerable to bad press. Not-for-profits depend on donations for the bulk of their revenues. They depend on people to give without receiving anything tangible in return (unlike most businesses). And the givers must have trust in the particular organization, trust that the contributions will be well spent, that beneficiaries will receive the maximum benefit, that administrative costs will be held low. Consequently, when publicity surfaces that causes such trust to be questioned, the impact can be devastating. Contributions can quickly dry up or be shunted to other charities.

With governmental bodies, of course, their perpetuation is hardly at stake with bad publicity. However, administrators can be recalled, impeached, or not reelected.

CONSIDER

Can you add to these learning insights?

QUESTIONS

1. How do you feel, as a potential or actual giver to United Way campaigns, about Aramony's "high living"? Would these allegations affect your gift giving? Why or why not?
2. What prescriptions do you have for thwarting arrogance in not-for-profit and/or governmental organizations? Be as specific as you can, and support your recommendations.
3. How do you personally feel about the coercion that some organizations exert for their employees to contribute substantially to the United Way? What implications, if any, emerge from your attitudes about this?
4. Given the information supplied about the dictatorial relationships between Girl Scout councils and the local volunteers—and recognizing that such anecdotal information may not be truly representative—what do you see as the pros and cons of Girl Scout cookie drives? On balance, is this marketing fund-raising effort still desirable, or might other alternatives be better?
5. "Since there is no bottom-line evaluation for performance, not-for-profits have no incentives to control costs and prudently evaluate expenditures." Discuss.
6. How would you feel, as a large contributor to a charity, if you learned that it spent $10 million for advertising? Discuss your rationale for this attitude.
7. Do you think the UWA's action after Aramony left was the best way to salvage the public image? Why or why not? What else might have been done?

INVITATION TO ROLE PLAY

1. You are an advisor to Elaine Chao, who has taken over the scandal-ridden United Way. What advice do you give her for as quickly as possible restoring the confidence of the American public in the integrity and worthiness of this preeminent national charity organization?
2. You are a member of the board of governors of United Way. Allegations have surfaced about the lavish lifestyle of the highly

regarded Aramony. Most of the board members, being corporate executives, see nothing at all wrong with his perks and privileges. You, however, feel otherwise. How do you convince the other board members of the error of condoning Aramony's activities? Be as persuasive as you can in supporting your position.

3. You are the parent of a Girl Scout, who has assiduously worked to sell hundreds of boxes of cookies. You now realize that her efforts and that of thousands of other girls are primarily supporting a bloated central and regional bureaucracy, and not the local troops. You feel strongly that this situation is an unacceptable use of child labor. Describe your proposed efforts to institute change.

INVITATION TO RESEARCH

What is the situation with the United Way today? Are local agencies contributing to the national? Have donations matched or exceeded previous levels? Has Elaine Chao restored public confidence? Did William Aramony receive his multimillion dollar severance package?

CHAPTER 4

Perrier: Ill-handling
of Adversity

On a Friday in early February 1990, the first news reached Perrier executive suites that traces of benzene had been found in its bottled water. Ronald Davis, president of the Perrier Group of America, ordered a sweeping recall of all bottles in North America. Just a few days later, Source Perrier S.A., the French parent, expanded the recall to the rest of the world while the company sought to identify the source of the problem and correct it.

Although at first view such a reaction to an unexpected crisis seems zealous and the ultimate in customer concern and social responsibility, a deeper study reveals marketing mistakes of major proportions.

BEFORE

In late 1989, Ronald Davis, 43-year-old president of Perrier's U.S. operations, had reason to be pleased. During his 10-year tenure, Perrier's U.S. sales had risen from $40 million to more than $800 million at retail, which was a significant 25 percent of the company's worldwide sales. He was also proud of his firm being depicted in a May 1989 issue of *Fortune* as one of six companies that compete best. *Fortune* captions: "These are companies you don't want to come up against in your worst nightmare. In the businesses they're in, they amass crushing market share."[1]

A company report in 1987 described the French source, a spring in Vergeze, as follows:

---

[1] Bill Saporito, "Companies That Compete Best," *Fortune* (May 22, 1989): 36ff.

One of Perrier's identifying qualities is its low mineral (particularly sodium) content. This is because the water spends only a short time filtering through minerals. While flowing underground, the water meets gas flowing vertically through porous volcanic rocks. This is how Perrier gets its fizz . . . the company assured us that production has never been limited by the source output. The company sells approximately one billion bottles of which 600 million are exported.[2]

Davis recognized that he was in two businesses, albeit both involved bottled water: (1) sparkling water, in the famous green bottle, which he had been successful in positioning as an adult soft drink with a French mystique, an alternative to soft drinks or alcohol; and (2) still water, a tap-water replacement, with the product delivered to homes and offices and dispensed through watercoolers. This latter business he saw as more resembling package delivery such as UPS and Federal Express, and less akin to pushing soft drinks. Accordingly, he emphasized quality of professional service for his route drivers. While best known for the green-bottled Perrier, a mainstay of most restaurants and bars, the company owned nine other brands of bottled water, including Poland Spring, Great Bear, Calistoga, and Ozarka.

At a price of 300 to 1200 times that of tap water, bottled water was the fastest growing segment of the U.S. beverage industry (see Table 4.1). Perrier controlled 24 percent of the total U.S. bottled-water business. Of the imported-bottled-water sector, the green bottle dominated with almost 50 percent of the market, although this market share had fallen when more competitors attempted to push into the rapidly growing market. In the 1980s more than 20 firms had taken a run at the green bottle, but without notable success; these included such behemoths as Coca-Cola, PepsiCo, and

Table 4.1   Average Annual Growth of Beverage Sales, 1985–1989

Beverage Type	Percent of Growth
Bottled water	+11.1
Soft drinks	+ 3.2
Milk	+ 1.5
Tea	+ 1.2
Beer	+ 0.4
Coffee	− 0.4
Wine	− 2.0
Distilled spirits	− 2.6

Source: Beverage Marketing Corporation, as reported in Fortune (Apr. 23, 1990): 277.

[2]B. Facon, Source Perrier—Company Report (Nov. 13, 1987): 4.

Anheuser-Busch. Now Davis was more concerned with expanding the category and was trying to shift the brand's image from chic to healthy, so as to make the brand more acceptable to the "masses."

THE CRISIS

The North American Recall

Davis, as he prepared his five-year plan in early 1990, wrote that competing in the 1990s would require not strategic planing, but "flexibility planning."[3] In retrospect, he seemed to be prophetic.

As he was fine-tuning his plan, the first news trickled in that a lab in North Carolina had discovered traces of benzene, a carcinogen, in some of the bottles. That same day, February 9, he ordered Perrier removed from distribution in North America.

Source Perrier officials were soon to inform reporters that the company believed the contamination occurred because an employee had mistakenly used cleaning fluid containing benzene to clean the production-line machinery that fills bottles for North America. Frederik Zimmer, managing director of Source Perrier, said that the machinery in question had been cleaned and repaired over the weekend. But in another news conference, Davis announced that he expected Perrier to be off the market for 2 to 3 months.

Such a long absence was seen by some marketing observers as potentially devastating to Perrier, despite its being the front-runner of the industry. Al Ries, chairman of a consulting firm and well-known business writer, was quoted in a *Wall Street Journal* article as saying: "If I were Perrier, I would make a desperate effort to reduce that time as much as possible, even if I had to fly it in on 747s from France."[4]

Without doubt, competitors were salivating at a chance to pick up market share of the $2.2 billion annual U.S. sales. Major competitors included Evian and Saratoga, both owned by BSN of France, and San Peligrino, an Italian import. In 1989 PepsiCo had begun test marketing $H_2OH!$, and in January 1990, Adolph Coors Company introduced Coors Rocky Mountain Sparkling Water. The Perrier absence was expected to accelerate their market entry.

Despite competitive glee at the misfortune of Perrier, some in the industry were concerned. They feared that consumers would forsake bottle water altogether, with its purity now being questioned. Would the public be as willing to pay a substantial premium for any bottled brand? See the following box for a discussion of the relationship between *price and quality*.

---

[3]Patricia Sellers, "Perrier Plots Its Comeback," *Fortune* (April 23, 1990): 277.
[4]Alix M. Freedman and Thomas R. King, "Perrier's Strategy in the Wake of Recall," *Wall Street Journal* (Feb. 12, 1990): B1.

INFORMATION BOX

IS QUALITY BEST JUDGED BY PRICE?

We as consumers today have difficulty in judging the quality of competing products. With their complex characteristics and hidden ingredients, we cannot rely on our own expertise to determine the best. So, what sources of information can we use? We can rely on our past experiences with the brand; we can be swayed by our friends and neighbors, we might be influenced by advertising and salespeople (but more and more we become skeptical of their claims); we can study *Consumer Reports* and other consumer information publications. But all of these sources are flawed in that the experience and information usually is dated, and is a limited sample—usually of 1—so that we can seriously question how representative the experience is.

Most people judge quality by price: the higher the price, the better the quality. But such a price/quality perception sets us up. While it may be valid, it also may not be. With the publicity about the impurity of Perrier, we are brought to the realization that paying many times the price of tap water gives us no assurance of better quality, as measured by purity.

Is a price/quality misperception limited mostly to bottled water, do you think? How about liquor? Designer clothes? Perfume?

Worldwide Recall

A few days later, the other shoe fell. After reports of benzene being found in Perrier bottles in Holland and Denmark, on February 14, Source Perrier expanded its North American recall to the rest of the world and acknowledged that all production lines for its sparkling water had been contaminated in recent months by tiny amounts of benzene.

At a news conference in Paris, company officials acknowledged for the first time that benzene occurs naturally in Perrier water and that the current problem came about because workers failed to replace filters designed to remove it. This was a critical reversal of previous statements that the water was tainted only because an employee mistakenly used cleaning fluid containing benzene to clean machinery. Zimmer even went further, revealing that Perrier water naturally contains several gases, including benzene, that have to be filtered out.

The company insisted that its famous spring was unpolluted. But now questions were being raised about this and about contradictory statements made about the problem. For example, how widespread was the contamination? Was benzene a naturally occurring phenomenon, or does it represent man-made pollution? Suspicions were tending toward the man-made origin.

While benzene occurs naturally in certain foods, it is more commonly found as a petroleum-based distillate used in many manufacturing processes.

Particularly surprising was the rather nonchalant attitude of Perrier executives. Zimmer, the president, even suggested that "all this publicity helps build the brand's renown."[5]

Ronald Davis was quick to point out that the company did not have to recall its entire 70-million-bottle U.S. inventory. After all, health officials both in the U.S. and France had noted that the benzene levels found in Perrier did not pose any significant health risk. The major risk really was to the image of Perrier: it had gone to great lengths to establish its water as naturally pure. And while not particularly dangerous, it was certainly not naturally pure—as all the world was finding out from the publicity about it. Add to this the undermining of the major attraction of bottled water that it was safer than ordinary tap water, and the recall and subsequent publicity assumed more ominous proportions.

THE COMEBACK

It took until mid-July before Perrier was again widely available in the United States; this was 5 months rather than the expected 3 months. Still, Davis was confident that Perrier's sales would return to 85 percent of normal by the end of 1991. Actually, he was more worried about short supply than demand. He was not sure the one spring in Vergeze, France, would be able to replace the world's supply before the beginning of 1991.

Davis's confidence in the durability of the demand stemmed from his clout with retailers, where the brand does a majority of its business. He believed the brand's good reputation, coupled with the other brands marketed by Perrier that had replaced some of the supermarket space relinquished by Perrier, would bring quick renewal. To help this, he wrote letters to 550 CEOs of retail firms, pledging heavy promotional spending. The marketing budget was increased from $6 million to $25 million for 1990, with $16 million going into advertising and the rest into promotions and special events. A highly visible discount strategy was instituted, which included a buy-two, get-one-free offer. Supermarket prices had dropped, with bottles now going for $0.89 to $0.99, down from $1.09 to $1.19. To win back restaurant business, a new 52-member sales force supplemented distributor efforts. However, a setback of sorts was the Food and Drug Administration order to drop the words "naturally sparkling" from Perrier labels.

---

[5]Alix M. Freedman and Thomas R. King, "Perrier Expands North American Recall to Rest of Globe," *Wall Street Journal* (Feb. 15, 1990): B1.

Still, a recent consumer survey indicated that 84 percent of Perrier's U.S. drinkers intended to buy the product again.[6] Davis could also take heart from the less-than-aggressive actions of his competitors during the hiatus. None appeared to have strongly reacted, although most improved their sales considerably. The smaller competitors proved to be short of marketing money and bottling capacity and apparently were fearful that a beleaguered Perrier would negatively affect the overall market. Big competitors, such as PepsiCo and Coors, who were introducing other bottled waters, somehow also appeared reluctant to move in aggressively.

CONSEQUENCES

By the end of 1990, however, it was clear that Perrier was not regaining market position as quickly and completely as Davis had hoped. Now more aggressive competitors were emerging. Some, such as Saratoga, La Croix, and Quibell, had experienced major windfalls in the wake of the recall. Evian, in particular, a nonsparkling water produced by the French firm BSN S.A., was the biggest winner. Through aggressive marketing and advertising it had replaced Perrier by the end of 1990 as the top-selling imported bottled water.

Perrier's sales had reached only 60 percent of prerecall levels, and its share of the imported bottled-water market had sunk to 20.7 percent from the 44.8 percent of one year earlier. While the Perrier Group of America expected to report a sales gain for 1990 of 3.7 percent, this was largely because of the strong performance of such domestic brands as Calistoga and Poland Spring.

Particularly worrisome for Davis was the slow return of Perrier to bars and restaurants, which had formerly accounted for about 35 percent of its sales. A sampling of comments of restaurant managers, as reported in such prestigious papers as the *Wall Street Journal* and *Washington Post,* were far from encouraging. For example:

The manager of the notable Four Seasons restaurant in New York City said his patrons had begun to shift to San Pellegrino: "I think Perrier is finished," he said. "We can write it off."[7]

The general manager of Spago Restaurant in Los Angeles said: "Now consumers have decided that other brands are better or at least as good, so Perrier no longer holds the monopoly on water." And Spago no longer carries Perrier.[8]

[6]Sellers, "Perrier Plots," 278.

[7]Freedman and King, "Perrier's Strategy," B3.

[8]Alix M. Freedman, "Perrier Finds Mystique Hard to Restore," *Wall Street Journal* (Dec. 1, 1990): B1.

Le Pavillon restaurant in Washington, D.C., switched to Quibell during the recall, and has not gone back to Perrier. "Customers still ask for Perrier, but it's a generic term like Kleenex, and customers aren't unhappy to get a substitute."[9]

Evian

David Daniel, 34, was Evian's U.S. CEO since June 1988. He joined the company in 1987 as the first director of marketing at a time when the American subsidiary was a two-person operation. By 1990 there were 100 employees.

Daniel came from PepsiCo, and his background was marketing. He saw Evian's sphere to be portable water that is good for you, a position well situated to capitalize on the health movement. He was particularly interested in broadening the distribution of Evian, and he sought out soft-drink and beer distributors, showing them that their basic industries were only growing at 1 to 3 percent a year, while bottled water was growing at over 10 percent per year. In 1989, Evian sales doubled to $65 million, with $100 million in sight for 1990. The attractiveness of such growth to these distributors was of no small moment.

Daniel made Evian the most expensive water on the market. He saw the price as helping Evian occupy a certain slot in the consumer's mind—remember the price/quality perception discussed earlier. For example, at a fancy grocery in New York's West Village, a 1-liter bottle of Evian sold for $2.50; the city charges a fraction of a penny for a gallon of tap water[10]—a lot of perceived quality in that. This type of pricing along with the packaging that made Evian portable—plastic nonbreakable bottles and reusable caps—were seen as keys in the selling of bottled water.

Then, late in 1990, Evian benefited greatly from the Persian Gulf War, with free publicity from several newspapers and from all three national TV networks: GIs were shown gulping water from Evian bottles.

ANALYSIS

Was the massive recall overkill, or was it a prudent necessity? Did it show a concerned corporate citizen, or rather a panicked executive? Were consumers impressed with the responsibleness of the company, or were they more focused on its carelessness? These questions are all directed at the basic impact of the recall and the subsequent actions and admissions: Was it to have favorable, neutral, or unfavorable public reactions?

Perrier did *not* have to recall its product. It was a North Carolina county laboratory that first noticed the excessive amounts of benzene in Perrier and

---

[9]Lori Silver, "Perrier Crowd Not Taking the Waters," *Washington Post* (July 4, 1990): 1.
[10]Seth Lubove, "Perched Between Perrier and Tap," *Forbes* (May 14, 1990): 120.

ISSUE BOX

ARE BOTTLED WATER CLAIMS BUNK?[11]

The bottled water industry came under serious attack in April 1991. As if the Perrier massive recall was not enough, now a congressional panel with wide media coverage accused the Food and Drug Administration of "inexcusably negligent and complacent oversight of the bottled-water industry." Despite its high price, the panel said, bottled water may be less safe than tap water. The panel noted that although consumers pay 300 to 1200 times more for bottled water than for tap water, 25 percent of all bottled water comes from public drinking water sources. For example:

> Lithia Springs Water Company touts its "world's finest" bottled mineral water as "naturally pure" and recommends its special Love Water as an "invigorator" before bedtime. Yet, it was found to be tainted with bacteria.

> Artisia Waters, Inc., promotes its "100% pure sparkling Texas Natural Water." But it comes from the same underground source that San Antonio uses for its municipal water supply.

Furthermore, the FDA released a list of 22 bottled-water recalls because of contaminants such as kerosene and mold. For the most part, these went unnoticed by consumers, being overshadowed by the Perrier recall.

At issue: Are we being hoodwinked? Debate two positions: (1) the bottled-water industry really is a throwback to the snake-oil charlatans of the last century; and (2) a few unscrupulous or careless bottlers are denigrating the image of the entire industry, an industry that is primarily focused on health and purity.

---

reported its findings to the state authorities. The state agriculture and health departments did not believe that a recall was necessary, but they did insist on issuing a health advisory, warning that Perrier should not be consumed until further tests could be made. It was the state's plan to issue the health advisory that was reported to Davis on the afternoon of the critical day, February 9. He announced the recall later that same day.

We are left to wonder: Perhaps a full and complete recall was not needed. Perhaps things could have been worked out entirely satisfactorily with less drastic measures. Given that a recall meant a 3- to 5-month absence from the marketplace, should it not have been the action of last resort?

But let us consider Davis's thought process on that ill-fated afternoon in February. He did not know the source of the problem; he certainly had

---

[11]Examples are taken from Bruce Ingersoll, "FDA Finds Bunk in Bottled-Water Claims," *Wall Street Journal* (Apr. 10, 1991): B1.

no reason to suspect that it emanated from the spring in southern France or that it was a worldwide problem. He probably considered it of less magnitude. Perhaps he thought of the total North American recall as a gesture showing the concerned thinking of the management of this product that had developed such a reputation of health and purity and, yes, status. Only with the experience after the fact do we know the error of this decision: that it was to result in a 5-month absence from the hotly competitive market; that it was to result in revelations of far more serious implications than a simple employee error or even a natural occurrence largely beyond the company's control.

So, perhaps Davis's drastic decision was fully justified and prudent. But it turned out to be confounded by circumstances he did not envision.

A lengthy complete absence from the marketplace is a catastrophe of rather monumental proportions—all the more so for a product that is habitually and frequently consumed, in Perrier's case, sometimes several times daily. Such an absence forces even the most loyal customers to establish new patterns of behavior, in this case switching brands. Once behavior becomes habituated, at least for some people, a change back becomes less likely. This is especially true if the competitive offerings are reasonably similar and acceptable. Anything that Perrier could have done to lessen the time away from the market would have been desirable—regardless of expense.

Perhaps the biggest problem for Perrier concerned the false impressions, and even outright deception, that the company had conveyed regarding the purity of its product. Now, in the wake of this total recall and the accompanying publicity, all was laid bare. Company officials in France had to own up that the contamination had occurred "in recent months," and not suddenly and unexpectedly on February 9.

But more than this, under intense pressure from the media to explain what caused the problem, Source Perrier ultimately conceded that its water does not bubble up pure, already carbonated and ready to drink, from its renowned spring in southern France. Instead, contrary to the image that it had spent tens of millions of dollars to promote, the company extracts the water and carbon dioxide gas separately, and must pipe the gas through charcoal filters before combining it mechanically with the water to give the fizz. Without the filters, Perrier water would contain benzene and, even worse, would taste like rotten eggs.

Finally, the public relations efforts were flawed. Source Perrier officials issued a confusing series of public statements and clarifications. Early on, the company tried to maintain the mystique of Perrier by concealing information about the cause of the contamination and by blaming it on a mistake by cleaning personnel in using an oily rag, which could have contained some benzene, to wipe equipment used for bottles to be shipped to the

United States. But the spokespeople knew the problem was more fundamental than that.

An aura of nonchalance was conveyed by corporate executives and reported in the press. This was hardly in keeping with a serious problem having to do with the possible safety of customers. Furthermore, Source Perrier relied mainly on media reports to convey information to consumers. Misinformation and rumors are more likely with this approach to public relations than in a more proactive strategy of direct company advertisement and statements.

The reputation of Perrier was on the ropes. And top management seemed unconcerned about the probability of severe public image damage. The following box discusses the topic of ignoring possible image damage.

INFORMATION BOX

IGNORING POSSIBLE NEGATIVE IMAGE CONSEQUENCES

We can identify several factors that induce a firm to ignore public image considerations until sometimes too late. First, a firm's public image often makes a nonspecific impact on company performance. The cause-and-effect relationship of a deteriorating image is virtually impossible to assess, at least until and unless image problems worsen. Image consequences may be downplayed because management is unable to single out the specific profit impact.

Second, an organization's image is not easily and definitively measured. Although some tools are available for tracking public opinion, they tend to be imprecise and of uncertain validity. Consequently, image studies are often spurned or given short shrift relative to more quantitative measures of performance.

Third, it is difficult to determine the effectiveness of image-building efforts. While firms may spend thousands, and even millions, of dollars for institutional and image-building advertising, measures of the effectiveness of such expenditures are inexact and also of questionable validity. For example, a survey may be taken of attitudes of a group of people before and after the image-building campaign is run. Presumably if a few more people profess to be favorably disposed toward the company after the campaign than before, this is an indication of its success. But an executive can question how much this really translates into sales and profits.

Given the near impossibility of measuring the effectiveness of image-enhancing promotion, how do you account for the prevalence of institutional advertising, even among firms that have no image problems?

WHAT CAN BE LEARNED?

Exiting a market for several months or more poses critical risks, particularly for a habitually consumed product. To allow new habits to be established and new loyalties to be created not only among consumers but also dealers may be impossible to fully recover from. This is especially true if competing products are comparable, and if competitors are aggressive in seizing the proffered opportunity. Since a front-runner is a target anyway, abandoning the battlefield simply invites competitive takeover.

Deception discovered and grudgingly admitted destroys a mystique. No mystique is forever. Consumer preferences change, competitors become more skilled at countering, or perhaps a firm becomes complacent in its quality control or innovative technology. These conditions act to nibble away at a mystique and eventually destroy it. As in the case of Perrier, where long-believed images of a product, its healthfulness and purity, are suddenly revealed to be false—that the advertising was less than candid and was even deceptive—then any mystique comes tumbling down and is unlikely to ever be regained. This scenario can only be avoided if the publicity about the deception or misdeed is not widespread. But, with a popular product such as Perrier, publicity reaches beyond business journals to the popular press. Such is the fate of large, well-known firms.

A price/quality misperception strongly exists. Without doubt, most consumers judge quality by price: the higher the price, the higher the quality. Is a $2.50 liter of Evian better quality than a gallon of tap water costing a fraction of a cent? Perhaps. But is it a hundred times better? And yet many people embrace the misconception that price is the key indicator of quality, and are consequently taken advantage of every day.

An industry catering to health is particularly vulnerable to a few unscrupulous operators. We, the general public, are particularly vulnerable to claims for better health, beauty, and youthfulness. It is human nature to reach out, hopefully, for the false promises that can be made about such important personal concerns. We become gullible in our desire to find ways to change our condition. And so we have become victims of quacks and snake-oil charmers through the ages. Governmental agencies try to exercise strong monitoring in these areas, but budgets are limited, and all claims cannot be investigated. As recent congressional scrutiny has revealed, the bottled-water industry had long been overlooked by governmental watchdogs. Now this is changing, thanks at least partly to the Perrier recall.

Should an organization have a crisis-management team? Perrier did a poor job in its crisis management. Would a more formal organizational unit devoted to this have handled things better, instead of leaving it to top executives unskilled in handling catastrophes? The issue can hardly be answered simply and all-inclusively. Crises occur rarely; and a serious crisis may never happen to a particular organization. A crisis team then would have to be composed of executives and staff who have other primary responsibilities. And their decisions and actions under fire may be no better than a less formal arrangement. For severe crises—and Perrier's was certainly that—top executives who bear the ultimate responsibility therefore have to be the final decision makers. Some will be cooler under fire than others, but this usually cannot be fully ascertained until the crisis occurs. More desirable for most organizations would seem to be contingency plans, with plans formulated for various occurrences, including the worst scenarios. With such action plans drawn up under more normal conditions, better judgments are likely to result.

CONSIDER

Can you think of other learning insights from this case?

QUESTIONS

1. How could the public relations efforts of Perrier have been better handled?
2. Discuss the desirability of Perrier's price-cutting during its comeback.
3. Whom do you see as the primary customers for Perrier? For Evian? For other bottled waters? Are these segments likely to be enduring in their commitment to bottled water?
4. Why do you think the big firms, such as Coca-Cola, PepsiCo, and Coors, have been so slow and unaggressive in entering the bottled-water market?
5. Are we being hoodwinked by bottled-water claims and images?
6. "The success of bottled water in the United States, unlike the situation in many countries of the world where bottled water is often essential for good health, attests to the power of advertising." Evaluate this statement.
7. Is the consumer appeal of bottled water largely attributable to an image developed of sophistication and status?

INVITATION TO ROLE PLAY

1. Put yourself in the position of Ronald Davis on the afternoon of February 9, 1990. The first report of benzene found by a Carolina lab

has just come in. What would you do? Be as specific as you can, and describe the logic behind your decisions.
2. How would you attempt to build up or resurrect the mystique of Perrier after the recall?

INVITATION TO RESEARCH

Johnson & Johnson (J & J) had to make a major recall of its Tylenol when some of the capsules were found to have been poisoned. Research the efforts of J & J in its crisis, and compare them with those of Perrier. What conclusions can you draw?

PART II

MARKETING STRATEGY MISTAKES

CHAPTER 5

IBM: A Giant Fails To Cope

On January 19, 1993, International Business Machines Corporation (IBM) reported a record $5.46 billion loss for the fourth quarter of 1992 and a deficit for the entire year of $4.97 billion, the biggest annual loss in American corporate history. (General Motors recorded a 1991 loss of $4.45 billion, after huge charges for cutbacks and plant closings. And Ford Motor Company reported a net loss of more than $6 billion for 1992, but that was a noncash charge to account for the future costs of retiree benefits.) The cost in human lives, as far as employment was concerned, was also consequential, because some 42,900 had been laid off during 1992, with an additional 25,000 planned to go in 1993. In its fifth restructuring, seemingly endless rounds of job cuts and firings had eliminated 100,000 jobs since 1985. Not surprisingly, IBM's share price, which was above $100 in the summer of 1992, closed at $48.375, an 11-year low. And yet IBM had long been the ultimate blue-chip company, reigning supreme in the computer industry. How could its problems have surfaced so suddenly and so violently?

THE ROAD TO INDUSTRY DOMINANCE

"They hired my father to make a go of this company in 1914, the year I was born," said Thomas J. Watson, Jr. "To some degree I've been a part of IBM ever since."[1] Watson took over his father's medium-sized company in 1956 and built it into a technological giant. Retired for almost 19 years by 1992, he now was witnessing the company in the throes of its greatest adversity.

---

[1]Michael W. Miller, "IBM's Watson Offers Personal View of the Company's Recent Difficulties," *Wall Street Journal* (December 21, 1992): A3.

IBM had become the largest computer maker in the world. With its ever-growing revenues, since 1946 it had become the bluest of blue-chip companies. It had 350,000 employees worldwide and was one of the largest U.S.-based employers. Its 1991 revenues had approached $67 billion, and while profits had dropped some from the peak of $6.5 billion in 1984, its common stock still commanded a price-to-earnings ratio of over 100, making it a darling of investors. In 1989, it ranked first among all U.S. firms in market value (the total capitalization of common stock, based on the stock price and the number of shares outstanding), fourth in total sales, and fourth in net profits.[2]

During the days of Watson, IBM was known for its centralized decision making. Decisions affecting product lines were made at the highest levels of management. Even IBM's culture was centralized and standardized, with strict behavioral and dress codes. For example, a blue suit, white shirt, and dark tie was the public uniform, and IBM became widely known as "Big Blue."

One of IBM's greatest assets was its research labs, by far the largest and costliest of their kind in the world, with staffs that included three Nobel Prize winners. IBM treated its research and development (R & D) function with tender, loving care, regularly budgeting 10 percent of sales for this forward-looking activity: For example, in 1991, the R & D budget was $6.6 billion.

The past success of IBM and the future expectations for the company with a seeming stranglehold over the technology of the future, made it a favorite of consultants, analysts, and market researchers. Management theorists from Peter Drucker to Tom Peters (of *In Search of Excellence* fame) lined up to analyze what made IBM so good. And the business press regularly produced articles of praise and awe for IBM.

Alas, the adulation was to abruptly change by 1992. Somehow, insidiously, IBM had gotten fat and complacent over the years, and now the devil had to be paid. (In a later case in this book, that of motorcycle maker Harley Davidson, we encounter a similar situation of complacency coming with longstanding market dominance.) IBM's problems, however, went deeper, as we will explore in the next section.

CHANGING FORTUNES

Perhaps the causes of the great IBM debacle of 1992 started in the early 1980s with a questionable management decision. The problems may have been more deep-rooted than any single decision; perhaps they were more a consequence of the bureaucracy that often typifies behemoth organizations (Sears and General Motors faced somewhat similar worsening problems), in the growing layers of policies, and entrenched interests.

---

[2]"Ranking the Forbes 500s," *Forbes* (April 30, 1990): 306.

In the early 1980s, two little firms, Intel and Microsoft, were upstarts, just emerging in the industry dominated by IBM. Their success by the 1990s can be largely attributed to their nurturing by IBM. Each got a major break when it was "anointed" as a key supplier for IBM's new personal computer (PC). Intel was signed on to make the chips, and Microsoft, the software. The aggressive youngsters proceeded to set standards for successive PC generations, and in the process wrested from IBM control over the PC's future. And the PC was to become the product of the future, shouldering aside the giant mainframe that was IBM's strength.

As IBM began losing ground in one market after another, Intel and Microsoft were gaining dominance. Ten years before, in 1982, the market value of stock of Intel and Microsoft combined had amounted to about one-tenth of IBM's. By October 1992, their combined stock value had surpassed IBM's; by the end of the year, they had topped IBM's market value by almost 50%. See Table 5.1 for comparative operating statistics of IBM, Intel, and Microsoft in recent years. Table 5.2 shows the market valuation of IBM, Intel, and Microsoft from 1989 to 1992, the years before and during the collapse of investor esteem.

Table 5.1   Growth of IBM and the Upstarts, Microsoft and Intel, 1983–1992 (in $ millions)

	1983	1985	1987	1989	1991	1992
IBM:						
Revenues	$40,180	$50,056	$54,217	$62,710	$64,792	$67,045
Net income	5,485	6,555	5,258	3,758	(2,827)	(4,970)
% of Revenue	13.6%	13.1%	9.7%	6.0%	—	—
Microsoft:						
Revenues	$ 50	$ 140	$ 346	$ 804	$ 1,843	$ 2,759
Net Income	6	24	72	171	463	708
% of Revenue	12.0%	17.1%	20.8%	21.3%	25.1%	25.7%
Intel:						
Revenues	$ 1,122	$ 1,365	$ 1,907	$ 3,127	$ 4,779	$ 5,192
Net Income	116	2	176	391	819	827
% of Revenue	10.3%	0.1%	9.2%	12.5%	17.1%	15.9%

Sources: Company annual statements, most 1992 figures are from "Annual Report of American Industry," *Forbes* (January 4, 1993): 115–16.

Commentary: Note the great growth of the "upstarts" in recent years, both in revenues and in profits, compared with IBM. Also note the great performance of Microsoft and Intel in profit as a percent of revenues.

Table 5.2   Market Value and Rank of IBM, Microsoft, and Intel among All U.S. Companies, 1989 and 1992

	Rank 1989	1992	Market Value 1989	($ millions) 1992
IBM	1	13	$60,345	$30,715
Microsoft	92	25	6,018	23,608
Intel	65	22	7,842	24,735

Source: "The *Forbes* Market Value 500," *Forbes* Annual Directory Issue (April 13, 1990): 258–59; and *Forbes* (April 26, 1993): 242. The market value is the per share price multiplied by the number of shares outstanding for all classes of common stock.

Commentary: The market valuation reflects the stature of the firms in the eyes of investors. Obviously, IBM has lost badly during this period, while Microsoft and Intel have more than tripled their market valuation, almost approaching that of IBM. Yet, IBM's sales were $65.5 million in 1992, against Microsoft sales of $3.3 million and Intel sales of $5.8 million.

Defensive Reactions of IBM

As the problems of IBM became more visible to the entire investment community, Chairman John Akers sought to institute reforms to turn the behemoth around. His problem—and need—was to uproot a corporate structure and culture that had developed when IBM had no serious competition.

A cumbersome bureaucracy stymied the company from being innovative in a fast-moving industry. Major commitments still went to high-margin mainframes, but these mainframes were no longer necessary in many situations, given the computing power of desktop PCs. IBM had problems in getting to market quickly with the technological innovations that were revolutionizing the industry. In 1991 Akers warned of the coming difficulties before an unbelieving group of IBM managers: "The business is in crisis."[3] He attempted to push power downward, to decentralize some of the decision making that for decades had resided at the top. His more radical proposal was to break up IBM—to divide it into 13 divisions and to give each more autonomy. He sought to expand the services business and make the company more responsive to customer needs. And perhaps most important, he saw a crucial need to pare costs by cutting the fat from the organization.

The need for cost cutting was evident to all but the entrenched bureaucracy. IBM's total costs grew 12 percent a year in the mid-1980s, but revenues were not keeping up with this growth.[4] Part of the plan for reducing costs involved cutting employees, which violated a cherished tradition dating back to Thomas Watson's father and the beginning of IBM: a promise

[3]David Kirkpatrick, "Breaking Up IBM," *Fortune* (July 27, 1992): 44.
[4]David Kirkpatrick, "Breaking Up IBM," 53.

never to lay off IBM workers for economic reasons.[5] (Most of the downsizing was indeed accomplished by voluntary retirements and attractive severance packages, but eventually outright layoffs became necessary.)

The changes decreed by Akers would leave the unified sales division untouched. But each of the new product group divisions would act as a separate operating unit, with financial reports broken down accordingly. Particularly troubling to Akers was the recent performance of the personal computer (PC) business. At a time when demand, as well as competition, was burgeoning for PCs, this division was languishing. Early in 1992 Akers tapped James Cannavino to be head of the $11 billion Personal Systems Division, which also included workstations and software.

IBM PCs

PCs had been the rising star of the company, despite the fact that mainframes still accounted for about $20 billion in revenues. But in 1990, market share dropped drastically as new competitors offered PCs at much lower prices than IBM; many experts even maintained that these clones were at least equal in quality. Throughout 1992, IBM had been losing market share in an industry price war. Even after it had attempted to counter Compaq's price cuts in June, IBM's prices still remained as much as one-third higher. Even worse, IBM had announced new fall models, and this curbed sales of current models. At the upper end of the PC market, firms such as Sun Microsystems and Hewlett-Packard were bringing out more powerful workstations that tied PCs together with minicomputers and mainframe computers. James Cannavino faced a major challenge in bringing back the PC to a powerful competitive entity.

Cannavino planned to streamline operations by slicing off a new unit to focus exclusively on developing and manufacturing PC hardware. By so doing, he would cut PCs loose from the rest of Personal Systems and the workstations and software. This, he believed, would create a streamlined organization that could cut prices often, roll out new products several times a year, sell through any kind of store, and provide customers with whatever software they wanted, even if it was not IBM's.[6] Such autonomy was deemed necessary in order to respond quickly to competitors and opportunities, without having to deal with the IBM bureaucracy.

[5]Miller, "Watson Offers Personal Views," A4.
[6]"Stand Back, Big Blue—And Wish Me Luck," *Business Week* (August 17, 1992): 99.

THE CRISIS

On January 25, 1993, John Akers announced that he was stepping down as IBM's chairman and chief executive. He had lost the confidence of the board of directors. Until mid-January, Akers had seemed determined to see IBM through its crisis, at least until he would reach IBM's customary retirement age of 60, which would be December 1994. But the horrendous $4.97 billion loss in 1992 changed that, and investor and public pressure mounted for a top management change. The fourth quarter of 1992 was particularly shocking, brought on by weak European sales and a steep decline in sales of minicomputers and mainframes. Now IBM's stock sank to a 17-year low, below $46 per share.

Other aspects of the operation were also emerging to accentuate IBM's fall from grace: most notably, the jewel of its operation, its mainframe processors and storage systems.

For 25 years IBM had dominated the $50 billion worldwide mainframe industry. In 1992 overall sales of such equipment grew at only 2 percent, but IBM experienced a 10 percent to 15 percent drop in revenue. At the same time, its major mainframe rivals—Amdahl and Unisys—had sales gains of 48 percent and 10 percent, respectively.[7]

The fact was becoming clear that IBM was seriously lagging behind in developing new computers that could outperform the old ones—such as IBM's old System/390. Competitors' products exceeded IBM's not only in absolute power but in prices—as much as a tenth or less per unit of computing. For example, with IBM's mainframe computers, customers paid approximately $100,000 for each MIPS, or the capacity to execute 1 million instructions per second, the rough gauge of computing power. Hewlett-Packard offered similar capability at a cost of only $12,000 per MIPS. Similarly, AT&T's NCR unit could sell for $12.5 million a machine that outperformed IBM's $20 million ES/9000 processor complex.[8]

In a series of full-page advertisements appearing in such business publications as the *Wall Street Journal,* IBM defended the mainframe and attacked the MIPS measure of computing power:

> One issue surrounding mainframes is their cost. It's often compared using dollars per MIPS with the cost of microprocessor systems, and on that basis mainframes lose. But . . . dollars per MIPS alone is a superficial measurement. The real issue is function. Today's appetite for information demands serious network and systems management, around-the-clock availability, efficient mass storage and genuine data security. MIPS alone provides none of these, but IBM

---

[7]John Verity, "Guess What: IBM Is Losing Out in Mainframes, Too," *Business Week* (February 8, 1993): 106.

[8]Verity, "Guess What," 106.

mainframes have them built in, and more fully developed than anything available on microprocessors.[9]

On March 24, 1993, 51-year-old Louis V. Gerstner, Jr., was named the new chief executive of IBM. The 2-month search for a replacement for Akers had captivated the media, with speculation ranging widely. The choice of an outsider caught many by surprise: Gerstner had been CEO of RJR Nabisco, a food and tobacco giant, but this was a far cry from a computer company. And IBM had always prided itself on promoting from within—for example, John Akers—and most IBM executives were life-long IBM employees. Not all analysts supported the selection of such an outsider. While most did not criticize the board for going outside IBM to find a replacement for Akers, some questioned going outside the computer industry or other high-tech industries. Geoff Lewis, senior editor of *Business Week*, fully supported the choice. He had suggested the desirability of bringing in some outside managers to Akers in 1988:

> Akers seemed shocked—maybe even offended—by my question. After a moment, he answered: "IBM has the best recruitment system anywhere and spends more than anybody on training. Sometimes it might help to seek outsiders with unusual skills, but the company already has the best people in the world."[10]

See the following box for a discussion of promotion from within.

ANALYSIS

In examining the major contributors to IBM's fall from grace, we will break down the analysis into predisposing or underlying factors, resultants, and controversies.

Predisposing Factors

Cumbersome Organization. As IBM grew with its success, it became more and more bureaucratic. One author described it as "big and bloated." Another used the phrase "inward-looking culture that kept them from waking up on time."[11] Regardless of phraseology, the facts were that by the late 1980s the IBM organization could not bring new machines quickly into the

---

[9]Taken from advertisement, *Wall Street Journal* (March 5, 1993): B8.
[10]Geoff Lewis, "One Fresh Face at IBM May Not Be Enough," *Business Week* (April 12, 1993): 33.
[11]Jennifer Reese, "The Big and the Bloated: It's Tough Being No. 1," *Fortune* (July 27, 1992): 49.

ISSUE BOX

SHOULD WE PROMOTE FROM WITHIN?

A heavy commitment to promoting from within, as had long characterized IBM and other firms as well, is sometimes derisively called "inbreeding." The traditional argument against it maintains that an "inbred" organization is not alert to needed changes and that it is enamored with the status quo, "the way we have always done it." Proponents of promotion from within talk about the motivation and great loyalty it engenders, with every employee knowing that he or she has a chance of becoming a high-level executive.

However, the opposite course of action—that is, heavy commitment to filling important executive positions with outsiders—plays havoc with morale of trainees and lower level executives and destroys the sense of continuity and loyalty. A middle ground seems preferable: filling many executive positions from within, promoting this idea to encourage both the achievement of present executives and the recruiting of trainees, and at the same time bringing strong outsiders into the organization where their strengths and experiences can be most valuable.

Do you think there are particular circumstances where one or the other extreme regarding promotion from within might be best? Discuss.

---

market and was unable to make the fast pricing and other strategic decisions of its smaller competitors. Too many layers of management, too many vested interests, a tradition-ridden mentality, and a gradually emerging contentment with the status quo shackled it in an industry that some thought to be mature, but which in reality had important sectors still gripped by burgeoning change. As a huge ship requires a considerable time and distance to turn or to stop, so the IBM behemoth found itself at a competitive disadvantage to smaller, hungrier, more aggressive, and above all, more nimble firms. And impeding all efforts to effect major changes was the typical burden facing all large and mature organizations: resistance to change. See the following information box for a discussion of this phenomenon.

Overly Centralized Management Structure. Often related to a cumbersome bureaucratic organization is rigid centralization of authority and decision making. Certain negatives may result when all major decisions have to be made at corporate headquarters rather than down the line. Decision making is necessarily slowed, because headquarters executives feel they must investigate fully all aspects, and because they are not personally involved with the recommendation, they tend to be not only skeptical but critical. More than this, the typical conservatism of higher management—divorced from the intimacy of the problem or the opportunity—may curb the enthusiasm and creativity of lower-level executives. The motivation and morale needed for a

---

INFORMATION BOX

RESISTANCE TO CHANGE

People as well as organizations have a natural reluctance to embrace change. Change is disruptive. It can destroy accepted ways of doing things and familiar authority–responsibility relationships. It makes people uneasy, because their routines will likely be disrupted; their interpersonal relationships with subordinates, coworkers, and superiors may well be modified. Positions that were deemed important before the change may be downgraded. And persons who view themselves as highly competent in a particular job may be forced to assume unfamiliar duties.

Resistance to change can be combatted by good communication with participants about forthcoming changes. Without such communication, rumors and fears can assume monumental proportions. Acceptance of change can be facilitated if employees are involved as fully as possible in planning the changes, if their participation is solicited and welcomed, and if assurance can be given that positions will not be impaired, only changed. Gradual rather than abrupt changes also make a transition smoother, as participants can be initially exposed to the changes without drastic upheavals.

In the final analysis, however, needed changes should not be delayed or canceled because of their possible negative repercussions on the organization. If change is necessary, it should be initiated. Individuals and organizations can adapt to change, but it may take some time.

The worst change an employee may face is layoff. And when uncertainty exists as to when the next layoff will occur, and to whom, total morale may sink to the pits, devastating productivity. Discuss how the necessity of upcoming layoffs might best be handled.

---

climate of innovative-mindedness and creativity is stifled under a bureaucratic attitude of "don't take a chance" and "don't rock the boat."

The Three C's Mindset of Vulnerability. Firms that have been well entrenched in their industry and that have dominated it for years tend to fall into a particular mindset that leaves them vulnerable to aggressive and innovative competitors. (We will also encounter this syndrome in a later case, Harley Davidson, the motorcycle maker.)

The following "three C's" are detrimental to a front-runner's continued success:

Complacency

Conservatism

Conceit

Complacency is smugness: A self-satisfied firm, content with the status quo, may no longer be hungry and eager for growth. *Conservatism* characterizes a management that is wedded to the past, to the traditional, to the way things have always been done. Managers see no need to change because nothing is different today (e.g., "Mainframe computers are the models of the industry and will always be."). Finally, *conceit* further reinforces the myopia of the mindset: conceit for present and potential competitors. A belief that "we are the best" and "no one else can touch us" can easily permeate an organization when everything has been going well for years.

With the three C's mindset, there is no incentive to undertake aggressive and innovative actions. There is growing disinterest in such important facets of the business as customer relations, servicing, and even quality control. Furthermore, there is little interest in developing innovative new products that may cannibalize—that is, take business away from—existing products or disrupt entrenched interests. (We will discuss cannibalization in more detail shortly.)

Result

Overdependence on High-Margin Mainframes. The mainframe computers had long been the greatest source of market power and profits for IBM. But the conservative and tradition-minded bureaucracy could not accept the reality that computer power was now becoming a desktop commodity. Although a market still existed for the massive mainframes, it was limited and had little growth potential; the future belonged to desktop computers and workstations. And to these areas, in a lapse of monumental proportions, IBM relinquished its dominance. First the minicomputers opened up a whole new industry, one with scores of hungry competitors. But the cycle of industry creation and decline started anew by the early 1980s as personal computers began to replace minicomputers in defining new markets and fostering new competitors. The mainframe was not replaced, but its markets became more limited, and cannibalization became the fear. See the following information box.

Neglect of Software and Service. At a time when software and service had become ever more important, IBM still had a fixation on hardware. In 1992 services made up only 9 percent of IBM's revenue. Criticisms flowed:

> "Technology is becoming a commodity, and the difference between winning and losing comes in how you deliver that technology. Service will be the differentiator."

> "As a customer, I want a supplier who's going to make all my stuff work together."

INFORMATION BOX

CANNIBALIZATION

Cannibalization occurs when a company's new product takes away some business of its existing product. The new product success consequently does not contribute its full measure to company revenues because some sales will be switched from older products. The amount of cannibalization can range from virtually none to almost total. In this latter case, then, the new product simply replaces the older product, with no real sales gain achieved. If the new product is less profitable than the older, the impact, and the fear, of cannibalization becomes all the greater.

For IBM the PCs and the other equipment smaller than mainframes would not come close to replacing the bigger units. Still, some cannibalizing was likely. And the profits on the lower priced computers were many times less than those of mainframes.

The argument can justifiably be made that if the company does not bring out such new products, the competitors will, and it is better to compete with one's own products. Still, the threat of cannibalization can cause a hesitation, a blink, in a full-scale effort to rush to market an internally competing product. This reluctance and hesitation needs to be guarded against, lest the firm find itself no longer in the vanguard of innovation.

Assume the role of vocal and critical stockholder at the annual meeting. What arguments would you introduce for a crash program to rush the PC to market, and damn any possible cannibalizing? What contrary arguments would you expect, and how would you counter them?

"The job is to understand the customer's needs in detail."[12]

The sales force had become reluctant to sell low-margin open systems if it could push proprietary mainframes or minicomputers, regardless of customers' needs.

Bloated Costs. Indicative of the fat that had insidiously grown in the organization, IBM cut some 42,900 jobs in 1992, thankfully all through early retirement programs. An additional 25,000 people were expected to be laid off in 1993, some without the benefit of early retirement packages. Health benefits for employees were also scaled down. Manufacturing capacity was reduced 25 percent, and two of three mainframe development labs were closed. But perhaps the area of greatest bloat was R & D.

---

[12] Kirkpatrick, "Breaking Up IBM," 49, 52.

The Diminishing Payoff of Massive R & D Expenditures. As noted earlier, IBM spent heavily on research and development, often as much as 10 percent of sales, as shown in Table 5.3. Its research labs were by far the largest and costliest of their kind in the world.

And IBM labs were capable of inventing amazing things. For example, they recently developed the world's smallest transistor, at 1/75,000th the width of a human hair.

Somehow, with all these R & D resources and expenditures, IBM lagged in transferring its innovation to the marketplace. The organization lacked the ability to quickly translate laboratory prototypes into commercial triumphs. Commercial R & D is wasted without this translation.

Controversies

Questionable Decisions. No executive has a perfect batting average of good decisions. Indeed, most executives do well to bat more than 500—that is, to have more good decisions than bad decisions. But, alas, this is all relative. So much depends on the importance and the consequences of these decisions.

IBM's made a decision of monumental long-term consequences in the early 1980s. At that time, IBM delegated to two upstart West Coast companies the task of being a key supplier for its new personal computer. Thus, it gave away the chance to control the personal computer industry. Over the next 10 years, each of the two young firms was to develop a near-monopoly—Intel in microprocessors and Microsoft in operating-systems software—by setting standards for successive PC generations. Instead of keeping such developments proprietary, that is, within its own organization, in an urge to save developmental time, IBM gave these two small firms a golden opportunity that both grasped to the fullest. By 1992 Intel and Microsoft had emerged as the computer industry's most dominant firms.

Table 5.3 IBM Research and Development Expenditures As a Percent of Revenues, 1987–1991

	1987	1988	1989	1990	1991
Revenues ($mil)	$54,217	$59,681	$62,710	$64,792	$67,045
Research, development, and engineering costs	5,434	5,925	6,827	6,554	6,644
Percent of revenues	10.0%	9.9%	10.9%	10.1%	9.9%

Source: Company annual reports.
Commentary: Where has been the significant contribution from such heavy investment in R & D

And yet the decision is still controversial. It saved IBM badly needed time in bringing its PC to market. And as computer technology becomes ever more complex, not even an IBM can be expected to have the ability and resources to go it alone. Linking up with competitors offers better products and services and a faster flow of technology today, and it seems the wave of the future.

Former IBM CEO Thomas Watson, Jr., has also criticized his successors, Frank Cary and John Opel, for phasing out rentals and selling the massive mainframe computer outright. Originally, purchasers could only lease the machines, thus giving IBM a dependable cushion of cash each year ("my golden goose," Mr. Watson called it).[13] Doing away with this renting left IBM and John Akers a newly volatile business, just as the industry position began worsening. Akers, just installed as CEO, was thus left with a hostile environment without the cushion or support of steady revenues coming from such rentals. So Watson's argument goes. But the counterposition is that selling quickly brought needed cash into company coffers. Furthermore, it is unlikely, given the more competitive climate that was emerging in the late 1980s, that big customers would continue to tolerate the leasing arrangement when they could own their machines, if not from IBM, from another supplier whose machines were just as good, if not better.

Breaking Up IBM. The general consensus of management experts favored the reforms of Akers to break Big Blue up into 13 divisions and give them increasing autonomy—even to the point that shares of some of these new Baby Blues might be distributed to stockholders. The idea is not unlike that of Japan's *keiretsu*, in which groups of companies with common objectives but with substantial independence seek and develop business individually.

The assumption in favor of such a break up is that the sum of the parts is greater than the whole, that the autonomy and motivation will bring more total revenues and profits. But these hypothesized benefits are not ensured. At issue is whether the good of the whole would be better served by suboptimizing some business units—that is, by limiting profit maximization of some units in order to have the highest degree of coordination and cooperation. Giving disparate units of an organization goals of individual profit maximization lays the seeds for intense intramural competition, with cannibalization and infighting likely. IBM has embarked on a program of decentralization and intramural competition. But will gross profit margins deteriorate even more with such competition? Is the whole better served by a less intensely competitive internal environment? That is the issue.

[13]Miller, "Watson Offers Personal Views," A4.

POSTSCRIPT

By June 1994 IBM stock was trading in the range of $62 to $63 per share, a significant comeback from the low $40s it had sunk to in fall 1993 and the low $50s when Lou Gerstner took IBM's top job in April 1993. Part of this rise was due to a $496 million operating profit for the fourth quarter of 1993. Part of it reflected new investor confidence that IBM was turning itself around, sparked by a market share gain in personal computers. Is such investor confidence misguided?

It perhaps is too soon to tell if IBM has truly been turned around. After all, in one year's time, can any leader impose major constructive changes on a tradition-ridden behemoth? But other positive signs are emerging. Notable among them is the fact that although IBM has let go some 180,000 employees worldwide since 1986, it has recently hired over 1300 professionals, including 36 new executives. "We want fresh blood at every level," said IBM's new human resources chief, Gerald Czarnecki. "New ideas, new ways of seeing the world."[14]

WHAT CAN BE LEARNED?

Beware of the cannibalization phobia. We have just set the parameters of the issue of cannibalization—that is, how far a firm should go in developing products and encouraging intramural competition that will take sales away from other products and units of the business. The issue is particularly troubling when the part of business that is likely to suffer is the most profitable in the company. And yet cannibalization should not even be an issue. At stake is the forward-leaning of the company, its embracing of innovation and improved technology, and its competitive stance. Unless a firm has an assured monopoly position, it can expect competitors to introduce advances in technology and/or new efficiencies of productivity and customer service.

In general we can conclude that no firm should rest on its laurels. Firms must introduce improvements and change as soon as possible, hopefully ahead of the competition, without regard to any possible impairment of sales and profits of existing products and units.

The need to be "lean and mean" (sometimes called "acting small"). The marketplace is uncertain, especially in high-tech industries. In such environments a large firm needs to be as responsive and flexible as smaller firms. It must avoid layers of management, limiting policies, and a tradition-bound

[14]Brigid McMenamin, "What Kind of Duck Are You?" *Forbes* (Mar. 14, 1994): 126-28; David C. Churbuck, "Cassandra Strikes Again," *Forbes* (Feb. 14, 1994): 45; Judith H. Dobrzynski, "Rethinking IBM," *Business Week* (Oct. 4, 1993): 86-97; and Catherine Arnst et al., "IBM Watchers Still find Plenty to Criticize," *Business Week* (Oct. 4, 1993): 96-97.

mindset. Otherwise our big firm is like the behemoth vessel, unable to stop or change course without losing precious time and distance. But how can a big firm keep the maneuverability and innovative-mindedness of a smaller firm? How can it remain "lean and mean" with increasing size?

We can identify certain conditions or factors of lean and mean firms:

1. They have simple organizations. Typically, they are decentralized, with decision making moved lower in the organization. This discourages the buildup of cumbersome bureaucracy and staff, which tends to add both increasing overhead expenses and the red tape that stultifies fast reaction time.

   A simple organization is a relatively flat one, with fewer levels of management than complex firms. This also has certain desirable consequences. Overhead is greatly reduced with fewer executives and their expensive staffs. But communication is also improved, since higher executives are more accessible and directions and feedback are less distorted because of more direct communications channels. Even morale is improved because of the better communications and accessibility to leaders of the organization.

2. They encourage new ideas. A major factor in the inertia of large firms is the managers who see their power threatened by new ideas and innovative directions. Consequently, real creativity is stymied by not being appreciated; often it is even discouraged.

   A firm that wishes to be lean and mean must seek new ideas. This implies giving rewards and recognition for creativity but, even more, acting upon the worthwhile ideas. Few things are more thwarting to creativity in an organization than pigeon-holing the good ideas of eager employees.

3. They move participation in planning as low in the organization as possible. Important employees and lower-level managers should be involved in decisions concerning their responsibilities, and their ideas should receive reasonable weight in final decisions. Performance goals and rewards should be moved as low in the organization as possible. Such an organizational climate encourages innovation, improves motivation and morale, and can lead to the fast reaction time that characterizes small organizations.

4. They have minimum frills, even austerity, at the corporate level. This quality does characterize some highly successful and proactive large organizations. Two of our most successful firms today, Wal-Mart and Southwest Airlines, epitomize this philosophy. A no-frills manage-

ment orientation is the greatest corporate model for curbing frivolous costs throughout an organization.

Beware the "king of the hill" three C's mindset. As a firm gains dominance and maturity, it must guard against conservatism, complacency, and conceit. Usually these three C's set in at the highest levels and eagerly filter down to the rest of the organization. As discussed earlier, this mindset leaves a firm highly vulnerable to smaller and hungrier competitors. And so the "king of the hill" is toppled.

Although top management usually initiates such a mindset, top management can also lead in inhibiting it. The lean and mean organization is anathema to the three C's mindset. If we can curb bureaucratic buildup, then the seeds are thwarted. Perhaps most important in preventing this mindset is encouragement of innovative thinking throughout the organization as well as a policy of bringing in fresh blood from outside the organization to fill some positions. A strict adherence to promotion from within is inhibiting.

We can overcome adversity! Perhaps the most valuable lesson that any organization, and its interested publics, can embrace is that adversity is not forever. Firms can come back—as we will describe later in this book. IBM can come back and become a strong player in its industry. With the computer technology market broadening and evolving, it may never achieve its former dominant position of the 1960s and 1970s—all lost ground may not be regained. But it can prosper again and become an organization to be proud of. Managements of any consequence, and with any resources, should be capable of learning from their mistakes. Mistakes should be valuable learning experiences, leading the way to better performance and decisions in the future.

CONSIDER

What additional learning insights do you see as emerging from the IBM case?

QUESTIONS

1. Assess the pro and con arguments for the 1982 decision to delegate to Microsoft and Intel a foothold in software and operating systems. (Keep your perspective to that of the early 1980s; don't be biased with the benefit of hindsight.)
2. Do you see any way that IBM could have maintained its nimbleness

and technological edge as it grew to a $60 billion company? Reflect on this, and be as creative as you can.

3. "Tradition has no place in corporate thinking today." Discuss this statement.

4. Playing devil's advocate (one who takes an opposing position for the sake of argument), can you defend the position that the problems besetting IBM were not its fault, that they were beyond its control?

5. Would you say that the major problems confronting IBM are marketing rather than organizational issues? Why or why not?

6. Which of the three C's do you think was most to blame for IBM's problems? Why?

INVITATION TO ROLE PLAY

1. As the new CEO brought in to turnaround IBM in 1993, what do you propose to do? (State any assumptions you find necessary, but keep them reasonable. And don't be swayed by what actually happened. Perhaps better actions could have been taken.) Be as specific as you can, and also discuss the constraints likely to face your turnaround program.

2. You are a marketing consultant reporting to the CEO in the late 1980s. IBM is still racking up revenue and profit gains. But you detect serious emerging weaknesses. What do you advise management to do at this time? (Make any assumptions you feel necessary, but state them clearly.) Persuasively explain your rationale.

INVITATION TO RESEARCH

What is the present situation of IBM? Has the great turnaround occurred? What major corrective decisions were made?

CHAPTER 6

Sears: Faltering to Competitors

On January 25, 1993, Sears announced that after 107 years, the company would no longer offer its venerable catalog. In its long history, the catalog had become part of the American heritage, at least that of rural and small-town America. It was known as the "wish book," as its well-used pages spurred the dreams of countless children and their parents and stimulated their aspirations for a better life.

At the time of the announcement, the catalog was a $3.3 billion operation. Yet it was a source of recurring losses in recent years, losses that a reeling giant could no longer sustain. The closing would cost 3,400 full-time and 16,500 part-time jobs.[1]

Heavy costs of production and operation at a time of declining demand crippled the catalog's ability to maintain profitability. Perhaps a bigger factor in its demise was the inroads of Wal-Mart stores into rural towns (see Chapter 18 for the Wal-Mart case). Consumers could now find a wide variety of goods at lower prices. Yet many other catalogs of all kinds are flourishing. Perhaps the Sears catalog was symptomatic of the problems facing its parent.

HISTORY

Richard W. Sears founded the R. W. Sears Watch Company in 1886 in Minneapolis. A year later, Alvah C. Roebuck joined the company, and the firm moved to Chicago. The corporate name, Sears, Roebuck and Company, was formalized in 1893.

---

[1]"History Collides With The Bottom Line," *Business Week* (Feb. 8, 1993): 34.

In the early years, the chief business was selling watches by mail order to people in small towns and rural areas. The assortment of goods rapidly expanded, and by 1896 a first general catalog of over 500 pages was published. It was not until 1925, almost 40 years after the founding, that General Robert E. Wood, then a senior vice president, experimented with a retail store in Chicago. Its success laid the groundwork for the retail expansion to come.

Expansion was rapid. By the end of 1927, Sears had 27 stores in operation, three times the number in the previous years. In 1931 Sears retail stores sales exceeded mail-order sales for the first time, contributing 53.4 percent of total sales. And the growth continued, slackening only during World War II. See Table 6.1 for the growth in retail stores for selected years.

General Wood formed a major subsidiary in 1931: Allstate Insurance Company. At first it operated only by mail, but in a few years it took sales locations in Sears stores. In his long tenure at the helm of Sears, General Wood also instituted a major store location policy after World War II. Instead of locating additional stores in crowded downtowns, he pioneered the idea of locating in outlying areas with an abundance of free parking. And the expansion continued. Table 6.2 shows sales and income statistics for Sears and its two major competitors from 1938 to 1955. By now, Sears was the largest retailer, as it was to remain for over 50 years.

Sears made some important nonretail acquisitions in 1981 by bringing in Coldwell Banker, the nation's largest residential real estate broker, and Dean Witter Reynolds, the fifth biggest U.S. brokerage house. They set up shop in the rich trafficways of Sears stores in the same marketing mode as

Table 6.1   Number of Retail Stores, 1925–1988

Year	Number of Stores
1925	1
1927	27
1928	192
1933	400
1941	600
1948	632
1970	827
1975	858
1979	864
1985	799
1988	824

Source: Sears annual reports.
Commentary: Note the great growth in the number of stores up until the early 1970s, then a gradual decline, until by the 1980s there were fewer stores than a decade earlier. This reflects that poorly performing stores were being closed. But it also reflects that few new stores were being opened despite the fact that retail space of all retailers doubled during the 1970s and 1980s.

Table 6.2 Sales and Income Statistics for Sears, Ward, and Penney, 1938–1954

Years	Ward Sales (000)	Ward Net Income (000)	Sears Sales (000)	Sears Net Income (000)	Penney Sales (000)	Penney Net Income (000)
1938	$ 414,091	$ 19,210	$ 537,242	$ 30,828	$ 257,971	$ 13,799
1942	632,709	22,353	915,058	29,934	490,356	18,058
1944	595,933	20,677	852,597	33,866	533,374	17,159
1946	654,779	22,932	1,045,359	35,835	676,570	35,495
1948	1,158,675	59,050	1,981,536	107,740	885,195	47,754
1950	1,084,436	47,788	2,168,928	108,207	949,712	44,931
1952	1,106,157	54,342	2,657,408	111,895	1,072,266	37,170
1954	999,123	41,195	2,981,925	117,882	1,107,157	43,617

Source: Moody's and company annual reports for respective years.
Commentary: Note the fading of Ward during this period. This reflects the no-growth policy of Ward chairman, Sewell Avery, after World War II. Ward was never again to be a significant factor, as Sears continued to surge ahead as the biggest retailer.

the highly profitable Allstate Insurance subsidiary. In 1985 Sears celebrated its 100th birthday, and a year later, it introduced the soon-to-be-successful Discover credit card.

But trouble was on the horizon for the huge firm and its key retail sector. Its major competitors now were not Ward and Penney, but two discounters, Wal-Mart and Kmart. By the end of the 1980s, these two would wrest Sears from its long-held position as largest retailer, while Sears struggled to define its identity in a changed environment.

EDWARD A. BRENNAN

The preservation of the traditional greatness of Sears had to loom large in the mind of Edward A. Brennan, chairman and chief executive of the behemoth retail conglomerate, as events unfolded in late 1992. He was a third-generation Sears man and had for more than a decade guided its somehow-faltering destiny. His rise to top position had the flavor of a legend.

Born in Chicago in 1934 to a family wedded to Sears virtually from the company's beginnings—a grandfather had worked beside Richard Sears, the company's founder—Brennan graduated from Marquette University with a degree in business administration in 1955. He left another job to join Sears in 1956, taking a drastic cut in pay of $4,000 to become a salesman in the Madison, Wisconsin, store. Progress was fast. By 1958 he was running the Sears store in Oshkosh, Wisconsin, and by the end of 1959 he was transferred to the Sears headquarters in Chicago. In 1967 he was again made manager of a store, this time in Baltimore's black ghetto, where his performance came to the attention of Edward Telling, the manager of the eastern territory. In 1969 Telling promoted Brennan to one of the biggest stores in the territory, and the following year made him assistant general manager of the New York group of stores. And his star continued to rise.

Invariably in his new positions Brennan distinguished himself by converting losing or mediocre operations to top profit generators. He accepted so many transfers that he once owned homes in three cities. In 1977 he became executive vice president of the southern territory, consisting of 13 groups and 150 stores, and with the promotion also became a member of the company's board of directors. In 1978 the south moved from third to first among territories in profitability, and on March 12, 1980, Telling, then chairman of the company, named Brennan president of Sears and chief operating officer of the merchandising group.

With this achievement Brennan was viewed as a 46-year-old "boy wonder," who had vaulted over senior executives, putting in 90-hour weeks as he moved from territory to territory, store to store. (The work ethic of the Brennan family also carried over to his younger brother, Bernard, who, after becoming a Sears buyer, eventually wound up as head of Montgomery Ward, Sears' long-time merchandising rival.)

Somehow, Brennan's success pattern, based on hard work and a firm dedication to his company, proved vulnerable in this top corporate job. Perhaps no one could have resurrected the company in the dynamic environment of the 1980s. Or perhaps the task could have been better performed by an outsider, someone not part of the glory days of Sears.

The basic thrust of Sears' merchandising policies had been to provide standard-quality goods at low prices, thereby appealing to low- and middle-income Americans, although several times the company had tried to upgrade and become fashion-oriented for more affluent customers. These attempts had little success; indeed, in the process of such upgrading, Sears risked losing its mainstream customers.

When Brennan took over as president in 1980, his emphasis was on quality, assortment, and service:

> We've adopted quality as our number one strategy for the years ahead . . . The customer also expects to go into a store and find that store fully stocked. The customer wants good service. It's the store that puts all those things together best that will get the best market share.[2]

Brennan continued to centralize major policy decisions in Chicago and began revamping stores with more aisles, lower ceilings, and better displays. He introduced such national apparel brands as Levis, Wrangler, and Wilson to

---

[2] Joseph Winski, "New President Hopes to Strike Balance at Sears," *Chicago Tribune* (March 17, 1980): 10, sec. 5.

supplement the house brands, such as Craftsman tools, Kenmore appliances, and Diehard batteries, which had strong consumer acceptance. However, the merchandise group continued to slip in profits and market share.

In Brennan's tenure the financial services areas began contributing the bulk of the growth in sales and profits. The company was close to achieving the goal of meeting both the shopping and financial services needs of middle America, a strategy sometimes described as "socks and stocks." Revenues of financial services had grown from $9.5 billion in 1982 to $26 billion in 1991. Even more impressive, the profits of financial services had reached $1.1 billion in 1991, far outstripping the merchandising group profits of $486 million. See Table 6.3 for the trend in relative profits of these two areas. Despite the profitable growth of financial services, the erosion of the core merchandising business had to be troubling.

Brennan, who had been elected chairman and chief executive in 1985, by no means ignored the retailing end of the business. He introduced the first "store of the future" in King of Prussia, Pennsylvania, in 1982, shortly after assuming the presidency. By 1989 all Sears stores fit this more modern prototype. He had tried various programs to promote the clothing end of the business, using supermodel Cheryl Tiegs and tennis star Yvonne Goolagong, to spur apparel sales, but with no apparent success. He even tried "everyday low prices," the strategy used by Wal-Mart and Kmart on customers tired of the "sales" game. This was announced with much fanfare in 1989. Unfortunately, it also bombed, as the high overhead structure of Sears did not allow it to give its customers rock-bottom prices. Despite the disappointments of these strategic ventures, let us note a great potential advantage that retail chain organizations have, as described in the following box.

Table 6.3   Contribution of Total Net Income of Financial Services and Merchandising Group, 1970–1991 (in millions)

Year	Net Income	Financial		Merchandising	
		Amount	%	Amount	%
1970	468	125	27	343	73
1975	523	129	25	394	75
1977	838	474	57	364	43
1979	830	549	66	281	34
1982	861	429	50	432	50
1985	1,294	528	41	766	59
1988	1,454	930	64	524	36
1991	1,586	1,100	69	486	31

Source: Sears annual reports.

Commentary: Note the increasingly subordinate role in corporate profits of the merchandising group in recent years, falling to only 31 percent of total in 1991, the lowest ever.

INFORMATION BOX

ADVANTAGES OF CHAINS: OPPORTUNITY FOR EXPERIMENTATION

An organization with numerous similar outlets has an unparalleled opportunity for experimenting with new ideas in the quest for what might be most productive and compelling. Prospective strategy changes can be tested with a few stores, any promising modifications determined, and the success of the strategy ascertained from concrete sales and profits results. All this can be done with relatively little risk since only a few outlets of the total chain are involved, and the strategy can be adopted throughout the organization only if results look favorable. Such experimentation is hardly possible for the firm with few comparable units, which describes most manufacturers, and consequently its risks in making major strategic changes are greater.

How would you design an experiment for a chain organization? Be as specific as you can, and make any assumptions needed.

The great strength of the Sears retail operation had long been its home improvement area—paint, power tools, siding, hardware, tires. These durable goods accounted for almost 70 percent of Sears' revenues from merchandise. But now even this was suffering. Such upstart competitors as Home Depot and Builders Square robustly gained market share at Sears' expense.

SEPTEMBER 30, 1992

In a special meeting, Sears directors approved a program to spin off the Dean Witter Financial Services Group, most of its Coldwell Banker real-estate holdings, and 20 percent of its Allstate insurance unit. The moves would reduce Sears' heavy debt by $3 billion. Essentially, Sears would be taken back to where it was in 1981, when Brennan first assumed the office of president, except that Sears's retail business had lost its dominance in the ensuing years.

The idea of spinning off subsidiaries was nothing new; it had been urged by some shareholders in the past. The assumption behind any such move is that the whole of the company is worth less than the sum of its parts. Therefore, shareholders would benefit. Some estimates were that the breakup of the company could bring $80 to $90 a share, versus the low $40s for the entire firm.[3]

Still, the suddenness and the completeness of the directors' decision was surprising, and Sears became the center of attention in the business

---

[3]Jeff Bailey, "Sears Stock Fails to Show Further Rally," *Wall Street Journal* (Oct. 1, 1992): A4. Also, Robert A.G. Monks, "Sears and the Shareholder," *Wall Street Journal* (Oct. 1, 1992): A16.

press. Besides the slowly deteriorating state of the retail business, several other factors probably led to the abrupt decision. In recent months, Sears auto centers had received bad publicity about overcharging customers, as we will describe in the next section. In addition, Hurricane Andrew had resulted in huge claims for the Allstate unit. And on September 25, Moody's Investors' Services lowered Sears' credit rating.

The decision was also described in headlines as a "humbling move for Brennan," since he had been the architect of most of the diversification efforts.[4] Despite the plaudits of some Sears investors and a strong $3.375 rise in the stock price the next day, serious concerns could be raised.

Spinning off the healthiest sectors of the business would mean that the underperforming retail sector would no longer be buttressed by financial support. The weaknesses of its operation would be all the more visible to the public and could hardly be hidden in corporate total statistics. With the retail operation unlikely to be quickly—if ever—turned around, Sears was going with its losers and getting rid of its winners.

ACCUSATIONS OF FRAUD AT SEARS AUTO CENTERS

On June 12, 1992, national publications reported that the California Department of Consumer Affairs had accused Sears of systematically over-charging auto-repair customers. The agency even went so far as to propose revoking the company's license to operate its automotive centers in the state.

The year-long undercover investigation had been prompted by a grow-ing number of consumer complaints. For example:

> Ruth Hernandez of Stockton, California, went to Sears to buy new tires for her 1986 Honda Accord. The Sears mechanic insisted that she also needed new struts at a cost of $419.95. Shocked, she sought a second opinion, and another auto-repair store told her the struts were fine. Hernandez was livid and she returned to Sears where a sheepish mechanic admitted the diagnosis was wrong. "I keep thinking," Hernandez reflected, "how many other people this has happened to."[5]

The Department of Consumer Affairs found that its agents were over-charged at Sears Centers nearly 90 percent of the time by an average of $233. The department said that repairmen were pressured to overcharge by Sears' punitive sales quotas. "This is a flagrant breach of the trust and confidence

---

[4]Gregory A. Patterson and Francine Schwadel, "Sears Suddenly Undoes Years of Diversifying Beyond Retailing Field," *Wall Street Journal* (Sept. 30, 1992): A1.

[5]Example taken from Keven Kelly, "How Did Sears Blow This Gasket?" *Business Week* (June 29, 1992): 38.

the people of California have placed in Sears for generations," said Jim Conran, director of the department. "Sears has used trust as a marketing tool, and we don't believe they've lived up to that trust."[6]

The Sears case may be the biggest fraud action ever against an auto-repair firm. Although the investigation was conducted in California, the findings seemingly represented a much more widespread problem, perhaps involving Sears's 850 auto repair centers nationwide.

At first Sears vigorously contested the allegations. It called the accusations by California regulators politically motivated and denied any fraud. It accused regulators of trying to gain support at a time when they were threatened by severe budget cuts. Sears' lawyers held this position for several days. But the crisis intensified, especially a few days later when New Jersey regulators said that they, too, had found overcharges common in Sears shops.

Sears soon adopted a more conciliatory stance. It took out full-page ads in major newspapers in the form of a letter from Chairman Brennan, who expressed deep concern about the problem and pledged that Sears would satisfy all its customers: "With over two million automotive customers serviced last year in California alone, mistakes may have occurred. However, Sears wants you to know that we would never intentionally violate the trust customers have shown in our company for 105 years." But auto service sales dropped 15 percent. And this was a division that had produced 9 percent of Sears' merchandising groups revenues and had been one of the fastest growing and most profitable business units in recent years, servicing 20 million vehicles in 1991.[7]

To appease the critics and assure the public of its honesty, Sears pledged to stop using the quota and commission system for its auto center employees and to substitute a full salary plan. However, on March 7, 1994, *Wall Street Journal* disclosed that Sears was quietly reinstating sales incentives in some auto centers. Jim Thornton, Sears automotive vice president, defended the use of commissions and cited safeguards he said should prevent a recurrence of the 1992 problems. "We don't believe all commission is bad," he said.[8]

WHAT WENT WRONG?

Sears merchandising efforts represent a classic example of nonresponse to a changing environment. While Brennan made some efforts to institute change—

---

[6]Tung Yin, "Sears is Accused of Billing Fraud at Auto Centers," *Wall Street Journal* (June 12, 1992): B1, B6.

[7]Gregory A. Patterson, "Sears's Brennan Accepts Blame for Auto Flap," *Wall Street Journal* (June 23, 1992): B1, B12.

[8]Gilbert Fuchsberg, "Sears Reinstates Sales Incentives in Some Centers," *Wall Street Journal* (March 7, 1994): B1.

store of the future, brand-name merchandise, and everyday low prices, for example—these were really only surface gestures of little consequence.

Of much more import, Sears allowed aggressive competitors to capture ever more market share. It ignored sweeping changes in demographics and shopping habits, under the assumption that the Sears way of doing business was unassailable. Yet all the while Sears was losing business: to department stores who offered customers more ambience; to discounters and specialty stores such as Toys R Us, Home Depot, and Circuit City Stores that focused on a single category of goods but offered huge assortments at low prices; and to Wal-Mart and Kmart stores that offered the widest possible variety of goods at prices that Sears simply could not match. See the following box for a discussion of the need for environmental monitoring.

In its many decades of retail dominance, Sears had built up a bureaucratic organizational structure. This seems to be a natural evolution for organizations as they achieve great size and dominance over decades.

The natural consequence of Sears's organization structure was not only that it failed to respond well to a rapidly changing environment, but also

---

INFORMATION BOX

NEED FOR ENVIRONMENTAL MONITORING

A firm must be alert to changes in the business environment: changes in customer preferences and needs, in competition, in the economy, and even in international events, such as nationalism in Canada, OPEC machinations, and economic and social changes in Eastern Europe. Many of the mistakes in the book are at least partly attributable to a failure to recognize how the business environment was changing and that unchanging policies were no longer appropriate.

How can a firm such as Sears, or IBM for that matter, remain alert to subtle and insidious as well as more obvious changes? A firm must have sensors constantly monitoring the environment. The sensor may reside in a marketing or economic research department, but in many instances such a formal organizational entity is not really necessary to provide primary monitoring. Executive alertness is essential. Few changes occur suddenly and without warning. Companies can get feedback from customers, from sales representatives, from suppliers; can keep abreast of the latest material and projections in business journals; and can observe what is happening in stores, in advertising, in pricing, and in the introduction of new technologies. These sources can provide sufficient information about the environment and how it is changing. Sensors of the environment can be organized and formal, or they can be strictly informal and subjective. But it is surprising and disturbing how many executives overlook, disregard, or are not even aware of important changing environmental factors that presage changes in their present and future business.

How would you go about ensuring that your firm has adequate sensors of the marketplace?

that it was burdened with such a high overhead that it was unable to match the prices of its most aggressive competitors. For example, in 1991 Sears spent 29.2 percent of its revenues on salaries, light bills, advertising, and other routine costs. At the same time, Kmart's expenses amounted to 19.6 percent of sales, and Wal-Mart's were even less, at 15.3 percent.[9] So Sears was left somewhere in a sterile middle between department stores and discount stores. By no means did it offer the ambience and fashion atmosphere of good department stores, and it certainly could not profitably match the prices of its discount competitors. One could wonder whether Sears had become an anachronism, an impotent throwback to an earlier time now sadly out of place and competitively vulnerable.

Perhaps Sears let its attention shift too much away from its core retail business in its quest for diversification into financial services. Brennan was the second Sears chairman to see the stores as a great vehicle for disseminating certain kinds of consumer services in addition to merchandise. Certainly, the logic seemed inescapable. See the following box.

In the last decade at least, the basic business of Sears appears to have been relatively neglected, as attention turned more to services. Perhaps this would also have happened without such diversification. It could well be argued that the lack of substantial change and innovation in the retail operation resulted from a smug and complacent organization (we have certainly encountered this situation before, and we will again). Some telling statistics support the conclusion that the retail sector was badly neglected, whatever the reasons might have been.

During the late 1970s and the 1980s, U.S. store space doubled. Yet Sears failed to add retail space in this period. (See Table 6.1 for the trend in number of stores.) Instead, it concentrated on closing unprofitable stores and remodeling others. Naturally, it lost market share. Its share of sales of department-store-type merchandise in the United States dropped to less than 6 percent from more than 8 percent.[10] And Sears catalog sales also stagnated, despite a boom in catalogs of all kinds during this period.

The 1980s was also marked as a time of rapid expansion of specialty stores, stores featuring limited lines of merchandise but great depth within the categories. Some of these were highly successful, such as Limited, Gap, and such discount specialty stores as Toys R Us and Kids R Us. Sears dabbled a bit with specialty stores during this period, opening Business Systems Centers, separate paint and hardware stores, a small chain of eye-care products, and one petite women's clothing chain. And it acquired the Western

---

[9]Stephanie Strom, "Further Prescriptions for the Convalescent Sears," *New York Times* (Oct. 1, 1992): D1.

[10]Patterson and Schwadel, "Sears Suddenly Undoes Years," A16.

INFORMATION BOX

SHOULD RETAILERS DIVERSIFY INTO SERVICES?

Although merchandising of services may seem far afield from traditional retailing and its merchandising of goods, in some ways consumer services are natural areas for expansion. Especially is this true for the retailer with a reputation for dependability and a sizable body of loyal customers with active charge accounts. Sears led most retailers in such diversifications. Much of the success of Sears in promoting its home repair and appliance servicing, and even its auto service, was due to its image of reliability, honest work, and guaranteed satisfaction. Many customers saw these characteristics sorely needed in repair industries, where honest work and dependability were usually lacking. They trusted Sears. (Unfortunately, such trust received a setback in mid-1992 when publicity, as we have seen, surfaced that Sears auto centers had been overcharging customers—just like the rest of the industry in the thinking of many consumers.)

Financial services—insurance, investments, real estate—are viewed by many middle-class Americans as just as arcane and subject to abuse as repair services. It seemed natural that a trusting relationship regarding Sears' quality and dependability could be transferred also to this area. And indeed there was a mutual compatibility, as the success of financial services in the Sears organization has proven.

Unfortunately, corporate executives from Brennan on down perhaps became too enamored with this end of the total operation. In the process, they let Sears' core business slip, perhaps irretrievably.

On balance, was the diversification of Sears all that wise?

Given that the core business is not neglected in the promotion of services, do you see any other dangers in such diversification?

Auto chain of auto supplies stores. But the efforts seemed too little and too late to capitalize on this specialty store trend.

POSTSCRIPT

Although Sears' dreams of again becoming the number-one retailer in the United States are unlikely ever to become reality, the fortunes of Sears are beginning to look up. Brennan had wanted to build a financial services and retailing empire, but he was forced to abandon the dream, sell Dean Witter and Coldwell Banker units, and focus on Sears' retail business. With the help of Saks Fifth Avenue executive Arthur Martinez, he eliminated the catalog and trampled other Sears traditions as talented executives came to Sears from outside. Better marketing and merchandising resulted. In 1993 sales were just over $50 billion, with profits of almost $2.5 billion.[11]

[11] Joyce M. Rosenberg, "Kmart Execs Facing Some Tough Choices," *Cleveland Plain Dealer* (June 7, 1994): 14C; "The *Forbes* 500 Ranking," *Forbes* (April 25, 1994): 290.

WHAT CAN BE LEARNED?

Neglect core business at your peril. Unless the prospects for a firm's core business are so bleak that resources and efforts need to be shifted, it is a monumental mistake to neglect the core. This is where a company's expertise is; it is the focal point of the heritage of success. The core should not be neglected in the quest for exciting but often unproven new ventures, ventures that have to be built up over time by trial and error. Sears was guilty of this: It shifted attention from retail goods to financial services. Although these diversifications were successful, the deemphasis of the flagship part of its business may never be surmounted.

Again, beware the "king of the hill" three C's mindset. In the preceding case we encountered this destructive trio that weaken frontrunners: conservatism, complacency, and conceit. As IBM's responsiveness to changing conditions was stymied because of this pervasive orientation, so has Sears' been. In Chapter 5, we discussed how a large and mature organization can guard against such a mindset. You may want to review this.

Can great size be achieved without becoming a bureaucratic organization? The bureaucratic stage is a natural evolution as a firm becomes larger and more dominant in its industry, but companies can guard against it. A firm can seek an adaptive organizational structure, emphasizing decentralization, minimizing rules and procedures, creating an open and flexible division of labor, establishing a wide span of control, and emphasizing informal and personal rather than formal and impersonal coordination. So a firm *can* avoid becoming a ponderous and high overhead organization. But it takes a strong top management commitment, a commitment to minimize the insularity of the executive suite and avoid cultivating more staff positions.

CONSIDER

What additional learning insights can you gain from the Sears case?

QUESTIONS

1. Do you think Sears' retail business can be turned around? Why or why not?
2. How would you propose streamlining the Sears bureaucratic organization? Be as specific as you can. If you need to make assumptions, state them clearly.
3. What is your opinion of the Sears auto repair centers? Do you think their overcharging was less than, worse than, or about the same as their competitors'? What led you to this opinion?

4. A common practice of repair people in all areas is to replace some parts that are still workable with new parts. This, of course, raises the price of the repair. But is this really such a bad practice? After all, the new parts should assure longer trouble-free use of the car.
5. Overreliance on promotion from within often is more harmful than desirable in an organization. Evaluate the promotion of Ed Brennan.
6. Evaluate the 1993 decision to drop the Sears catalog. What arguments can you see for keeping it?
7. "We don't believe all commission is bad," said Jim Thornton, the Sears official in charge of its auto centers, in 1994. Evaluate this statement.

ROLE PLAY

1. It is 1980, and you are the staff assistant to the president of Sears. You sense that major shifts in retailing are emerging and that Sears needs to change if it is to keep its market dominance.
   a. What research do you recommend for tracking competitive thrusts?
   b. Based on what we know in 1994, what actions should Sears have undertaken in the 1980s? Do you think these efforts would have been successful in preserving market dominance? Why or why not?
2. You are executive assistant to Edward Brennan, CEO of Sears. He wants to institute sweeping reforms in the auto repair operations. What arguments can you give him not to push the panic button, but to institute only very modest changes? What counterarguments do you expect?

INVITATION TO RESEARCH

What is the current situation with Sears? Is Brennan still the CEO? Have sweeping changes been started? Has the auto repair business had any more negative publicity?

CHAPTER 7

Borden: Letting Brand Franchises Sour

Elsie the cow has long been the symbol of Borden, the largest producer of dairy products. But Borden grew well beyond dairy products to become a diversified food processor and marketer. Decades of children cherished its Cracker Jacks candied popcorn with a gift in every box; its Creamette pasta is the leading national brand, and it has strong regional brands as well. Lady Borden ice cream, milk, and frozen yogurt are well known, as are other dairy brands, national and regional. Even Elmer's glue belongs to the Borden family. With its well-known brands, Borden experienced solid growth in sales and profits for years and became a $7 billion company. Then in 1991, fortunes took a turn for the worse, and dark days were upon Borden. Top management had somehow allowed its brand franchises—the public recognition and acceptance of its brands—to deteriorate. Regaining lost ground was to prove no easy matter.

PRELUDE TO THE DARK DAYS

Borden was founded in 1857 by Gail Borden, Jr., a former Texas newspaperman. It sold condensed milk during the Civil War and later diversified into chemicals. In the 1960s Borden acquired such food brands as Cracker Jack and ReaLemon. Because of the wide earnings swings of cyclical chemical prices, Eugene J. Sullivan, the CEO, intensified the shift into consumer products in the 1970s.

In November 1991 Anthony S. D'Amato took the helm at Borden. He succeeded Romeo J. Ventres, a good friend, who convinced the board when he retired in 1991 that his protege, D'Amato, was the ideal successor. The two men, however, had sharply different management styles. Ventres was an idea man who had great faith in his top managers and gave them free rein. D'Amato was blunt, profane, and believed in personally becoming deeply involved in operations. D'Amato's different management approach was not well received by some Borden top managers, and the company went downhill fast under D'Amato's chairmanship.

But the seeds of Borden's problems were sowed before D'Amato took the helm. Ventres had dreamed of transforming Borden from a rather unexciting conglomerate into a major food marketer. Between 1986 and 1991, Ventres spent nearly $2 billion on 91 acquisitions. "We were hurriedly buying companies for the sake of buying companies," said one Borden executive. In its rush to move quickly on its acquisition program, the company sometimes spent as little as two weeks researching an acquisition candidate before making a decision.[1]

Some acquisitions turned out to be real losers. For example, in 1987 Borden purchased Laura Scudder potato chips for nearly $100 million. Unfortunately, major union problems led Borden to close all of Laura Scudder's California plants only a year after the purchase. Borden then shifted production to a plant in Salt Lake City, only to encounter high costs and quality control problems it could not correct. In 1993 it sold Laura Scudder for less than $20 million. All told, this fiasco cost Borden nearly $150 million.

Most acquisitions were small and medium-sized regional food and industrial companies. Ventres' strategy was to obtain growth by marketing these regional brands beyond their regular market areas. By consolidating manufacturing and distribution, he thought Borden could become the low-cost producer of a variety of product lines, thereby gaining more clout in the marketplace.

In the late 1980s this strategy seemed to work well. With its acquisitions, company sales grew 54 percent between 1985 and 1988. Earnings climbed even sharper to 61 percent, the most rapid growth in the company's history. (See Table 7.1.) Regional marketing and tailoring products to local tastes seemed a potent strategy.

In 1987, *Fortune* magazine featured Borden as a model of corporate performance. It termed the company "a consumer products brute" and extolled "some 40 acquisitions over two years that have made Borden, already the world's largest dairy company, the nationwide king of pasta and the second-largest seller of snack foods behind PepsiCo's Frito-Lay." The regional brand strategy was praised as motivating regionals to create new products as well as borrow from one another. For example, in just 6 weeks, Snacktime, one of Borden's new regional brands, developed Krunchers!, a kettle-cooked

---

[1]Kathleen Deveny and Suein L. Hwang, "A Defective Strategy of Heated Acquisitions Spoils Borden Name," *Wall Street Journal* (Jan. 18, 1994): A4.

Table 7.1   Revenues and Net Income, 1983–1989

	Revenues (in $millions)	% Change	Net Income (in $millions)	% Change
1989	7,593	4.8	(61)	
1988	7,244	11.2	312	16.9
1987	6,514	30.2	267	19.7
1986	5,002	6.1	223	14.9
1985	4,716	3.2	194	1.5
1984	4,568	7.1	191	1.1
1983	4,265	—	189	—

Source: Company reports.
Commentary: Growth was steady during most of these years, but it really accelerated in 1987 and 1988. No wonder the 1987 *Fortune* article spoke in glowing terms about Borden.

potato chip differentiated from those made the conventional way through continuous frying. The chip became an instant success, generating $17 million in annual sales.[2]

In 1987, the milk business was among the most profitable in the industry. Borden, with its Elsie the cow symbol, was able to charge more than competitors could, which was surprising for a commodity such as milk, which is virtually the same product whatever cow it comes from. The company insisted that its high quality and service standards made the "Borden difference." But when asked exactly what that difference was, a veteran dairyman in a succinct quote said, "About a buck a gallon."[3] Perhaps this was a portent of what was to come.

Premonitions

Flaws in the execution of the strategy were beginning to emerge by end of the 1980s. In the race to expand the food portfolio, the company had ignored some of the well-known and successful brands it already had. For example, it had sold ice cream under the Lady Borden label for decades, but it ignored the golden opportunity in the 1980s to extend the line into super-premium ice cream, which was becoming highly popular. Borden showed the same negligence in not aggressively developing new products for many of its other strongest brand names. (See the following box for a discussion of the effective brand extension strategy.) And one could wonder how much longer the price premium charged for milk and Lady Borden ice cream could hold up as the company moved into the skeptical 1990s.

[2]Bill Saporito, "How Borden Milks Packaged Goods," *Fortune* (Dec. 21, 1987): 139–44.
[3]Saporito, "How Borden Milks Packaged Goods," 142.

INFORMATION BOX

BRAND EXTENSION

Brand extension can be a particularly effective use of branding. It is a strategy of applying an established brand name to new products. As a result, customer acceptance of the new products is more likely because of customer familiarity and satisfaction with the existing products bearing the same name. This reduces the risk of new-product failure. Today about one-half of new consumer products use some form of brand extension, such as the same product in a different form, a companion product, or a different product for the same target market.

The more highly regarded a brand is by customers, the better candidate it is for brand extension—provided that a new product will not hurt its reputation and has some relevance to it. The strong favorable image of the Lady Borden brand made it ideal for such brand extension. A favorable image should be zealously protected from being cheapened or having its perception of good value undermined. Discuss why brand extension may not always work.

Borden was now finding difficulty in digesting its hodgepodge of acquisitions. (Table 7.2 shows the broad range of food and nonfood products and the business segment contributions to total sales and profits as of 1992.) It continued to operate as a conglomeration of unintegrated businesses and thereby proved to be neither as efficient as major competitors nor as able to amass marketing clout.

By the time D'Amato took over, the company was clearly ailing. By the end of 1991, sales had declined 5 percent from the previous year, and net income had fallen 19 percent. D'Amato quickly tried to consolidate the loosely structured organization, but all his efforts seemed only to make matters worse.

D'AMATO'S FUTILITY

Shortly after becoming CEO, D'Amato tried to better integrate the morass of consumer food businesses. He wanted to tighten up and centralize the widely decentralized company, with its "dozens of independent fiefdoms." Even corporate offices were scattered between New York City and the hub of the company's operations in Columbus, Ohio. Such geographical distance suited the hands-off management style of Ventres, who rarely got involved in day-to-day operations and spent most of his time at Borden's small Park Avenue offices in New York. D'Amato moved to centralize far-flung operations in Columbus. There he involved himself deeply in day-to-day operations. He increasingly saw the need to eliminate or sell many of Borden's small regional businesses while focusing most efforts on building national brands: a reversal of the strategy of Ventres.

Table 7.2   Business Segment Contributions to Total Company Sales and Earnings, 1992

	Sales	Operating Profits
Grocery[a]	26%	42%
Snacks and International Consumer[b]	26	18
Dairy[c]	20	5
Packaging and Industrial[d]	28	35

[a]Grocery products include North American pasta and sauces (Creamette, Prince, Dutch Maid, Goodman's, Classico, Aunt Millie's); niche grocery products (Eagle-brand condensed milk, Campfire marshmallows, Cracker Jack candied popcorn); refrigerated products (Borden cheese); and food service operations.
[b]Snacks and International Consumer products include Borden's worldwide sweet and salty snacks (Borden, Wise, Snack Time!); other food products outside the United States and Canada (Weber sweet snacks, KLIM milk powder, Lady Borden ice cream); and films and adhesives in the Far East.
[c]Dairy products, including milk, ice cream, and frozen yogurt, are sold under national and branded labels, which include Borden, Lady Borden, Meadow Gold, Viva, and Eagle.
[d]Packaging and Industrial products include consumer adhesives (Elmer's glue); wallcoverings; plastic films and packaging products (Proponite food packaging film, Resinite and Sealwrap vinyl food-wrap films); and foundry, industrial, and specialty resins.
Source: Company public information.

Analysts initially applauded D'Amato's strategy for turning Borden around, but their praise was short-lived. Results failed to meet expectations and even brought new problems.

D'Amato was especially wedded to the notion that the brand recognition of certain brands should allow the company to charge a premium price. For example, Borden's own research had shown that 97 percent of consumers recognized Borden as a leading milk brand.[4] D'Amato saw this as supporting such a premium price. Then, in early 1992, raw milk prices dropped by about one-third. Borden doggedly held its prices while competitors lowered theirs to reflect the drop in commodity prices. Before long, Borden began losing customers, who were realizing that milk is milk. Good brand recognition did not insulate a national brand from lower priced competition of other national brands and private brands. See the following box for a discussion of the battle between national and private brands.

D'Amato opted to tough out the loss of market share, expecting that higher profit margins would offset somewhat lower sales. Only after almost a year of steadily declining sales did he abandon the premium-pricing policy. By then sales had fallen so drastically that the milk division was operating at a loss.

Another marketing mistake involved misuse of advertising. In his strategy to build up Borden's major brands, D'Amato had boosted marketing

[4]Elizabeth Lesly, "Why things Are So Sour At Borden," *Business Week* (Nov. 22, 1993): 82.

INFORMATION BOX

THE BATTLE OF THE BRANDS: PRIVATE VERSUS NATIONAL

Wholesalers and retailers often use their own brands—commonly referred to as private brands—in place of or in addition to the national brands of manufacturers. Private brands usually are offered at lower selling prices than nationally advertised brands, yet they typically give dealers more per-unit profit since they can be bought on more favorable terms, partly reflecting the promotional savings involved. Some firms, such as Sears and Penney, used to stock mostly their own brands. Thus, they had better control over repeat business since satisfied customers could repurchase the brand only through the particular store or chain.

With private brands directly competing with manufacturers' brands, often at a more attractive price, you may ask why manufacturers sell some of their output to retailers under a private brand. A major reason is to minimize idle plant capacity. Manufacturers can always rationalize that if they refuse private-label business, someone else will not, and competition with private brands will continue. Other manufacturers welcome private-brand business because they lack the resources and know-how to enter the marketplace effectively with their own brands.

As we come into the 1990s, more knowledgeable and frugal consumers are realizing that private brands often offer the best value. National consumer brands are being hurt. Recognizing this new intense competition, some manufacturers of branded goods, led by makers of cigarettes and disposable diapers, in 1993 rolled back the price differentials over private brands of their national labels. Borden management had difficulty accepting the idea that the price premiums of its national brands were no longer sustainable if market share was to be maintained.

Do you think the popularity of private brands will continue once the country moves fully out of recession?

How do you personally feel about private brands?

---

efforts for Creamette, the leading national pasta brand. With the sizable promotional expenditures, the brand's sales rose 1.6 percent in 1992. This may have seemed like a significant increase but for the fact that, nationally, pasta sales rose 5.5 percent.

How could the promotional efforts have been so ineffective? Unbelievably, most of the advertising featured recipes aimed at increasing pasta consumption, rather than at building selective demand for the Creamette brand.

Making the marketing efforts for Creamette even more misguided, Borden neglected its regional pasta brands, such as Anthony's in the West and Prince in the Northeast. These sales slumped, so that total division sales were down $600 million in the first 9 months of 1993. D'Amato admitted the mistake: "There was a very strong desire to make Creamette the one bigger brand beyond anything else. That's a great objective, [but] when you do it at the expense of your strong regional brands, maybe it doesn't make any sense."[5]

The snack food division also bedeviled D'Amato. He planned to launch a national Borden brand of chips and pretzels in the expectation that this could replace many of the company's regional snack brands. Combining the regionals' manufacturing and distribution costs under a single brand should enable Borden both to cut costs and also gain marketing muscle. The company tested its new snack line in Michigan, but results were only mediocre. Unfortunately, Borden was going up against PepsiCo's Frito-Lay and Anheuser-Busch's Eagle Snacks—major entrenched national brands. It could not wedge its way in. The company finally refocused its efforts to attempt to build up regional brands such as Jay's and Wise. But they were ineffective or too late.

THE CHANGING OF THE GUARD

D'Amato's sweeping strategy to rejuvenate the ailing Borden left the company worse off than before. Two of its four divisions, dairy and snacks, were operating at losses. Its other two divisions, grocery products and chemicals, could not take up the slack. On October 27, 1993, Standard and Poor downgraded much of Borden's debt. Since the beginning of 1993, Borden's share price had plummeted 43 percent.

In June 1993 D'Amato hired Ervin R. Shames, 53, as president and heir apparent. Whereas D'Amato's background had been in chemical engineering for most of his 30 years with Borden, Shames was an experienced food marketer, having spent 22 years in the industry, holding top positions with General Foods USA and Kraft USA. He most recently had been chair, president, and chief executive of Stride Rite Corporation. In making Shames president, D'Amato gave him a compensation package that exceeded those of Borden's other top executives, including himself.

Shames and D'Amato now attempted to correct Borden's problems together. They quickly stopped offering deals to retailers to encourage heavier end-of-quarter shipments. While these deals temporarily boosted sales, they hurt profits and also stole business from the next quarter.

Shames and D'Amato accelerated the examination of Borden's various businesses. Teams of management consultants and financial advisers helped with the evaluation. As a consequence, morale among managers, who feared drastic changes, plummeted almost to the point of paralysis.

In October 1993 the independent directors of the board considered the possibility of selling the entire company. But the efforts proved futile. Hanson

---

[5] Lesly, "Why Things Are So Sour," 84.

PLC and RJR Nabisco briefly appeared interested, but talks broke down. Several other possible buyers, including Nestle SA, also looked over Borden's portfolio of businesses but declined to negotiate. The weak condition of Borden was proving a major hindrance to any buyout. It likely would have to solve its own problems without outside help.

Shames and D'Amato believed that the biggest problem was the fact that the company was spread too thin in too many mediocre businesses. Although it was unlikely that the entire company could be sold at this time, still certain parts should be salable. They had to decide which should be sold if the company was to be streamlined enough to reverse the consequences of its haphazard and even confused former growth mentality. An early recognized candidate for pruning was the $1.4 billion chemical business. This had little relevance with the core food properties, but still it was a major profit generator, as shown in Table 7.2.

D'Amato was not to see the conclusions of his latest efforts to turn around Borden. On December 9, 1993, the board of directors fired him and left Shames in charge. At the same time, D'Amato's predecessor and former supporter, R. J. Ventres, resigned from his board seat. Operating results through 1993 were a disaster, as shown in Table 7.3.

RECOVERY EFFORTS

Shames announced a $567 million restructuring plan on January 5, 1994. It included the sale of the salty snacks division and other niche grocery lines. The dividend was also slashed for the second time in 6 months. In a speech to security analysts, Shames identified four reasons for Borden's problems: lack of focus, insufficient emphasis on brand names, absence of first-rate executives and managers, and a tangled bureaucracy. He vowed to purge weak managers and increase advertising with much greater focus on core lines, notably pasta, the namesake dairy products, and industrial businesses such as adhesives and wallcoverings. For example, he planned to increase advertising for pasta from $2 million to $8 million for 1994 and to focus on

Table 7.3   Operating Performance, 1990–1993

	Revenues (in $millions)	% Change	Net Income (in $millions)	% Change
1993	6,600[a]	(7.6)	(593)[a]	
1992	7,143	(1.3)	(253)	
1991	7,235	(5.2)	295	(19.0)
1990	7,633	—	364	—

[a]Estimates.
Source: Borden.

the company's faded regional brands. The pasta would also be cross-marketed with Classico, the successful premium pasta sauce.

Shames also pledged to bring Borden from last place among food companies to the top 25 percent. See Table 7.4 for a ranking of Borden with other major competitors as of the beginning of 1994. He began bringing in a new management team, many of them his former colleagues. In a major shake-up, three senior managers announced their early retirement: the chief financial officer, the general counsel, and the former executive vice president in charge of the struggling snack food and international consumer products unit.[6]

Some security analysts were encouraged by Shames' speech. They believed that Borden's bringing in an experienced outsider—at the time, Shames had been with the company for only 7 months—showed that the company was truly committed to the drastic changes needed for a turnaround. Other people were more skeptical. After all, Borden has been "restructuring" for five years. "Who's to say the latest plan will work any better than previous ones?" Joanna Scharf, an analyst with S. G. Warburg & Co., was among such skeptics: "I found some of [Shames] remarks heartening. However, this is not something that is going to turn around in six months." And she maintained she was not going to change her advice to investors to sell the stock.[7]

Table 7.4 Comparison of Borden and Major Competitors, 5-year Average, 1988–1993

	Return on Equity	Sales Growth	Earnings per Share
General Mills	42.8%	10.0%	10.4%
Kellogg	31.8	10.2	11.6
H. J. Heinz	25.4	5.8	8.6
Quaker Oats	24.6	4.9	12.2
Sara Lee	21.1	6.2	16.1
Hershey Foods	18.4	7.1	8.3
Campbell Soup	16.5	5.3	NM[a]
Dole	11.7	11.7	−5.4
Borden	5.8	1.3	NM

[a]*NM*, Not meaningful.

Source: Industry statistics as reported in *Forbes* (Jan. 3, 1994): 152–54.

Commentary: Borden's poor performance compared with that of its major peers is starkly indicated here, with Borden dead last in 5-year average return on equity, sales growth, and earnings per share.

[6]Suein L. Hwang, "Borden Aides Leaving as Part of Shake-Up," *Wall Street Journal* (Feb. 15, 1994): A4.

[7]Vindu P. Goel, "Putting Elsie Back on Track," *Cleveland Plain Dealer* (January 23, 1994): 1-E, 5-E.

ANALYSIS

Acquiring other businesses is a common growth strategy. Through acquisitions a company can quickly achieve a relatively large size, bypassing the time needed to develop such new ventures internally. By acquiring already proven businesses, the buyer can obtain personnel and management experienced to run such businesses effectively.

Several problems, however, can occur in such buyouts: First, a buying firm may pay too much and be saddled with heavy debt and interest overhead. Second, the acquisition may prove incompatible with the buyer's existing resources and strategy. In such a situation, it may find great difficulty in integrating the new enterprise with existing operations and making it a profit contributor.

In the 1980s Ventres, D'Amato's predecessor, took on $1.9 billion in debt to acquire 91 regional food and industrial companies. He had hoped to build these up to be regional powerhouses and to marry efficiencies of scale in manufacturing with the marketing nimbleness of regional operations. By centralizing production in the most efficient plants, costs should be lowered and profits enhanced. And there was always the potential for a regional brand to take off and be worthy of national distribution. This was the theory behind many of Borden's acquisitions in the 1980s.

Unfortunately, theory and practice did not meld well. The businesses were never integrated and continued to operate autonomously with diverse and often competing brands. Production never achieved the efficiency of most of the large competitors, and Borden still lacked their marketing clout. It also encountered great problems in allocating advertising among the diverse brands: Which should be given strong support, and why? And should the other brands be allowed to languish?

Compounding its problems with unwise and unassimilated acquisitions, Borden management grievously misjudged the mood of the market. It overestimated consumers' willingness to pay premium prices for its most popular brands. Borden's stubbornness in maintaining high prices for Lady Borden milk at the very time when raw milk prices were collapsing simply invited competitors to increase their market share at Borden's expense. Attempts to raise ice cream prices backfired as well.

The early 1990s, a period of recession and considerable unemployment and fear of layoffs, brought a new consumer recognition that many national brands were not much, if any, better than competing private brands. Many national-brand manufacturers, faced with declining sales in the face of strong private-label competition, began price rollbacks. So it was not surprising that Borden found difficulty with a changed marketing environment. What was surprising was its slowness to adapt to these changing conditions.

With so many brands in its portfolio stable, reflecting nearly 100 recent acquisitions, Borden lost focus. Key brands were often not sufficiently championed. Brand extensions, such as one for Lady Borden ice cream, were often overlooked or only half-heartedly attempted. One wonders how many opportunities were ignored by a management team whose attention was caught up in a frenzy for acquisitions.

POSTSCRIPT

Coming into the second half of 1994, we see little to suggest that Borden is on the verge of a turnaround. Perhaps the consequences of the disastrous acquisitions binge of the 1980's are far too deep rooted for any quick fixes, even by the most capable top executive. The only hint of a possible resolution to Borden's problems is personnel related. Since Ervin Shames took over as CEO in late 1993, he has brought in six new executives for top posts. A number of these hail from his alma mater, Philip Morris's Kraft General Foods unit. Will such fresh blood do the trick?[9]

WHAT CAN BE LEARNED?

Beware an unfocused strategy. An unfocused strategy often accompanies too much unrelated diversification. A firm has difficulty deciding what it is, other than being a conglomerate. Not many managements cope well with a lot of diversification, although many have tried to. Often such acquisitions become candidates for sale some years later, thus confirming flawed acquisition decisions.

In Borden's case most of the acquisitions were related to its major food business. But there were too many, and they were not integrated into the main corporate structure. Such diffusion of resources and uncoordinated marketing efforts made it difficult indeed to achieve either cost savings or a unified and powerful approach to the marketplace.

How much decentralization? Here we are confronted with the negative consequences of too much decentralization or autonomy. Borden acquisitions' autonomy led to lack of coordination and great inefficiency.

Does this have to be true? Or can decentralization work without causing loss of control and efficiency? Can intrafirm competition among semi-independent units lead to greater performance incentive? The answer is yes, decentralization is often far more desirable than centralization. For example, we saw in the IBM's efforts to move away from its centralized bureaucratic

[9]Suein L. Hwang, "Borden Taps Van Meter, Ex-Official of Georgia-Pacific, for Two Top Posts," *Wall Street Journal* (June 17, 1994): B2.

organization toward more decentralization. Still, there are degrees of decentralization. Too much uncontrolled autonomy led to Borden's problems. There has to be some focus and common purpose along with sufficient controls to prevent unpleasant surprises. But in the final analysis, the issue depends on the competence of the managers. If they are highly competent, then an organization will likely thrive under decentralization. If they are incompetent, as appeared to be the case with Borden, then decentralization can be a disaster.

Run with your winners. Although any firm wants to develop new products and bring them to fruition as soon as possible, it must not neglect its older products and brands that are doing well, that are winners. Advertising and other marketing efforts, such as brand extension, should not be curtailed as long as the products are growing and profitable. Marketing commitments should perhaps even be increased for such winners, since favorable growth trends often can continue for a long time. Alas, Borden sometimes exercised the opposite strategy: It cut back on its winners and directed resources to futilely trying to build up weak regional brands.

But we should not completely condemn Borden for ignoring its winners. It threw all its advertising support behind Creamette, the leading national brand of pasta. But Creamette's sales failed to take off. Meantime, Borden's strong regional brands—in particular, Prince in the Northeast and Anthony's in the West—stagnated with no support. D'Amato must have thought "damned if you do and damned if you don't." But there were reasons for the lack of success with the Creamette advertising, as we will examine next.

For mature products, beware using primary-demand advertising. Despite a strong boost in marketing efforts for Creamette in 1992, the brand's sales rose only 1.6 percent. At the same time total U.S. pasta sales rose 5.5 percent.[8] Was this poor showing the fault of the product? Hardly, since it was the leading national pasta brand. Rather, the advertising was at fault. Most of it was built around recipes that did more to promote pasta consumption than to promote the superior qualities of Creamette. In other words, a primary-demand theme was used rather than selective-demand theme stressing the merits of a particular brand. Because primary-demand advertising helps the industry and all competitors, it is best used with new products in a young growth industry. Primary-demand advertising is seldom appropriate in a mature industry. The results of the advertising efforts for Creamette confirm this. Shouldn't Borden managers have been more savvy? They should never have approved such a theme for an advertising campaign.

[8]Lesly, "Why Things Are So Sour," 84.

CONSIDER

Do you see any other learning insights coming from this case?

QUESTIONS

1. Do you think the problems in Borden's acquisition strategy stemmed from a flaw in the basic concept or in the execution? Support your position.
2. Is primary-demand advertising ever advisable for a mature product? If so, under what circumstances?
3. Prince is a strong regional pasta brand in the Northeast. What would it take to convert it into a national brand? Should Borden have attempted this?
4. Should Borden have made a strong effort to create a presence in the private brand market? Why or why not?
5. Critics have decried Borden's lack of focus. What does this mean? How can the criticisms best be resolved?
6. "After firing D'Amato, the board one month later adopted virtually the same restructuring plan he had proposed. What an injustice!" Discuss.
7. How much of a price premium do you think national brands ought to command over private brands? Justify your position.

INVITATION TO ROLE PLAY

1. It is 1984 and you are the assistant to the president. He has asked you to design a growth plan for the next decade. What are your recommendations? Take care to avoid the pitfalls that actually beset the company.
2. It is early 1994. You are the assistant to the new CEO, Erwin Shames. The company is in sorry straits. What do you propose to enable your boss to meet his pledge to boost Borden from the bottom of the food company heap to the top 25 percent?

INVITATION TO RESEARCH

Has Shames been successful yet in resurrecting Borden to the top 25 percent of its industry? What has happened to Borden stock prices? What major changes have happened? Is Shames still CEO?

CHAPTER 8

Maytag: A Bungled Promotion in England

The atmosphere at the annual meeting in the little Iowa town of Newton had turned contentious. As Leonard Hadley faced increasingly angry questions from disgruntled shareholders, a thought crossed his mind: "I don't deserve this!" After all, he had been CEO of Maytag Corporation for only a few months, and this was his first chairing of an annual meeting. But the earnings of the company had been declining every year since 1988, and in 1992 Maytag had had a $315.4 million loss. No wonder the stockholders in the packed Newton High School auditorium were bitter and critical of their management. But there was more. Just the month before, the company had suffered the public embarrassment and costly atonement resulting from a monumental blunder in the promotional planning of its United Kingdom subsidiary.

Hadley doggedly saw the meeting to its close and limply concluded, "Hopefully, both sales and earning will improve this year."[1]

THE FIASCO

In August 1992, Hoover Limited, Maytag's British subsidiary, had launched this travel promotion: Anyone in the United Kingdom buying more than £100 (UK pounds) worth of Hoover products (about $150) before the end of January 1993 would get two free round-trip tickets to selected European destinations. For £250 worth of Hoover products, buyers could get two free round-trip tickets to New York or Orlando.

---

[1]Richard Gibson, "Maytag's CEO Goes Through Wringer at Annual Meeting," *Wall Street Journal* (April 28, 1993): A5.

A buying frenzy resulted. Consumers had quickly figured out that the value of the tickets easily exceeded the cost of the appliances necessary to be eligible for them. By the tens of thousands, Britons rushed out to buy just enough Hoover products to qualify. Appliance stores were emptied of vacuum cleaners. The Hoover factory in Cambuslang, Scotland, that had been making vacuum cleaners only 3 days a week was suddenly placed on a 24-hour, 7-days-a-week production schedule—an overtime bonanza for the workers. What a resounding success for a promotion! Hoover managers, however, were unhappy.

Hoover had never expected more than 50,000 people to respond. And of those responding, it expected far fewer would go through all the steps necessary to qualify for the free trip and really take it. But more than 200,000 not only responded but qualified for the free tickets. The company was overwhelmed. The volume of paperwork created such a bottleneck that by the middle of April only 6,000 people had flown. Thousands of others either never got their tickets, were unable to get the dates requested, or waited for months without hearing the results of their applications. Hoover established a special hotline to process customer complaints, and these were coming in at 2,000 calls a day. But the complaints quickly spread, and the ensuing publicity brought charges of fraud and demands for restitution. This raises the issue of loss leaders. How much should we use loss leaders as a promotional device? This topic is discussed in the following box.

Maytag dispatched a task force to try to resolve the situation without jeopardizing customer relations any further. But it acknowledged that it was "not 100% clear" that all eligible buyers would receive their free flights.[2] The ill-fated promotion was a staggering blow to Maytag financially. It took a $30 million charge in the first quarter of 1993 to cover unexpected additional costs linked to the promotion. Final costs were expected to exceed $50 million, which would be 10 percent of UK Hoover's total revenues. This was especially damaging for a subsidiary acquired only 4 years before, that had yet to produce a profit.

Adding to the costs were problems with the two travel agencies involved. The agencies were to obtain low-cost space-available tickets and would earn commission selling "packages," including hotels, rental cars, and insurance. If consumers bought a package, Hoover would get a cut. However, despite the overwhelming demand for tickets, most consumers declined to purchase the package, thus greatly reducing support money for the promotional venture. So Hoover had greatly underestimated the likely response and overestimated the amount it would earn from commission payments.

---

[2] James P. Miller, "Maytag U.K. Unit Finds a Promotion Is Too Successful," *Wall Street Journal* (March 31, 1993): A9.

ISSUE BOX

SHOULD WE USE LOSS LEADERS?

Leader pricing is a type of promotion with certain items advertised at a very low price—sometimes even below cost, in which case they are known as *loss leaders*—in order to attract more customers. The rationale is that such customers are likely to purchase other regular-price items as well, increasing total sales and profits. If customers do not purchase enough other goods at regular prices to more than cover the losses incurred from the attractively priced bargains, then the loss leader promotion is ill advised. Some critics maintain that the whole idea of using loss leaders is absurd: The firm is just "buying sales" with no regard for profits.

While UK Hoover did not think of its promotion as a loss leader, in reality it was: The company stood to lose money on every sale if the promotional offer was taken advantage of. Unfortunately for its effectiveness as a loss leader, the likelihood of customers purchasing other Hoover products at regular prices was remote, and the level of acceptance was not capped, so losses were permitted to multiply. The conclusion has to be that this was an ill-conceived idea from the beginning. It violated these two conditions of loss leaders: They should stimulate sales of other products, and their losses should be limited.

Do you think loss leaders really are desirable under certain circumstances? Why or why not?

If these cost overruns had added greatly to Maytag and Hoover's customer relations and public image, the expenditures would have seemed more palatable. But with all the problems the best that could be expected would be to lessen the worst of the agitation and charges of deception. And this was proving to be impossible. The media, of course, salivated at the problems and were quick to sensationalize them:

> One disgruntled customer, who took aggressive action on his own, received the widest press coverage, and even became a folk hero. Dave Dixon, claiming he was cheated out of a free vacation by Hoover, seized one of the company's repair vans in retaliation. Police were sympathetic: they took him home, and did not charge him, claiming it was a civil matter.[3]

Heads rolled. Initially, Maytag fired three UK Hoover executives involved, including the president of Hoover Europe. At the annual meeting

---

[3] "Unhappy Brit Holds Hoover Van Hostage," *Cleveland Plain Dealer* (June 1, 1993): D1; and Simon Reeve and John Harlow, "Hoover is Sued Over Flights Deal," *London Sunday Times* (June 6, 1993).

Mr. Hadley also indicated that others might lose their jobs before the cleanup was complete. He likened the promotion to "a bad accident...and you can't determine what was in the driver's mind."[4]

Receiving somewhat less publicity was the fact that corporate headquarters allowed executives of a subsidiary such wide latitude that they could saddle parent Maytag with tens of millions of dollars in unexpected costs. Did not top corporate executives have to approve ambitious plans? A company spokesman said that operating divisions were "primarily responsible" for planning promotional expenses. Although the parent may review such outlays, "if they're within parameters, it goes through."[5] This raises the issue, discussed in the following box, of how loose a rein foreign subsidiaries should be allowed.

BACKGROUND ON MAYTAG

Maytag is a century-old company. The original business, formed in 1893, manufactured feeder attachments for threshing machines. In 1907 the company moved to Newton, Iowa, a small town 30 miles east of Des Moines, the capital city. Manufacturing emphasis turned to home laundry equipment and wringer-type washers.

A natural expansion of this emphasis occurred with the commercial laundromat business in the 1930s, when coin meters were attached to Maytag washers. Rapid growth of these coin-operated laundries took place in the United States during the late 1950s and early 1960s. The increased competition and soaring energy costs of the 1970s hurt laundromats. In 1975 Maytag introduced new energy-efficient machines and "home style" stores that rejuvenated the business.

The Lonely Maytag Repairman

For years Maytag reveled in a marketing coup, with its washers and dryers enjoying a top-quality image, thanks to ads in which a repairman laments his loneliness because of Maytag's trouble-free products. The result of this dependability and quality image was that Maytag could command a price premium: "Their machines cost the same to make, break down as much as ours—but they get $100 more because of the reputation," grumbled a competitor.[6]

---

[4]Gibson, "CEO Goes Through Wringer," A5.
[5]Miller, "Maytag UK Unit," A9.
[6]Brian Bremmer, "Can Maytag Clean Up Around the World?" *Business Week* (Jan. 30, 1989): 86.

ISSUE BOX

HOW LOOSE A REIN FOR A FOREIGN SUBSIDIARY?

In a decentralized organization, top management delegates considerable decision-making authority to subordinates. Such decentralization—often called a "loose rein"—tends to be more marked with foreign subsidiaries, such as UK Hoover. Corporate management in the United States understandably feels less familiar with the foreign environment and more willing to let the native executives operate with fewer constraints than a domestic subsidiary has. In the Maytag/Hoover situation, decision-making authority by British executives was evidently extensive, and corporate Maytag exercised little operational control, being content to judge performance by ultimate results achieved. Major deviations from expected performance goals, or widespread traumatic happenings—both of which happened to UK Hoover—finally grained corporate management attention.

Extensive decentralization has many advantages: First, top management effectiveness can be improved because time and attention is freed for presumably more important matters; second, subordinates are permitted more self-management, which should improve their competence and motivation; and third, in foreign environments, native managers presumably understand their unique problems and opportunities better than corporate management, located thousands of miles away, possibly can. But the drawbacks are as we have seen: parameters within which subordinate managers operate can be so wide that serious miscalculations may not be stopped in time. Because top management is ultimately responsible for all performance, including actions of subordinates, it faces greater risks with extensive decentralization.

"Since the manager is ultimately accountable for whatever is delegated to subordinates, then a free rein reflects great confidence in subordinates." Discuss.

During the 1970s and into the 1980s, Maytag continued to capture 15 percent of the washing machine market and enjoyed profit margins about twice that of competitors. Table 8.1 shows operating results for the period 1974 to 1981. Whirlpool was the largest factor in the laundry equipment market, with a 45 percent share, but this was largely because of sales to Sears under the Sears brand.

Acquisitions

For many years, until his retirement December 31, 1992, Daniel J. Krumm had influenced Maytag's destinies. He had been CEO for 18 years and chairman since 1986, and his tenure with the company encompassed 40 years. In that time the home-appliance business had encountered some drastic

Table 8.1   Maytag Operating Results, 1974–1981 (in $ millions)

	Net Sales	Net Income	Percent of Sales
1974	$229	$21.1	9.2%
1975	238	25.9	10.9
1976	275	33.1	12.0
1977	299	34.5	11.5
1978	325	36.7	11.3
1979	369	45.3	12.3
1980	346	35.6	10.2
1981	409	37.4	9.1
Average net income percent of sales: 10.8%		

Source: Company operating statistics.
Commentary: These years show a steady, though not spectacular, growth in revenues and a generally rising net income, except for 1980. Of particular interest is the high net income percentage of sales, averaging 10.8% over the 8-year period, with a high of 12.3%.

changes. The most ominous occurred in the late 1980s with the merger mania, in which the threat of takeovers by hostile raiders often motivated heretofore conservative executives to greatly increase corporate indebtedness, thereby decreasing the attractiveness of their firms. Daniel Krumm was one of these running-scared executives, as rumors persisted that the company was a takeover candidate.

Largely as a defensive move, Krumm pushed through a deal for a $1 billion buyout of Chicago Pacific Corporation (CPC), a maker of vacuum cleaners and other appliances with $1.4 billion in sales. As a result, Maytag was burdened with $500 million in new debt. Krumm defended the acquisition as giving Maytag a strong foothold in a growing overseas market. CPC was best known for the Hoover vacuums it sold in the United States and Europe. Indeed, so dominant was the Hoover brand in England that many people did not vacuum their carpets, but "hoovered the carpet." CPC also made washers, dryers, and other appliances under the Hoover brand, selling them exclusively in Europe and Australia. In addition, it had six furniture companies, but Maytag sold these shortly after the acquisition.

Krumm had been instrumental in transforming Maytag, the number four U.S. appliance manufacturer—behind General Electric, Whirlpool, and Electrolux—from a niche laundry-equipment maker into a full-line manufacturer. He had led an earlier acquisition spree in which Maytag had expanded into microwave ovens, electric ranges, refrigerators, and freezers. Its brands now included Magic Chef, Jenn-Air, Norge, and Admiral. The last years of Krumm's reign, however, were not marked by great operating results. As shown in Table 8.2, revenues showed no gain in the 1989–1992 period, while income steadily declined.

Table 8.2   Maytag Operating Results, 1989–1992

	Revenue	Net Income	% of Revenue
	(000,000)		
1989	$3,089	131.0	4.3%
1990	3,057	98.9	3.2
1991	2,971	79.00	2.7
1992	3,041	(315.4)	(10.4)

Source: Company annual reports.
Commentary: Note the steady erosion of profitability, while sales remained virtually static. For a comparison with profit performance of earlier years, see Table 8.1 and the net-income-to-sales percentages of this more "golden" period.

Trouble

Although the rationale for internationalizing seemed inescapable, especially in view of a recent wave of joint ventures between U.S. and European appliance makers, the Hoover acquisition was troublesome. It was a major brand in England and in Australia, but Hoover had only a small presence in Continental Europe. Yet this was where the bulk of the market was, with some 320 million potential appliance buyers.

The probabilities of the Hoover subsidiary capturing much of the European market were hardly promising. Whirlpool was strong, having 10 plants there in contrast to Hoover's two plants. Furthermore, Maytag faced entrenched European competitors such as Sweden's Electrolux, the world's largest appliance maker; Germany's Bosch-Siemens; and Italy's Merloni Group. And General Electric had also entered the market with joint ventures. Europeans' fierce loyalty to domestic brands raised further questions as to the ability of Maytag's Hoover to penetrate the European market without massive promotional expenditures, and maybe not even then.

Australia was something else. Hoover had a good competitive position there, and its refrigerator plant in Melbourne could easily be expanded to include Maytag's washers and dryers. Unfortunately, the small population of Australia limited the market to only about $250 million for major appliances.

Britain accounted for one-half of Hoover's European sales. But at the time of the acquisition, its major appliance business was only marginally profitable. This was to change: After the acquisition it became downright unprofitable, as shown in Table 8.3 for the years 1990 through 1992, as it struggled to expand in a recession-plagued Europe. The results for 1993, of course, will reflect the huge loss for the promotional debacle. Hardly an acquisition made in heaven.

Maytag's earlier acquisitions also were becoming soured. Its acquisitions of Magic Chef and Admiral were diversifications into lower-priced appliances, and these acquisitions did not meet expectations. But they left

Maytag's balance sheet and its cash flow weakened (see Table 8.4). Perhaps more serious, Maytag's reputation as the nation's premier appliance maker became tarnished. Meanwhile, General Electric and Whirlpool were attacking the top end of its product line. As a result, Maytag found itself in the number three or number four position in most of its brand lines.

ANALYSIS

Flawed Acquisition Decisions

The long decline in profits after 1989 should have triggered strong concern and corrective action. And perhaps it did, but the action was not effective because the decline continued, culminating in a large deficit in 1992 and serious problems in 1993. As shown in Table 8.2, the acquisitions brought neither revenue gains nor profitability. One suspects that in the rush to fend off potential raiders in the late 1980s, the company bought businesses it might never have bought under more sober times and that it also paid too much for these businesses. Further, they cheapened Maytag's proud quality image.

Table 8.3   Operating Results of Maytag's Principal Business Components, 1990–1992

	Revenue (000,000)	Income[a] (000)
1990		
North American Appliances	$2212	$221,165
Vending	191	25,018
European Sales	497	(22,863)
1991		
North American Appliances	2183	186,322
Vending	150	4,498
European Sales	486	(865)
1992		
North American Appliances	2242	129,680
Vending	165	16,311
European Sales	502	(67,061)

[a]This is operating income, that is, income before depreciation and other adjustments.
Source: Company annual reports.
Commentary: While these years had not been particularly good for Maytag in growth of revenues and income, the continuing, and even intensifying, losses in the Hoover European operation had to be troublesome. And this was true even before the ill-fated early 1993 promotional results.

Table 8.4   Long-Term Debt as a Percent of Capital from Maytag's Balance Sheets, 1986–1991

Year	Long-Term Debt/Capital
1986	7.2%
1987	23.3
1988	48.3
1989	46.8
1990	44.1
1991	42.7

Source: Company annual reports.

Commentary: The effect of acquisitions, in particular that of the Chicago Pacific Corporation, can be clearly seen in the buildup of long-term debt. In 1986 Maytag was virtually free of such commitments; 2 years later its long-term debt ratio had increased almost sevenfold.

Who Can We Blame in the UK Promotional Debacle?

Corporate Maytag management was guilty of a common fault in its acquisitions. It gave newly acquired divisions a loose rein, letting them continue to operate independently with few constraints: "After all, these executives should be more knowledgeable about their operations than corporate headquarters would be." Such confidence is sometimes misguided. In the UK promotion, Maytag management would seem as derelict as management in England. Planning guidelines or parameters were far too loose and undercontrolled. That subsidiary management could burden the parent with $50 million of unexpected charges, and to have such a problem erupt with no warning, borders on the absurd.

Finally, the UK executives' planning for this ill-conceived travel promotion defies all logic. They vastly underestimated the demand for the promotions offer and greatly overestimated paybacks from travel agencies on the package deals. Yet it took no brilliant insight to realize that the value of the travel offer exceeded the price of the appliance—indeed, 200,000 customers rapidly arrived at this conclusion—and that such a sweetheart of a deal would be irresistible to many. Hoover management should have seen that the promotion could prove to be extremely costly to the company. Was it a miscalculation or complete naivete on the part of executives and their staffs, who should have known better?

How Could the Promotion Have Avoided the Problems?

The great problem resulting from an offer that was too good could have been avoided without scrapping the whole idea. A cost-benefit analysis would have provided at least a perspective as to how much the company should spend to achieve certain benefits, such as increased sales, greater consumer interest, and favorable publicity. See the following information box for a more detailed discussion of the important planning tool of a cost-benefit analysis.

INFORMATION BOX

COST-BENEFIT ANALYSIS

A cost-benefit analysis is a systematic comparison of the costs and benefits of a proposed action. Only if the benefits exceed the costs would we normally have a "go" decision. The normal way to make such an analysis is to assign dollar values to all costs and benefits, thus providing a common basis for comparison.

Cost-benefit analyses have been widely used by the Department of Defense in evaluating alternative weapons systems. In recent years such analyses have been sporadically applied to environmental regulation and even to workplace safety standards. As an example of the former, a cost-benefit analysis can be used to determine if it is socially worthwhile to spend $X million to meet a certain standard of clean air or water.

Many business decisions lend themselves to a cost-benefit analysis. It provides a systematic way of analyzing the inputs and the probable outputs of particular major alternatives. While in the business setting some of the costs and benefits can be quantitative, they often should be tempered by nonquantitative inputs to reach the broadest perspective. Schermerhorn suggests considering the following criteria in evaluating alternatives:[7]

- *Benefits.* What are the benefits of using the alternatives to solve a performance deficiency or take advantage of an opportunity?
- *Costs.* What are the costs to implement the alternatives, including direct resource investments as well as any potential negative side effects?
- *Timeliness.* How fast will the benefits occur and a positive impact be achieved?
- *Acceptability.* To what extent will the alternatives be accepted and supported by those who must work with them?
- *Ethical soundness.* How well do the alternatives meet acceptable ethical criteria in the eyes of multiple stakeholders?

What numbers would you assign to a cost-benefit analysis for Maytag Hoover's plan to offer the free airline tickets, under an assumption of 5000 takers? 20,000 takers? 100,000 takers? 500,000 takers? (Make any assumptions needed as to costs.) What would be your conclusions for these various acceptance rates?

---

[7]John R. Schermerhorn, Jr., *Management for Productivity*, 4th ed. (New York: Wiley, 1993), 164.

A cost-benefit analysis should certainly have alerted management to the possible consequences of various acceptance levels and to the significant risks of high acceptance. However, the company could have set limits on the number of eligibles: perhaps the first 1000, or the first 5000. Doing this would have held or capped the costs to reasonably defined levels and avoided the greater risks. Or the company could have made the offer less generous, perhaps by upping the requirements or by lessening the premiums. Such more moderate alternatives would still have made an attractive promotion, but not the major uncontrolled catastrophe that happened.

WHAT CAN BE LEARNED?

In planning, consider a worst-case scenario. There are those who preach the desirability of positive thinking, confidence, and optimism, whether it be in personal lives, athletics, or business practices. But expecting and preparing for the worst has much to commend it, since a person or a firm is then better able to cope with adversity, avoid being overwhelmed, and make prudent decisions. And if the risks outweigh probable benefits, then the alternative ought to be scrapped or modified.

Apparently the avid acceptance of the promotional offer was a complete surprise; no one dreamed of such demand. Yet was it so unreasonable to think that a very attractive offer would meet wild acceptance?

In using loss leaders, put a cap on potential losses. Loss leaders, as we noted earlier, are items promoted at such an attractive price that the firm loses money on every sale. The expectation, of course, is that the customer traffic generated by such attractive promotions will increase sales of other regular profit items so that total profits will be increased.

The risks of uncontrolled or uncapped loss leader promotions is vividly shown in this case. For a retailer who uses loss leaders, the loss is ultimately capped as the inventory is used up. With UK Hoover there was no cap. The moral is clear: Attractive loss leader promotions should be capped, such as at the first 100 or the first 1000 or for one week only. Otherwise the promotion should be made less attractive.

Beware giving unproven foreign subsidiaries loose rein. Although moving more authority down into the ranks of the organization is often desirable and stimulates better motivation and management development than centralization, it can be overdone. At the extreme, where divisional and subsidiary executives have virtually unlimited decision-making authority and can run their operations as virtual dynasties, then corporate management essentially abdicates its authority. Such looseness in an organization endangers cohesiveness; it tends to obscure common standards and objectives; and it can even dilute unified ethical standards.

Such extreme looseness of organizational structure is not uncommon with acquisitions, especially foreign ones, under the assumption that they were operating successfully before the acquisition and have the greater expertise because of their experience. International operations are often given more freedom of scope than domestic operations, simply because such executives are presumed to have more first-hand knowledge of their environment than the parent executives.

Still, there should be limits on how much freedom these divisional and subsidiary executives should be permitted—especially when their operations have not been notably successful. In Maytag's case, the UK subsidiary had lost money every year since it was acquired. One would expect prudent corporate management to have condoned less decentralization and tighter supervision under such circumstances.

The power of a cost-benefit analysis. For major decisions, executives have much to gain from a cost-benefit analysis. It forces them to systematically tabulate and analyze the costs and benefits of particular courses of action. They may find that likely benefits are so uncertain as to not be worth the risk. If so, now is the time to realize this, rather than after substantial commitments have already been made.

Without doubt, regular use of cost-benefit analyses for major decisions improves executives' batting averages for good decisions. Even though some numbers may have to be judgmental, especially as to probable benefits, the process of making this analysis forces a careful look at alternatives and most likely consequences. For more important decisions, input from diverse staff people and executives will bring greater power to the analysis.

CONSIDER

What additional learning insights can you add?

QUESTIONS

1. How could the promotion of UK Hoover have been better planned and designed? Be as specific as you can.
2. Given the fiasco that did occur—in particular, the huge unexpected demand—how do you think Maytag should have responded?
3. "Firing the three top executives of UK Hoover is unconscionable. It smacks of a vendetta against European managers by an American parent. After all, their only 'crime' was a promotion that was too successful." Comment on this statement.

4. Do you think Leonard Hadley, the Maytag CEO for only 2 months, should be soundly criticized for the UK situation? Why or why not?
5. Please speculate: Why do you think this UK Hoover fiasco happened in the first place? What went wrong?
6. Evaluate the decision to acquire Chicago Pacific Corporation (CPC). Do this both for the time of the decision and for now—after the fact— as a post mortem. Defend your overall conclusions.
7. Use your creativity: Can you devise a marketing strategy for UK Hoover to become more of a major force in Europe?

INVITATION TO ROLE PLAY

1. You have been placed in charge of a task force sent by headquarters to England to coordinate the fire-fighting efforts in the aftermath of the ill-fated promotion. There is neither enough productive capacity nor enough airline seats available to handle the demand. How do you propose to handle this situation? Be as specific as you can, and defend your recommendations.
2. As a staff vice president at corporate headquarters, you have been charged to develop companywide policies and procedures that will prevent such a situation from ever occurring again. What do you recommend?

INVITATION TO RESEARCH

How was the promotional disaster finally resolved? What was the final impact on company image and profits? Has the European operation been brought into the black as yet? How has the stock market price of Maytag changed since early 1993?

CHAPTER 9

Euro Disney: A Successful Format Does Not Transfer Well to Europe

With high expectations Euro Disney opened just outside Paris in April 1992. Success seemed ensured. After all, the Disneylands in Florida, California, and, most recently, Japan were all spectacular successes. But somehow all the rosy expectations became a delusion. The opening results cast even the future continuance of Euro Disney into doubt. How could what seemed so right be so wrong? What mistakes were made.

PRELUDE

Optimism

Perhaps a few early omens should have raised some cautions. Between 1987 and 1991, three $150 million amusement parks had opened in France with great fanfare. All had fallen flat, and by 1991 two were in bankruptcy. Now Walt Disney Company was finalizing its plans to open Europe's first Disneyland early in 1992. This would turn out to be a $4.4 billion enterprise sprawling over 5000 acres 20 miles east of Paris. Initially it would have six hotels and 5,200 rooms, more rooms than the entire city of Cannes, and lodging was expected to triple in a few years as Disney opened a second theme park to keep visitors at the resort longer.

Disney also expected to develop a growing office complex, one only slightly smaller than France's biggest, La Defense, in Paris. Plans also called for shopping malls, apartments, golf courses, and vacation homes. Euro Disney would tightly control all this ancillary development, designing and building nearly everything itself, and eventually selling off the commercial properties at a huge profit.

Disney executives had no qualms about the huge enterprise, which would cover an area one-fifth the size of Paris itself. They were more worried that the park might not be big enough to handle the crowds:

> "My biggest fear is that we will be too successful." "I don't think it can miss. They are masters of marketing. When the place opens it will be perfect. And they know how to make people smile—even the French."[1]

Company executives initially predicted that 11 million Europeans would visit the extravaganza in the first year alone. After all, Europeans accounted for 2.7 million visits to the U.S. Disney parks and spent $1.6 billion on Disney merchandise. Surely a park in closer proximity would draw many thousands more. As Disney executives thought more about it, the forecast of 11 million seemed most conservative. They reasoned that since Disney parks in the United States (population of 250 million) attract 41 million visitors a year, then if Euro Disney attracted visitors in the same proportion, attendance could reach 60 million with Western Europe's 370 million people. Table 9.1 shows the 1990 attendance at the two U.S. Disney parks and the newest Japanese Disneyland, as well as the attendance-population ratios.

Adding fuel to the optimism was the fact that Europeans typically have more vacation time than do U.S. workers. For example, five-week vacations are commonplace for French and German employees, compared with two to three weeks for U.S. workers.

The failure of the three earlier French parks was seen as irrelevant. Robert Fitzpatrick, Euro Disneyland's chairman, stated, "We are spending 22 billion French francs before we open the door, while the other places spent 700 million. This means we can pay infinitely more attention to details—to costumes, hotels, shops, trash baskets—to create a fantastic place. There's just too great a response to Disney for us to fail."[2]

Nonetheless, a few scattered signs indicated that not everyone was happy with the coming of Disney. Leftist demonstrators at Euro Disney's stock offering greeted company executives with eggs, ketchup, and "Mickey Go Home" signs. Some French intellectuals decried the pollution of the country's cultural ambiance with the coming of Mickey Mouse and company: They called the park an American cultural abomination. The mainstream press also seemed contrary, describing every Disney setback "with

---

[1] Steven Greenhouse, "Playing Disney in the Parisian Fields," *New York Times* (Feb. 17, 1991): Section 3: 1, 6.
[2] Greenhouse, "Playing Disney," 6.

Table 9.1   Attendance and Attendance/Population Ratios, Disney Parks, 1990

	Visitors Population (millions)		Ratio
United States			
Disneyland (Southern California)	12.9	250	5.2%
Disney World/Epcot Center (Florida)	28.5	250	11.4%
Total United States	41.4		16.6%
Japan			
Tokyo Disneyland	16.0	124	13.5%
Euro Disney	?	310[a]	?

[a]Within a two-hour flight.
Source: Euro Disney, Amusement Business Magazine.
Commentary: Even if the attendance/population ratio for Euro Disney is only 10 percent, which is far below that of some other theme parks, still 31 million visitors could be expected. Euro Disney "conservatively" predicted 11 million the first year.

glee." And French officials in negotiating with Disney sought less American and more European culture at France's Magic Kingdom. Still, such protests and bad press seemed contrived, unrepresentative, and certainly not predictive. Company officials dismissed the early criticism as "the ravings of an insignificant elite."[3]

The Location Decision

In the search for a site for Euro Disney, Disney executives examined 200 locations in Europe. The other finalist was Barcelona, Spain. Its major attraction was warmer weather, but its transportation system was not as good as that around Paris, and it lacked level tracts of land of sufficient size. The clincher for the Paris decision was its more central location. Table 9.2 shows the number of people within 2 to 6 hours of the Paris site.

Table 9.2   Number of People Within 2–6 Hours of the Paris Site

Within a 2-hour drive	17 million people
Within a 4-hours drive	41 million people
Within a 6-hour drive	109 million people
Within a 2-hour flight	310 million people

Source: Euro Disney, Amusement Business Magazine.
Commentary: The much more densely populated and geographically compact European continent makes access to Euro Disney much more convenient that it is in the United States.

[3]Peter Gumbel and Richard Turner, "Fans Like Euro Disney But Its Parent's Goofs Weigh the Park Down," *Wall Street Journal* (March 10, 1994): A12.

The beet fields of the Marne-la-Vallee area was the choice. Being near Paris seemed a major advantage, since Paris was Europe's biggest tourist draw. And France was eager to win the project to help lower its jobless rate and also to enhance its role as the center of tourist activity in Europe. The French government expected the project to create at least 30,000 jobs and to contribute $1 billion a year from foreign visitors.

To entice the project, the French government allowed Disney to buy up huge tracts of land at 1971 prices. It provided $750 million in loans at below-market rates, and it spent hundreds of millions of dollars on subway and other capital improvements for the park. For example, Paris's express subway was extended out to the park; a 35-minute ride from downtown cost about $2.50. A new railroad station for the high-speed Train a Grande Vitesse was built only 150 yards from the entrance gate. This enabled visitors from Brussels to arrive in only 90 minutes. And once the English Channel tunnel opened in 1994, even London would be only 3 hours and 10 minutes away. Actually, Euro Disney was the second largest construction project in Europe, second only to construction of the English Channel tunnel.

Financing

Euro Disney cost $4.4 billion. Table 9.3 shows the sources of financing, in percentages. The Disney Company had a 49 percent stake in the project, which was the most that the French government would allow. For this stake it invested $160 million, while other investors contributed $1.2 billion in equity. The rest was financed by loans from the government, banks, and special partnerships formed to buy properties and lease them back.

The payoff for Disney began after the park opened. The company receives 10 percent of Euro Disney's admission fees and 5 percent of the food and merchandise revenues. This is the same arrangement as Disney has with the Japanese park. But in the Tokyo Disneyland, the company took no ownership interest, opting instead only for the licensing fees and a percentage of

Table 9.3 Sources of Financing for Euro Disney (percent)

Total to Finance: $4.4 billion	100%
Shareholders equity, including $160 million from Walt Disney Company	32
Loan from French government	22
Loan from group of 45 banks	21
Bank loans to Disney hotels	16
Real estate partnerships	9

Source: Euro Disney.

Commentary: The full flavor of the leverage is shown here, with equity comprising only 32 percent of the total expenditure.

the revenues. The reason for the conservative position with Tokyo Disney-land was that Disney money was heavily committed to building the Epcot Center in Florida. Furthermore, Disney had some concerns about the Tokyo enterprise. This was the first non-American and the first cold-weather Disneyland. It seemed prudent to minimize the risks. But this turned out to be a significant blunder of conservatism, because Tokyo became a huge suc-cess, as the following box discusses in more detail.

Special Modifications

With the experiences of the previous theme parks, and particularly that of the first cold-weather park in Tokyo, Disney construction executives were able to bring state-of-the-art refinements to Euro Disney. Exacting demands were placed on French construction companies, and a higher level of per-formance and compliance resulted than many thought possible to achieve. The result was a major project on time, if not completely on budget. In con-trast, the Channel tunnel was plagued by delays and severe cost overruns.

One of the things learned from the cold-weather project in Japan was that more needed to be done to protect visitors from such weather problems as wind, rain, and cold. Consequently, Euro Disney's ticket booths were pro-tected from the elements, as were the lines waiting for attractions, and even the moving sidewalk from the 12,000-car parking area.

Certain French accents—and British, German, and Italian accents as well—were added to the American flavor. The park has two official lan-guages, English and French, but multilingual guides are available for Dutch, Spanish, German, and Italian visitors. Discoveryland, based on the science fiction of France's Jules Verne, is a new attraction. A theater with a full 360-degree screen acquaints visitors with a sweep of European history. And, not the least modification for cultural diversity, Snow White speaks German, and the Belle Notte Pizzeria and Pasticceria are right next to Pinocchio.

Disney had foreseen that it might encounter some cultural problems. This was one of the reasons for choosing Robert Fitzpatrick as Euro Disney's president. He is American but speaks French, knows Europe well, and has a French wife. However, he was unable to establish the rapport needed and was replaced in 1993 by a French native. Still, some of his admonitions that France should not be approached as if it were Florida fell on deaf ears.

RESULTS

As the April 1992 opening approached, the company launched a massive communications blitz aimed at publicizing the fact that the fabled Disney experience was now accessible to all Europeans. Some 2,500 people from

---

INFORMATION BOX

THE TOKYO DISNEYLAND SUCCESS

Tokyo Disneyland opened in 1983 on 201 acres in the eastern suburb of Urazasu. It was arranged that an ownership group, Oriental Land, would build, own, and operate the theme park with advice from Disney. The owners borrowed most of the $650 million needed to bring the project to fruition. Disney invested no money but receives 10 percent of the revenues from admission and rides and 5 percent of sales of food, drink, and souvenirs.

Although the start was slow, Japanese soon began flocking to the park in great numbers. By 1990 some 16 million a year passed through the turnstiles, about one-fourth more than visited Disneyland in California. In fiscal year 1990, revenues reached $988 million with profits of $150 million. Indicative of the Japanese preoccupation with things American, the park serves almost no Japanese food, and the live entertainers are mostly American. Japanese management even apologizes for the presence of a single Japanese restaurant inside the park: "A lot of elderly Japanese came here from outlying parts of Japan, and they were not very familiar with hot dogs and hamburgers."[4]

Disney executives were soon to realize the great mistake they made in not taking substantial ownership in Tokyo Disneyland. They did not want to make the same mistake with Euro Disney.

Would you expect the acceptance of the genuine American experience in Tokyo to be indicative of the reaction of the French and Europeans? Why or why not?

---

various print and broadcast media were lavishly entertained while being introduced to the new facilities. Most media people were positively impressed with the inauguration and with the enthusiastic spirit of the staffers. These public relations efforts, however, were criticized by some for being heavy-handed and for not providing access to Disney executives.

As 1992 wound down after the opening, it became clear that revenue projections were, unbelievably, not being met. But the opening turned out to be in the middle of a severe recession in Europe. European visitors, perhaps as a consequence, were far more frugal than their American counterparts. Many packed their own lunches and shunned the Disney hotels. For example, a visitor named Corine from southern France typified the "no spend" attitude of many: "It's a bottomless pit," she said as she, her husband, and their three children toured Euro Disney on a 3-day visit. "Every time we turn around, one of the kids wants to buy something."[5] Perhaps investor expectations, despite the logic and rationale, were simply unrealistic.

[4]James Sterngold, "Cinderella Hits Her Stride in Tokyo," *New York Times* (Feb. 17, 1991): 6.
[5]"Ailing Euro Disney May Face Closure," *Cleveland Plain Dealer* (Jan. 1, 1994): E1.

Indeed, Disney had initially priced the park and the hotels to meet revenue targets and had assumed demand was there, at any price. Park admission was $42.25 for adults—higher than at the American parks. A room at the flagship Disneyland Hotel at the park's entrance cost about $340 a night, the equivalent of a top hotel in Paris. It was soon averaging only a 50 percent occupancy. Guests were not staying as long or spending as much on the fairly high-priced food and merchandise. We can label the initial pricing strategy at Euro Disney as *skimming pricing*. The following box discusses skimming and its opposite, penetration pricing.

Disney executives soon realized they had made a major miscalculation. Whereas visitors to Florida's Disney World often stayed more than 4 days, Euro Disney—with one theme park compared to Florida's three—was proving to be a 2-day experience at best. Many visitors arrived early in the morning, rushed to the park, staying late at night, then checked out of the hotel the next morning before heading back to the park for one final exploration.

The problems of Euro Disney were not public acceptance (despite the earlier critics). Europeans loved the place. Since the opening it attracted just under 1 million visitors a month, thus easily achieving the original projections. Such patronage made it Europe's biggest paid tourist attraction. But the large numbers of frugal patrons did not come close to enabling Disney to meet revenue and profit projections and cover a bloated overhead.

Other operational errors and miscalculations, most of these cultural, hurt the enterprise. A policy of serving no alcohol in the park caused consternation in a country where wine is customary for lunch and dinner. (This policy has since been reversed.) Disney thought Monday would be a light day and Friday a heavy one and allocated staff accordingly, but the reverse was true. It found great peaks and valleys in attendance: The number of visitors per day in the high season could be ten times the number in slack times. The need to lay off employees during quiet periods came up against France's inflexible labor schedules.

One unpleasant surprise concerned breakfast. "We were told that Europeans don't take breakfast, so we downsized the restaurants," recalled one executive. "And guess what? Everybody showed up for breakfast. We were trying to serve 2,500 breakfasts at 350-seat restaurants. The lines were horrendous."[6]

Disney failed to anticipate another demand, this time from tour bus drivers. Restrooms were built for 50 drivers, but on peak days 2,000 drivers were seeking the facilities. "From impatient drivers to grumbling bankers, Disney stepped on toe after European toe.[7]

[6]Gumbel and Turner, "Fans Like Euro Disney," A12.
[7]Gumbel and Turner, "Fans Like Euro Disney," A12.

INFORMATION BOX

SKIMMING AND PENETRATION PRICING

A firm with a new product or service may be in a temporary monopolistic situation. If there is little or no present and potential competition, more latitude in pricing is possible. In such a situation (and, of course, Euro Disney was in this situation), one of two basic and opposite approaches may be taken in the pricing strategy: skimming or penetration.

Skimming is a relatively high-price strategy. It is the most tempting where the product or service is highly differentiated because it yields high per-unit profits. It is compatible with a quality image. But it has limitations. It assumes a rather inelastic demand curve, in which sales will not be appreciably affected by price. And if the product or service is easily imitated (which was hardly the case with Euro Disney), then competitors are encouraged because of the high profit margins.

The penetration strategy of low prices assumes an elastic demand curve, with sales increasing substantially if prices can be lowered. It is compatible with economies of scale, and it discourages competitive entry. The classic example of penetration pricing was the Model T Ford. Henry Ford lowered his prices to make the car within the means of the general public, expanded production into the millions, and in so doing realized new horizons of economies of scale.

Euro Disney correctly saw itself in a monopoly position; it correctly judged that it had a relatively inelastic demand curve with customers flocking to the park regardless of rather high prices. What it did not reckon with was the shrewdness of European visitors: Because of the high prices they shortened their stay, avoided the hotels, brought their own food and drink, and bought only sparingly the Disney merchandise.

What advantages would a lower price penetration strategy have offered Euro Disney? Do you see any drawbacks?

For the fiscal year ending September 30, 1993, the amusement park had lost $960 million, and the future of the park was in doubt. (as of December 31, 1993, the cumulative loss was 6.04 billion francs, or $1.03 billion). Walt Disney made $175 million available to tide Euro Disney over until the next spring. Adding to the problems of the struggling park were heavy interest costs. As depicted in Table 9.3, against a total cost of $4.4 billion, only 32 percent of the project was financed by equity investment. Some $2.9 billion was borrowed primarily from 60 creditor banks, at interest rates running as high as 11 percent. Thus, the enterprise began heavily leveraged, and the hefty interest charges greatly increased the overhead to be covered from operations. Serious negotiations began with the banks to restructure and refinance.

ATTEMPTS TO RECOVER

The $921 million lost in the first fiscal year represented a shortfall of more than $2.5 million a day. The situation was not quite as dire as these statistics would seem to indicate. Actually, the park was generating an operating profit, but nonoperating costs were bringing it deeply into the red.

Still, operations were far from satisfactory although they were becoming better. It had taken 20 months to smooth out the wrinkles and adjust to the miscalculations about demand for hotel rooms and the willingness of Europeans to pay substantial prices for lodging, meals, and merchandise. Operational efficiencies were slowly improving.

By the beginning of 1994, Euro Disney had been made more affordable. Prices of some hotel rooms were cut—for example, at the low end, from $76 per night to $51. Expensive jewelry was replaced by $10 T-shirts and $5 crayon sets. Luxury sit-down restaurants were converted to self-service. Off-season admission prices were reduced from $38 to $30. And operating costs were reduced 7 percent by streamlining operations and eliminating over 900 jobs.

Efficiency and *economy* became the new watchwords. Merchandise in stores was pared from 30,000 items to 17,000, with more of the remaining goods being pure U.S. Disney products. (The company had thought that European tastes might prefer more subtle items than the garish Mickey and Minnie souvenirs, but this was found not so.) The number of different food items offered by park services was reduced more than 50 percent. New training programs were designed to remotivate the 9,000 full-time permanent employees, to make them more responsive to customers and more flexible in their job assignments. Employees in contact with the public were given crash courses in German and Spanish.

Still, as we have seen, the problem had not been attendance, although the recession and the high prices had reduced it. Still, some 18 million people passed through the turnstiles in the first 20 months of operation. But they were not spending money as people did in the U.S. parks. Furthermore, Disney had alienated some European tour operators with its high prices, and it diligently sought to win them back.

Management had hoped to reduce the heavy interest overhead by selling the hotels to private investors. But the hotels had an occupancy rate of only 55%, making them unattractive to investors. Although the recession was a factor in such low occupancy rates, a significant part of the problem lay in the calculation of lodging demands. With the park just 35 minutes from the center of Paris, many visitors stayed in town. About the same time as the opening, the real estate market in France collapsed, making the hotels unsalable in the short term. This added to the overhead burden and confounded the business plan forecasts.

While some analysts were relegating Euro Disney to the cemetery, few remembered that Orlando's Disney World showed early symptoms of being a disappointment. Costs were heavier than expected, and attendance was below expectations. But Orlando's Disney World turned out to be one of the most profitable resorts in North America.

PROGNOSIS

Euro Disney has many things going for it, despite the disastrous early results. In May 1994 a station on the high-speed rail running from southern to northern France opened within walking distance of Euro Disney. This should help fill many of the hotel rooms too ambitiously built. The summer of 1994, the 50th anniversary of the Normandy invasion, brought many people to France. Another favorable sign for Euro Disney is the English Channel tunnel's opening in 1994, which potentially could bring a flood of British tourists.

Furthermore, the recession in Europe is bound to end, and with it should come renewed interest in travel. As real estate prices become more favorable, hotels can be sold and real estate development around the park spurred.

Even as Disney Chairman Michael Eisner threatened to close the park unless lenders restructured the debt, Disney increased its French presence, opening a Disney store on the Champs Elysees. The likelihood of a Disney pullout seemed remote, despite the posturing of Eisner, since royalty fees could be a sizable source of revenues even if the park only breaks even after servicing its debt. With only a 3.5 percent increase in revenues in 1995 and a 5 percent increase in 1996, these could yield $46 million in royalties for the parent company. "You can't ask what does Euro Disney mean in 1995. You have to ask what does it mean in 1998."[8]

ANALYSIS

Euro Disney, as we have seen, fell far short of expectations in the first 20 months of its operation, so far short that its continued existence was even questioned. What went wrong?

External Factors

A serious economic recession that affected all of Europe undoubtedly was a major impediment to meeting expectations. As noted before, it adversely af-

---

[8]Lisa Gubernick, "Mickey N'est Pas Fini," *Forbes* (Feb. 14, 1994): 43.

fected attendance—although still not all that much—but drastically affected spending patters. Frugality was the order of the day for many visitors. The recession also affected real estate demand and prices, thus saddling Disney with hotels it had hoped to sell at profitable prices to eager investors to take the strain off its hefty interest payments.

The company assumed that European visitors would not be greatly different from those visitors, foreign and domestic, of U.S. Disney parks. Yet, at least in the first few years of operation, visitors were much more price conscious. This suggested that those within a 2- to 4-hour drive of Euro Disney were considerably different from the ones who traveled overseas, at least in spending ability and willingness.

Internal Factors

Despite the decades of experience with the U.S. Disney parks and the successful experience with the new Japan park, Disney still made serious blunders in its operational planning, such as the demand for breakfasts, the insistence on wine at meals, the severe peaks and valleys in scheduling, and even such mundane things as sufficient restrooms for tour bus drivers. It had problems in motivating and training its French employees in efficiency and customer orientation. Did all these mistakes reflect an intractable French mindset or a deficiency of Disney management? Perhaps both. But Disney management should have researched all cultural differences more thoroughly. Further, the park needed major streamlining of inventories and operations after the opening. The mistakes suggested an arrogant mindset by Disney management: "We were arrogant," concedes one executive. "It was like 'We're building the Taj Mahal and people will come—on our terms.'"[9]

The miscalculations in hotel rooms and in pricing of many products, including food services, showed an insensitivity to the harsh economic conditions. But the greatest mistake was taking on too much debt for the park. The highly leveraged situation burdened Euro Disney with such hefty interest payments and overhead that the breakeven point was impossibly high, and it even threatened the viability of the enterprise. See the following box for a discussion of the important inputs and implications affecting breakeven, and how these should play a role in strategic planning.

Were such mistakes and miscalculations beyond what we would expect of reasonable executives? Probably not, with the probable exception of the crushing burden of debt. Any new venture is susceptible to surprises and the need

---

[9]Gumbel and Turner, "Fans Like Euro Disney," A12.

INFORMATION BOX

THE BREAKEVEN POINT

A breakeven analysis is a vital tool in making go/no go decisions about new ventures and alternative business strategies. This can be shown graphically as follows:

Below the breakeven point, the venture suffers losses; above it, the venture becomes profitable.

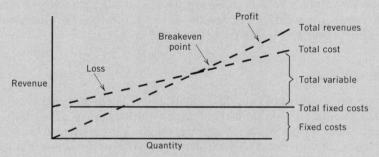

Let us make a hypothetical comparison of Euro Disney with its $1.6 billion in high interest loans (some of these as high as 11 percent) from the banks, and what the situation might be with more equity and less borrowed funds.

For this example, let us assume that other fixed costs are $240 million, that the average interest rate on the debt is 10 percent, and that average profit margin (contribution to overhead) from each visitor is $32. Now let us consider two scenarios: (a) the $1.6 billion of debt, and (b) only $0.5 billion of debt.

The number of visitors needed to breakeven are determined as follows:

$$\text{Breakeven} = \frac{\text{Total fixed costs}}{\text{Contribution to overhead}}$$

Scenario (a):   Interest $= 10\% \,(\$1{,}600{,}000{,}000) = \$160{,}000{,}000$

Fixed costs $=$ Interest $+ \$240{,}000{,}000$

$= 160{,}000{,}000 + 240{,}000{,}000$

$= \$400{,}000{,}000$

Breakeven $= \dfrac{\$400{,}000{,}000}{\$32} = 12{,}500{,}000$ visitors needed to breakeven

Scenario (b):   Interest $= 10\% \,(500{,}000{,}000) = \$50{,}000{,}000$

Fixed costs $= 50{,}000{,}000 + 240{,}000{,}000$

$= \$290{,}000{,}000$

$$\text{Breakeven} = \frac{\$290,000,000}{\$32} = 9,062,500 \quad \text{visitors needed to breakeven}$$

Because Euro Disney expected 11 million visitors the first year, it obviously was not going to breakeven while servicing $1.6 billion in debt with $160 million in interest charges per year. The average visitor would have to be induced to spend more, thereby increasing the average profit or contribution to overhead.

In making go/no go decisions, many costs can be estimated quite closely. What cannot be determined as surely are the sales figures. Certain things can be done to affect the breakeven point. Obviously it can be lowered if the overhead is reduced, as we saw in scenario b. Higher prices also result in a lower breakeven because of greater per-customer profits (but would probably affect total sales quite adversely). Promotion expenses can be either increased or decreased and affect the breakeven point, but they probably also have an impact on sales. Some costs of operation can be reduced, thus lowering the breakeven. But the hefty interest charges act as a lodestone over an enterprise, greatly increasing the overhead and requiring what may be an unattainable breakeven point.

Does a new venture have to break even or make a profit the first year to be worth going into? Why or why not?

to streamline and weed out its inefficiencies. While we would have expected such to have been done faster and more effectively from a well-tried Disney operation, European, and particularly French and Parisian, consumers and employees showed different behavior and attitude patterns than expected.

The worst sin that Disney management and investors could make would be to give up on Euro Disney and not to look ahead 2 to 5 years. A hint of the future promise was Christmas week of 1993. Despite the first year's $920 million in red ink, some 35,000 packed the park most days. A week later on a cold January day, some of the rides still had 40-minute waits.

POSTSCRIPT

On March 15, 1994, an agreement was struck aimed at making Euro Disney profitable by September 30, 1995. The European banks would fund another $500 million and make concessions such as forgiving 18 months' interest and deferring all principal payments for 3 years. In return, Walt Disney Company agreed to spend about $750 million to bail out its Euro Disney affiliate. Thus, the debt would be halved, with interest payments greatly reduced. Disney

[10]Brian Coleman and Thomas R. King, "Euro Disney Rescue Package Wins Approval," *Wall Street Journal* (March 15, 1994): A3, A5.

also agreed to eliminate for 5 years the lucrative management fees and royalties it received on the sale of tickets and merchandise. Although the continuance of the park is thus ensured, some analysts still believed Euro Disney needs a planned second park to make the investment a major success.[10]

The problems of Euro Disney were not resolved by mid-1994. The theme park and resort near Paris remained troubled. However, a new source for financing had emerged: A member of the Saudi Arabian royal family had agreed to invest up to $500 million for a 24 percent stake in Euro Disney. Prince Alwaleed had shown considerable sophistication in investing in troubled enterprises in the past. Now, his commitment to Euro Disney showed a belief in the ultimate success of the resort.[11]

WHAT CAN BE LEARNED?

Beware the arrogant mindset, especially when dealing with new situations and new cultures. French sensitivities were offended by Disney corporate executives who often turned out to be brash, insensitive, and overbearing. A contentious attitude by Disney personnel alienated people and aggravated planning and operational difficulties. "The answer to doubts or suggestions invariably was, Do as we say, because we know best."[12]

Such a mindset is a natural concomitant to success. It is said that success breeds arrogance, but this inclination must be fought against by those who would spurn the ideas and concerns of others. For a proud and touchy people, the French, this almost contemptuous attitude by the Americans fueled resentment and glee at Disney miscues. It did not foster cooperation, understanding, or the willingness to smooth the process. One might almost speculate that had not the potential economic benefits to France been so great, the Euro Disney project might never have been approved.

Great success may be ephemeral. We often find that great successes are not lasting, that they have no staying power. Somehow the success pattern gets lost or forgotten or is not well rounded. Other times an operation grows beyond the capability of the originators. Hungry competitors are always in the wings, ready to take advantage of any lapse. As we saw with Euro Disney, having a closed mind to new ideas or to needed revisions of an old success pattern—the arrogance of success—makes expansion into different environments more difficult and even risky.

---

[11]Richard Turner and Brian Coleman, "Saudi to Buy as Much as 24% of Euro Disney," *The Wall Street Journal* (June 2, 1994): A3.
[12]Gumbel and Turner, "Fans Like Euro Disney," A1.

While corporate Disney has continued to have strong success with its other theme parks and its diversifications, competitors are moving in with their own theme parks in the United States and elsewhere. We may question whether this industry is approaching saturation, and we may wonder whether Disney has learned from its mistakes in Europe.

Highly leveraged situations are extremely vulnerable. During most of the 1980s, many managers, including corporate raiders, pursued a strategy of debt financing in contrast to equity (stock ownership) financing. Funds for such borrowing were usually readily available, heavy debt had income tax advantages, and profits could be distributed among fewer shares so that return on equity was enhanced. During this time a few voices decried the overleveraged situations of many companies. They predicted that when the eventual economic downturn came, such firms would find themselves unable to meet the heavy interest burden. Most lenders paid little heed to such lonesome voices and encouraged greater borrowing.

The widely publicized problems of some of the raiders in the late 1980s, such as Robert Campeau, who had acquired major department store corporations only to find himself overextended and unable to continue, suddenly changed some expansionist lending sentiments. The hard reality dawned that these arrangements were often fragile indeed, especially when they rested on optimistic projections for asset sales, for revenues, and for cost savings to cover the interest payments. An economic slowdown hastened the demise of some of these ill-advised speculations.

Disney was guilty of the same speculative excesses with Euro Disney, relying far too much on borrowed funds and assuming that assets, such as hotels, could be easily sold off at higher prices to other investors. As we saw in the breakeven box, hefty interest charges from such overleveraged conditions can jeopardize the viability of the enterprise if revenue and profit projections fail to meet the rosy expectations.

Be judicious with the skimming price strategy. Euro Disney faced the classical situation favorable for a skimming price strategy. It was in a monopoly position, with no equivalent competitors likely. It faced a somewhat inelastic demand curve, which indicated that people would come almost regardless of price. So why not price to maximize per-unit profits? Unfortunately for Disney, the wily Europeans circumvented the high prices by frugality. Of course, a severe recession exacerbated the situation.

The learning insight from this example is that a skimming price assumes that customers are willing and able to pay the higher prices and have no lower-priced competitive alternatives It is a faulty strategy when many customers are unable, or else unwilling, to pay the high prices and can find a way to experience the product or service in a modest way.

CONSIDER

Can you think of other learning insights from this case?

QUESTIONS

1. How could the company have erred so badly in its estimates of the spending patterns of European customers?
2. How could a better reading of the impact of cultural differences on revenues have been achieved?
3. What suggestions do you have for fostering a climate of sensitivity and goodwill in corporate dealings with the French?
4. How do you account for the great success of Tokyo Disneyland and the problems of Euro Disney? What are the key contributory differences?
5. Do you believe that Euro Disney might have done better if located elsewhere in Europe rather than just outside Paris? Why or why not?
6. "Mickey Mouse and the Disney park are an American cultural abomination." Evaluate this critical statement.
7. Consider how a strong marketing approach might be made to both European consumers and agents, such as travel agents, tour guides, even bus drivers.

INVITATION TO ROLE PLAY

1. As the staff assistant to the president of Euro Disney, you already believe before the grand opening that the plans to use a skimming pricing strategy and to emphasize luxury hotel accommodations are ill advised. What arguments would you marshal to persuade the company to offer lower prices and more moderate accommodations? Be as persuasive as you can.
2. It is 6 months after opening. Revenues are not meeting target, and a number of problems have surfaced and are being worked on. The major problem remains, however, that the venture needs more visitors and/or higher expenditures per visitor. Develop a marketing strategy to improve the situation.

INVITATION TO RESEARCH

What is the situation with Euro Disney today? Are the optimistic expectations now being realized, or are dire predictions still prevalent?

CHAPTER 10

Coca-Cola's Classic Blunder: The Failure of Marketing Research

On April 23, 1985, Roberto C. Goizueta, chairman of Coca-Cola, made a momentous announcement. It was to lead to more discussion, debate, and intense feelings than perhaps ever before resulting from one business decision.

"The best has been made even better," he proclaimed. After 99 years, the Coca-Cola Company had decided to abandon its original formula in favor of a sweeter variation, presumably an improved taste, which was named "New Coke."

Not even 3 months later, public pressure brought the company to admit it had made a mistake, and that it was bringing back the old Coke under the name "Coca-Cola Classic." It was July 11, 1985. Despite $4 million and two years of research, the company had made a major miscalculation. How could this have happened with such an astute marketer? The story is intriguing and provides a number of sobering insights, and it has a happy ending for Coca-Cola.

THE HISTORY OF COCA-COLA

Early Days

Coca-Cola was invented by a pharmacist who rose to cavalry general for the Confederates during the Civil War. John Styth Pemberton settled in Atlanta after the war and began putting out patent medicines such as Triplex Liver Pills and Globe of Flower Cough Syrup. In 1885 he registered a trademark for French Wine Coca, "an Ideal Nerve and Tonic Stimulant." In 1886, Pemberton unveiled a modification of French Wine Coca that he called

Coca-Cola, and began distributing this to soda fountains in used beer bottles. He looked on the concoction less as a refreshment than as a headache cure, especially for people who had overindulged in food or drink. By chance, one druggist discovered that the syrup tasted better when mixed with carbonated water.

When his health failed and Coca-Cola failed to bring sufficient money to meet his financial obligations, Pemberton sold the rights to Coca-Cola to a 39-year-old pharmacist, Asa Griggs Candler, for a paltry $2300. The destitute Pemberton died in 1988 and was buried in a grave that went unmarked for the next 70 years.

Candler, a small-town Georgia boy born in 1851 (and hence too young to be a hero in the Civil War), had planned to become a physician but he changed his mind after observing that druggists made more money than doctors. He struggled for almost 40 years until he bought Coca-Cola, but then his fortunes changed profoundly. In 1892 he organized the Coca-Cola Company, and a few years later downgraded the therapeutic qualities. At the same time, he developed the bottling system that still exists, and for 25 years he almost singlehandedly guided the drink's destiny.

Robert Woodruff and the Maturing of the Coca-Cola Company

In 1916, Candler left Coca-Cola to run for mayor of Atlanta. The company was left in the hands of his relatives, who, after only 3 years, sold it to a group of Atlanta businessmen for $25 million. Asa was not consulted, and he was deeply distraught. The company was then netting $5 million. By the time of his death in 1929, annual profits were approaching the $25 million sale price. The group who bought Coca-Cola was headed by Ernest Woodruff, an Atlanta banker. Coke today still remains in the hands of the Woodruff family. Under the direction of the son, Robert Winship Woodruff, Coca-Cola became not only a household word within the United States, but one of the most recognized symbols the world over.

Robert Woodruff grew up in affluence but believed in the virtues of personal achievement and effort. As a young man, he ignored his father's orders to return to Emory College to complete the remaining years of his education. He wanted to earn his keep in the real world and not "waste" 3 years in school. Eventually in 1911 he joined one of his father's firms, the newly organized Atlantic Ice & Coal Company, as a salesperson and a buyer. But he and his father violently disagreed again, this time over the purchase by Robert of trucks from White Motors to replace the horse-drawn carts and drays of the day. Ernest fired his son and told him never to return home again. So Robert promptly joined White Motors. At the age of 33, he had become the nation's top truck sales representative and was earning $85,000 a year. But then he heeded the call to come home.

By 1920 the Coca-Cola Company was threatened by bankruptcy. An untimely purchase of sugar just before prices plummeted had resulted in a staggering amount of borrowing to keep the company afloat. Bottler relations were at an all-time low because the company had wanted to raise the price of syrup, thus violating the original franchise contracts in which the price had been permanently fixed. In April of 1923, Robert was named president, and he cemented dealer relationships, stressing his conviction that he wanted everyone connected with Coca-Cola to make money. A quality control program was instituted and distribution was greatly expanded: By 1930, there were 64 bottlers in 28 countries.

During World War II, Coke went with the GIs. Woodruff saw to it that every man in uniform could get a bottle of Coca-Cola for 5 cents whenever he wanted, no matter what the cost to the company. Throughout the 1950s, 1960s, and early 1970s, Coca-Cola ruled the soft-drink market, despite strong challenges by Pepsi. It outsold Pepsi by two to one. But this was to change.

BACKGROUND OF THE DECISION

Inroads of Pepsi, 1970s and 1980s

By the mid-1970s, the Coca-Cola Company was a lumbering giant. Performance reflected this. Between 1976 and 1979, the growth rate of Coca-Cola soft drinks dropped from 13 percent annually to a meager 2 percent. As the giant stumbled, Pepsi Cola was finding heady triumphs. First came the "Pepsi Generation." This advertising campaign captured the imagination of the baby boomers with its idealism and youth. This association with youth and vitality greatly enhanced the image of Pepsi and firmly associated it with the largest consumer market for soft drinks.

Then came another management coup, the "Pepsi Challenge," in which comparative taste tests with consumers showed a clear preference for Pepsi. This campaign led to a rapid increase in Pepsi's market share, from 6 to 14 percent of total U.S. soft-drink sales.

Coca-Cola, in reaction, conducted its own taste tests. Alas, these tests had the same result—people liked the taste of Pepsi better, and market share changes reflected this. As Table 10.1 shows, by 1979 Pepsi had closed the gap on Coca-Cola, having 17.9 percent of the soft-drink market, to Coke's 23.9 percent. By the end of 1984, Coke had only a 2.9 percent lead, while in the grocery store market it was now trailing by 1.7 percent. Further indication of the diminishing position of Coke relative to Pepsi was a study done by Coca-

Table 10.1   Coke and Pepsi Shares of Total Soft-Drink Market 1950s–1984

	Mid-1950s Lead	*1975 % of Market*	*Lead*	*1979 % of Market*	*Lead*	*1984 % of Market*	*Lead*
Coke	Better than	24.2	6.8	23.9	6.0	21.7	2.9
Pepsi	2 to 1	17.4		17.9		18.8	

Sources: Thomas Oliver, *The Real Coke, the Real Story* (New York: Random House, 1986), pp. 21, 50; "Two Cokes Really Are Better Than One—For Now," *Business Week* (Sept. 9, 1985): 38.

Cola's own marketing research department. This showed that in 1972 18 percent of soft-drink users drank Coke exclusively, while only 4 percent drank only Pepsi. In 10 years, the picture had changed greatly: only 12 percent now claimed loyalty to Coke, while the number of exclusive Pepsi drinkers almost matched, with 11 percent. Figure 10.1 shows this graphically.

What made the deteriorating comparative performance of Coke all the more worrisome and frustrating to Coca-Cola was that it was outspending Pepsi in advertising by $100 million. It had twice as many vending machines, dominated fountains, had more shelf space, and was competitively priced. Why was it still losing market share? The advertising undoubtedly was not as effective as that of Pepsi, despite vastly more money spent. And this raises the question: How can we measure the effectiveness of advertising? See the box on page 134 for a discussion.

The Changing of the Guard

J. Paul Austin, the chairman of Coca-Cola, was nearing retirement in 1980. Donald Keough, the president for Coca-Cola's American group, was expected to succeed him. But a new name, Roberto Goizueta, suddenly emerged.

Goizueta's background was far different from that of the typical Coca-Cola executive, He was not from Georgia, was not even southern. Rather, he was the son of a wealthy Havana sugar plantation owner. He came to the United States at age 16 to enter an exclusive Connecticut preparatory school, Cheshire Academy. He spoke virtually no English when he arrived, but by using the dictionary and watching movies, he quickly learned the language—and became the class valedictorian.

He graduated from Yale in 1955 with a degree in chemical engineering and returned to Cuba. Spurning his father's business, he went to work in Coke's Cuban research labs.

Goizueta's complacent life was to change in 1959 when Fidel Castro seized power and expropriated foreign facilities. With his wife and their three children, he fled to the United States, arriving with $20. With Coca-Cola he soon became known as a brilliant administrator, and in 1968 he was brought to company headquarters. In 1980 Goizueta and six other executives were made vice chairmen and began battling for top spot in the company.

CEO J. Paul Austin, soon to retire because of Alzheimer's disease, favored an operations man to become the next CEO. But he was overruled by Robert Woodruff, the 90-year-old patriarch. In April 1980, the board of directors approved Woodruff's recommendation of Goizueta for the presidency. When Goizueta became chairman of the board in March 1981, Donald Keough succeeded him as president.

Shortly after, Goizueta called a worldwide managers' conference in which he announced that nothing was sacred to the company anymore, that change was imminent, and that they had to accept that. He also announced ambitious plans to diversify beyond the soft-drink industry.

In a new era of change announced by a new administration, the sacredness of the commitment to the original Coke formula becomes tenuous, and the ground was laid for the first flavor change in 99 years.

Marketing Research

With the market share erosion of the late 1970s and early 1980s, despite strong advertising and superior distribution, the company began to look at the product itself. Evidence was increasingly suggesting that taste was the single most important cause of Coke's decline. Perhaps the original secret formula needed to be scrapped. And so Project Kansas began.

Under Project Kansas in 1982 some 2000 interviews in 10 major markets were conducted to investigate customers' willingness to accept a different

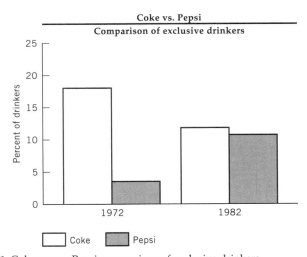

Figure 10.1. Coke versus Pepsi: comparison of exclusive drinkers.

INFORMATION BOX

HOW DO WE MEASURE THE EFFECTIVENESS OF ADVERTISING?

A firm can spend millions of dollars for advertising, and it is only natural to want some feedback of the results of such an expenditure: To what extent did the advertising really pay? Yet, many problems confront the firm trying to measure this.

Most of the methods for measuring effectiveness focus not on sales changes but on how well the communication is remembered, recognized, or recalled. Most evaluative methods simply tell which ad is the best among those being appraised. But even though one ad may be found to be more memorable or to create more attention than another, that fact alone gives no assurance of relationship to sales success. A classic example of the dire consequences that can befall advertising people as a result of the inability to directly measure the impact of ads on sales occurred in December 1970:

> In 1970, the Doyle Dane Bernbach advertising agency created memorable TV commercials for Alka-Seltzer, such as the "spicy meatball man," and the "poached oyster bride." These won professional awards as the best commercials of the year and received high marks for humor and audience recall. But in December the $22 million account was abruptly switched to another agency. The reason? Alka-Seltzers sales had dropped somewhat. Of course, no one will ever know whether the drop might have been much worse without these notable commercials.

So, how do we measure the value of millions of dollars spent for advertising? Not well. Nor can we determine what is the right amount to spend for advertising, versus what is too much or too little.

Can a business succeed without advertising? Why or why not?

Coke. People were shown storyboards and comic strip-style mock commercials and were asked series of questions. One storyboard, for example, said that Coke had added a new ingredient and it tasted smoother, while another said the same about Pepsi. Then consumers were asked about their reactions to the "change concept": for example, "Would you be upset?" and "Would you try the new drink?" Researchers estimated from the responses that 10 to 12 percent of Coke drinkers would be upset, and that one-half of these would get over it, but one-half would not.

While interviews showed a willingness to try a new Coke, other tests disclosed the opposite. Small consumer panels or focus groups revealed strong favorable and unfavorable sentiments. But the technical division persisted in trying to develop a new, more pleasing flavor. By September 1984 it thought it had done so. It was a sweeter, less fizzy cola with soft, sticky taste due to a higher sugar content from the exclusive use of corn syrup sweetener that is sweeter than sucrose. This was introduced in blind taste tests, where consumers were not told what brand they were drinking. These tests were highly encouraging. The new flavor substantially beat Pepsi, whereas in previous blind taste tests Pepsi had always beaten Coke.

As a result, researchers estimated that the new formula would boost Coke's share of the soft-drink market by 1 percentage point. This would be worth $200 million in sales.

Before adopting the new flavor, Coca-Cola invested $4 million in the biggest taste test ever. Some 191,000 people in more than 13 cities were asked to participate in a comparison of unmarked various Coke formulations. The use of unmarked colas was intended to eliminate any bias toward brand names. Fifty-five percent of the participants favored New Coke over the original formula, and it also beat out Pepsi. The research results seemed to be conclusive in favor of the new formula.

The Go Decision

While the decision was made to introduce the new flavor, a number of ancillary decisions had to be reconciled. For example, should the new flavor be added to the product line, or should it replace the old Coke? It was felt that bottlers generally would be opposed to adding another cola. After considerable soul-searching, top executives unanimously decided to change the taste of Coke and take the old Coke off the market.

In January 1985, the task of introducing the new Coke was given to McCann-Erickson advertising agency. Bill Cosby was to be the spokesperson for the nationwide introduction of the new Coke scheduled for April. All departments of this company were gearing their efforts for a coordinated introduction.

On April 23, 1985, Goizueta and Keough held a press conference at Lincoln Center in New York City in order to introduce the new Coke. Invitations had been sent to the media from all over the United States, and some 200 newspaper, magazine, and TV reporters attended the press conference. However, many of them came away unconvinced of the merits of the new Coke, and their stories were generally negative. In the days ahead, the news media's skepticism was to exacerbate the public nonacceptance of the new Coke.

The word spread quickly. Within 24 hours, 81 percent of the U.S. population knew of the change, and this was more people than were aware in July 1969 that Neil Armstrong had walked on the moon.[1] Early results looked good; 150 million people tried the new Coke, and this was more people than had ever before tried a new product. Most comments were favorable. Shipments to bottlers rose to the highest percent in 5 years. The decision looked unassailable. But not for long.

---

[1] John S. Demott, "Fiddling with the Real Thing," *Time* (May 6, 1985): 55.

AFTERMATH OF THE DECISION

The situation changed rapidly. While some protests were expected, these quickly mushroomed. In the first 4 hours, the company received about 650 calls. By mid-May, calls were coming in at a rate of 5000 a day, in addition to a barrage of angry letters. The company added 83 WATS lines and hired new staff to handle the responses. People were speaking of Coke as an American symbol and as a long-time friend that had suddenly betrayed them. Some threatened to switch to tea or water. Here is a sample of the responses.[2]

> The sorrow I feel knowing not only won't I ever enjoy real Coke, but my children and grandchildren won't either...I guess my children will have to take my word for it.
>
> It is absolutely TERRIBLE! You should be ashamed to put the Coke label on it. ...This new stuff tastes worse than Pepsi.
>
> It was nice knowing you, You were a friend for most of my 35 years. Yesterday I had my first taste of new Coke, and to tell the truth, if I would have wanted Pepsi, I would have ordered a Pepsi not a Coke.

In all, more than 40,000 such letters were received that spring and summer. In Seattle, strident loyalists calling themselves Old Coke Drinkers of America laid plans to file a class action suit against Coca-Cola. People began stockpiling the old Coke. Some sold it at scalper's prices. When sales in June did not pick up as the company had expected, bottlers demanded the return of old Coke.

The company's research also confirmed an increasing negative sentiment. Before May 30, 53 percent of consumers said they liked the new Coke. In June, the vote began to change, with more than one-half of all people surveyed saying they did not like the new Coke. By July, only 30 percent of the people surveyed each week said they liked the new Coke.

Anger spread across the country, fueled by media publicity. Fiddling with the formula for the 99-year-old beverage became an affront to patriotic pride. Robert Antonio, a University of Kansas sociologist, stated, "Some felt that a sacred symbol had been tampered with."[3] Even Goizueta's father spoke out against the switch when it was announced. He told his son the move was a bad one and jokingly threatened to disown him. By now company executives began to worry about a consumer boycott against the product.

---

[2]Thomas Oliver, *The Real Coke, the Real Story* (New York: Random House, 1986), 155–156.
[3]John Greenwald, "Coca-Cola's Big Fizzle," *Time* (July 22, 1985): 48.

Coca-Cola Cries "Uncle"

Company executives now began seriously thinking about how to recoup the fading prospects of Coke. In an executive meeting, the decision was made to take no action until after the Fourth of July weekend, when the sales results for this holiday weekend would be in. Results were unimpressive. The decision was announced to the public on July 11th, when top executives walked onto the stage in front of the Coca-Cola logo to make an apology to the public, without admitting that New Coke had been a total mistake.

Two messages were delivered to the American consumer. First, to those who were drinking the new Coke and enjoying it, the company conveyed its thanks. The message to those who wanted the original Coke was that "we heard you," and the original taste of Coke is back.

The news spread fast. ABC interrupted its soap opera, *General Hospital,* on Wednesday afternoon to break the news. In the kind of saturation coverage normally reserved for disasters or diplomatic crises, the decision to bring back old Coke was prominently reported on every evening network news broadcast. The general feeling of soft-drink fans was joy. Democratic Senator David Pryor of Arkansas expressed his jubilation on the Senate floor: "A very meaningful moment in the history of America, this shows that some national institutions cannot be changed."[4] Even Wall Street was happy. Old Coke's comeback drove Coca-Cola stock to its highest level in 12 years.

On the other hand, Roger Enrico, president of Pepsi-Cola USA, said: "Clearly this is the Edsel of the 80s. This was a terrible mistake. Coke's got a lemon on its hand and now they're trying to make lemonade."[5] Other critics labeled this the "marketing blunder of the decade."[6]

WHAT WENT WRONG?

The most convenient scapegoat, according to the consensus, was the marketing research that preceded the decision. Yet Coca-Cola spent about $4 million and devoted 2 years to the marketing research. About 200,000 consumers were contacted during this time. The error in judgment was surely not from want of trying. But when we dig deeper into the research efforts, some flaws become apparent.

---

[4]Greenwald, "Coca-Cola's Big Fizzle," 48.
[5]Greenwald, "Coca-Cola's Big Fizzle," 49.
[6]"Coke's Man on the Spot," *Business Week* (July 29, 1985): 56.

Flawed Marketing Research

The major design of the marketing research involved taste tests by representative consumers. After all, the decision point involved a different-flavored Coke, so what could be more logical than to conduct blind taste tests to determine the acceptability of the new flavor, not only versus the old Coke but also versus Pepsi? And these results were significantly positive for the new formula, even among Pepsi drinkers. A clear "go" signal seemed indicated.

But with the benefit of hindsight some deficiencies in the research design were more apparent—and should have caused concern at the time. The research participants were not told that by picking one cola, they would lose the other. This turned out to be a significant distortion: Any addition to the product line would naturally be far more acceptable to a loyal Coke user than would be a complete substitution, which meant the elimination of the traditional product.

While three to four new tastes were tested with almost 200,000 people, only 30,000 to 40,000 of these tests involved the specific formula for the new Coke. The research was geared more to the idea of a new, sweeter cola than the final formula. In general, a sweeter flavor tends to be preferred in blind taste tests. This is particularly true with youth, the largest drinkers of sugared colas, and the group that had been drinking more Pepsi in recent years. Furthermore, preferences for sweeter tasting products tend to diminish with use.[7]

Consumers were asked whether they favored change as a concept, and whether they would likely drink more, less, or the same amount of Coke if there were a change .But such questions could hardly prove the depth of feelings and emotional ties to the product.

Symbolic Value

The symbolic value of Coke was the sleeper. Perhaps this should have been foreseen. Perhaps the marketing research should have considered this possibility and designed the research to map it and determine the strength and durability of these values—that is, would they have a major effect on any substitution of a new flavor?

Admittedly, when we get into symbolic value and emotional involvement, any researcher is dealing with vague and nebulous attitudes. But various attitudinal measures have been developed to measure the strength or degree of emotional involvement, such as the *semantic differential*.

---

[7]"New Coke Wins Round 1, but Can It Go the Distance?" *Business Week* (June 24, 1985): 48.

INFORMATION BOX

MARKETING TOOL: THE SEMANTIC DIFFERENTIAL

An important tool in attitudinal research, image studies, and positioning decisions is the *semantic differential*. It was originally developed to measure the meaning that a concept—perhaps a political issue, a person, a work of art, or in marketing, a brand, product, or company—might have for people in terms of various dimensions. As first presented, the instrument consisted of pairs of polar adjectives with a seven-interval scale separating the opposite members of each pair. For example:

Good —— —— —— —— —— —— —— Bad

The various intervals from left to right would then represent degrees of feeling or belief ranging from extremely good to neither good nor bad, to extremely bad.

This instrument has been refined to obtain greater sensitivity through the use of descriptive phrases. Example of such bipolar phrases for determining the image of a particular brand of beer are:

Something —— —— —— —— —— —— —— Just another
special   drink

American —— —— —— —— —— —— —— Foreign
flavor   flavor

Really peps —— —— —— —— —— —— —— Somehow doesn't
you up   pep you up

The number of word pairs varies considerably but may be as many as 50 or more. Flexibility and appropriateness to a particular study are achieved by constructing tailor made word and phrase lists.

Semantic differential scales have been used in marketing to compare images of particular products, brands, firms, and stores against competing ones. The answers of all respondents can be averaged and then plotted to provide a "profile," as shown below for three competing beers on four scales (actually, a firm would probably use 20 or more scales in such a study).

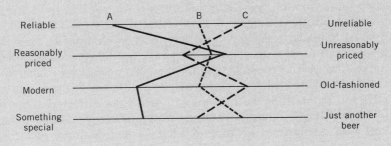

In this profile, brand A shows the dominant image over its competing brands in three of the four categories; however, the negative reaction to its price should alert the company to review pricing practices. Brand C shows a negative image especially regarding the reliability of its product. The old fashioned image may or may not be desirable, depending on the type of customer being sought; at least the profile indicates that brand C is perceived as being distinctive from the other two brands. Probably the weakest image of all is that of brand B; respondents viewed this brand as having no distinctive image, neither good nor bad. A serious image-building campaign is desperately needed if brand B is to compete successfully; otherwise, the price may have to be dropped to gain some advantages.

Simple, easy to administer and analyze, the semantic differential is useful not only in identifying segments and positions where there might be opportunities because these are currently not well covered by competitors, but it is also useful to a well-established firm—such as Coca-Cola—to determine the strength and the various dimensions of attitudes towards its product. Semantic differential scales are also useful in evaluating the effectiveness of a changed marketing strategy, such as a change in advertising theme. Here the semantic differential could be administered before the campaign and again after the campaign, and any changes in perceptions pinpointed.

Develop eight semantic differential scales for soft drinks, and then profile Coke and Pepsi. What differences do you perceive in the two brands? Are they important? Do you see any soft-drink untapped opportunities?

Herd Instinct

A natural human phenomenon asserted itself in this case—the herd instinct, the tendency of people to follow an idea, a slogan, a concept, to "jump on the bandwagon." At first, acceptance of the new Coke appeared to be reasonably satisfactory. But as more and more outcries were raised—fanned by the press—about the betrayal of the old tradition (somehow this became identified with motherhood, apple pie, and the flag), public attitudes shifted vigorously against this perceived unworthy substitute. And the bandwagon syndrome was fully activated. It is doubtful that by July 1985 Coca-Cola could have done anything to reverse the unfavorable tide. To wait for it to die down was fraught with danger—for who would be brave enough to predict the durability and possible heights of such a protest movement?

Could, or should, such a tide have been predicted? Perhaps not, at least as to the full strength of the movement. Coca-Cola expected some resentment. But perhaps it should have been more cautious, and have considered a "worst case" scenario in addition to what seemed the more probable, and been prepared to react to such a contingency.

WHAT CAN BE LEARNED?

The inconstancy of taste. Taste tests are commonly used in marketing research, but I have always been skeptical of their validity. Take beer, for example. I know of few people—despite their strenuous claims—who can in blind taste tests unerringly identify which is which among three of four disguised brands of beer. We know that people tend to favor the sweeter in taste tests. But does this mean that such a sweeter flavor will always win out in the marketplace? Hardly. Something else is operating with consumer preference other than the fleeting essence of a taste—unless the flavor difference is extreme.

Brand image usually is a more powerful sales stimulant. Advertisers consistently have been more successful in cultivating a desirable image or personality for their brands or the types of people who use them, than by such vague statements as "better tasting."

Don't tamper with tradition. Not many firms have a 100-year-old tradition to be concerned with, or even 25, or even 10. Most products have much shorter life cycles. No other product has been so widely used and so deeply entrenched in societal values and culture as Coke.

The psychological components of the great Coke protest make interesting speculation. Perhaps, in an era of rapid change, many people wish to hang on to the one symbol of security or constancy in their lives—even if this is only the traditional Coke flavor. Perhaps many people found this protest to be an interesting way to escape the humdrum, by "making waves" in a rather harmless fashion, and in the process to see if a big corporation might be forced to cry "uncle."

One is left to wonder how many consumers would even have been aware of any change in flavor had the new formula been quietly introduced without fanfare. But, of course, the advertising siren call of "New!" would have been muted.

So, do we dare tamper with tradition? In Coke's case the answer is probably not, unless done very quietly, but then Coke is unique.

Don't try to fix something that isn't broken. Conventional wisdom may advocate that changes are best made in response to problems, that when things are going smoothly the success pattern or strategy should not be tampered with. Perhaps. But perhaps not.

Actually, things were not going all that well for Coke by early 1985. Market share had steadily been declining to Pepsi for some years. Vigorous promotional efforts by Pepsi featuring star Michael Jackson had increased the market share of regular Pepsi by 1.5 percent in 1984, while regular Coke was dropping 1 percent.[8] Moreover, regular Coke had steadily been losing market position in supermarkets, dropping almost 4 percent between 1981 and 1985. And foreign business, accounting for 62 percent of total soft-drink volume for Coca-Cola, was showing a disappointing growth rate.[9]

So there was certainly motivation for considering a change. And the obvious change was to introduce a somewhat different flavor, one more congruent with the preference of younger people who were the prime market for soft drinks. I do not subscribe to the philosophy of "don't rock the boat" or "don't change anything until virtually forced to." However, Coca-Cola had another option.

Don't burn your bridges. The obvious alternative was to introduce the new Coke, but still keep the old one. This could be called "don't burn your bridges." Of course, in July Roberto Goizueta brought back the old coke after some months of turmoil and considerable corporate embarrassment and competitive glee—which was soon to turn to competitive dismay. The obvious drawback for having two Cokes was dealer resentment at having to stock an additional product in the same limited space, and bottler concern at having a more complicated production run. Furthermore, there was the real possibility that Pepsi would emerge as the number one soft drink due to two competing Cokes—and this would be an acute embarrassment for Coca-Cola.

The ineffectiveness of sheer advertising dollars. Coca-Cola was outspending Pepsi for advertising by $100 million, but its market share in the late 1970s and early 1980s continued to erode to Pepsi. Pepsi's campaigns featured the theme of the "Pepsi Generation" and the "Pepsi Challenge." The use of a superstar such as Michael Jackson also proved to be more effective with the target market of soft drinks than Bill Cosby for Coca-Cola. Any executive has to be left with the sobering realization that the sheer number of dollars spent on advertising does not guarantee competitive success. A smaller firm can still outdo a larger rival.

The power of the media. The press and broadcast media can be powerful influencers of public opinion. With new Coke, the media undoubtedly exacerbated the herd instinct by publicizing the protests to the fullest. After all, this was news. And news seems to be spiciest when an institution or person can be criticized or found wanting. The power of the press should also be sobering to an executive and ought to be one of the factors considered along with certain decisions that may affect the public image of the organization.

[8] "Pepsi's High-priced Sell Is Paying Off," *Business Week* (Mar. 4, 1985): 34–35.
[9] "Is Coke Fixing a Cola That Isn't Broken?" *Business Week* (May 6, 1985): 47.

Aftermath

Forced by public opinion into a two-cola strategy, the company found the results to be reassuring. By October 1985 estimates were that Coke Classic was outselling New Coke by better than 2 to 1 nationwide, but by 9 to 1 in some markets; restaurant chains, such as McDonald's, Hardee's, Roy Rogers, and Red Lobster had switched back to Coke Classic.

For the full year of 1985, sales from all operations rose 10 percent and profits 9 percent. In the United States Coca-Cola soft-drink volume increased 9 percent, and internationally 10 percent. Profitability from soft drinks decreased slightly, representing heavier advertising expenses for introducing New Coke and then reintroducing old Coke.

Coca-Cola's fortunes continued to improve steadily if not spectacularly. By 1988 it was producing 5 of the 10 top-selling soft drinks in the country, and now had a total 40 percent of the domestic market to 31 percent for Pepsi.[10]

Because the soft-drink business was generating about $1 billion in cash each year, Roberto Goizueta had made a number of major acquisitions, such as Columbia Pictures and the Taylor Wine Company. However, these had not met his expectations, and the company disposed of them. Still, by 1988 there was a hoard of $5 billion in new cash and debt capacity, and the enticing problem now was how to spend it.

Table 10.2   1986 Family of Cokes

Kinds	Millions of Cases
Total of one cola in 1980	1,310.5
1986	
Coca-Cola Classic	1,294.3
Diet Coke	490.8
Coke	185.1
Cherry Coke	115.6
Caffeine-Free Diet Coke	85.6
Caffeine-Free Coke	19.0
Diet Cherry Coke	15.0

Source: "He Put the Kick Back into Coke," *Fortune* (Oct. 26, 1987): 48.

The most successful diversifications were in the soft-drink area. As recently as 1981 there had been only one Coke, and not too many years before, only one container—the 6/12-oz glass bottle. By 1987, only one-tenth

[10] "Some Things Don't Go Better with Coke," *Forbes* (Mar. 21, 1988): 34–35.

of 1 percent of all coke was sold in that bottle.[11] Classic is the best-selling soft drink in the United States, and Diet Coke was the third largest selling. New Coke was being outsold by Classic about seven to one. Table 10.2 shows the total sales volume, expressed as millions of cases, of the family of Coke.

The future for Coca-Cola looked bright. Per capita soft-drink consumption in the United States rose significantly in the 1980s.[12]

	Per Capita Consumption	Percent Increase
1980	34.5 gal.	—
1986	42 gal.	22

The international potential was great. The per capita consumption outside the United States was 4 gallons. Yet 95 percent of the world's population lives outside the United States.

CONCLUSION

Some called New Coke a misstep, others a blink. At the time there were those who called it a monumental blunder, even the mistake of the century. But it hardly turned out to be that. As sales surged, some competitors accused Coca-Cola of engineering the whole scenario, in order to get tons of free publicity. Coke executives stoutly denied this, and admitted their error in judgment. For who could foresee, as *Fortune* noted, that the episode would "reawaken deep-seated American loyalty to Coca-Cola."[13]

CONSIDER

Can you think of other learning insights arising from this case?

QUESTIONS

1. How could Coca-Cola's marketing research have been improved? Be as specific as you can.
2. When a firm is facing a negative press, as Coca-Cola was with the new Coke, what recourse does the firm have? Support your conclusions.

[11] "He Put the Kick Back into Coke," *Fortune* (Oct. 26, 1987): 47–56.
[12] *Pepsico 1986 Annual Report*, 13.
[13] "He Put the Kick," p. 48.

3. Do you think Coca-Cola would have been as successful if it had introduced the new Coke as an addition to the line, and not as a substitute for the old Coke? Why or why not?
4. "If it's not broken, don't fix it." Evaluate this statement.
5. Do you think Coca-Cola engineered the whole scenario with the new Coke, including fanning public protests, in order to get a bonanza of free publicity? Defend your position.
6. Would you, as a top executive at Coca-Cola, have "caved in" as quickly to the protests? Would you have "toughed it out" instead?
7. Given the inability to judge very closely the effectiveness of advertising expenditures, why do you suppose so many firms still spend millions and millions of dollars for advertising? Is it faith?

INVITATION TO ROLE PLAY

1. Assume that you are Robert Goizueta and that you are facing increasing pressure in early July 1985 to abandon the new Coke and bring back the old formula. However, your latest marketing research suggests that only a small group of agitators is making all the fuss about the new cola. Evaluate your options, and support your recommendations to the board.
2. You are the public relations director of Coca-Cola. It is early June 1985, and you have been ordered to "do something" to blunt the negative publicity. What ideas can you offer that might counter or replace the negatives with positive publicity?

INVITATION TO RESEARCH

Who is winning the cola battle in the 1990s? How would you assess future possibilities?

CHAPTER 11

Adidas: Underestimating Competitors

Here is one of the great classic cases of a frontrunner's underestimating the dangers of competitive intrusion into its markets. Though this occurred two decades ago, the learning insights are far from dated.

In the early 1970s, Adidas dominated the running-shoe industry. It had done so for decades. It stood on the threshold of one of the biggest surges of popularity for its market that any recreational pursuit had ever known. Millions of people were to take up running or jogging in the next few years; other millions of nonrunners would be buying and wearing running shoes because they were comfortable, and because they conveyed an aura of fitness and youth—an image that most people were not averse to emulating.

Did Adidas cash in on this recreational boom of the century? In one of the classic instances of miscalculation, it underestimated the U.S. market. (It still was to dominate in other parts of the world.) Even worse, it underestimated the entry and aggressiveness of U.S. competitors. Most of these competitors were to be upstart firms that had not even been around at the beginning of the decade. In just a few years, Adidas was to be pushed aside by one of the fastest growing firms outside the computer industry: Nike.

HISTORICAL BACKGROUND

Rudolf and Adolf Dassler began making shoes in Herzogenaurach, Germany, shortly after World War I. Adolf, known as Adi to his family, was the innovator, and Rudolf was the marketer who sold his brother's creations. The brothers achieved only moderate success at first, but then in 1936 a big breakthrough came. Jesse Owens agreed to wear their shoes in the Olympics and won his medals in front of Hitler, the German nation, and the world. The lucrative association of shoes with a famous athlete was to trigger a marketing strategy that Adidas—and other athletic shoe manufacturers—was to practice from that point on.

In 1949 the brothers had a falling out and never again spoke to each other outside court. Rudolf took one-half the equipment and left his brother for the other side of town, where he set up the Puma Company. Adolf established the Adidas Company from the existing firm ("Adidas" was derived from his nickname and the first three letters of his surname). Rudolf and his Pumas never quite caught up with Adolf's Adidas, but they did become number two in the world.

Adolf was constantly experimenting with new materials and techniques to develop stronger yet lighter shoes. He tested thorny sharkskin in attempts to develop abrasive leather for indoor flats. He tried kangaroo leather to toughen the side of shoes.

The first samples of Adidas footwear were shown at the Helsinki Olympic Games of 1952. Then in 1954 the German soccer team, equipped with Adidas footwear, won the World Cup over Hungary. The shoes were definitely a factor in the win, because Dassler had developed a special stud to screw into the shoes that allowed good footing on the muddy playing field that day; Hungary's shoes did not give the same traction.

Dassler's many innovations in the running-shoe industry included four-spiked running shoes, track shoes with a nylon sole, and injected spikes. He developed a shoe that allowed an athlete to choose from 30 different variations of interchangeable spike elements that could be adapted to an indoor or outdoor track as well as to natural or artificial surfaces.

With its great variety of superior products, Adidas dominated in the widely publicized international showcase events. For example, at the Montreal games, Adidas-equipped athletes accounted for 82.8 percent of all individual medal winners.[1] This was tremendous publicity for the company, and sales rose to $1 billion worldwide.

But competitors were entering the marketplace. Prior to 1972 Adidas and Puma had practically the entire athletic shoe market to themselves. Although this was changing, Adidas seemingly had built up an insurmountable lead, providing footwear for virtually every type of sporting activity, as well as diversifying into other sports-related product lines: shorts, jerseys, leisure suits, and track suits; tennis and swimwear; balls for every kind of sport; tennis racquets and cross-country skis; and the popular sports bag that carried the Adidas name as a prominently displayed status symbol.

---

[1]Norris Willett, "How Adidas Ran Faster," *Management Today* (Dec. 1979): 58.

Though the position of Adidas seemed unassailable in the early 1970s, this vision of dominance proved to be an illusion. See the following box for a discussion of the dangers of severe new competition in easy-entry industries.

MARKETING STRATEGY

The marketing strategy originated by the Dassler brothers became the guiding influence for the entire industry. The Dasslers had long used international athletic competition as a testing ground for their products. Many years of feedback from these athletes led to continued design changes and improvements. Agreements were entered into with professional athletes to use their products. However, Adidas's strength was in international and Olympic events in which the participants were amateurs, and such endorsement contracts were more often made with national sports associations than with the individuals.

Because of the lead of Adidas and Puma, endorsement contracts with athletes have become commonplace. For example, every player in the National Basketball Association is under contract to at least one manufacturer. The going rate for an endorsement contract today ranges from $500 to $150,000. The athlete must wear a certain brand and appear in various promotional activities. It has become an industry practice to spend about 80 percent of the advertising budget for endorsements and 20 percent for media advertising. The distinctive logos that all manufacturers have developed is key to the effectiveness of these endorsement contracts. Such logos permit immediate identification of product; fans and potential customers can see the product actually in use by the famous athlete. These logos also permit effective product diversification into apparel, bags, and so on.

To increase volume quickly, companies sought production facilities where shoes could be made cheaply and in great quantities, in areas such as Yugoslavia and the Far East. Medium-size firms in such countries were therefore signed up as licensees, and goods were produced to specifications. Great outlays for plants and equipment were thus avoided, so costs could be kept low.

Finally, Adidas led the running-shoe industry into offering a very wide variety of shoe styles—shoes to fit all kinds of running activities, from various kinds of races to training shoes. Shoes were also offered for every type of runner and running style. The great variety of offerings, more than 100 different styles and models for Adidas, was to be exceeded only by Nike as it charged to capture the U.S. market.

THE 1970s RUNNING MARKET

During the late 1960s and early 1970s the environment affecting the running-shoe industry changed dramatically and positively. Americans were increas-

---

INFORMATION BOX

EASY-ENTRY DANGERS TO FRONTRUNNERS

Certain industries are vulnerable to competitive entry. In such easy-entry industries, would-be competitors face no huge investment or technological requirements. With neither monetary barriers nor unique expertise as constraints, the only concern left is marketing. The dominant firm probably has a commanding marketing presence, has customer acceptance, and seemingly has the resources to maintain its market dominance. Should would-be competitors be dismayed at the likelihood of failure in facing such an entrenched and formidable foe?

Perhaps they should be; perhaps the embryonic Nike should have been. Undoubtedly it did not realize the vulnerability of the long-dominant Adidas. Probably it initially hoped to get only some of the crumbs left by Adidas. And perhaps this is what should have happened, but Adidas let down its guard. In an industry with no major investment and technological requirements, marketing strengths are not always sufficient to protect against aggressive competitors intent on toppling the "king of the hill." And if the frontrunner blinks or lets down its guard, the vulnerability increases—especially in a suddenly growing market, which becomes especially attractive to newcomers.

The moral: Frontrunners in easy-entry industries are precariously positioned against new competitors. They must constantly be on guard.

What are some examples of industries that have major barriers to entry? Are such firms insulated from new competition?

---

ingly concerned with physical fitness. Millions of previously unathletic people were searching for easy ways to exercise. The spark that ignited the booming interest may have been the 1972 Munich Olympics. Millions of television viewers watched Dave Wottle defeat Russian Evgeni Arzanov in the 800-meters and Frank Shorter win the prestigious marathon. But the groundwork for the running boom had been laid before. The idea of fitness perhaps first came to the attention of the general public in a trail-blazing book by Dr. Kenneth Cooper, *Aerobics*, which sold millions of copies and gave scientific evidence of the physical benefits of a running (or jogging) regimen. A little less than 10 years later, another book with monumental impact, *The Complete Book of Running*, by James Fixx, also sold millions of copies and was on the best seller list for months.

Through the decade of the 1970s the number of joggers increased. Estimates by the end of the decade were that 25 million to 30 million Americans were joggers, while another 10 million wore running shoes around home and town.[2] The number of shoe manufacturers also increased. The original

[2] "The Jogging Shoe Race Heats Up," *Business Week* (Apr. 9, 1979): 125.

three—Adidas, Puma, and Tiger—were joined by new U.S. brands: Nike, Brooks, New Balance, Etonic, and even J.C. Penney, Sears, and Converse. To sell and distribute these new shoes, specialty shoe stores such as Athlete's Foot, Athletic Attic, and Kinney's Foot Lockers sprouted up nationwide. New magazines catering to this market were starting up and showing big increases in circulation: for example, *Runner's World*, *The Runner*, and *Running Times*. These helped the advertising media to reach runners with no wasted coverage.

COMPETITION

The Beginning of Nike

Phil Knight was a miler of modest accomplishments. His best time was a 4:13, hardly in the same class as the below-4:00 world-class runners. But he had trained under the renowned coach Bill Bowerman at the University of Oregon in the late 1950s. Bowerman had put Eugene, Oregon, on the map in the 1950s when year after year he turned out world-record-setting long-distance runners. Bowerman was constantly experimenting with shoes, because of his theory that an ounce off a running shoe might make enough difference to win a race.

In the process of completing his MBA at Stanford University, Phil wrote a research paper based on the theory that the Japanese could do for athletic shoes what they were doing for cameras. After receiving his degree in 1960, Knight went to Japan to seek an American distributorship from the Onitsuka Company for Tiger shoes. Returning home, he took samples of the shoes to Bowerman.

In 1964 Knight and Bowerman went into business. They each put up $500 and formed the Blue Ribbon Shoe Company, sole distributor in the United States for Tiger running shoes. They put the inventory in Knight's father-in-law's basement, and they sold $8000 worth of these imported shoes that first year. Knight worked by days as a Cooper & Lybrand accountant, while at night and on weekends he peddled these shoes mostly to high school athletic teams.

Knight and Bowerman finally developed their own shoe in 1972 and decided to manufacture it themselves. They contracted the work out to Asian factories where labor was cheap. They named the shoe Nike after the Greek goddess of victory. At that time they also developed the "swoosh" logo, which was highly distinctive and subsequently was placed on every Nike products. The Nike shoe's first appearance in competition came during the 1972 Olympic trials in Eugene, Oregon. Marathon runners persuaded to wear the new shoes placed fourth through seventh, whereas Adidas wearers finished first, second, and third in these trials.

On a Sunday morning in 1975, Bowerman began tinkering with a waffle iron and some urethane rubber, and he fashioned a new type of sole, a "waffle" sole whose tiny rubber studs made it more springy than those of other shoes currently on the market. This product improvement—seemingly so simple—gave Knight and Bowerman an initial impetus. The marketing strategy that propelled Nike to the top in the U.S. market was more imitative than innovative, however. It was patterned after that of Adidas. But the result was that the imitator outdid the originator.

Nike's Charge

The new "waffle sole" developed by Bowerman proved popular with runners, and this, along with the favorable market, brought 1976 sales to $14 million, up from $8.3 million the year before, and from only $2 million in 1972.

Nike stayed in the forefront of the industry with its careful research and development of new models. By the end of the decade Nike was employing almost 100 people in the research and development section of the company. Over 140 different models were offered in the product line, some of these the most innovative and technological advanced on the market. This diversity came from models designed for different foot types, body weights, running speeds, training schedules, sexes, and different levels of skills.

By the late 1970s and early 1980s, demand for Nikes was so great that 60 percent of its 8000 department store, sporting goods, and shoe store dealers gave advanced orders, often waiting six months for delivery. This gave Nike a big advantage in production scheduling and inventory costs. Table 11.1 shows the phenomenal growth of Nike, with sales rising from $14 million in 1976 to $694 million only 6 years later. Table 11.2 shows the market shares in the U.S. market for the beginning of 1979. By then Nike was the market leader with 33 percent of the market; within 2 years it had taken an even more commanding lead, with approximately 50 percent of the total market.[3]

Table 11.1   Nike Sales Growth, 1976–1981

Year	Sales $ (in millions)	Percent Change from Previous Year
1976	$14	—
1977	29	107
1978	71	145
1979	200	182
1980	370	35
1981	458	70
1982	694	34

Source: Company annual reports.

[3]"Joggings' Fade Fails to Push Nike Off Track," *Wall Street Journal* (Mar. 5, 1981): 25.

Table 11.2   U.S. Running-Shoe Market Shares, 1978

	Percentage of Total U.S. Market
Nike	33
Adidas	20
Brooks	11
New Balance	10
Converse	5
Puma	5

Source: Compiled from various published material, including "The Jogging-Shoe Race Heats Up," *Business Week* (Apr. 9, 1979): 125.

Adidas's share was falling, well below that of Nike, and it also had U.S. firms such as Brooks and New Balance to worry about.

In 1980 Nike went public, and Knight became an instant multimillionaire, reaching the coveted *Forbes* Richest Four Hundred Americans with a net worth estimated at just under $300 million.[4] Bowerman, at 70, had sold most of his stock earlier and owned only 2 percent of the company, worth a mere $9.5 million.

In the January 4, 1982, edition of *Forbes* in the "Annual Report on American Industry," Nike was rated number one in profitability over the previous 5 years, ahead of all other firms in all other industries.[5]

Ingredients of Nike's Success

Unquestionably, Nike faced an extraordinarily favorable primary demand in the 1970s. Nike was positioned to take advantage of this, and indeed most of the running-shoe manufacturers had impressive gains during those years. But Nike's success went far beyond simple coasting with favorable primary demand. Nike outstripped all its competitors, including the heretofore dominant Adidas. Nike was able to overcome whatever aura or mystique such foreign producers as Adidas, Puma, and Tiger had had.

Nike as it began to reach its potential, offered an even broader product line than Adidas, which had pioneered with a great variety of shoe styles. A broad product line can have its problems; it can be overdone, hurt efficiency, and greatly add to costs. Most firms are better advised to pare their product line, to prune their weak products so that adequate attention and resources can be directed to the winners. Here we see the disavowal of such a policy, and yet Nike was one of the great successes of the decade, largely at the expense of Adidas. What is a prudent product mix?

[4]"The Richest People in America—The *Forbes* Four Hundred," *Forbes* (Fall 1983): 104.
[5]*Forbes* (Jan. 4, 1982): 246.

Although Nike may have violated some product-mix concepts, let us recognize what it accomplished and at what cost. By offering a great variety of styles, prices, and uses, Nike was able to appeal to all kinds of runners; it was able to convey the image of the most complete running-shoe manufacturer of all. In a rapidly evolving industry in which millions of runners of all kinds and abilities were embracing the idea, such an image became very attractive. Furthermore, in a rapidly expanding market, Nike found that it could tap the widest possible distribution with its breadth of products. It could sell its shoes to conventional retailers, such as department stores and shoe stores, and it could continue to do business with the specialized running-shoe stores. It could even be only moderately concerned about discounters getting some Nike shoes since there were certainly enough styles and models to go around—different models for different types of retail outlets, and everyone could be happy.

Short production runs and many styles generally add to production costs, but perhaps in Nike's case this was less of a factor. Most of the shoe production was contracted out—some 85 percent to foreign, mostly Far Eastern, factories. Short production runs were less of an economic deterrent where many foreign plants were contracting for part of the production.

Early on Nike placed a heavy emphasis on research and technological improvement. It sought ever more flexible and lighter weight running shoes that would be protective but also give the athlete—world-class or slowest amateur—the utmost advantage that running-shoe technology could provide. Nike's commitment to research and development was evident in the approximately 100 employees working in this area, many of whom held degrees in biomechanics, exercise physiology, engineering, industrial design, chemistry, and related fields. The firm also engaged research committees and advisory boards, including coaches, athletes, athletic trainers, equipment managers, podiatrists, and orthopedists who met periodically with the firm to review designs, materials, and concepts for improved athletic shoes. Activities included high-speed photographic analyses of the human body in motion, the use of athletes on force plates and treadmills, wear testing using over 300 athletes in an organized program, and continual testing and study of new and modified shoes and materials. Some $2.5 million was spent in 1980 on product research, development, and evaluation, and the 1981 budget was approximately $4 million. For such an apparently simple thing as a shoe, this was a major commitment to research and development.

Nike attempted no major deviation from the accepted and successful marketing strategy norm of the industry. This norm was established several decades before by Adidas. In summary, it primarily involved testing and development of better running shoes, a broad product line to appeal to all segments of the market, a readily identifiable trademark or motif prominently displayed on all products, and the use of well-known athletes and prestigious athletic events to show off the products in use. Even the contracting out of much of the production to low-cost foreign factories was not unique to Nike. But Nike used these proven techniques better and more aggressively than any of its competitors, even Adidas.

ADIDAS'S MISTAKES: WHAT WENT WRONG?

Adolph Dassler died in 1978. Perhaps this was a factor in Adidas's lessening of its aggressiveness, although the management transition after his death appeared to have gone very smoothly. And actually Nike had made its big inroads by this time. No, perhaps we have to seek further to find a suitable explanation of a front-runner stumbling to give the lead to someone coming from far back in the pack.

Undoubtedly, Adidas underestimated the growth of the market for running shoes. For a firm that had been four decades in the business and had always seen the stability of slow growth during those years, a skepticism about the extent and duration of the "boom" would have seemed most reasonable. And Adidas was not alone in misjudging the market opportunity. Some of the U.S. firms that were traditionally strong in the lower priced athletic shoe industry, notably Converse and Uniroyal's Keds, were caught flat-footed in the race to bring new and technologically improved models to the market. These major producers of tennis shoes and sneakers (Converse made two-thirds of U.S. basketball shoes) also vastly underestimated the potential and did not direct strong efforts toward this market until they were completely outclassed by Nike and several other U.S. manufacturers.

In gearing an operation for rapid growth, companies focus on sales forecasting as a vital element of the planning and preparation for handling the opportunity at hand. All aspects of a firm's operation are necessarily based on the sales estimates for the coming period(s); for example, production planning, facilities, inventories, sales staff, and advertising efforts. But when sales are reaching uncharted territory, the firm faces the dilemma of optimistic versus conservative sales projections as the following box discusses.

It seems evident that Adidas, in addition to underestimating the market potential, also underestimated the aggressiveness of Nike and the other U.S. manufacturers. Perhaps this was a natural consequence after being the market leader with a seemingly unassailable position. After all, foreign brands in many product lines command a mystique and attraction that no domestic brands can. And then, how could small U.S. manufacturers, starting practically from scratch, pose any serious threats to the more than three decades of seasoned experience of Adidas? So, the perception of U.S. firms as mere weak opportunists seemed reasonable.

INFORMATION BOX

OPTIMISTIC VERSUS CONSERVATIVE SALES FORECASTS IN RAPIDLY EXPANDING MARKETS

The sales forecast—the estimate of sales for the period(s) ahead—serves a crucial role, since it is the starting point for all planning and budgeting. When markets are volatile and rapidly growing, it presents some high-risk alternatives: Should we be optimistic or conservative?

If the forecasts are conservative, the danger that the firm faces when its market begins to boom is that it cannot keep up with demand and cannot expand its resources sufficiently to handle the potential. It simply does not have enough manufacturing capability and sales staff. The result, invariably is to abdicate a good share of this growing business to competitors who are willing and able to match their capability and marketing efforts to the demands of the market.

On the other hand, for a firm facing burgeoning demand, the judgment should be made whether this is likely to be a short-term fad or a more permanent situation. You can see how easily a firm can permit itself to become overextended in the buoyancy of booming business, only to see the collapse of the market actually jeopardizing its viability.

When a firm is operating under extreme conditions of uncertainty, forecasted and actual results should be carefully monitored and the forecast adjusted upward or downward as indicated by empirical sales data.

"If we guess wrong and overcommit, we may lose the company; on the other hand, if we guess wrong and undercommit, we have lost nothing." Comment.

But we know that U.S. manufacturers were not weak opportunists striving for a stray bone. Nike among others saw an opportunity, seized it, and charged. Perhaps this happening is less a reflection of Adidas's deficiencies than it is a credit to Nike. But we can still raise doubts about Adidas's role in the Nike inroads. Should not Adidas have been more alert in such an easy-to-enter industry? After all, neither the technology nor the plant investment requirements were enough to preclude other firms from entering the arena. Should not the front-runner have recognized this ease of competitive entry and acted aggressively to discourage it—especially in a market that was increasing geometrically? Strong promotional efforts, new product introductions, a step-up in research and development, sharper pricing practices, expanding the channels of distribution—these actions might not have prevented competition, but given the resources of the market leader, they should have lessened the inroads. But Adidas did not take aggressive counteractions until its dominance had been severely breached.

WHAT CAN BE LEARNED?

Effective imitation without innovation or greater resources can lead to success. Of course, imitation must be judicious. A strategy worth imitating should be historically successful. In the case of the running-shoe industry, the successful strategy of Adidas in offering many models, in associating its brand with major athletic events and athletes themselves, in constantly seeking new products, was proved over a long period. All running-shoe manufacturers followed the same strategy, but Nike did it better.

While being imitative, a firm must develop its own identity. Successful imitation is not a slavish effort to be identical. Only the successful policies, standards, and actions are imitated. A tottering Burger Chef could have improved its lot by imitating some of the successful policies of McDonald's, particularly with respect to operational standards, but it would have been a mistake to have copied the golden arches, modifying them to become pink or green. With effective imitation there is still room to develop a distinctive image, trademark, or logo, and to establish an organization and management alert to new opportunities.

The front-runner is vulnerable, particularly in easy-entry industries with rapidly expanding markets. We will see later that a dominant firm in a supposedly nongrowth industry can still be vulnerable. The ability of Honda to convert motorcycles to a growth industry and outdistance Harley Davidson is a business marvel. The front-runner is much more vulnerable in a rapidly growing industry. If the investment in technological know-how and financial resources to enter the industry are not great, the vulnerability of the front-runner increases. This situation characterized the running-shoe industry in the 1970s.

The industry leader tends toward complacency. Sharply rising demand is reassuring and lulling. Sales will be increasing sharply for the industry leader during such a time, but increasing sales may mask a declining market position in which competitors are gaining at the expense of the dominant firm.

In an expanding market, beware of judging performance on increases in sales rather than market share. Market share refers to the percentage of total industry sales accounted for by an individual firm. A market share analysis evaluates company performance by measuring it relative to that of competitors. Changes in market share from preceding periods, expecially when these changes show a worsening competitive position, should induce strenuous efforts to ascertain the cause and take corrective action. When a market is expanding, such as the running-shoe market, market share changes need to be carefully monitored to prevent loss of competitive advantage.

The critical lapse of Adidas, faced with the growing strength of Nike and its American contemporaries, and the greatly increasing industry potential, suggests a need for a better monitoring of demand and competitive factors. Alert executives should be able to detect nascent changes by encouraging systematic feedback from those closest to the market—sales representatives, dealers, and suppliers alike—by keeping abreast of latest trade journal statistics and commentaries, and by monitoring other sources described below. There must also be a willingness to act on significant changes in industry conditions, but such willingness is often difficult for veteran firms since it requires disassociating themselves from perspectives and practices of a different past.

Sources of Market Share Data. Market-share analysis requires information on sales of competing brands and firms in the market. Fortunately, it is usually not difficult to obtain such information in most industries, although some costs are involved. Trade associations or trade publications provide reasonably accurate sales figures for many industries. While such information may not include brand breakdowns, a firm can determine its share of the total market and define important trends. Government agencies provide data for other industries, such as automotive, liquor, and insurance, from mandatory reports including new car registrations and excise and other tax data.

There are syndicated services that provide consumer-goods manufacturers various measure of competitive brand positions. Two major services are:

1. A. C. Nielsen Company conducts store audits in grocery, drug, and certain other fields, and also buys computer tapes from supermarkets equipped with electronic scanning cash registers.
2. Market Research Corporation of American (MRCA) gathers information on expenditures through a panel of consumers who maintain a record of their purchases in diaries.

Caution in the Use of Market Data. Although market-share information is a valuable management tool, it should not be used as the primary or only measure of marketing performance. It ignores profitability, and this is a major flaw. Too much emphasis on increasing market share often leads to rash sales growth at the expense of profits. Executives can be motivated in this direction because their prestige is bound up with company size and growth relative to other firms in the industry. Heavy advertising or concentration on short-term sales at the expense of more satisfied customers and dealers will increase market share, but profitability may be adversely affected.

The great value of market share measurements is that they identify possible problem areas that need further investigation. Perhaps there is a satisfactory explanation for an initial decline in market share. For example, it might be caused by a large sale in an adjacent period, or perhaps it might be due to a temporary production slowdown for a model change. On the other hand, a declining market share may indicate a serious problem that needs prompt corrective action in order to prevent a loss in competitive position that can never be regained.

In coping with product life-cycle uncertainties, be flexible in order to avoid unacceptable risks. Every firm needs to react with its environment and the subtle and not-so-subtle changes taking place. This is especially important when the product life cycle is uncertain in scope and duration.

The uncertainties about the extent and durability of the life cycle led Converse and Keds, the two biggest makers of low-priced athletic shoes, to move far too slowly into the running-shoe market, and they never gained much ground. Had the bubble burst, had the running boom been a short-lived phenomenon, would Nike have been able to maintain its viability in a greatly diminished market? We think so. Several years before the leveling off and maturing of the market, Nike diversified into related but different products. It kept production flexible by contracting the greater portion of its manufacturing to foreign factories. Consequently, it did not establish a large infrastructure with high fixed costs and vulnerability to falling demand.

No one is immune from mistakes; success does not guarantee continued success. Many executives and administrators fool themselves into thinking success begets continued success. It is not so! No firm, market leader or otherwise, can afford to rest on its laurels, to disregard a changing environment and aggressive but smaller competitors. Adidas had as commanding a lead in this industry as IBM had in computers. But it was overtaken and surpassed by Nike, a rank newcomer, and a domestic firm with few resources in an era when foreign brands (of beer, watches, cars) had a mystique and attraction for affluent Americans that few domestic brands could achieve. But Adidas let down its guard at a critical point. In the same way, Nike later lagged because of its underestimation or unawareness of the marketing opportunity in aerobic dancing.

Would Nike have achieved its success if Adidas had been more aggressive? Was a major part of the Nike success due not to its own efforts but to the deficiencies of Adidas? Perhaps this is a realistic assessment. We would have to answer this hypothetical question by conceding that Nike probably would not have been nearly as successful if Adidas had not dropped its guard. On the other hand, with a rapidly expanding market and easy entry, Nike could have entered successfully and become a viable and profitable operation.

Aftermath

If is difficult for firms to maintain a pattern of success. A few firms have done so year after year, even decade after decade—McDonald's most readily comes to mind here, but even this stalwart has shown signs of slipping in recent years. Most firms have their time of success, find success slipping away, and become ordinary enterprises. With Nike the pendulum began swinging back in 1983, the year that the running-shoe industry peaked. The decline in running-shoe demand was not so much a result of fewer people running, but a consequence of less use of running shoes for casual dress. In addition, the market began to fragment, with shoes for aerobics, basketball, and tennis competing with running shoes for shelf space. As it turned out, Nike made the same planning mistake Adidas had a decade earlier: underestimating an opportunity. Nike was late into the fast-growing market for shoes worn for the aerobic dancing that was sweeping the country, fueled by best-selling books by Jane Fonda and others. And Reebok had emerged to challenge Nike for first spot in the athletic-shoe industry. By the early 1990s, the two firms were neck and neck, commanding 50 percent of the U.S. market. But Adidas was till on top in Europe. And now Nike and Reebok were marshalling their resources to seek further growth in Europe.

CONSIDER

Do you see any other learning insights for this case?

QUESTIONS

1. Do you think Adidas could have successfully blunted the charge of Nike? Why or why not?
2. In what ways do the age and experience of a firm tend to induce myopia and resistance to change?
3. "The success of Nike was strictly fortuitous and had little to do with powerful marketing strategy." Evaluate this statement.
4. Discuss the pros and cons of optimistic versus conservative sales forecasts for a hot new product.
5. Do you think Nike would have done better to be more innovative in its initial approach to the running-shoe market rather than being so imitative?
6. What would you hypothesize accounts for Adidas's ability to maintain its dominance in Europe when it was so vulnerable in the United States?

7. In recent years Nike has moved strongly to develop markets fro running shoes in the Far East, particularly in China. Discuss how Nike might go about stimulating such undeveloped markets.

INVITATION TO ROLE PLAY

1. As an Adidas executive, how to you propose to counter the initial thrusts at your market share by Nike and other U.S. running-shoe manufacturers?

2. As an executive for a medium-sized U.S. running-shoe manufacturer, you recognize that the long overdue lessening of the popularity of running is beginning to take place. What strategy recommendations do you make now that the primary demand curve is moving down?

INVITATION TO RESEARCH

Is the popularity of running and jogging waning today? What are the newest strategy shifts in the athletic shoe industry today? Who has the greatest market share?

CHAPTER 12

Osborne Computer: Short-Lived Product Uniqueness

Only rarely may a new firm hit the jackpot: a meteoric rise surpassing even the most optimistic expectations of founders and inventors. In the heady excitement of great growth anything seems possible. It is tantalizing to think that such an enterprise is invincible to competition. Alas, sometimes such stars can come tumbling back to earth and to reality. Perhaps no better example can be found in modern business annals than the almost vertical rise and collapse of Osborne Computer Corporation. Founded in 1981, the business was booming at a $100 million clip—in barely 18 months. But on September 14, 1983, the company sought protection from creditors under Chapter 11 of the Bankruptcy Code.

ADAM OSBORNE

Adam Osborne was born in Thailand, the son of a British professor, and spent his earliest years in India. His parents were disciples of a maharishi, although Adam was educated in Catholic schools. Later he was sent to Britain for schooling, and in 1961 at the age of 22 he moved to the United States. He obtained a Ph.D in chemical engineering at the University of Delaware and then worked for Shell Development Company in California.

Osborne and Shell soon parted company, the bureaucratic structure frustrating him. He became interested in computers, and in 1970 he set up his own computer consulting company. The market for personal computers began to mushroom in the mid-1970s, and he emerged a guru. He had a computer column, "From the Fountainhead," for *Interface Age*, and he began making speeches and building a reputation. He wrote a book geared to the mass market, *Introduction to Microcomputers*, which was turned down by a publisher. Osborne published the book himself, and it sold 300,000 copies. By 1975 his publishing company had put out some 40 books on microcomputers, nearly a dozen of which Osborne had written himself. In 1979 he sold the publishing company to McGraw-Hill, but agreed to stay as a consultant through May 1982.

Osborne was thus in a position to take full advantage of the growth of the microcomputer industry. But he had also angered many in the industry with his stinging criticisms and bold assertions. In particular, he spoke out sharply against the pricing strategies of the personal computer manufacturers, contending that they were ignoring the mass market by constantly raising prices with every new feature added.

Osborne himself came to be the subject of some of the most colorful copy of the industry. Tall and energetic, he possessed a strong British accent to go along with his volubility, his charm, and his supreme confidence. He seemed to epitomize the new breed of entrepreneurs drawn to the epicenter of new high-tech industry, the so-called Silicon Valley in California.

Early in 1981 Osborne put his criticisms and assertions to the test. To a chorus of skeptics he announced plans to manufacture and market a new personal computer: one priced well below the competition. His first machines were ready for shipping by that July, and before long the skeptics were running for the hills. Now Osborne could prove that he was a doer, and not merely a talker.

INDUSTRY BACKGROUND

In the early 1970s, computers ranged from small units to very large units, with prices reaching limits affordable only to the well-heeled firms. The industry was dominated by one company, IBM, which held 70 percent of the market. All the other firms in the industry were scrambling for small shares. IBM seemed to have an unassailable advantage because it had the resources for the heaviest marketing expenditures in the industry as well as the best research and development. The firm with the masterful lead in a rapidly growing industry has ever-increasing resources over its lesser competitors, who can hardly hope to catch up and seemingly must be content to chip away at the periphery of the total market.

The computer industry had been characterized by rapid technological changes since the early 1960s. By the early 1970s, however, the new technology being introduced generally involved peripheral accessories, and not major changes in main units.

Before the advent of microelectronics technology, which made smaller parts possible, computers were very costly and complicated. It was not economically feasible for one person to interact with one computer. The processing power at that time existed only in a central data processing installation, and for those who could not afford to have their own computer, time-sharing services were available. The minicomputer industry began in 1974 when a few small firms began using memory chips to produce small computer systems as do-it-yourself kits for as low as $400. These proved popular, and other companies began to build microcomputers designed for the affluent hobbyist and small-business owner.

In 1975 microcomputer and small-business computer shipments went over the $1 billion mark. As the mainframe market began to mature, the microcomputer industry was starting its rocketing ascendancy. In 1975 the first personal computer reached the market.

Personal computers can be defined as easy-to-use desktop machines that are microprocessor based, have their own power supply, and are priced below $10,000. By using various software packages, these computers can be customized to serve the needs of businesses and a variety of professionals such as accountants, financial analysts, scientists, and educators, as well as the sophisticated individual at home. It should be noted that the minicomputer grew up without IBM, the company that dominated mainframe computers and accounted for two-thirds of all computer revenues in the mid-1970s. And one of the great success stories of the century had occurred with personal computers. Apple Computer was started in a family garage on $1300 capital in 1976. By 1982 sales were $583 million, and Steven Jobs, a college dropout who was the cofounder at age 21, had become one of the richest people in America, with a net worth exceeding $225 million.[1]

Portable computers are a subset of personal computers, being, as the name implies, lightweight and relatively easy to carry. Actually, three categories of portable computers are recognized by the industry: (1) handheld; (2) portable, which have a small display screen, limited memory, and weigh between 10 and 20 pounds; and (3) transportable, which have bigger screens and memories and weight more than 20 pounds. Osborne was in the third group.

THE OSBORNE STRATEGY

Osborne had discerned a significant niche in the portable computer market: "I saw a truck-size hole in the industry, and I plugged it," he said.[2] He hired Lee Felsenstein, a former Berkeley radical, to design a powerful unit that

---

[1]For more details of the Apple success story, see Robert F. Hartley, *Marketing Successes,* 2nd ed. (New York: Wiley, 1990) 214–229.

[2]"Osborne: From Brags to Riches," *Business Week* (Feb. 22, 1982) 86.

weighed only 24 pounds and could be placed in a briefcase small enough to fit under an airline seat. It was the first portable business computer; the other portable computers had been of much more limited sophistication. And it sold for $1795, which was hundreds of dollars less than other business-oriented computers, and half the price of an Apple. He was able to sell for this price by running a low-overhead operation. For example, he hired Georgette Psaris, then 25, and made her vice president of sales and marketing. Her office was in a chilly former warehouse. He was able to achieve economies of scale, and also to capitalize on the declining prices of semiconductor parts. The computers were assembled from standard industry components. The display screen was small, only 5 inches across, and there was no color graphics capability. Osborne himself admitted, "The Osborne 1 had no technology of consequence. We made the purchasing decision convenient by bundling hardware and needed software in one price."[3]

To cut costs on software, Osborne employed no programmers. This was a drastic departure from other personal computer makers. Instead, he relied entirely upon independent software companies to provide programs written in the popular programming language. To reduce software costs still further, Osborne gave some software suppliers equity in the company. The result was that Osborne was able to provide almost $1500 worth of software packages as part of the $1795 system price.

Osborne had a flair for showmanship. One of his first triumphs was in the 1981 West Coast Computer Fair in San Francisco. In place of the rather ordinary booths and displays of the other computer makers, he took a substantial part of his venture capital to build a Plexiglas booth that towered toward the ceiling. The Osborne Company logo, the "Flying O," dominated the show.

He believed that mass distribution was a key to success. By 1982 he had signed an agreement with Computerland Corporation, the largest computer retailer. This extended Osborne's distribution by doubling in one swoop the number of retail stores carrying his computer. The Osborne 1 was proving to be a hot item, with sales hitting $10 million by the end of 1981, the first year of operation in which the first computer had not even been shipped until July. By the end of 1982, after only 18 months of operation, annual sales were soaring to $100 million. Predictions were made that "most of the Osborne management team would be millionaires by the time they're 40 or even 30,"[4] and their earlier bare-bones operating style was forsaken.

By 1983 some 750 retail outlets were stocking the company's portables: the Computerland chain, Xerox's retail stores, Sears' business center, and

---

[3] "Osborne Bytes the Distribution Bullet," *Sales & Marketing Management* (July 4, 1983): 34.
[4] Steve Fishman, "Facing Up to Failure," *Success* (Nov. 1984): 48.

such department stores as Macy's. And early in 1983, 150 office-equipment dealers with experience in selling the most advanced copiers also were added, thus enabling Osborne to reach small- and medium-sized businesses.

In summary, Osborne was the first to sell such computers in mass quantities, and his efforts expanded the market greatly.

MARCHING INTO 1983

By early 1983 Osborne began to loosen his grip on the company, under pressure from his investors. If was felt that the growing operation—it already had 800 employees—required a professional management that Osborne and his early hires were not. Osborne was an entrepreneur and not an administrator, and the two abilities are quite different. To protect the company's front-running position—estimated at an 80 to 90 percent market share—Robert Jaunich II, president of Consolidated Foods, was hired to head up Osborne Computer as president and chief executive officer. Adam Osborne moved up to chairman. Jaunich had turned down offers at Apple and Atari because he felt that these firms would not give him enough control. He also sacrificed a $1 million incentive to remain at Consolidated Foods, so he must have felt strongly that the opportunities and potential of Osborne far surpassed his other options.

Jaunich moved quickly to decentralize the management structure. Georgette Psaris, vice president of marketing, was moved into a newly created position as vice president of strategic planning. She was replaced by Joseph Roebuck, lured from Apple Computer, where he had been marketing director. Fred Brown, the director of sales for Osborne, was elevated to vice president of sales, and David Lorenzen, a consultant for Osborne, was made director of marketing services, with responsibility for dealer-support programs.

The distribution strategy, which Adam Osborne had considered one of the strengths of the venture, was refined. The computer-store outlets were continued, but some alternative channels were instituted as well. A major addition was an affiliation with Harris Corporation's computer systems division to act as a national distributor for contacting major firms. Harris was a $1.7 billion minicomputer firm whose computer systems divisions had some 70 salespeople and 1200 support personnel, including systems analysts. To protect Osborne's smaller clients, Harris agreed to handle only large orders of 50 units or over.

Other sales targets were United Press International (UPI), the news service, where Osborne planned to sell portables to the 1000 subscriber newspapers as personal workstations. Brown, the vice president of sales also began exploring other distribution possibilities, including independent sales organizations, airlines, and hotel chains.

As competitors started to enter the portable market, offering cheaper and fancier machines than the Osborne 1, the firm began readying itself to broaden its product line. An even cheaper version of the Osborne 1, the Vixen, was being prepared. And an Executive 1 was unveiled in the spring of 1983, with an Executive 2 planned for late summer. These offered more storage capacity and larger screens than Osborne 1. The Executive 1 could serve as a terminal to communicate with a mainframe, thereby enabling users to work with larger databases and to handle more complicated jobs. This was to have a $2495 price tag with some $2000 worth of software, including word processing, an electronic spreadsheet, and database management. The Executive 2, at $3195, was promoted as compatible with IBM's hot-selling personal computer, the IBM PC.

In 1982 Osborne spent $3.5 million on advertising. This included $1.5 million in consumer magazines and $500,000 on spot TV, with $1.5 million in business publications. Plans were laid to continue heavy advertising in order to reinforce the product differentiation. The sales force was also being expanded to keep pace with the growing firm. An eight-person salesforce was to be supplemented by an additional 30 to 40 people, thereby permitting more specialized selling. Instead of being generalists selling to all types of customers, sales was to be organized by specialists who concentrated either on retail or nonretail accounts. Brown explained this rationale: "Retailers . . . need help on such things as point-of-sale displays to stimulate the guy who comes in off the street. Dealers call on purchasing and data-processing departments and need advice on direct mail campaigns."[5]

The sky seemed to be the limit. Osborne was predicting revenues of $300 million for 1983. And when he made one of his frequent trips abroad, he was received by ambassadors and prime ministers, most of whom wanted stock in his company, He was the head of the fastest growing company Silicon Valley had ever seen—growing even faster than Apple.

PREMONITION

The first premonition of trouble came to Adam Osborne on April 26, 1983. He was giving a seminar in Colorado when he received a call. "Over the weekend considerable losses were discovered," he was told. "That's not possible," he is reported to have said.[6]

The news of earlier profit figures being in error was particularly ominous because of its timing. On April 29 a public stock offering was planned. This was designed to raise about $50 million, and it would have made the top executives of Osborne rich. How would this news of losses instead of profits affect the stock offering? Adam Osborne had to wonder.

---

[5] "Osborne Bytes," 36.
[6] Fishman, "Facing Up to Failure," 51.

Actually, the few days Adam had been away from the office, the bad news had been building up. In the first two months of the fourth fiscal quarter (the fiscal year ended February 1983), pretax profits had been reported that ran $300,000 ahead of company projections. And in February the company racked up an all-time high in shipments, all these with supposed very high profit margins. Projections had been that profits in February would be in the neighborhood of $750,000 for that month alone, and the future seemed even brighter.

But the heady optimism was to rapidly disappear. By late March the results for February showed, instead of a profit, a loss of more than $600,000 for the month, reflecting charges against new facilities as well as heavy promotional spending. For the entire fiscal year a loss of $1.5 million was incurred, despite revenues of slightly more than $100 million.

The worst was still to come. On April 21, Jaunich, the CEO, had learned that later data showed that the company would have a $1.5 million loss for the February quarter, and a $4 million loss for the full year. The chief reasons seemed to be excessive inventories of old stock that the company did not even realize it had, liabilities in software contracts, and the need for greater bad debt and warranty reserves. Jaunich still planned to move ahead with the filing for the stock offering, although certainly the attractiveness of stock in the company was rapidly diminishing.

On April 24, Jaunich was informed that the losses would be even greater: $5 million for the quarter and $8 million for the year, thanks to further unrecorded liabilities and more inventory problems.

That same day Jaunich decided to scrap the offering, despite heavy pressure to find another underwriter to bring the stock to market. Now every report blackened the situation still further. The final report for the year showed a loss of more than $12 million. Heavy losses continued over the next months, as further adjustments in inventories and reserves became necessary. Adam Osborne's house of cards was close to collapsing.

Osborne had had no trouble attracting seed money from venture capitalists before—indeed, venture capital firms had been clamoring to participate. But now that the company's earnings problems had come to light, such funding was drying up. A few investors still had hopes, and Osborne found another $11 million in June. But an additional $20 million that the company considered necessary to speed a competitive product from drawing board to market could not be found.

Black Friday

Sporadic employee layoffs had been occurring since late spring as the company desperately tried to improve its cash flow. The climax came on Friday,

September 16. On the previous Tuesday the company had filed for protection from creditor lawsuits under Chapter 11 of the federal Bankruptcy Code. The company filed its petition after three creditors filed two lawsuits saying Osborne owed them a total of $4.7 million. Osborne's petition stated that it owed secured and unsecured creditors about $45 million while its assets were $40 million.

Osborne's employees had to expect the worst when a meeting was abruptly called in the company cafeteria. Top management then announced that more than 300 workers, about 80 percent of the company staff still remaining, were to be immediately "furloughed." Final paychecks were issued and the workers were given two hours to empty their desks and vacate the company offices.

News of the company's Chapter 11 filing and near total shutdown shocked the industry, even though Osborne's recently sagging sales and the consequent need for cash were well known. The company had made strenuous efforts to raise money, especially after July shipments had turned soft and the banks were pressing it to improve its shrinking capital base. But venture capitalists appeared to have fled the industry because a serious shakeout was occurring, not only for Osborne but for other personal computer firms as well. The market was just not able to support some 150-plus microcomputer companies.

POSTMORTEM

Internal Factors

Adam Osborne was an entrepreneur, not a professional manager. Perhaps this accounted for most of the problems that were to befall his company. So often it seems that the entrepreneurial personality is incompatible with the manager-type person who must necessarily be engrossed with the nitty-gritty details and day-to-day controls over operations. Osborne had never managed more than 50 people, and the organization had grown to almost 20 times that size. He operated under a "fire fighting" perspective, with no advanced planning, dealing with problems as they arose. "I had no professional training whatsoever in finance or business management," Osborne admitted.[7]

The board of directors of Osborne and the venture capitalists who had contributed mightily to the fledgling enterprise certainly brought about sufficient pressure to persuade Adam Osborne to step aside and turn over the operations responsibilities to a professional manager, Robert Jaunich, early in 1983. But this was apparently too late to rectify the damage that had already been done. Perhaps 6 months earlier . . . ?

[7]Jaye Scholl, "Osborne's Back Byting," *Barrons* (July 26, 1984): 26.

Some of the mistakes made are inexcusable from the standpoint of any prudently run operation. Perhaps they can be explained as due to the heady excitement that can accompany rapidly rising sales and the subsequent euphoria that clouds rational judgments and expectations. Other mistakes can be credited to simple miscalculations—which any firm could be guilty of—as to the impact of competitors of all kinds, and particularly the rapidity with which the awesome IBM could enter the market and dominate it.

Lack of controls was the most obvious failing of the company. It had no efficient means of monitoring inventories of finished products. Consequently, managers did not know how much inventory they had. They did not know how much they were spending, or needed to spend. Information management was sorely lacking—and this in a company whose product was primarily geared to aiding information management. While rapid growth can be accompanied by growing pains and some difficulty in keeping abreast of booming operations, in Osborne's case the lack was abysmal and accounted for supposed profits suddenly being revealed instead as devastating losses. There were other examples of incompetence: unrecorded liabilities, with some bills never handed over to the accounting department; no reserves established for the shutdown of a New Jersey plant that was producing computers with a 40 percent failure rate; and a shortage of capital set aside to pay for a new European headquarters on Lake Geneva in Switzerland.

Lack of controls permitted expenses to run rampant. "Everybody was trying to buy anything they wanted," said one former Osborne employee.[8] When Jaunich finally took over the managerial reins, he clamped down hard on expenses, but perhaps it was too late.

By spring of 1983 marketing miscalculations had reduced cash flow to a trickle. Osborne had planned to introduce a new computer, the Executive, but he made the grievous mistake of announcing it too soon. While the Executive was not supposed to compete against the original Osborne 1, many dealers saw it as doing just that. Upon learning of the new machine in April, many canceled their orders for the Osborne 1. This in itself necessitated heavy inventory writeoffs, since the Osborne was not planned to be phased out. Compounding the problems, the Executive was delayed and not ready for initial shipments until May. April was a month, consequently, with practically no sales.

Another major mistake was failing to realize just how short the *product life cycle* could be in this volatile industry, and how quickly a competitive advantage—the low price, portability, and bundling of software—could be countered by competitors and even improved upon. (See the box on page

---

[8] "Shaken Osborne Computer Seeking Suitor in the Face of Possible Failure," *Wall Street Journal* (Sept. 12, 1983): 35.

171.) Other companies, notably KayPro and Compaq, entered the market with low-priced portable computers and at least as much bundled software. But the biggest impact was that of IBM. It introduced its personal computer in late 1981, and it quickly became the industry standard against which other computers were judged. Osborne turned out to be slow in reacting and adopting IBM's state-of-the-art-technology. Furthermore, Osborne was slow in coming up with a model that was compatible with the IBM personal computer at home or in the office. Scores of other computer companies jumped to produce IBM compatible computers, while Osborne lagged, and suddenly its product was not selling. Hardly a year after coming to market, the formerly popular Osborne computer with its tiny screen was practically obsolete.

One new product developed by Osborne was obsolete before it was even introduced. The Vixen was originally scheduled for introduction in December 1982. It was 10 pounds lighter and an even cheaper version of the Osborne 1. A poorly designed circuit board caused production delays, and the project was finally scrapped as company resources were at last redirected to an Executive model, an IBM-compatible unit with a larger screen. The Osborne production delays and the speed with which IBM took over the personal computer market were tough to cope with.

External Factors

The environment for personal-computer makers was rapidly becoming unhealthy by 1983. A major shakeout for the more than 150 small manufacturers in this industry was inevitable. A major factor behind the proliferation of firms was a tidal wave of venture capital. Early winners such as Apple Computer had dazzled investors and led to the perception of a "can't lose" industry. It became almost too easy to start a new computer company. "As a result, a whole series of 'me too' companies have been started. They are developing products that do not have a unique feature or competitive advantage. They don't stand a chance," one venture capitalist said.[9] Only the strongest firms were likely to survive. And yet, in size and with its head start, Osborne should have been one of the survivors.

While demand by businesses and consumers alike for small computers was rapidly increasing, so was cutthroat competition. Price-cutting and shrinking profit margins were inevitable. And certainly dealers' shelves could hardly accommodate more than a few brands.

The first presentiment of worsening problems for the industry came early in 1983 when three big manufacturers of low-priced home computers, Atari, Texas Instruments, and Mattel, reported first-half losses totaling more

[9] "Trouble in Computer Land," *Newsweek* (Sept. 26, 1983): 73.

INFORMATION BOX

THE PRODUCT LIFE CYCLE

Just as people and animals do, products go through states of growth and maturity—that is—life cycles. They are affected by different competitive conditions at each stage, ranging often from no competition in the early stages to intense competition later on. We can recognize four stages in a product's life cycle: introduction, growth, maturity, and decline.

Figure 12.1 depicts three different product life cycles. Number 1 is that of a standard item in which sales take some time to develop and then eventually begin

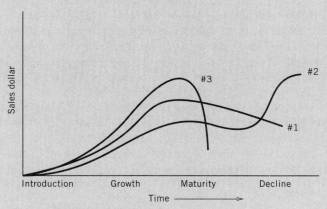

Figure 12.1. The product life cycle.

a slow decline. Number 2 shows a life cycle for a product in which a modification of the product or else the uncovering of a new market rejuvenates the product so that it takes off on a new cycle of growth (the classic examples of such remarketing are Listerine, originally sold as a mild external antiseptic, and Arm & Hammer Baking Soda, which was remarketed as a deodorizer). Number 3 shows the life cycle for a fad product or one experiencing rapid technological change and intense competition. Notice its sharp rise in sales and the abrupt downturn.

In certain industries the competitive environment is volatile enough that some products quickly become obsolete—this is more a characteristic of young industries, such as microcomputers, than of mature industries like steel. A host of competitors, drawn into the industry by the growing market and the relative ease of getting started, contribute to the short life cycle. Short life cycles can severely test any management. The organization must constantly be working on new product ideas, technological improvements, and greater production efficiency. But inventories must also be closely monitored so that they not be allowed to build up faster than the rate of sale. Otherwise, severe inventory writeoffs may become necessary because of obsolescence.

Most products nowadays have very short life cycles. Yet there are a few that have life cycles of decades. Can you name some of these long-lived products? What do you see as accounting for such longevity?

than half a billion dollars. Makers of higher priced computers tried to dissociate themselves from this low-end calamitous environment. But other well-known companies such as Victor Technologies, Fortune Systems, and Vector Graphics all reported shocking losses for the second quarter. Even Apple Computer saw its stock price sink nearly 34 points between June and September 1983.

Indicative of the price-cutting going on, Texas Instruments' 99/4A home computer, which sold for $525 when introduced in 1981, was retailing for $100 by early 1983. Yet, each 99/4A cost about $80 in parts and labor, to which must be added TI's overhead expenses, dealer profits, and marketing costs.[10]

Other computer makers were desperately struggling to revamp their production and marketing efforts. For example, after losing $1.7 million in the second quarter of 1983, Vector Graphic obtained a new $7 million line of credit to help it tailor its computers to such specialty markets as meeting the accounting needs of farmers.[11]

Now the problems of the industry dried up venture capital. Osborne was partly the victim of an external situation of which it had no control. These external factors were unforgiving of Osborne's internal mistakes.

AFTERMATH

Under Chapter 11 of the federal Bankruptcy Act, a company continues to operate but has court protection against creditors' lawsuits while working out a plan for paying its debts. By the end of 1984, Osborne was emerging from bankruptcy with most of its debts paid and two new machines to sell. Its retail network had shrunk from 800 dealers to about 50. Suppliers now demanded cash on delivery. And the firm was anathema to venture capitalists, who had lost $31 million when the company collapsed. Gone were the factories, the 1000-worker payroll, and the posh executive offices. But the lean, trimmed-down company had $10 to $30 million worth of tax-loss carryforwards. And its name and still-extant dealer network in Europe was a plus. Perhaps the biggest challenge it then faced was redeveloping its retail network: "Competition for shelf space is hot even for companies with no strikes against them. Retailers were left with a bad taste when the company

[10] "Behind the Shakeout in Personal Computers," *U.S. News & World Report* (June 27, 1983): 59–60.
[11] "Trouble in Computer Land." 73.

went Chapter 11," noted the president of a 40-store chain.[12] The new president was Ronald J. Brown, the former vice president of international operations who had engineered the company's restructuring.

Adam Osborne had left the company. He was now trying his entrepreneurial talents by marketing software, as well as organizing a defense against investor lawsuits. He wrote a book (publishing it himself, since major publishers were reluctant to), *Hypergrowth: The Rise and Fall of the Osborne Computer Corporation* (with John Dvorak), soundly criticizing Robert Jaunich. Georgette Psaris, Osborne's former vice president, noted:" I've gone from being a multimillionaire to being in the hole."[13] But she joined Adam Osborne in his new entrepreneurial endeavor.

WHAT CAN BE LEARNED?

Issue: How much growth to embrace. Here we have an example of the dangers of uncontrolled growth: Osborne's extremes are unique in business annals. And yet, shouldn't we "run with the ball" when we get that rare opportunity? The temptation is to expand operations as fast as possible. But there are times when caution is required.

Risks lie on all sides as we reach for these opportunities. When a market begins to boom and a firm is unable to keep up with demand without greatly increasing capacity and resources, it faces a dilemma: stay conservative in the expectation that the burgeoning potential will be short-lived, and thereby abdicate some of the growing market to competitors, or expand vigorously and take full advantage of the opportunity. If the euphoria is short-lived, and demand slows drastically, the firm is left with expanded capacity, more resource commitment than is needed, high interest and carrying costs, and perhaps even a jeopardized viability because of overextension. There is no one answer or solution to such uncertainties. Decision making in the chaotic times of technological breakthroughs and environmental changes is risky, challenging, and tremendously exciting.

Regardless of the commitment to a vision of great growth, a firm must build in organizational, accounting, and financial standards and controls, or find itself on treacherous footing. Without tight controls, cost gets out of hand, inventory buildup becomes an albatross, customer accounts may imprudently be allowed to become excessive and overdue, and, in the excitement of increasing sales, assumed profits in reality may be losses. Tight controls, especially over inventories and expenses, are essential.

---

[12] "Osborne Tries for Comeback in Computers," *Wall Street Journal* (Oct. 12, 1984): 27.
[13] "Trouble in Computer Land," 74.

New and rapidly growing industries are often characterized by particularly keen competition. New and rapidly growing industries present dangers far greater than those facing the entrant to more mature industries. Unless entry to the industry is exceedingly difficult because of high start-up costs or secure technological expertise, the new, rapidly growing industry is attractive to all kinds of firms and a host of investors. Such new industries are usually characterized by rapid product improvements and by severe price-cutting. A firm in such an industry must be aware of the potential shakeout. It may be better to resist expanding so fast that it becomes vulnerable to overcapacity and excessive inventory when the trauma of price-cutting begins. Competition invariably results in price-cutting as production efficiencies and technological improvements are advanced by competing firms. Where many firms enter the industry, the marginal ones will fall by the wayside, leaving the field to the more able firms with better management and greater resources. During the shakeout period, however, virtually all firms may find themselves losing money because of the severe price competition and the dumping of excess inventories. A stayer must be prepared to weather some rough times before the industry stabilizes.

The advantage of uniqueness may be short-lived. In such a new industry, we often find uniqueness to be short-lived. Osborne certainly had a unique product offering in its early months. But the firm vastly underestimated how quickly the uniqueness would be matched, and even surpassed, by competitors. Research and development efforts must not be delayed simply because a firm now has a successful product. The product life cycle can be very short in the turmoil of such new industries. Such short product life cycles necessitate very careful monitoring of production and inventories to stop them from expanding faster than current sales warrant. See the following box about *strategy countering by competitors.*

The possibility of cannibalization must not be ignored. The Osborne example shows the dangers of cannibalization carried to the extreme. Cannibalization refers to the process by which one product of the firm takes sales away from other products of the firm. Generally, new products succeed to some extent at the expense of other products in the line, but hopefully there will be enough new business to increase total sales. In Osborne's case, the foolish announcement of the new Executive computer—before it was even ready to go to market—practically killed sales for the older Osborne 1. Encountering a month and more of virtually no sales is more than most firms can endure.

On the other hand, to be so concerned about cannibalization that needed product improvements and additions are delayed or withheld from the market can also be costly. The classic example of the dangers of such delays is that of Gillette. It procrastinated introducing its higher quality stainless steel

---

INFORMATION BOX

STRATEGY COUNTERING BY COMPETITORS

Some strategies are easily duplicated or countered by competitors. Price-cutting is the most easily countered. It is easy to match a price cut, and it sometimes can be done within minutes. Similarly, a different package, such as bundling, or an extended warranty is easily matched by competitors. The low price of Osborne, its bundling of software, and even the portability of its product were quickly and easily met by competitors, and its profits were severely affected.

Other strategies are not so easily duplicated. Most such strategies pertain to either service consideration or a strong and positive company image. A reputation for quality and dependability is not easily countered, at least in the short run. A good company or brand image is hard to match since it usually results from years of good service and satisfied customers—and here, of course, Osborne was hampered by its newness.

The best strategies are those that offer something not easily countered, that have lasting effect, and that are reasonably compatible with the present image and resources of the company. In a volatile industry composed mostly of new and unproven firms, however, such insulation from competitors is rarely achieved. Strategy countering has to be expected and euphoric expectations tempered.

Knowing that strategy countering is likely in a new industry, what, if anything, can a firm do to cope?

---

blade for fear that this blade, which afforded more shaves than its highly profitable super blue blade, would seriously cannibalize the other product. Only when aggressive competitors introduced their own stainless steel blades did Gillette do so. Because of this hesitance in bringing forth an innovation and improvement in shaving, Gillette's market share of the double-edge blade market fell from 90 percent to 70 percent. The loss in competitive position was never fully regained.

CONSIDER

Can you think of any additional learning insights?

QUESTIONS

1. What kind of controls would you advise Osborne to have set up to prevent the debacle that befell it?
2. Did Osborne Computer Corporation have any unique strengths that could have enabled it to survive in this hotly competitive industry?

3. What factors account for the surge of competitors in the portable computer field? Should a prudent executive have anticipated this?
4. Discuss and evaluate the pros and cons of a heavy growth commitment for a small innovator in
   a. A personal computer adaptation
   b. Running shoes
   c. Discount-concept retailing
   d. A fast-food restaurant
5. How can a firm in a rapidly growing industry maintain controlled growth and thus guard against Osborne's frenzied growth mode? Are there any dangers in such controlled growth? (We define controlled growth as slower, more carefully planned growth.)
6. Why are new industries so frequently characterized by severe price competition and price cutting?
7. On balance, do you think any firm should attempt to guard against cannibalization?

INVITATION TO ROLE PLAY

1. Place yourself in the role of Adam Osborne in late 1982. Sales are exceeding your wildest expectations, yet you sense that IBM will soon be a factor in this market, as will many smaller firms. Plan your strategy for 1983 to protect the viability of your enterprise and pave the way for further growth.
2. As a management consultant, you have been called in by Robert Jaunich in late spring 1983. Company losses are mounting. You have been charged with developing recommendations to save the company.
3. As an entrepreneur seeking venture capital for a new and innovative personal computer company what persuasive arguments would you propose for a $500,000 initial request for funds? How would you counter the skeptic's query of how you could possibly compete with the might of IBM?

INVITATION TO RESEARCH

Is there still an Osborne Computer Corporation? Whatever became of Adam Osborne?

PART III

NOTABLE
TURNAROUNDS

CHAPTER 13

Chrysler's Great Reversal

Some said Lee Iacocca performed a miracle at Chrysler. Some said he should be president of the United States. Iacocca brought Chrysler to profitability by 1983 and to a strong performance for most of the decade. The reeling number-three automaker had been given new life and respectability. Like a phoenix, it had practically risen from its ashes.

IACOCCA TO THE RESCUE?

In November 1978, Lee A. Iacocca became president of Chrysler, at one time the fourth-largest industrial corporation in the United States. Iacocca brought to the enterprise and its hopes for survival his proven abilities of salesmanship, image building, and cost cutting, but many doubted that he would be able to save the company—indeed, whether anything could.

Iacocca embodied the great American success story. In an earlier era, this would have been dubbed a Horatio Alger tale, after the prominent fiction writer of rags-to-riches stories early in this century. Iacocca was the son of an Italian immigrant. He saw education as the route to success, and he went to Lehigh University and then on to Princeton for a master's degree in engineering. "In my day you went to college, not to go into government or to be a lawyer, but to embark on a career that paid you more money than the guy who didn't go. For 32 years I was motivated by money," said Iacocca.[1]

Iacocca started with the Ford Motor Company as a trainee in 1946 at $125 a week. As he moved upward through the Ford organization, he was

---

[1]"Off to the Races Again," *Fortune* (Dec. 4, 1979): 15.

responsible for introducing the trend-setting Mustang and later the Maverick, Pinto, and Fiesta. By 1977 he was president of Ford, earning $978,000 that year. Then, in July 1978, Henry Ford abruptly fired him. The falling out has been attributed to basic disagreement between Ford and Iacocca over the pace of downsizing cars. Iacocca wanted to move fast, whereas Ford, worried about the impact of such additional investment on short-term profits, wanted to move more slowly.

After Iacocca left Ford, John J. Riccardo, chief executive of Chrysler, offered him the presidency. In accepting this job, Iacocca turned down a dozen jobs that offered more money. But he was after a place in automotive history: "I might not only save a blue-chip company and 200,000 jobs, but also help the Big Three become an honest Big Three."[2]

THE CHRYSLER DILEMMA

Chrysler had long been the weakest of the Big Three automakers. Although a multibillion-dollar firm, it was smaller, less well financed, and less talented than General Motors and Ford. It had suffered major reversals in the early 1960s, in 1970, and in 1974 and 1975. The monumental problems affecting the very viability of the company in the later 1970s and early 1980s had their roots in the recession of 1974–75. At that time a severe drop in sales forced the company to make massive cuts in capital spending and, perhaps more serious, in engineers and designers. Delays in introducing new models and quality problems resulted. For example, Chrysler compacts Volare and Aspen were introduced in 1976 and subsequently went through eight recalls for defects. Many Chrysler fans who had been loyal through generations turned to other makes.

In 1978 Chrysler lost $205 million. By 1979 problems had worsened as gasoline prices rose sharply and the public began demanding small, fuel-efficient cars. Although Chrysler had some success with its subcompact Omni and Horizon, losses were over $1 billion, and the future of the company was in doubt.

Lobbying in Washington

Iacocca turned to Washington to bail out the company. He sought federal loan guarantees of $1.2 billion. Chrysler's lobbying had irresistible bipartisan appeal in a coming election because of the concentration of Chrysler workers and parts suppliers in such key states as Michigan, Ohio, Indiana, and five other states. The Carter administration strongly supported the loan-

---

[2]"Off to the Races," 15.

guarantee legislation, and Congress finally authorized not $1.2 billion, but $1.5 billion.

But Chrysler's problems continued, and its actual sales for 1980 were far worse than had been predicted, with the deficit an unbelievable $1.7 billion. Although the blame could be laid on such externals as a recession and mushrooming interest rates that affected consumers and dealers alike, the early failure of the widely touted new K-car was critical.

Iacocca reacted with an ambitious cost-cutting program designed to save the company $1 billion in 1981. He went back to the loan-guarantee board for another $400 million. And to help spur lagging demand, he offered rebates of $380 to $1200 a car in December 1980 and early 1981. See the following box for a discussion of this pricing strategy of using rebates.

THE GREAT STAKE IN THE K-CARS

During the darkest days, the hopes for the K-car—the Dodge Aries and the Chrysler Reliant—sustained Iacocca and the Chrysler organization. This was a front-wheel-drive vehicle with only four cylinders that afforded great fuel economy—25 miles per gallon in the city and 41 on the highway—but at the same time was roomy enough to seat a family of six. In contrast to other rather flimsy-looking compacts on the market at the time, the K-car appeared strong and solid. Although GM had an older X-car aimed at the economy market, it was not on a par with the K-car. Chrysler management believed it had a superior and attractive product aimed at an important segment of the market. It was seen as the last hope for Chrysler, or as Iacocca put it, "the light at the end of the tunnel," "the last train in the station; if we failed here, it was all over."[3]

But Chrysler had made a mistake. Introduced in October 1980, the cars were an acute disappointment. Production problems and limited supplies prevented a strong launch in dealer showrooms. The major mistake, however, was pricing too high. The base price was $5880, well below that of the principal domestic competitor, GM's Citation hatchback, at $6270. With survival at stake, Chrysler sent out most of its early K-cars loaded with expensive options—air conditioning, automatic transmissions, velour upholstery, and electric windows—that added several thousand dollars to the price. As a result, the car aimed at the economy market was no longer a low-priced car.

To its credit, Chrysler quickly recognized the problem. Interviews with people leaving dealer showrooms without placing orders confirmed their disappointment in not seeing the good buys they had expected. By year's end, Chrysler was producing more basic models, and sales improved. But now the economy threatened the comeback of the company.

---

[3]Lee Iacocca, *Iacocca* (New York: Bantam Books, 1984): 251-52.

INFORMATION BOX

REBATES

A rebate is a manufacturer's promise to return part of the purchase price directly to the purchaser. The rebate is usually given to consumers, although it can be offered to dealers instead in the expectation that they will pass some or all of the savings along to consumers.

Obviously the objective of a rebate is to increase sales by giving purchasers a lower price. But why not simply reduce prices? The rebate is used instead of a regular markdown or price reduction because it is less permanent than cutting the list price. Rebates can be quite effective in generating short-term business. But they may affect business negatively once the rebate has been lifted. In other words, they often "steal" from future sales.

As a consumer, would you prefer a rebate or a price reduction, or does it make any difference? On balance, do you think rebates are an effective marketing strategy?

By December 1980, the prime rate soared to 18.5 percent; two months earlier it had been 13.5 percent. Now cars, houses, furniture, and appliances were all unsalable. To try to spur sales during this time of almost unparalleled high interest rates, Iacocca led the auto industry in offering refunds to customers based on the difference between 13 percent and the prevailing interest rate at the time of purchase.

1981

Because of the slow start for the K-cars, Chrysler began 1981 in very bad shape and had to go back to Washington to draw another $400 million in loan guarantees. The consequent bad publicity devastated company sales as many potential customers, fearing that Chrysler would go out of business and not honor its warranties or be able to supply parts, switched to competitors' products. Throughout 1981 survival "was never more than a week-by-week proposition."[4]

In the darkest days of 1981, Iacocca proposed a merger with Ford. Since Ford at the time had nothing equivalent to Chrysler's K-car, such a merger seemed reasonable, with both firms standing to benefit. However, obstacles loomed. One was the personality question. Henry Ford had fired Iacocca from the presidency of Ford in 1978. Could he and Iacocca work together now? Another problem concerned antitrust laws: Would such a merger of the num-

---

[4]Iacocca, *Iacocca*, 256.

ber-two and number-three automakers violate restraint of trade and lessen competition? This problem seemed easier to resolve. Preliminary talks with Washington about such a merger were promising, especially since Chrysler was on the brink of failing. If the merger went through, the Ford/Chrysler combination would have the equivalent of 75 percent of GM's U.S. sales. Thus, the behemoths would be competing on close to equal footing.

The merger did not come to pass. Ford top management turned it down. We can only speculate whether Henry Ford, although retired, vetoed the idea, or whether Ford top managers shuddered at the thought of an aggressive Iacocca again being part of their organization.

As the bitter year of 1981, with its high interest rates and terrible economy, dragged to an end, Chrysler faced another crisis on November 1: It was down to its last million dollars. And it normally spent $50 million a day. In desperation the company persuaded most of its suppliers, including all the major ones, to extend credit terms. Iacocca sweated out meeting payrolls:

> There were times when I said: "God, we need to ship a thousand more cars to get this much cash or we can't meet . . . a $50-million payroll on Friday." Day by day, it was that close, and oh, the numbers were so big.[5]

In the end, the K-cars saved Chrysler. With their looks, their fuel economy, and their comfort, and now with the right balance of basics and options, consumers continued to buy them in tough economic conditions. It did not hurt either when *Motor Trend Magazine* named the Aries and Reliant cars of the year for 1981. But even with the K-car, Chrysler staggered to a $478.5 million loss for 1981.

1982 AND 1983—REBIRTH

By 1982 Iacocca had Chrysler poised for a recovery. By paring costs and improving efficiency, he had reduced the breakeven point from 2.3 million cars and trucks to only 1.1 million. He had reduced the workforce from 160,000 in 1979 to 80,000 in 1982. Iacocca had closed or consolidated 20 of the 60 plants, and more than 1000 dealers were gone. He had brought many new executives into the company: 15 of the top 28 officials had come on board in the previous 4 years. With the greatly reduced breakeven point, any sales beyond the 1.1 million would generate $2,500 profit per vehicle.[6]

However, the economy still lagged for most of 1982, improving only near the end of the year. Car sales moved up along with the economy and by the end of the year the company had eked out a modest operating profit,

[5] Iacocca, *Iacocca*, 262.
[6] "Can Chrysler Keep Its Comeback Rolling?" *Business Week* (Feb. 14, 1983): 134.

although net profit had not quite crept out of the red. Still, Chrysler had weathered the storm. And Iacocca was a hero.

The following year, 1983, the company made an operating profit of $925 million—the best in Chrysler's history—and a net profit of $302 million, or 2.3 percent of sales of some 413 billion. The good times were to continue. As shown in Table 13.1, the company rose from the depths to rack up impressive gains in revenues and profits until it again encountered problems in the late 1980s. Table 13.2 shows the comparative net profit percentage figures of Chrysler, General Motors, and Ford during these years. Figure 13.1 shows the percentage growth in revenues of Chrysler compared with GM and Ford from 1984 to 1992.

Table 13.1   Chrysler's Sales and Profit Performance, 1980–1988 (in $ millions)

	Sales	Net Profit	Percent Profit to Sales
1980	$ 8,600	($1,772)	(20.6%)
1981	9,972	(555)	(5.6)
1982	10,045	(69)	(0.7)
1983	13,240	526	4.0
1984	19,573	1,496	7.6
1985	21.255	1,635	7.7
1986	22,586	1,404	6.2
1987	26,277	1,290	4.9
1988	35,473	1,143	3.2

Source: Company public records.
Commentary: In these years we see a big increase in revenues, with sales rising more than four-fold from 1980 to 1988. The return to profitability is significant too, with five consecutive years of profits well over $1 billion, although the growth of profits to match the growth in sales does not happen. Table 13.4 for the years immediately after 1988 will show Chrysler's situation again worsening, but then also turning around.

Table 13.2   Comparison of Chrysler, General Motors, and Ford on Net Profit Margin, 1983–1988

	Chrysler	General Motors	Ford
1983	4.0%	5.0%	4.2%
1984	7.6	5.4	5.6
1985	7.7	4.1	4.8
1986	6.2	2.9	5.2
1987	4.9	3.5	6.5
1988	3.2	3.8	5.7

Source: Industry statistics.
Commentary: Note how much more profitable, as a percentage of sales, Chrysler can be in good years compared with its domestic competitors. Also note its deteriorating profitability condition by the late 1980s, especially compared with Ford.

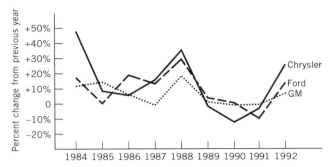

Figure 13.1. Comparison of Chrysler, General Motors, and Ford:
Year-to-Year Percent Changes in Revenues, 1984–1992.
(*Source*: Comparable public records.)
Commentary: Note the greater peaks and valleys of Chrysler's per-
formance.

With the turnaround publicly recognized, Iacocca moved swiftly to
secure more financial resources. In spring 1983 he made a new stock offering, and it was gobbled up. Originally, he had planned to sell 12.5 million
shares, but demand proved so strong that Chrysler issued 26 million shares.
The entire offering was sold out within the first hour at a market value of
$432 million. Investors now were salivating at the chance to participate in
the greatly improved prospects of Chrysler. Although additional stock offerings dilute the value of each outstanding share, investors in their optimism
disregarded this, as the stock price was bid up from $16⅝ at the time of the
offering, to $25 a few weeks later, and soon to $35.

Now awash in funds, Chrysler paid off $400 million—one-third of the
government loan guarantee—shortly after the stock sale. Just a few weeks
later, Iacocca paid back the entire loan, 7 years before it was due. Many
viewed this as rash, giving up over $800 million in cash so soon after the firm
was practically at death's door. But the well-publicized payback had great
psychological value for the company, its investors, and its present and
potential customers. It conclusively showed the confidence that Iacocca had
in Chrysler's future.

1984—ANOTHER COUP

The K-car saved Chrysler in the dark days. In 1984 another innovation
added fuel to the rejuvenation of Chrysler: the T115 minivan. At the time it
was an entirely new product, bigger than a station wagon but smaller than
a van. It held seven passengers, had front-wheel drive, and got 30 miles to
the gallon. And it fit into a normal garage.

Coming just a few years after the near-demise of the company, such an innovation seemed a wonderment: Where did Chrysler find the resources for such a project? Ah, it was not born from scratch, but had been first conceived at Ford, in 1974. Iacocca fell in love with the prototype and predicted a market of 800,000 a year. But Henry Ford would not approve it. Now at Chrysler, Iacocca could have a little retribution for being fired by Henry. Still, in 1980 Iacocca had to find $500 million to turn out this minivan that he and Harold Sperlich, who had helped design the Mustang at Ford and who had also come to Chrysler, had wanted to build at Ford. In a famous quote, Iacocca said during the critical days when the minivan idea surfaced: "The hell with what people say. Somehow we'll find a way to do it. For God's sake, let's not forget we're here to do cars."[7]

Favorable publicity abounded. *Connoisseur* magazine selected it as one of the most beautiful cars ever designed. *Fortune* called it one of the 10 most innovative products of the year. And car-buff magazines featured it on their covers, even months before it went on sale. Chrysler's four minivan nameplates began selling at a sustained rate of 30,000 per month.

THE NITTY GRITTY OF PRODUCTIVITY IMPROVEMENT

Basic production efficiencies occurring by the early 1980s paved the way for the revival to come. Richard Dauch, an ex-Big Ten football player, was a vehicle of change. Iacocca lured him away from Volkswagen in 1980, promising that he could modernize each plant when a new model was launched. Dauch's role model was Vince Lombardi: "Inspire 'em with speeches, but if they do not produce—kick tail and take names."[8]

At the start of the 1980s, the auto industry was ravaged by foreign competition, particularly Japanese. No automaker was worse than Chrysler: Its quality was in the pits at the same time that its production costs were the highest in the industry. Part of the problem was aged plants: For example, Dodge Main was built in 1910 and was eight stories tall, with an assembly line ponderously writhing from floor to floor amid half-assembled cars awaiting repairs or cannibalization for parts. Part of the problem was a heedless rush for production at any cost.

Dauch first worked to improve the most obvious deficiencies: squeaks and rattles. This meant adhering to tight specifications. In 5 years he quadrupled the number of robots and the computers that control them. He transformed the assembly line and introduced just-in-time inventory, under which parts arrive only as they are needed and in the order in which they

---

[7]John B. Judis, "Myth vs. Manager," *Business Month* (July 1990): 26.
[8]Alex Taylor III, "Lee Iacocca's Production Whiz," *Fortune* (June 22, 1987): 36.

will be used. By 1987 Dauch had invested $1.2 billion in new paint shops to give Chrysler products the finest finishes in the industry.

He worked assiduously to promote quality thinking among his employees, working closely with United Auto Workers officials. He upped the training of all workers; he gave them more say about overtime and vacations; he eliminated time clocks. In return he got greater flexibility in scheduling, and he gained a reputation as being tough but fair.

The result was a solid increase in productivity. The production lines by 1987 could deliver 8000 cars and trucks a day, versus 4500 in 1981. The number of labor-hours to build a vehicle went from 175 to 102. Absenteeism and friction were down sharply.

In other efforts to improve productivity, Chrysler scrutinized supplier relations and weeded out less efficient suppliers. Those remaining faced new specifications for quality, costs, and delivery. Car designs and especially number of options were simplified. For example, at one time Chrysler offered an unbelievable 19 million possible combinations of color, trim, and accessories; this was reduced to 42 options. Customers still had ample choices, and manufacturing costs were reduced $100 a car.[9]

A major move to reduce production costs and decrease the breakeven point for profitability was the basic K-car single platform strategy. As the company moved into the later 1980s, it was still using one basic engine, transmission, and underbody structure. Yet it had developed eight new models differentiated by sheet metal and distinctive market identities.

The idea of the single platform was born of desperation: Chrysler could not afford all-new models. But the engineering was so clever that most customers were not aware of the basic commonality. General Motors, on the other hand, was producing 19 distinct body structures for its 175 models. Yet most of these were so similar that it was often criticized for its look-alike cars. Still, how much longer could Chrysler continue selling its clones? Critics were becoming vocal against this long-lasting strategy, and sales of some models were beginning to suffer.

The payoff of the efforts at increasing productivity was monumental. After being lowest in quality and highest in costs in 1982, by 1986 Chrysler was near the top in reliability, durability, and fit-and-finish. It was credited with making a profit per vehicle of $1,057 in 1986, while Ford made $847 and GM only $157.[10] In the process, the competitive position of Chrysler as shown by its market share improved significantly, as shown in Table 13.3.

Iacocca had done it. He had resurrected a desperate company in the depths of the worst recession in one-half a century. By 1984 he was the

---

[9]Taylor, "Production Whiz," 40.
[10]Taylor, "Production Whiz," 36.

Table 13.3   Chrysler Market Share, 1983–1988

	Percentage of U.S. Car/Truck Market
1983	9.2%
1984	9.5
1985	11.2
1986	11.5
1987	10.8
1988	11.2

Source: Industry statistics.

Commentary: We see a significant improvement in competitive position during these years, although the growth trend stops in 1987.

author of the best-selling nonfiction hardcover book ever, his own autobiography, which sold almost 6 million copies and stayed on top of the best-seller lists for a year. He was the star of Chrysler's television commercials. He was a charismatic talk-show guest, an authentic American hero, even the object of a draft-Iacocca-for-president movement. One of his greatest honors was being appointed by President Reagan to oversee the restoration of the Statue of Liberty—this for a son of Italian immigrants who had come through Ellis Island. What kind of a leader was Iacocca? See the following box for a more detailed discussion of his leadership style.

TROUBLE AGAIN, LATE 1980S AND EARLY 1990S

After Iacocca's resurrection of Chrysler in the early 1980s, by 1988 the company was hurting again. Still wedded to the K-car frame, which was aging fast, it had to make cash rebates up to $2,500 to entice buyers. Even truck sales were faltering, such as the Dodge Ram, which had not been changed since 1962. To a large extent this reflected capital deprivation: Sufficient moneys were not put into new car and truck designs.

Admittedly, the company had brought out a variety of nameplates, marketing some 66 models during the 1980s. This was twice as many as Ford, which was twice as big. But Chrysler's many models led to customer confusion. And all these new nameplates, even including the popular minivan, used the same basic platform developed for the K-car in 1980. So, whether a $10,000 Shadow or Sundance or a $28,000 Chrysler Imperial, the basic foundation had the same engine, suspension, and underbody parts. Unfortunately, the press caught on and started denigrating Chrysler.

At the same time, the company was having serious problems assimilating the 1987 acquisition of American Motors Corporation (AMC) for $757 million. The crown jewel of the buyout was the Jeep line of sport-util-

---

INFORMATION BOX

IACOCCA'S LEADERSHIP STYLE

A super salesman, charismatic, politically skilled, decisive—these characteristics have been commonly attributed to Iacocca. He was also a demanding boss, quick to fire subordinates who didn't measure up to his standards. Still, his personality was such as to engender strong loyalty, with many of his managers following him to Chrysler from Ford. Unlike many top executives, he did not demand conformity, but even encouraged disagreement and eccentricity, seeing this as fuel for creativity. Also unlike most top executives, he readily abandoned organizational chains of command to solicit opinions of junior executives, auto dealers, line workers, and even union officials.

He was hardly a humble man, and his firing by Henry Ford was probably due to a bitter power struggle between two proud men, each unwilling to back down or compromise. Eventually, as we will see shortly, Iacocca's management focus at Chrysler became diluted as his attention shifted to other interests, and some critics did not treat him kindly.

Possibly one of his greatest strengths at Chrysler was his flexibility or adaptability. If a strategy was not working out, such as his diversifications, he could cut his losses. And in the late 1980s, in the face of strong opposition from his younger designers, Iacocca backed away from his position on styling issues.

In commenting on his future successor, Iacocca noted: "Somebody suggested . . . that I hire General Norman Schwarzkopf. He's a brilliant strategist and a hard worker . . . He knows objectives and he must know people, and he sure would have discipline. What else does an executive need?"[11] Discuss.

---

ity vehicles, selling at a steady 150,000 or so units annually. These units appealed to younger, more affluent buyers than the older, lower-income customers of Chrysler. Still, the company found itself saddled with the great inefficiencies that had bedeviled AMC. Payrolls burgeoned, and AMC's retired workers brought unfunded pension liabilities of $384 million. Another $1.4 billion debt arose from legal claims from Jeep rollover accidents. The aged AMC plants in Kenosha, Wisconsin, and Toledo, Ohio, depressed Chrysler's overall efficiency. In 1988 the Kenosha plant had to be closed, at a cost of more than $100 million. The AMC acquisition brought Chrysler's breakeven point up from 1.2 million units a year to 1.6 million. Table 13.4 shows Chrysler's operating performance in the later 1980s and the 1990s. Table 13.5 shows the net profit percentages of Chrysler and its domestic competitors.

---

[11]Alex Taylor III, "Can Iacocca Fix Chrysler—Again," *Fortune* (April 8, 1991): 53.

Table 13.4   Chrysler's Operating Performance, 1989–1992 (in $ millions)

	Sales	Net Profit	Percent Profit to Sales
1989	$34,922	$ 315	0.9%
1990	30,620	68	0.2
1991	29,370	(665)	(2.3)
1992	36,897	430	1.2

Source: Company public records.
Commentary: Here we see a new sales and profit decline and the beginning of a major and probably more durable turnaround in 1992.

Table 13.5   Comparison of Chrysler, General Motors, and Ford on Net Profit Margins, 1989–1992

	Chrysler	General Motors	Ford
1989	0.9%	3.4%	4.4%
1990	0.2	(1.6)	0.9
1991	(2.3)	(4.1)	(2.6)
1992	1.2	(0.5)	(0.5)

Source: Industry statistics.
Commentary: Although Chrysler faltered badly at the end of the 1980s, it was not alone by 1990. By 1992 only Chrysler had made it back into profitability.

The Iacocca Contribution to the Relapse of Chrysler

After Iacocca brought Chrysler back from the very brink of disaster from 1982 through 1984, his attention wandered from car making. In addition to his personal distractions—his best-selling autobiography, his charisma as a public figure, and his political ambitions—he succumbed to the wheeling and dealing machinations that characterized much of the 1980s. He went on an acquisitions binge.

Instead of investing Chrysler's newfound wealth in new models and improved production facilities, Iacocca found other uses for this money. To begin with, he was obsessed with the share price of Chrysler stock. It seemed a vast injustice to him to see growth stocks such as Xerox trading at price/earnings ratios of 15 to 20 while Chrysler was under 5. The prevailing climate of the time suggested that diversifications through acquisitions was the key to better Wall Street acceptance. Therefore, if Chrysler could become more than an auto company, its fortunes should soar.

Iacocca began his quest to boost Chrysler stock by spending $1.9 billion to buy up company stock, thus spreading the profits over fewer shares of stock. Then he moved on to acquisitions. Chrysler already owned 24 percent of Mitsubishi, and now he wanted other foreign relationships. He bought a 3.5 percent share in the Italian car company Maserati and with Maserati began joint development of a luxury sports car, the TC. In 1986 he upped

Chrysler's stake to 15.6 percent, with the option to purchase full control. In early 1987 he bought another Italian sports-car maker, Lamborghini. And later that year he made the major purchase of American Motors.

Iacocca made other acquisitions outside the car business, the business that was judged so unfavorably by investors. Iacocca bought four rental car companies—Dollar, General, Snappy, and Thrifty—to serve as captive customers for Chrysler's fleet sales. He had never quite gotten over his resentment of the government's loan guarantee board, which had forced him to sell the company's jets in order to get the vital loan guarantees. Now he got a measure of revenge by buying Gulfstream Aerospace for $637 million. And his sights expanded into defense contracting with the 1987 purchase of Electrospace Systems, a small defense electronics firm.

In 1987, Iacocca reorganized Chrysler as a holding company with three subsidiaries: Chrysler Motors, Chrysler Financial, and Chrysler Technologies. And he even considered moving corporate headquarters from the Detroit suburbs to Manhattan. At this time he was also seriously considering acquiring the E. F. Hutton brokerage house.

Iacocca, in his spending frame of mind, allotted more than $1 billion to the construction of a new Technology Center in Auburn Hills, Michigan. This state-of-the-art facility would house Chrysler's design and research operations.

He eventually tired of his diversification efforts, especially since they uniformly turned out to be unprofitable. He sold Gulfstream in 1990 for a good profit but could not sell Electrospace owing to defense cutbacks. The worst money loser was Maserati, on whose TC sports car he squandered more than $200 million.

The upshot of this spending and acquisition binge was that attention and resources were taken away from the heart of Chrysler's operation, the development of new models to compete in the mid-size and full-size sector of the auto market. The old K-car design, dating back to 1980, was long overdue for replacement.

ANOTHER COMEBACK, 1992 AND 1993

With Chrysler faltering again, an aging Iacocca turned his full attention back to the car business 7 years after retiring his company's horrendous bank debt. He and top company executives made a long-overdue 5-year commitment in 1988 to concentrate $15 billion on four high-visibility and potentially profitable new models of cars and trucks. Regardless of the economic climate, these were to receive top priority: a 1991 minivan, the 1993 Jeep Grand Cherokee, the 1993 LH sedans, and the 1994 T300 full-size pickup. To try to pay for the project, Iacocca had to unload some of his prior purchases and find other funding. The schedule was met, and Chrysler's viability seemed ensured.

Fearful that the company might not survive until the new models came out, especially if a recession were to occur first, Iacocca instituted a far-reaching austerity program to cut $3 billion from the company's $26 billion annual operating costs. Product development was totally reorganized and streamlined. Suggestions of outside suppliers were enlisted in the slimming operation. Budgets for marketing and advertising, dealer relations, and health care were trimmed. Perhaps most important, Iacocca wanted a climate of cost containment to permeate the organization at all levels. Some 24 percent of the white-collar work force had already been eliminated since 1987, with 3,000 more scheduled for 1991. The number of vice presidents was reduced to 23 from 36; layers of management—the levels of executives that separate the CEO from the factory floor—were reduced to 9 from the previous 11 (see the following box for a discussion of the implications of management layers and the concomitant span of control); the number of board members dropped to 13 from 18. Most management consultants were eliminated, as well as white-collar training, including Dale Carnegie courses. Even secretaries became "as scarce as rain in Baja."[12]

Iacocca was prescient. In the last 3 months of 1990, Chrysler's car and truck sales to dealers dropped 7.2 percent, which should have pushed the company into the red for the year. Instead, Chrysler registered a small profit for 1990, although it still racked up a $665 million loss in 1991. Still, Chrysler was able to survive that loss unscathed and still launch its new models on schedule in 1992. Then things improved greatly, with a $430 million profit in 1992. (See Table 13.4.) By 1993 the company was riding high. Now Chrysler's stock price per share was reflecting optimistic investor sentiments as it reached into the $40s by mid-1993, up from around $14 in early 1991.

Iacocca retired December 31, 1992, with a job well done. He said on TV: "When it's your last turn at bat, it sure is nice to hit a home run."[13] Robert J. Eaton, formerly with GM of Europe, replaced Iacocca as Chrysler chair.

THE JAPANESE PRESENCE

The Japanese invasion of the U.S. auto market has been phenomenal and for years left U.S. carmakers reeling. Somehow, Detroit had trouble adjusting its thinking to combatting the Japanese incursion; instead it wanted government protection, fighting to keep Japanese cars out.

In 1981 it received voluntary import restrictions, but the Japanese had already gained 20 percent of the U.S. car market. By 1982 Honda alone had sold 195,000 made-in-Japan Accords, making Accord the fourth most popu-

[12]Taylor, "Can Iacocca Fix Chrysler," 52.
[13]Alex Taylor III, "U.S. Cars Come Back," Fortune (Nov. 16, 1992): 85.

INFORMATION BOX

LEVELS OF MANAGEMENT AND THE TRADEOFF WITH SPAN OF CONTROL

The more levels of managers there are between the top executive and the lowest workers, the more higher executives are insulated from rank and file workers. Such insulation, or distance, frustrates communication, impedes rapport, and even damages the morale of the workers. It promotes a "them versus us" attitude. Perhaps the greatest disadvantage is that overhead costs rise substantially with each layer: high-salaried executives, their staffs, their offices, and their other perks. Yet in large organizations, many layers of management are seen as necessary if the span of control is to be reasonable.

One of the major principles of organization is that the span of control—the number of subordinates reporting to an executive—should be small enough to allow proper supervision. A number of factors can affect the optimum span. Obviously, the more experienced and able the executive is, as well as the subordinates, and the more stable and similar the operations are, the wider the span that can be adequately handled. But there is a limit to how many subordinates one person can supervise effectively. General conclusions are that higher management can supervise from 4 to 8 subordinates, whereas the span can reach 8 to 15 or more at the lower management levels. A span that is too wide will normally be narrowed by adding one or more management levels as shown below.

Wide span, one supervisory level:

General Manager

Store managers and headquarters executives

Moderate span, two supervisory levels:

General Manager

Regional Manager   Regional Manager   Headquarters staff

Moderate span, three supervisory levels:

General Manager

Regional Manager   Regional Manager   Headquarters staff

District Managers   District Managers

> Computers have made it possible to widen spans—and reduce the number of levels—by providing timely and abundant operating data. In a time of austerity, so-called "flat" organizations—that is, ones with few management levels, such as Wal-Mart and Southwest Airlines—have become models of effective organizational structures. The tradeoff is that workers in such flat organizations are less directly supervised. Sometimes, however, this is not so bad. Workers and lower level managers gain opportunity to act more independently, and this can increase job satisfaction and even advancement potential.
>
> What do you see as the likely consequences of the growing trend toward flat organizations?

lar car in the United States. Under pressure, Japan agreed to limit auto shipments to the United States to 1.68 million cars per year.

As we have seen with Chrysler—it also took place with the other U.S. automakers—the windfall profits between 1984 and 1988 were not committed to the core business, but were instead dissipated. Some companies spent their profits in diversifications having little relationship with the core business, as Iacocca did. Others spent money in acquiring small but prestigious European automakers, where profit was an illusion.

To their sorrow, the import restraints had two dire consequences for U.S. carmakers. First, Japanese manufacturers circumvented the import ceiling by assembling cars in U.S. plants. Honda led this trend, but soon other firms followed. By 1990 the Japanese were building 1.2 million cars and trucks in the United States.

The second consequence was the emergence of upscale Japanese autos. With restrictions on the number of cars, the Japanese moved to more expensive models, thus maximizing the profit on each car shipped. Honda's Acura led the way in 1985, and it was quickly followed by other luxury makes that successfully took highly profitable sales from U.S. carmakers.

During the 1980s U.S. firms scurried behind whatever protectionism they could muster; they repudiated the idea that they could compete nose-to-nose with the Japanese. This began to change by the 1990s.

By the early 1990s, Japanese firms had more than 30 percent of the U.S. car market. But problems were surfacing. In particular, the value of the Japanese yen had risen 65 percent between 1985 and 1990. This meant that Japanese cars would normally be that much more costly to customers than U.S. cars. However, Japanese manufacturers tried to counter this by cutting costs and keeping prices competitive without damaging the quality of their output.

The Japanese marketing strategy for luxury cars was awesome. For example, in 1989 Toyota introduced the Lexus, positioning it against the best of the Europeans, such as Mercedes, BMW, and Jaguar, and against domestic Cadillacs and Lincolns. Lexus dealers received as much as $7000 profit per car as incentive to lure customers with ultimate attention and service. Backed with great quality control, within months the Lexus had established itself as the "thinking man's luxury car," providing great performance without hassle, and unsurpassed maintenance.

By the early 1990s, U.S. carmakers finally began to recognize that they could compete against the Japanese, and even win. Part of the optimism stemmed from some economic problems that Japan was facing at home, but part also resulted from a long-overdue realization that U.S. workers could make cars nearly on par with the Japanese cars in quality and quality control.

As the country moved into 1993, the business press was trumpeting the troubles in Japan and the opportunity thus created for U.S. firms. Indeed, statistics bore out a resurgence. In 1992, Detroit gained nearly 2 points of market share, with a 72 percent share of the market for cars and light trucks. The light truck segment in particular was Detroit's coup. This segment had grown to a record 41.6 percent of all vehicles produced in 1992, as consumers replaced sedans with pickups, minivans, and sport-utility vehicles. And of this growing and lucrative market, Detroit gained 4 percent in market share in 1992, to a whopping 91 percent of the market.[14]

Meantime, in order to maintain a reasonable semblance of profits, Japanese producers were forced to raise their U.S. auto prices by 6.7 percent in 1992, versus Detroit's mere 1.2 percent. The problems in Japan worsened; by 1993 they were the worst since 1974, during the oil shock. Major firms were having record losses, and Nissan became the first major Japanese manufacturer to announce a plant shutdown. Lifetime job tenure was being abandoned. The book *Honorable Poverty* had become a best seller.[15]

U.S. automakers appeared to have learned an important lesson, one that had eluded them for the previous two decades of competition with Japan. They were holding prices down, bringing out new products faster, and paying more attention to quality standards in production. In addition, they were testing out intriguing new marketing ideas, notably no-haggling selling (see the following issue box), and offering standard packages of popular options at attractive prices.

Lest U.S. carmakers become too satisfied with their recent inroads against the Japanese, they apparently still have a considerable way to go to

---

[14]Kathleen Kerwin, "Is Detroit Pulling Up to Pass?" *Business Week* (January 11, 1993): 63.

[15]Robert Neff, "Fixing Japan," *Business Week* (March 29, 1993): 68-74. For the effect of this situation on the workforce, see Karen Lowry Miller, "Stress and Uncertainty: The Price of Restructuring," *Business Week* (Mar. 29, 1993): 74; also "Unemployment in Japan Doubly Hard on Workers," from *New York Times*, reported in *Cleveland Plain Dealer* (May 22, 1993): E2.

INFORMATION BOX

TO HAGGLE OR NOT TO HAGGLE OVER THE PRICE OF A CAR?

We have come to expect to haggle or negotiate over the price of a vehicle, whether new or used. It was the naive consumer indeed who did not try to get a better price than the one on the sticker. Invariably some customers would drive harder bargains than others, and some dealers were more eager to "deal" than others. But did most consumers really like this "challenge" of trying to best a car salesperson and the sales manager? And how could you really be sure that you had gotten the best deal?

Now, some car dealers—and one make of car, the Saturn—are testing the waters with no-haggling selling, in which a uniformly low price is offered to all customers, with no further negotiation or haggling accepted. (With trade-ins, of course, some negotiation is still possible.) This breaking away from the traditional is the source of some controversy. While many customers like the idea of not having to haggle, which can be traumatic for novices, others feel that they are not getting as good a price. Still, the very fact that it is being tested suggests that the U.S. auto industry is becoming more innovative, and even possibly more in tune with customer preferences.

How do you feel about no-haggling car buying? Why do you feel this way? What has been your previous experience in car purchasing?

---

match the quality of Japanese cars. The widely watched J. D. Power & Associates quality survey for 1993 listed the following as the top ten cars:[16]

Rank	Model
1	Lexus LS 400
2	Lexus SC 300/400
3	Infiniti J30
4	Infiniti Q45
4	Toyota Camry
6	Acura Legend
6	Ford Crown Victoria
8	Lexus ES 300
9	Toyota Paseo
10	Buick Park Avenue
10	Toyota Corolla
10	Toyota Tercel

Chrysler embarrassingly was not in the top ten, despite its widely heralded new LH sedans. It experienced another setback, also. Japan recalled

---

[16]J. D. Power & Associates, as published in Neal Templin, "Toyota Is Standout Once Again On J. D. Power's Quality Survey," *Wall Street Journal* (May 28, 1993): B1, B5.

more than one-half the Chrysler vehicles sold in that country from 1989 to 1993 because of possible brake failure.

ANALYSIS

In the great Chrysler comebacks, we are impressed with *the thin line* that can exist between failure—and even total loss of a company—and solid success and glittering acclaim. A few "ifs" dramatize this thin line:

If Iacocca had not been able to sell Washington on giving Chrysler the $1.5 billion loan guarantee, the "bailout," would the company have survived? The federal assistance was no foregone conclusion; indeed, many in Washington opposed it. Without the badly needed funds, it is doubtful the company could have survived intact.

If the K-car had not proved to be an outstanding success, it is unlikely the company could have remained viable, even with the federal guarantee. Iacocca himself admitted that the K-car "was the last train in the station . . . if we failed here, it was all over." Not only did the K-car provide needed sales and profits in the early 1980s, but it served as the basic structure for succeeding models into the next decade, thus enabling Chrysler to generate the cash flow to sustain the company and its options.

If the cost-cutting of Iacocca in the early 1990s had cut into too much bone and muscle, the weakened Chrysler would have been unable to take advantage of the surge to come a few years later. And again, as with the K-car, all the chips were resting on the market acceptance of a few new models. A risky situation this, but then Chrysler had few other choices.

By the mid-1980s, with success and wide acclaim surrounding him, Iacocca almost lost it. He forgot his focus. Instead of investing the now plentiful financial resources in new prototypes and models and in updating plant and equipment, he squandered billions of dollars on unwise diversifications and other endeavors. This *dilution of resources and focus* almost destroyed the company again.

Beyond squandering the company's financial resources, Iacocca also abandoned his own whole-hearted commitment to Chrysler. Other roads now beckoned him, and he left company operations in lesser hands as he pursued the heady life of a popular public figure. Fortunately for Chrysler and its employees, creditors, and investors, he was still around and able to come back again to save the company, after he had led it astray in the first place.

This brings us to one of the interesting anomalies of great leaders: their *inconsistencies of performance.* After making highly successful decisions and actions, they tend to let up, to rest on their laurels. Perhaps the reason may be that they have overcome the great challenge and now have lost interest in the more mundane. So they seek new challenges, ones for which they may not be as capable or certainly not as experienced.

WHAT CAN BE LEARNED?

The captain must pilot. After saving Chrysler, Iacocca left governing Chrysler to a number of "strong-willed, highly ambitious mavericks who had been derailed from the fast track at other companies."[17] Gerald Greenwald, Bennett Bidwell, and Robert Lutz came from Ford. And Iacocca promoted Sperlich, who had preceded him to Chrysler from Ford and who was instrumental in developing the K-car, to be the company's president. The four senior executives began feuding, with a particularly bitter struggle between Sperlich, the engineer, and Greenwald, the numbers man. Iacocca backed Greenwald, and lost his brilliant product designer. By the time Iacocca again took over the helm, the company was in disarray and badly behind in new product planning.

Delegation is the mark of the good executive. But it can be overdone and become abdication. When several executives are competing for the top spot, such abdication has been likened to a kingdom without a king, in which the various lords, formerly working together for the king, now fight among themselves for the throne.[18]

The lure of cosmetic changes. Chrysler was able to use cosmetic changes for its new models for years, building on the same basic platform developed for the K-car in 1980. As long as customers did not wise up and demand more substantial changes, this was a strategy of no small moment. It enhanced the profitability of Chrysler because of the low breakeven point for the new models, which were little different from previous ones. For any business, cosmetic rather than basic changes can be a key to greater profits. However, a considerable challenge is to know when to cash in your winnings before it is too late.

A winning hand eventually succumbs. Chrysler had had a winning hand with its K-car, but eventually and inevitably that car was superseded and outmoded. Unfortunately, Chrysler did not recognize this vulnerability in time and almost self-destructed for the second time in less than a decade. The lesson should be clear: A winning strategy, a successful product, is not forever. Times change, innovations make for obsolescence, competitors match and surpass the product, and customers become jaded. Chrysler and Iacocca eventually recognized the fallacy of K-car's enduring demand, and reacted, but it was close. The desirability of only cosmetic changes must be balanced with the periodic need to make more substantial ones. And this can be a narrow line.

---

[17]Judis, "Myth vs. Manager," 30.
[18]Judis, "Myth vs. Manager," 30.

Spread your risks. Chrysler and Iacocca represent the ultimate gamble: staking everything on one roll of the dice, for the K-car and later for the LH. Fortunately, the gamble paid off. But what if it had not? The company then would probably have succumbed. Admittedly, with the K-car, Iacocca had little choice. There were no resources left for spreading risks. Just as the gambler stakes everything on one roll of the dice, so Iacocca gambled with Chrysler's fortunes. And he became a hero because he won. But prudence suggests that management should avoid the "all or nothing" decision. The stakes are too great and the risks too uncertain for such a gamble.

CONSIDER

What additional learning insights do you see coming from the Chrysler roller coaster?

QUESTIONS

1. Do you think Chrysler could have survived without the government bailout? Why or why not? Playing the devil's advocate (one who takes an opposing position for the sake of helping determine the validity), what arguments would you present for Congress to reject giving such assistance?
2. "Iacocca was not a great manager, He simply lucked out." Discuss.
3. Defend Iacocca's acquisitions in the mid-1980s, particularly the four rental car companies, Lamborghini, the airplane company, and the stake in Maserati. Although these purchases did not work out profitably, as we know with the benefit of hindsight, were the decisions all that bad at the time?
4. During some of his darkest days, Iacocca seriously considered merging Chrysler with Ford, but Ford top executives would not consent. Given that the federal government would have approved, what do you see as the pros and cons of such a merger, (a) from the viewpoint of the companies involved, and (b) from the perspective of the general public?
5. Is stock price the best indicator of a corporation's worth?
6. Do you think Iacocca has built the foundation for Chrysler to be reasonably secure and an ever-growing presence in the U.S. auto industry? Array your pro and con arguments, and defend your conclusions.

INVITATION TO ROLE PLAY

1. How could Iacocca have better handled his stewardship of Chrysler?

Place yourself in his shoes in the 1980s.

2. You are the confidant of Hal Sperlich, the gifted developer of the Mustang for Iacocca at Ford and later of the K-car and the minivan for Chrysler. It is 1986, and your boss is fighting for a new car platform to replace the aging K-car platform. But Greenwald and his accounting and finance cronies oppose this as an unacceptable waste of company resources. What persuasive arguments can you marshall for Sperlich to try to win this key controversy? What courses of action do you recommend that he take?

INVITATION TO RESEARCH

How is Chrysler faring as we move beyond the early 1990s? Is Iacocca still a powerful voice? Have the Japanese rebounded from their hard times? Has the U.S. auto industry been able to gain ground on foreign automakers?

CHAPTER 14

Harley Davidson Fights Back, Finally

In the early 1960s, a staid and unexciting market was shaken up, was rocked to its core, by the most unlikely invader. This intruder was a smallish Japanese firm that had risen out of the ashes of World War II and was now trying to encroach on the territory of a major U.S. firm, a firm that had in the space of 60 years destroyed all of its U.S. competitors and now had a firm 70 percent of the motorcycle market.

Yet, almost inconceivably, in one-half a decade this market share was to fall to 5 percent, and the total market was to expand many times over what it had been for decades. A foreign invader had furnished a textbook example of the awesome effectiveness of carefully crafted marketing efforts. In the process, this confrontation between Honda and Harley Davidson was a harbinger of the Japanese invasion of the auto industry.

Eventually, by the late 1980s, Harley was to make a comeback. But only after more than two decades of travail and mediocrity.

THE INVASION

Sales of motorcycles in the United States were around 50,000 per year during the 1950s: Harley Davidson, Britain's Norton and Triumph, and Germany's BMW accounted for most of the market. By the turn of the decade, Honda had begun to penetrate the U.S. market. In 1960 fewer than 400,000 motorcycles were registered in the United States. While this was an increase of almost 200,000 from the end of World War II 15 years before, it was a rate of increase far below that of other motor vehicles. But by 1964, only 4 years later, the number had risen to 960,000; 2 years later it was 1.4 million; and by 1971 it was almost 4 million.

In expanding the demand for motorcycles, Honda instituted a distinctly different strategy. The major elements of this strategy were lightweight cycles and an advertising approach directed toward a new customer. Few firms have ever experienced such a shattering of market share as did Harley Davidson in the 1960s. (Although its market share declined drastically, its total sales remained nearly constant, indicating that it was getting none of the new customers for motorcycles.)

Reaction of Harley Davidson to the Honda Threat

Faced with an invasion of its staid and static U.S. market, how did Harley react to the intruder? It did not react! At least not until far too late. Harley Davidson considered itself the leader in full-size motorcycles. While the company might shudder at the image tied in with its product's usage by the leather jacket types, it took solace in the fact that almost every U.S. police department used its machines. Perhaps this is what led Harley to stand aside and complacently watch Honda make deep inroads into the American motorcycle market. The management saw no threat in Honda's thrust into the market with lightweight machines. The attitude was exemplified in this statement by William H. Davidson, the president of the company and son of the founder:

> Basically, we don't believe in the lightweight market. We believe that motorcycles are sport vehicles, not transportation vehicles. Even if a man says he bought a motorcycle for transportation, it's generally for leisure-time use. The lightweight motorcycle is only supplemental. Back around World War I, a number of companies came out with lightweight bikes. We came out with one ourselves. They never got anywhere. We've seen what happens to these small sizes.[1]

Eventually Harley recognized that the Honda phenomenon was not an aberration, and that there was a new factor in the market. The company attempted to fight back by offering an Italian-made lightweight in the mid-1960s. But it was far too late; Honda was firmly entrenched. The Italian bikes were regarding in the industry to be of lower quality than the Japanese bikes. Honda, and toward the end of the 1960s other Japanese manufacturers, continued to dominate what had become a much larger market than Harley Davidson had ever dreamed.

---

[1] Tom Rowan, "Harley Sets New Drive to Boost Market Share," *Advertising Age* (Jan. 29, 1973): 34–35.

AFTERMATH OF THE HONDA INVASION: 1965–1981

In 1965 Harley Davidson made its first public stock offering. Soon after, it faced a struggle for control. The contest was primarily between Bangor Punta, an Asian company, and AMF, an American company with strong interests in recreational equipment, including bowling products. In a bidding war, Harley Davidson's stockholders chose AMF over Bangor Punta, even though the bid was $1 less than Bangor's offer of $23 per share. Stockholders were leery of Bangor's reputation of taking over a company, squeezing it dry, and then scrapping it for the remaining assets. AMF's plans for expansion of Harley Davidson seemed more compatible.

But the marriage was troubled: Harley Davidson's old equipment was not capable of the expansion envisioned by AMF. At the very time that Japanese manufacturers—Honda and others—were flooding the market with high-quality motorcycles, Harley was falling down on quality. One company official noted that "quality was going down just as fast as production was going up."[2] Indicative of the depths of the problem at a demoralized Harley Davidson, quality control inspections failed 50 percent to 60 percent of the motorcycles produced. Only 5 percent of Japanese motorcycles failed their quality control checks.[3]

AMF put up with an average $4.8 million operating loss for 11 years. Finally, it called it quits and put the division up for sale in 1981. Vaughan Beals, vice president of motorcycle sales, still had faith in the company: He led a team that used $81.5 million in financing from Citicorp to complete a leveraged buyout. All ties with AMF were severed.

VAUGHAN BEALS

Beals was a middle-aged Ivy Leaguer, a far cry from what one might think of as a heavy motorcycle aficianado. He had graduated from MIT's Aeronautical Engineering School and was considered a production specialist.[4] But he was far more than that. His was a true commitment to motorcycles, personally as well as professionally. Deeply concerned with AMF's declining attention to quality, he achieved the buyout from AMF.

The prognosis for the company was bleak. Its market share, which had dominated the industry before the Honda invasion, now was 3 percent. In 1983 Harley Davidson would celebrate its 80th birthday; some doubted it

---

[2]Peter C. Reid, *Well Made in America—Lessons from Harley Davidson on Being the Best* (New York: McGraw-Hill, 1990), 10.

[3]Reid, "Well Made in America," 27.

[4]Rod Willis, "Harley Davidson Comes Roaring Back," *Management Review* (Mar. 1986): 20–27.

would still be around by then. Tariff protection seemed Harley's only hope, and massive lobbying paid off. In 1983 Congress passed a huge tariff increase on Japanese motorcycles. Instead of a 4 percent tariff, now Japanese motorcycles would be subject to a 45 percent tariff for the coming 5 years.[5]

The tariff gave the company new hope, and it slowly began to rebuild market share. Key to this was restoring confidence in the quality of its products. And Beals took a leading role in this. He drove Harley Davidsons to rallies, where he met Harley owners. There he learned of their concerns and their complaints, and he promised changes. At these rallies a core of loyal Harley Davidson users, called HOGs (for Harley Owners Group), were to be trailblazers for the successful growth to come.

Beals had company on his odyssey: Willie G. Davidson, grandson of the company's founder and the vice president of design. Davidson was an interesting contrast to the more urbane Beals. His was the image of a middle-aged hippie. He wore a Viking helmet over his long, unkempt hair, and a straggly beard hid some of his wind-burned face. With his aged leather jacket, Davidson fit in nicely at the HOG rallies.

THE STRUGGLE BACK

In December 1986 Harley Davidson asked Congress to remove the tariff barriers, more than a year earlier than originally planned. The company's confidence had been restored, and it believed it could now compete with the Japanese head to head.[6]

Production Improvements

Shortly after the buyout, Beals and other managers visited Japanese plants in Japan and Honda's assembly plant in Marysville, Ohio. They were impressed that they were being beaten not by "robotics, or culture, or morning calisthenics and company songs, [but by] professional managers who understood their business and paid attention to detail."[7] As a result, Japanese operating costs were as much as 30 percent lower than Harley's.[8]

Beals and his managers tried to implement some of the Japanese management techniques. They divided each plant into profit centers, assigning

---

[5]Robert L. Rose, "Vrooming Back," *Wall Street Journal* (Aug. 31, 1990): 1.

[6]"Harley Back in High Gear," *Forbes* (April 20, 1987): 8.

[7]Dexter Hutchins, "Having a Hard Time with Just-in-Time," *Fortune* (June 19, 1986): 65.

[8]John A. Saathoff, "Workshop Report: Maintain Excellence through Change," *Target* (Spring 1989): 3.

managers total responsibility within their particular area. Just-in-time (JIT) inventory and a materials-as-needed (MAN) system sought to control and minimize all inventories both inside and outside the plants. Quality circles (QCs) were formed to increase employee involvement in quality goals and to improve communication between management and workers. See the following box for further discussion of quality circles. Another new program called statistical operator control (SOC) gave employees the responsibility for checking the quality of their own work and making proper correcting adjustments. Efforts were made to improve labor relations by more sensitivity to employees and their problems as well as better employee assistance and benefits. Certain product improvements were also introduced, notably a new engine and mountings on rubber to reduce vibration. A well-accepted equipment innovation was to build stereo systems and intercoms into the motorcycle helmets.

The production changes between 1981 and 1988 caused some dramatic results:[9]

Inventory fell by 67 percent.

Productivity increased by 50 percent.

Scrap and rework fell 67 percent.

Defects per unit fell 70 percent.

In the 1970s the joke among industry experts was, "If you're buying a Harley, you'd better buy two—one for spare parts."[10] Now this had obviously changed, but the change still had to be communicated to consumers, and believed.

INFORMATION BOX

QUALITY CIRCLES

Quality circles were adopted by Japan in an effort to rid its industries of poor quality control and junkiness after World War II. Quality circles are worker-management committees that meet regularly, usually weekly, to talk about production problems, plan ways to improve productivity and quality, and resolve job-related gripes on both sides. They have been described as "the single most significant explanation for the truly outstanding quality of goods and services produced in Japan."[11] For example, Mazda had 2147 circles, with more than 16,000

---

[9]Hutchins, "Having a Hard Time," 66.
[10]Hutchins, "Having a Hard Time," 66.
[11]"A Partnership to Build the New Workplace," *Business Week* (June 30, 1980): 101.

employees involved. They usually consisted of seven to eight volunteer members who met on their own time to discuss and solve the issues that concerned them. In addition to making major contributions to increased productivity and quality, they provided employees an opportunity to participate and gain a sense of accomplishment.[12]

The idea—like so many ideas adopted by the Japanese—did not originate with them: It came from two American personnel consultants. The Japanese refined the idea and ran with it. Now American industry has rediscovered quality circles. Some firms have found them a desirable way to promote teamwork and good feelings and to avoid at least some of the adversarial relations stemming from collective bargaining and union grievances that must be negotiated.

Despite sterling claims for quality circles, they have not always worked out well. Some workers claim they smack of "tokenism" and are more a facade than anything practical. Questions are also raised as to how much lasting benefits such circles have, once the novelty has worn off. Others doubt that the time invested in quality circles by management and workers is that productive. And few U.S. workers accept the idea of participating in quality circles on their own time.

How would you feel about devoting an hour or more to quality circle meetings every week or so, on your own time? If your answer is "no way," do you think this is a fair attitude on your part? Why or why not?

Marketing Moves

Despite its bad times and its poor quality, Harley had a cadre of loyal customers almost unparalleled. Company research maintained that 92 percent of its customers remained with Harley.[13] Despite such hard core loyalists, however, the company had always had a serious public image problem. It was linked to an image of the pot-smoking, beer-drinking, woman-chasing, tattoo-covered, leather-clad biker: "When your company's logo is the number one requested in tattoo parlors, it's time to get a licensing program that will return your reputation to the ranks of baseball, hot dogs, and apple pie."[14]

Part of Harley's problem had been with bootleggers, who had helped ruin the name by placing it on unlicensed goods of poor quality. Now the company began to use warrants and federal marshalls to crack down on unauthorized uses of its logo at motorcycle conventions. And it began licensing its name and logo on a wide variety of products, from leather jackets to

[12] As described in a Mazda ad in *Forbes* (May 24, 1982): 5.
[13] Mark Marvel, "The Gentrified HOG," *Esquire* (July 1989): 25.
[14] "Thunder Road," *Forbes* (July 18, 1983): 32.

cologne to jewelry—even to pajamas, sheets, and towels. Suddenly retailers realized that these licensed goods were popular and were even being bought by a new customer segment, undreamed of until now: bankers, doctors, lawyers, and entertainers. These new customers soon expanded their horizons to include the Harley Davidson bikes themselves. They joined the HOGs, only now they became known as *Rubbies*—the rich urban bikers. And high prices for bikes did not bother them in the least.

Beals was quick to capitalize on this new market with an expanded product line with expensive heavyweights. In 1989 the largest motorcycle was introduced, the Fat Boy, with 80 cubic inches of V-twin engine and capable of a top speed of 150 MPH. By 1991 Harley had 20 models, ranging in price from $4,500 to $15,000.

The Rubbies brought Harley back to a leading position in the industry by 1989, with almost 60 percent of the super heavyweight motorcycle market; by the first quarter of 1993, this had become 63 percent. See Figure 14.1. The importance of this customer to Harley could be seen in the demographic statistics supplied by the *Wall Street Journal* in 1990: "One in three of today's Harley Davidson buyers are professionals or managers. About 60 percent have attended college, up from only 45 percent in 1984. Their median age is 35, and their median household income has risen sharply to $45,000 from $36,000 five years earlier."[15]

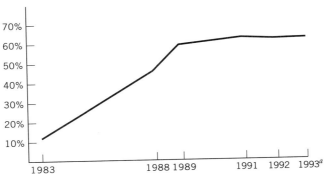

Figure 14.1. Harley Davidson's share of the U.S. heavyweight motorcycle market, selected years, 1983–1993.
(*Sources:* Company reports; R. L. Polk & Company; Gary Slutsker, "Hog Wild," *Forbes* (May 24, 1993): 45–46.)

aData as of first quarter 1993.

[15]Rose, "Vrooming Back," 1.

In 1989 Beals stepped down as CEO, turning the company over to Richard Teerlink, who was chief operating officer of the Motorcycle Division. Beals, however, retained his position as chairman of the board. The legacy of Beals in the renaissance of Harley was particularly notable for his bringing it out of the internal production orientation that had long characterized the firm. See the following information box for a discussion of an internal versus an external (marketing) orientation.

INFORMATION BOX

INTERNAL VS. EXTERNAL (MARKETING) ORIENTATION

Managers sometimes focus primarily on internal factors, such as technology and cost cutting. They subsequently see the key to attracting customers in improving production and distribution efficiency and lowering costs if possible. Henry Ford pioneered this philosophy in the early 1900s with his Model T. Harley stuck for decades with this orientation in the absence of competition. The internal orientation is most appropriate in three situations (with the third one often of unknown risk):

1. When demand for a product exceeds supply, such as in new technologies and in developing countries.
2. When the product cost is high and the market can be expanded only if costs can be brought down.
3. When there is a present lack of significant competition, and no competitive threat is expected either because of severe entry requirements to the industry or because the market is limited.

Obviously, Harley Davidson in the 1960s had made a major miscalculation with the third situation, assuming that the motorcycle market would be forever limited.

An external, or marketing, orientation recognizes the fallacy of the assumption that products will forever sell themselves "if we maintain our production and technological superiority." Looking outside the firm to the market environment results in giving major priority to determining customers' needs and wants, assessing how these may be changing as evidenced by shifts in buying patterns, and adapting products and services accordingly. The external focus also permits more responsiveness to other external forces that may be influencers, such as major competitive thrusts, changing laws and regulations, economic conditions, and the like. With such an external orientation, attention will more likely be directed to locating new opportunities brought about by changing conditions, rather than focusing on internal production and technology. Such an orientation is more geared to meeting and even anticipating change.

Do all firms need a marketing orientation? Can you think of any that probably do not and will not?

SUCCESS

By 1993 Harley Davidson had a new problem, one born of success. Now it could not even come close to meeting demand. Customers faced empty showrooms, except perhaps for rusty trade-ins or antiques. Waiting time for a new bike could be 6 months or longer, unless the customer was willing to pay a 10 percent or higher premium to some gray marketer advertising in biker magazines.

Some of the 600 independent U.S. dealers worried that these empty showrooms and long waiting lists would induce their customers to turn to foreign imports, much as they had several decades before. But other dealers recognized that somehow Beals and company had engendered a brand loyalty unique in this industry, and perhaps in all industries. Assuaging the lack of big bike business, dealers were finding other sources of revenues. Harley's branded line of merchandise, available only at Harley dealers and promoted through glossy catalogs, had really taken off. Buyers snapped up Harley black leather jackets at $500, fringed leather bras at $65, even shot glasses at $12—all it seemed to take was the Harley name and logo. So substantial was this ancillary business that in 1992 noncycle business generated $155.7 million in sales, up from $130.3 million in 1991.

Production

In one sense, Harley's production situation was enviable: It had far more demand than production capability. More than this, it had such a loyal body of customers that delays were not likely to turn many away to competitors. The problem, of course, was that full potential was not being realized.

Richard Teerlink, the successor of Beals, expressed the corporate philosophy to expanding quantity to meet the demand: "Quantity isn't the issue, quality is the issue. We learned in the early 1980s you do not solve problems by throwing money at them."[16]

The company increased output slowly. In early 1992 it was making 280 bikes a day; by 1993 it was up to 345 a day. With increased capital spending, goals were to produce 420 bikes a day, but not until 1996.

Export Potential

Some contrary concerns with Teerlink's conservative expansion plans surfaced in regard to international operations. The European export market beckoned. Harleys had become very popular in Europe, but the company had promised its domestic dealers that exports would not go beyond 30 per-

---

[16]Gary Slutsker, "Hog Wild," *Forbes* (May 24, 1993): 46.

cent of total production until the North American market was fully satisfied. Suddenly the European big-bike market grew by an astounding 33 percent between 1990 and 1992. Yet because of its production constraints, Harley could maintain only a 9 percent to 10 percent share of this market. In other words, it was giving away business to foreign competitors.

To enhance its presence in Europe, Harley opened a branch office of its HOG club in Frankfurt, Germany, for its European fans.

Specifics of the Resurgence of Harley Davidson

Table 14.1 shows Harley's trend in revenues and net income since 1982. The growth in sales and profits did not go unnoticed by the investment community. In 1990 Harley Davidson stock sold for $7 per share; in January 1993 it hit $39. Its market share of heavyweight motorcycles (751 cubic centimeters displacement and larger) had soared from 12.5 percent in 1983 to 63 percent by 1993. Let the Japanese have the lightweight bike market! Harley would dominate the heavyweights.

Harley acquired Holiday Rambler in 1986. As a wholly owned subsidiary, this manufacturer of recreational and commercial vehicles was judged by Harley management to be compatible with the existing motorcycle business as well as moderating some of the seasonality of the motorcycle business. The diversification proved rather mediocre. In 1992 Rambler accounted for 26 percent of total corporate sales, but only 2 percent of profits.[17]

Table 14.1 Harley Davidson's Growth in Revenue and Income 1983–1992 (in $ Millions)

Year	Revenue	Net Income
1982	$ 210	($25.1)
1983	254	1.0
1984	294	2.9
1985	287	2.6
1986	295	4.3
1987	685	17.7
1988	757	27.2
1989	791	32.6
1990	865	38.3
1991	940	37.0
1992	1100	54.0

Source: Company annual reports.
Commentary: The steady climb in sales and profits, except for a pause in 1985, is noteworthy. The total gain in revenues over these 11 years is 423.8 percent, while income has risen more than 50-fold since 1983.

[17]Company annual reports.

Big motorcycles, made in America by a single U.S. manufacturer, continued the rage. Harley's 90th anniversary was celebrated in Milwaukee on June 12, 1993. As many as 100,000 people, including 18,000 HOGs, were there to celebrate. Hotel rooms were sold out for a 60-mile radius. Harley Davidson was up and running.

ANALYSIS

One of Vaughan Beals's first moves after the 1981 leveraged buyout was to improve production efficiency and quality control. This became the foundation for the strategic regeneration moves to come. In this quest he borrowed heavily from the Japanese, in particular in cultivating employee involvement.

The cultivation of a new customer segment for the big bikes had to be a major factor in the company's resurgence. To some, that more affluent consumers embraced the big, flashy Harley motorcycles was a surprise of no small moment. After all, how could you have two more incompatible groups than the stereotyped black-jacketed cyclists and the Rubbies? Perhaps part of the change was due to high-profile people such as Beals and some of his executives, who frequently participated at motorcycle rallies and charity rides. Technological and comfort improvements in motorcycles and their equipment added to the new attractiveness. Dealers were also coaxed to make their stores more inviting.

Along with this, expanding the product mix not only made such Harley-branded merchandise a windfall for company and dealers alike, but also piqued the interest of upscale customers in motorcycles themselves. The company was commendably aggressive in running with the growing popularity of the ancillary merchandise and making it well over a $100 million revenue booster.

Some questions remain. How durable will be this popularity, both of the big bikes and the complementary merchandise, with this affluent customer segment? Will it prove to be only a passing fad? If such should be the case, then Harley needs to seek diversifications as quickly as possible. But its one major diversification, the Holiday Rambler Corporation, was no notable success. Diversifications often prove to be earnings disappointments compared with a firm's core business.

Another question concerns Harley's slowness in expanding production capability. Faced with a burgeoning demand, should a company go slowly, be carefully protective of quality, and refrain from heavy debt commitments? This has been Harley's most recent strategy. See the following issue box for a discussion of the wisdom of a slow-growth policy.

ISSUE BOX

HOW WISE IS A DELIBERATE SLOW-GROWTH POLICY?

This question could also be described as the issue between being conservative and being aggressive. On the one hand, with a conservative growth approach in a growing market, a firm risks being unable to expand its resources sufficiently to handle the potential, and it may have to abdicate a good share of the growing market to competitors who are willing and able to expand their capability to meet the demands of the market.

On the other hand, an aggressive strategy for growth becomes vulnerable if the growth is a short-term fad rather than a more permanent situation. A firm can easily become overextended in the buoyancy of booming business, only to see the collapse of such business jeopardize its viability.

Harley's conservative decision was undoubtedly influenced by concerns about expanding beyond the limits of good quality control. The decision, right or wrong, was probably also influenced by management's belief that Harley had a loyal body of customers who would not switch despite the wait. We might accept this latter hypothesis, but are customers likely to be less loyal in Europe?

Do you think Harley Davidson made the right decision to expand conservatively? Why or why not? Defend your position.

WHAT CAN BE LEARNED?

A firm can come back from adversity. The resurrection of Harley Davidson almost from the point of extinction proves that adversity can be overcome. It need not be fatal.

What does it take for a turnaround? Above all it takes a leader who has the vision and the confidence that things can be changed for the better. The change may not necessitate anything particularly innovative; it may involve only a rededication to basics, such as improved quality control or an improved commitment to customer service. But such a return to basics requires that a demoralized or apathetic organization be rejuvenated and remotivated. This is leadership of a high order. If the core business has still been maintained, there is at least a base to work from.

Preserve the Core Business at All Costs. Every viable firm has a basic core or distinctive position—sometimes called an *ecological niche*—in the business environment. This unique position may be due to its particular location or to a certain product. It may come from somewhat different operating methods or from the customers served. In these particular strengths, a firm is better than its competitors. This is the basic core of its survivability. Though it may diversify and expand far beyond this, it should not abandon its final bastion of strength.

Harley almost did this. Its core—and indeed, only—business was its heavyweight bikes sold to a limited and at the time not particularly savory customer segment, but one with surprising loyalty. Harley almost lost this core business by abandoning reasonable quality control to the point that its motorcycles became the butt of jokes. To his credit, upon assuming leadership Beals acted quickly to correct the production and employee motivation problems. With its core preserved, Harley could now pursue other avenues of expansion.

The power of a mystique. Few products are able to gain a mystique or cult following. Coors beer did back in the 1960s and early 1970s, when it became the brew of celebrities and the emblem of the purity and freshness of the West. In the cigarette industry, Marlboro rose to become the top seller on a somewhat similar advertising and image thrust: the Marlboro man. Perhaps the Ford Mustang had a mystique at one time. And then, somehow, the big bikes of Harley Davidson developed a mystique. The HOGs expanded to include the Rubbies: two disparate customer segments, but both loyal to their Harleys. The mystique led to "logo magic": Simply put the Harley Davidson name and logo on all kinds of merchandise, and watch the sales take off.

How does a firm develop (or acquire) a mystique? There is no simple answer, no guarantee. Certainly a company's product has to be unique and somehow different from competitors'. But this is hardly enough—indeed, most firms strive for this and never achieve a mystique. Image-building advertising, focusing on the type of person the firm is targeting, may help some. Perhaps even better is image-building advertising of the persons customers might wish to emulate. But the black-leather-jacketed, perhaps bearded, motorcyclist?

Perhaps in the final analysis, acquiring a mystique is more accidental and fortuitous than deliberate. Two lessons, however, can be learned about mystiques. First, do not expect them to last forever. Second, run with them as long as you can, and try to expand the reach of the name or logo to other goods, even unrelated ones, through licensing.

CONSIDER

What additional learning insights can you see coming from this Harley Davidson resurgence?

QUESTIONS

1. Do you think Beals's rejuvenation strategy for Harley Davidson was the best? Discuss and evaluate other strategies that he might have pursued.

2. How durable do you think the Rubbies' infatuation with the heavy-weight Harleys will be? What leads you to this conclusion?

3. A Harley Davidson stockholder criticizes present management: "It is a mistake of the greatest magnitude that we abdicate a decent share of the European motorcycle market to foreign competitors, simply because we do not gear up our production to meet the demand." Discuss.

4. Given the resurgence of Harley Davidson in the early 1990s, would you invest money in the company? Discuss, considering as many factors bearing on this decision as you can.

5. "Harley Davidson's resurgence is only the purest luck. Who could have predicted, or influenced, the new popularity of big bikes with the affluent?" Discuss.

6. "The tariff increase on Japanese motorcycles in 1983 gave Harley Davidson badly needed breathing room. In the final analysis, politics is more important than marketing in competing with foreign firms." What are your thoughts?

INVITATION TO ROLE PLAY

1. You are a representative of a mutual fund with a major investment in Harley Davidson. You are particularly critical of Vaughan Beals's visible presence at motorcycle rallies and his hobnobbing with black-jacketed cycle gangs. He maintains this is a fruitful way to maintain a loyal core of customers. Playing the devil's advocate (a person who opposes a position to establish its merits and validity), argue against Beals's practices.

2. As a vice president at Harley Davidson, you believe the recovery efforts should have gone well beyond the heavyweight bikes into lightweights. What arguments do you present for this change in strategy, and what specific recommendations do you make for such a new course of action? What contrary arguments do you expect? How will you counter them?

3. As a staff assistant to Vaughan Beals, you have been charged to design a marketing strategy to bring a mystique to the Harley Davidson name. How do you propose to do this? Be as specific as you can, and defend your reasoning.

INVITATION TO RESEARCH

What is the situation with Harley Davidson today? Has the strategy changed? Has penetration of the European market increased? Is the mystique still apparent?

PART IV

MARKETING SUCCESSES

CHAPTER 15

Microsoft: Harnessing Innovation

In the last few months of 1992, what had been increasingly evident throughout the year finally became indisputable: the passing of the leadership of IBM in the computer industry. As the *Wall Street Journal* described it on December 21, 1992, "The generational shift in the computer industry is unfolding . . . As leadership slips away from the old behemoth . . . it is being picked up by two young juggernauts—Intel Corp. and Microsoft Corp.—which both were nurtured by IBM."[1]

This case concerns one of these "young juggernauts," Microsoft, and its cofounder and leader, William H. Gates III, who by 1992 was the richest man in America, with a net worth of over $7 billion. He was then 36 years old, and a bachelor.

BILL GATES

Bill Gates was born on October 28, 1955, in Seattle, Washington. His father was a prominent attorney, and his mother was to become a regent of the University of Washington. Growing up in an affluent and socially prominent family, it was not long before his genius intellect became clearly evident. By 11 years of age, he was far ahead of his peers in math and science, and his parents enrolled him in Lakeside, a prep school noted for its rigorous academic environment. There he was exposed to the primitive com-

---

[1]Stephen Kreider Yoder, "How IBM's Heirs Plan to Expand Empires in Computer Industry," *Wall Street Journal* (Dec. 21, 1992): A1, A4.

puters of the day and became immediately hooked. He spent every spare moment with computers, and he even created a computer program at age 13.

On the math achievement test Lakeside gave its students, Gates was number one. He was later to score a perfect 800 on the math SAT, and was bound for Harvard.

Bill Gates would later tell a friend that he went to Harvard University to learn from people smarter than he was . . . and left disappointed.[2] When he arrived at Cambridge, Massachusetts, in fall 1973, he had no real sense of what he wanted to do with his life; although his academic major was prelaw, he had little interest in becoming a lawyer. Computers and the entrepreneurial opportunities emerging in a rapidly changing technology engrossed his attention (as did a mean game of poker) in these undergraduate years. It came as little surprise that he dropped out of Harvard in 1975 to cofound Microsoft Corporation with a longtime friend, Paul G. Allen. Microsoft became the most successful startup company in the history of American business, and it was to become the world's largest microcomputer software company. Bill Gates was 20 years old at its founding.

What kind of person is Bill Gates? Of his intellect and overall ability there is no question. Unlike many entrepreneurs, he seems also to have the talent to run a massive and growing operation. However, criticisms of his character and his personality have flourished:

> "Gates is tenacious. That's what's scary . . . he always comes back, like Chinese water torture. His form of entertainment is tearing people to shreds."

> "A bad personality and a great intellect. In a place like Harvard, where there are a lot of bright kids, when you are better than your peers, some tend to be nice and others obnoxious. He was the latter."

> "Bill Gates wants it all. And he's on his way to getting it."[3]

HISTORICAL DEVELOPMENT OF COMPUTER TECHNOLOGY

The modern computer was first developed in the 1940s during World War II. But the concept goes back to the 1800s when a mathematical genius, Charles Babbage, unsuccessfully tried to develop an "analytical machine" to solve mathematical equations. By the end of the century, however, people used punch cards to help tabulate information from the 1890 census. The machine used was designed by Herman Hollerith, a young engineer. Soon, punch cards became widely used in all kinds of office machines, and Hollerith's company would be absorbed by a New York firm destined to

---

[2] James Wallace and Jim Erickson, *Hard Drive* (New York: John Wiley, 1992), 53.
[3] Wallace and Erickson, *Hard Drive*, quotes listed on backpiece.

dominate the computer industry for almost a century—International Business Machines (IBM).

In the 1930s IBM had financed the development of a large computing machine, the Mark I, finished in 1944. It could multiply two 23-digit numbers in about 5 seconds. But it was an electromechanical machine with thousands of noisy relays serving as switching units.

A major improvement came with the vacuum tube. The first electronic digital computer, the ENIAC, was unveiled in 1946. It weighed 30 tons and took up more space than a two-car garage. But it could handle about 5,000 additions and subtractions per second, and in its final stages of completion it helped the physicists at Los Alamos build the first atomic bomb.

In 1947 came the big breakthrough in computing technology, the transistor, which could now replace the vacuum tube. These transistors, or semiconductors as they became known, were smaller, more reliable, and cheaper to make than the old vacuum tubes. The first semiconductors were made of crystals of germanium. Later, silicon became more popular.

Another technological breakthrough came in the late 1950s. It was found that networks of transistors could be etched on a single piece of silicon with thin metallic connectors. Such integrated circuits, or chips as they became known, provided the foundation for all modern electronics, and they made possible the development of much smaller, faster, and more powerful computers.

In the 1950s IBM was so dominant that the other makers of large, mainframe computers were called the seven dwarfs. They all made large mainframe computers that cost hundreds of thousands of dollars, needed many technicians to service them, and also required careful and controlled access to minimize dust, temperature, and humidity contaminants. Now, with the advances in technology and the development of the semiconductor, more practical and accessible computers—minicomputers—were possible. But in a grievous error IBM elected not to enter this new market.

Thus, it provided an unimaginable opportunity for new computer companies. Digital Equipment Corporation quickly became the leader, establishing the minicomputer market in 1965 when it introduced its PDP-8 (shorthand for Program Data Processor), which cost $18,500. It abandoned the traditional method of data input through punch cards fed into the machine; instead, the user could communicate with the computer via a keyboard.

In 1971 Intel developed the microprocessor. A microchip made it possible to encode the entire central processing unit of a computer onto a silicon chip no larger than a thumbnail. Somehow, this step was not undertaken by the large corporations, such as Digital Equipment Corporation and IBM, with their financial and technological resources. Instead, it was left to entrepreneurs, to people like Bill Gates, Steve Jobs of Apple, and similar men, usually young, with vision and a hunger for achievement.

THE MAKING OF MICROSOFT

In 1974 MITS (Micro Instrumentation and Telemetry Systems), a small company in Albuquerque, New Mexico, built Altair, the first personal computer to have any real impact on the market. Although it had serious shortcomings, its low price stimulated considerable demand from hobbyists who had dreamed of having their own personal computer, even if they had to tediously assemble it.

Bill Gates and Paul Allen, friends from high school, developed a BASIC software program for the Altair that greatly enhanced its marketability. In order to carry out negotiations with MITS, Gates and Allen formed a partnership called Micro-Soft (for microcomputer software; the hyphen was later dropped) in July 1975. Their business objective was to develop languages for the Altair and for other microcomputers that were bound to appear soon on the market. Thus, Microsoft was the first company formed for the specific purpose of producing software for such computers.

In spring 1977 Microsoft had six employees and moved into eighth floor offices in downtown Albuquerque. But for the microcomputer industry to take off it needed more reliable machines, and these began to appear in 1977—notably the TRS-80 by Tandy, the PET by Commodore, and the Apple II. Microsoft now expanded its product line beyond BASIC, with Fortran in July 1977 and later COBOL and Pascal.

By the end of 1978, Microsoft had doubled its sales over the previous year, reaching its first million, and it now had 13 employees. Allen and Gates shared the executive tasks. Since both were from Washington, it was perhaps inevitable that as Microsoft grew larger they would opt to move it to Seattle, which they did in summer 1978. Most employees moved with the company. For 1979 sales reached $2.5 million, with worldwide sales of BASIC passing 1 million copies. Microsoft was poised for its major breakthrough.

In 1980 IBM was the uncontested leader in the computer world, with sales of $28 billion. But it was not yet a player in the personal computer market. Unable to buy out a suitable firm already in this business, such as Apple, IBM decided to go ahead internally but to follow Apple's strategy of encouraging software development by independent firms.

Microsoft and IBM signed a contract November 6, 1980, for Microsoft to provide software programs. Such a collaboration was particularly significant: The industry giant was asking a small firm with a 25-year-old president to work with it in a major new developmental effort.

By mid-1981, Microsoft had 100 employees, with 35 of these involved with the IBM project. IBM accepted the operating system created by Microsoft, and MS-DOS became the official system of the IBM PC. IBM announced its first microcomputer on August 12, 1981, and it was available in stores 2 months later.

It now remained for Microsoft to make MS-DOS the standard for the industry. Less than a year after the IBM PC was announced, a number of other manufacturers also were adapting to the MS-DOS. It began to catch on even more quickly in 1983 when Lotus released a spreadsheet program which operated only under MS-DOS. In just 3 months, Lotus 1-2-3 became the best-selling software package for spreadsheets for 16-bit machines, and this was a great boost for MS-DOS machines. By the end of 1983, 500,000 copies of MS-DOS had been sold, about 400,000 of them through IBM. Microsoft sales for the year reached $69 million, and the firm had grown to 383 employees. MS-DOS was now available for more than 60 computer systems, and other computer manufacturers were touting the "IBM compatibility" of their products—that is, their ability to run software written for the PC.

Going Public

Experts wondered why Gates waited so long to take Microsoft public. Success had continued unabated, and by 1986 its basic software was running millions of IBM personal computers and clones. By now it had myriad versions of computer languages and fast-selling applications programs such as spreadsheets and word-processing packages for IBM, Apple, and other personal computers.

Gates had stood firm in 1983 when two of his archcompetitors, Lotus and Ashton-Tate, had floated stock worth a total of $74 million. He did not budge in 1984 and 1985 when three other microcomputer software companies sold $54 million of stock. He did not budge, even though going public with a successful venture was the path to great riches.

Gates' reasons for procrastination were rather simple. Growing up in affluence, he valued control of his time and his company more than personal wealth. And unlike his competitors, Microsoft was not dominated by venture capital investors eager to harvest some of their gains. Besides, the business "gushed" cash, as *Fortune* phrased it.[4] Pretax profits were running as high as 34 percent of sales, and Microsoft needed no outside money to expand.

But by 1986 a public offering seemed necessary and desirable. Gates had been selling his managers and technical experts shares and stock options, and with over 500 people owning shares, this would be enough to force the company to register with the Securities and Exchange Commission (SEC). At this point it seemed prudent to sell enough shares to enough investors to create a liquid market, so that trading would not be difficult.

On March 13, 1986, shares were offered at $21. By the end of the first day of trading, some 2.5 million shares had changed hands, and the price of

---

[4]Bro Uttal, "Inside the Deal That Made Bill Gates $350,000,000," *Fortune* (July 21, 1986): 24.

Microsoft's stock stood at $27.75. This was soon to zoom to $35.50 before settling back to $31.25. Microsoft raised $61 million, and the public put a market value of $350 million on the 45 percent stake Bill Gates retained, making him one of the richest Americans. In subsequent years, he became the richest American of all, as the growth and value of Microsoft stock doubled and tripled.

DOMINANCE

A 1991 article in *Forbes* magazine bore the title, "Can Anyone Stop Bill Gates?"[5] The article noted that Microsoft was "massacring its competitors" and that it seemed to be heading for a near monopoly in the software industry. In the time since the article appeared, Microsoft has certainly not faltered—during this same time period, the behemoth of the computer industry, IBM itself, has fared badly as described in Chapter 5, with its stock price collapsing amid layoffs of tens of thousands of employees and billion-dollar writeoffs as part of a major restructuring.

The road to market dominance for Microsoft was MS-DOS. This software system guided the inner workings of almost all of the 40 million IBM PCs and IBM-compatible personal computers in existence as of 1991. With MS-DOS standard for almost any PC, a constant stream of royalties was pouring into the company, providing high profits and furnishing ample funds for research and further developments in the forefront of technology, such as Windows.

The goal of Windows was to transform MS-DOS from a monochrome, arcane, text-based environment into a multicolor, user-friendly, graphics-based environment. Achieving this was not easy. The project began in September 1981, and after a number of embarrassing delays from announced scheduled introductions, it finally came out in November 1985. However, success was far from immediate. Few machines at that time could do justice to this new environment, either in their color monitors or in their operational capability. For example, for a PC with two disk drives, Windows was unbearably slow.

Windows was to set company records for the greatest number of development hours. More than 24 developers devoted all their time to Windows for more than 3 years, and this did not include testing and documentation time. By the time it was released, Windows had had four product managers and three development directors.[6]

---

[5] Kathleen K. Wiegner and Julie Pitta, "Can Anyone Stop Bill Gates?" *Forbes* (Apr. 1, 1991): 108–14.

[6] Daniel Ichbiah and Susan L. Knepper, *The Making of Microsoft* (Rocklin, CA: Prima Publishing, 1991), 192.

Just a few years later, Windows became Microsoft's best-selling software. By 1992 Microsoft was selling more than 1 million copies of its Windows program per month. This all but cemented the program's position as the standard operating system for computer users. Table 15.1 shows the great increase in Microsoft's sales and profits since it went public in 1986. Note how well the percentage growth rates in sales and profits per year have been maintained, despite the increasing size of the firm. As any firm grows larger, it has more and more difficulty holding the percentage growth rate.

As of the beginning of 1993, Microsoft planned to introduce a new operating system, called Windows NT, thereby building on the runaway success of its Windows program. The Windows NT would continue to offer everything in the Windows operating system but would add a multitude of other features, such as the ability to run many programs simultaneously, to safeguard against unauthorized use, to use vast amounts of memory, to tie many machines into networks, and to run on "multiprocessing" systems that link many chips together.[7]

Both Microsoft and Intel, the premier maker of chips, were operating under the cloud of possible antitrust rulings for building virtual monopolies with products so heavily protected by patents and copyrights that legal duplication was practically impossible for competitors. With the operating system and the microprocessor being a PC's most crucial components, any PC buyer who wanted a powerful machine able to run the biggest selection of software had to go the Intel-Microsoft route. The likelihood of competitors being able to break through seemed ever more remote as Microsoft and Intel grew ever larger, were able to pour more and more funds into research, and were able to spread their costs over millions of units, making them the lowest-cost producers of the most advanced technological products. Table 15.2 shows the growth in sales revenues of Microsoft and its major competi-

Table 15.1   Microsoft's Growth in Sales and Profits, 1986–1992 (in $ thousands)

Year ended June 30	Net Revenues	Percent Increase	Net Income	Percent Increase
1986	$ 197,514	40.7%	$ 39,254	62.9%
1987	345,890	75.1	71,878	83.1
1988	590,827	70.8	123,908	54.2
1989	803,530	36.0	170,538	47.1
1990	1,183,446	47.3	279,186	63.7
1991	1,843,432	55.8	462,743	65.7
1992	2,758,725	49.7	708,060	55.9

Source: Company annual reports.

[7]Yoder, "Heirs Plan to Expand," 1.

Table 15.2   Sales Revenues for Major PC Software Companies, 1987–1992 (in $ millions)

Company	1987	1988	1989	1990	1992
Borland	$ 38	$ 82	$ 91	$ 227	$ 474
Computer Associates	309	709	1,030	1,348	1,688
Lotus Development	396	469	557	685	903
Microsoft	346	591	831	1,183	2,759
Novell	—	—	422	498	860
Oracle	131	282	584	971	1,241

Source: Business Week 1000 Companies, 1990, 1991, 1992; and *Forbes* (January 4, 1993): 118.

tors in the PC software industry. By 1992 the growth of Microsoft had far exceeded that of its competitors, leaving it well over a billion dollars larger than its largest competitor, Computer Associates, much larger than Lotus, and with a growth rate far outstripping these competitors.

Whether the FTC eventually constrains the market dominance of Microsoft and its ally, Intel, remains to be seen.

ANALYSIS

Undoubtedly the initial success of Microsoft reflects Bill Gates's brilliant technological expertise coupled with a tenacious entrepreneurial business sense. But whereas most entrepreneurs are unable to transfer entrepreneurial talent to the organizational ability needed to manage large-scale operations, Gates seemed able to make the transference with ease. But let us go beyond the personal talents of the man and examine specific contributors to the runaway success of Microsoft.

A Distinctive and Overpowering Product

The early development of the DOS operating program gave Microsoft a major competitive edge. How durable and encompassing this edge would be was not clear, but Bill Gates was able to sell it to the mighty IBM and to persuade IBM to let him sell the program to all comers, thus allowing other manufacturers to make PC clones. The ensuing competition drove down prices, intensified innovation, and left Microsoft in the center of an $83-billion-a-year industry worldwide. While competitors struggled to match or surpass the DOS program, they were unable to make any significant inroads. Buttressed by good patent protection and ever stronger commitment to research and development, Microsoft remained unassailable. See Table 15.3 for the growth in research and development expenditures from 1986 through 1992. Note in particular the heavy commitment as a percent of sales.

Part of the durability of Microsoft's operating system is simple economics. Computer users have heavy sunk costs that act as a barrier to entry for new software. For a new operating system to be widely accepted, it would force users to throw out their old application software and buy new versions, in the process incurring sizable costs of additional software as well as substantial retraining. Consequently, Gates is the sought-after partner with hardware makers that no small firm can be.

A further competitive advantage of Microsoft today is that it is selling items that have very low marginal costs of production. For example, the first copy of a program may cost $20 million for research and development. But additional copies may cost only $20 for the disk and the manual.[8] Consequently, Microsoft projects such a major cost advantage that newcomers, no matter how much they might like to discount in order to enter the market, are hardly likely to be successful.

Staying in the Technological Forefront

Better than any other firm that has grown to relatively large size, Microsoft has been able to maintain its vitality and innovativeness. Perhaps reflecting the leadership of Gates, the creativity flair has flourished.

Largely credited with this has been the organizing of small, independent "business units" of programmers and marketers, each geared to specific business goals. The groups are small enough that Gates can easily interact with the key members. Each of these groups is responsible for a particular type of software. Business unit managers (BUMs) monitor how their products stack up against competitors in all aspects, from a program's technical

Table 15.3   Microsoft Growth in Expenditures for Research and Development, 1986–1992 (in $ thousands)

Year ended June 30	Research and Development Expenditures	Percentage Increase	Percent of Sales
1986	$ 20,523	—	10.4%
1987	38,076	85.5%	11.0
1988	69,776	83.3	11.8
1989	110,220	56.0	13.7
1990	180,615	63.9	15.3
1991	235,386	30.3	12.8
1992	352,153	49.6	12.8

Source: Company annual reports.

[8] Example taken from Wiegner and Pitta, "Can Anyone Stop Bill Gates," 110.

sophistication to financial and productivity information their rivals make public. Woe to the unit that does not outperform its competitors.

Business units commonly employ brainstorming to provide ideas for new products, and Gates frequently joins programmers in such sessions. "It's very important to me and to the guys that work for us that Microsoft feel like a small company, even though it isn't one anymore," says Gates.[9] See the following box for a more detailed discussion of brainstorming.

In a rapidly growing company such as Microsoft, an esprit de corps is not surprising. Turnover is low. But Microsoft works its employees hard, with many putting in 75-hour weeks, especially during shipment deadlines for new products. Pay is not particularly high; even Gates paid himself only $190,000 a year in 1990. There are few perks, and no one has a company car. But the company is generous with stock options, and the great increases in company share prices have made dozens of programmers paper millionaires.

Does Microsoft Have Any Threats

Defensive alliances between competitors aimed at combatting Microsoft are possible and are evolving. For example, Lotus and Novell attempted a defensive merger into a company that would have been Microsoft's size, but the deal fell through at the time. Hewlett-Packard and Sun Microsystems are united in battling Microsoft over industry standards for linking different programs.

Microsoft's relationship with a battered IBM has cooled. Perhaps as a result, in 1992 IBM and Apple started a joint venture called Taligent Inc., directly challenging Microsoft in computer operating systems. Taligent will run applications originally written for Apple's Macintosh or IBM's OS/2 as well as applications developed in the future that automate common tasks. This should cut into Microsoft's market share.

In the past Microsoft has been notorious for rushing products to market too quickly, before all the bugs have been worked out. This happened with its original word-processing program, with Windows, and with several other software endeavors. While the problems eventually were corrected, customers may still be conditioned to skip the first version of a new product.

Added to these possible problems of unknown magnitude is the threat of antitrust action, as Microsoft gains an ever more monopolistic position.

Perhaps these threats are gnat-like. But the king of the hill is always the target. Should Microsoft let its guard down on the technological forefront, not anticipate and act quickly enough in potentially promising new directions, then the king of the hill may be supplanted.

---

[9] Brenton Schlender, "How Bill Gates Keeps the Magic Going," *Fortune* (June 18, 1990): 83.

INFORMATION BOX

BRAINSTORMING

Brainstorming is a technique to stimulate group creativity. A group—five to eight seems to be the best size—comes together for the sole purpose of producing ideas, and the more ideas, the better. At this point the quality and practicality of ideas is not a factor: The group simply seeks the greatest number. In a conducive environment, such as when there is no need to impress a boss and no hint of criticism, one idea tends to spark other ideas.

Only after the brainstorming session is over should any efforts be made to cull, evaluate, and select the most acceptable ideas. Alex Osborn, the father of brainstorming, and probably the foremost authority on developing creativity, lists these four rules for effective brainstorming:[10]

1. Criticism is ruled out.
2. Free-wheeling is welcomed; the wilder the idea, the better.
3. Quantity is desired; the greater the number of ideas, the more likely some useful ones will be found.
4. Combination and improvement are sought; participants are encouraged to build on or modify the ideas of others.

The problems should be as specific as possible, and ideally should be limited to one a session. One hour seems to be about the ideal length for such sessions. Brainstorming can be useful, even with participants who are not creative, in producing usable ideas. Osborn describes one typical session in which participants produced 136 ideas in 40 minutes. In addition to stimulating ideas, some of which, one hopes, will be worthy of further development, brainstorming can also be used as a training device to develop the creativity of the individual participants.

For which of the following situations would you expect brainstorming to be most effective, and why?

1. Sales in a particular territory have fallen drastically from last year.
2. Your firm is ready to introduce a new product and is planning its promotional campaign.
3. Your firm wishes to open a new retail outlet and wonders where best to locate it.

POSTSCRIPT

Bill Gates, the most eligible of all bachelors, finally got married on January 1, 1994. Many had predicted that he eventually would marry some famous person from show business; instead he married a marketing manager.

[10] Alex F. Osborn, *Applied Imagination*, 3rd ed. (New York: Scribner's, 1963).

For 1993 sales were just under $4 billion, with net income almost $1 billion, a revenue and earnings growth of 35 percent from the previous year. The company was now moving aggressively into the next hot market, software for the home and children.

Indications were that the Justice Department was intensifying its antitrust investigation of the world's largest software company and would continue to do so for many months. "They're just learning about our business," said Gates. "We've only sent them like a million pieces of paper. They need a million more." This investigation was initially started by the Federal Trade Commission, investigating several charges: (1) that Microsoft undercut rivals through pricing low and preannouncing products (thus helping other firms to quickly bring to market their own ancillary products to those sold by Microsoft) and (2) that it exploited its control of the DOS and Windows programs, vital to the operations of most personal computers, to prevent computer makers from outfitting their machines with rival programs. The FTC deadlocked on whether to take legal action. In late 1993 the Justice Department took over the case.[11]

WHAT CAN BE LEARNED?

Great riches can come from going public with a successful venture.
We saw in this case how Bill Gates became a billionaire—and a few years later the richest American—after he took Microsoft public by issuing stock. He had founded Microsoft in 1975 and waited until 1986 to take it public. Criticism had abounded that he should have done this years earlier, but Gates was not all that interested in personal wealth. In another example of entrepreneurial success, Steven Jobs took his fledgling firm, Apple, public in 1980, only 4 years after he had started it in the family garage, and by 1983 it was worth well over $200 million.

While Gates and Jobs have extraordinary success stories, on smaller scales many small businesses can find themselves attractive to investors seeking growth companies that often offer far greater potential than the behemoths can. If the founder of the business keeps a substantial block of the company's stock, the payoff in the investing public's appraisal of the value of the enterprise can be mind boggling.

Again, beware the "king of the hill" mental trap. As we have seen with IBM and Harley Davidson in particular—firms that became dominant in their particular industry sector and felt unassailable—dominant firms tend to fall

[11]G. Pascal Zachary, "Microsoft Aides to be Deposed in U.S. Probe," *The Wall Street Journal* (June 6, 1993): A3, A6; "America's Most Admired Corporations," *Fortune* (Feb. 7, 1994): 58, 129; "Annual Report of American Industry," *Forbes* (Jan. 3, 1994): 120; and Kathy Rebello et al., "Is Microsoft Too Powerful?" *Business Week* (Mar. 1, 1993): 82-88.

into a particular mindset that leaves them vulnerable to aggressive and innovative competitors. We have called this vulnerability the *three C's syndrome of failure:* complacency, conservatism, and conceit.

To review, *complacency* is smugness, and it typifies the self-satisfied firm content with the status quo and no longer hungry and eager for growth.

Conservatism characterizes a management that is wedded to the past, to the traditional, to the ways things have always successfully been done: "There is no need to change because nothing is different today."

Finally, *conceit* for present and potential competitors can further reinforce the myopia of the managerial perspective. A belief that "we are the best" and that "no one else can touch us" can easily permeate an organization when everything has been going well for years.

These attitudes, which originate with top management, can reduce commitment to consistency of quality, create an aloofness to customer needs and concerns, and allow a lack of innovativeness in seeking new markets and substantially improved products. Also there often is decreased emphasis on pricing for good value and more on maximizing per-unit profits. Thus, the foundation is laid for vulnerability to the aggressive competitor "foolish" enough to challenge a seemingly entrenched dominant firm.

At this time Microsoft certainly shows none of the symptoms of the three C's. But this could come if it takes for granted its mastery of the software and applications market. Remember once-mighty IBM. The frontrunner must maintain constant vigilance to avoid the king-of-the-hill mental trap, with its three C's.

Be aware of the risks if you are a minor player in a high-growth arena. In a high-growth industry, the entrenched, dominant firm has the advantage (despite the eventual danger of a king-of-the-hill mindset, as just described). The dominant firm in such a situation is generating rapidly increasing sales and profits and is able to invest heavily in research and development. Where technology is rapidly changing, this is a major competitive advantage. The firm with low market share faces the need for heavy investment, not only in research and development but also in its promotion budget and its pursuit of distributors as well as other aspects of its marketing strategy. It may have to slash prices to hold or gain market share, and this cuts drastically into profits. The esteemed Boston Consulting Group Matrix, described in the following box, designates such a situation for the low-market-share firm as a question mark: that is, should it even remain in the industry against the formidable odds it faces and the major investments required to be a player?

Of course, there is the possibility that the frontrunner will stumble and become complacent and too conservative. But decades may elapse before the king-of-the-hill mindset may make this frontrunner vulnerable.

INFORMATION BOX

THE BOSTON CONSULTING GROUP MATRIX

The Boston Consulting Group, a leading management consulting firm, has boiled down the major strategy decisions a firm faces to only four, depending on the firm's competitive position in a particular industry and the growth of that industry. Accordingly, a firm's major business categories can be classified as stars, question marks, cash cows, and dogs. Figure 15.1 presents the matrix of this concept.

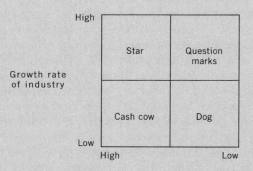

Relative market dominance compared to largest competitor
(market share)

Figure 15.1. Matrix of a firm's major business categories.
Star, dominant market position in a high-growth industry.
Question mark, weak market position in a high-growth industry.
Cash cow, dominant market position in a low-growth industry.
Dog, weak market position in a low-growth industry.

A different strategy implementation is recommended for each of these business categories, as follows:

Category	Strategy Implementation
Stars	*Build.* In a dominant market position and a rapidly growing industry, more investment and long-term profit goals are recommended, even if they come at the expense of short-term profitability.
Question Marks	*Build or Divest.* The decision whether to commit more resources to building such products into leaders or to divest and use company resources elsewhere is not easily

made. It may depend on the strength of major competitors and how well-heeled the company is: For example, a firm may decide it cannot provide sufficient financing to achieve the growth it needs, given the competition.

Cash Cows

Harvest. When in a dominant position in a low-growth industry, the recommended strategy is to reap the harvest of a strong cash flow. Only enough resources should be reinvested to maintain competitive position.

Dogs

Divest. There is no use wasting resources on poor competitive positions in low-growth industries. The recommended strategy is to sell or liquidate this business.

Microsoft is obviously in a star situation, with its dominant position in a high-growth industry. Inroads by smaller competitors thereby become very difficult as they face the question mark scenario.

Do you see any limitations to the Boston Consulting Group's model?

CONSIDER

Can you identify additional learning insights that could be applicable to other firms in other situations?

QUESTIONS

1. Bill Gates has an informal management style, even in his choice of clothes, and he is emulated by the rest of the organization. Evaluate such informality in a large corporation, especially related to its marketing presence.
2. Assess the future prospects of Microsoft using a SWOT analysis (i.e., strengths, weaknesses, opportunities, and threats).
3. If Microsoft's stock price should plummet in a severe stock market decline, do you think Gates will have trouble motivating his employees, given their long working hours, few perks, and relatively low wages?
4. Many other firms in the forefront of a rapidly expanding industry have lost their competitive advantage, perhaps because they have become less hungry, or because the three C's syndrome has crept in. Do you see any reasons why Microsoft would steer clear of the same disincentives for performance excellence?
5. We have just discussed two rather contradictory theories of market dominance: the three C's syndrome of vulnerability and the Boston

Consulting Group's matrix of the invulnerability of a star. What is your position on this issue? Which is correct, and under what circumstances?

6. "The success of Microsoft is not so much a credit to Bill Gates as a flawed miscalculation by IBM." Evaluate this statement.

INVITATION TO ROLE PLAY

1. Lotus Corporation has been quite successful with its Lotus 10203 spreadsheets. But it has been left in the dust by Microsoft with its Windows software. How would you, as chief executive of Lotus, attempt a comeback, or at least attempt to maintain a competitive position? (To answer this question in depth you may need to research more specifically the products of Lotus and their uses.)

2. As Bill Gates, you are aware of the dangerous king-of-the-hill mindset. How do you combat it in your organization?

INVITATION TO RESEARCH

1. Compare and contrast the two highly successful young entrepreneurs, Steve Jobs and Bill Gates.

2. What is the situation with Microsoft today? Are there any threats on its horizon?

CHAPTER 16

Southwest Airlines: "Try to Match Our Prices"

In 1992 the airlines lost a combined $2 billion, matching a dismal 1991 and bringing their three-year red ink total to a disastrous $8 billion. Three carriers—TWA, Continental, and America West—were operating under Chapter 11 bankruptcy, and others were lining up to join them. But one airline, Southwest, was profitable as well as rapidly growing— with a 25 percent sales increase in 1992 alone. Interestingly enough, this was a low-price, bare bones operation run by a flamboyant CEO, Herb Kelleher. He had found a niche, a strategic window of opportunity, and oh, how he had milked it! See the following box for further discussion of a strategic window of opportunity and its desirable accompaniment, a SWOT analysis.

HERBERT D. KELLEHER

Herb Kelleher impresses one as an eccentric. He likes to tell stories, often with himself as the butt of the story, and many involve practical jokes. He admits he sometimes is a little scatterbrained. In his cluttered office, he displays a dozen ceramic wild turkeys as a testimonial to his favorite brand of whiskey. He smokes five packs of cigarettes a day. As an example of his zaniness, he painted one of his 737s to look like a killer whale in celebration of the opening of Sea World in San Antonio. Another time, during a flight he had flight attendants dress up as reindeer and elves, while the pilot sang Christmas carols over the loudspeaker and gently rocked the plane. Kelleher

---

INFORMATION BOX

STRATEGIC WINDOW OF OPPORTUNITY AND SWOT ANALYSIS

A strategic window is an opportunity in the marketplace not presently well served by competitors that fits well with the firm's competencies. Strategic windows often last for only a short time (although Southwest's strategic window has been much more durable) before they are filled by alert competitors.

Strategic windows are usually found by systematically analyzing the environment, examining the threats and opportunities it holds. The competencies of the firm, its physical, financial, and people resources—management and employees and their strengths and weaknesses—should also be assessed. The objective is to determine what actions might or might not be appropriate for that particular enterprise and its orientation. This is commonly known as a SWOT analysis: analyzing the strengths and weaknesses of the firm and assessing the opportunities and threats in the environment.

This analysis may be a formal part of the planning process, or it may also be informal and even intuitive. We suspect that Herb Kelleher instinctively sensed a strategic window in short hauls and lowest prices. Although he must have recognized the danger that his bigger competitors would try to match his prices, he believed that with his simplicity of operation he would be able to make a profit while bigger airlines were racking up losses.

Why do you think the major airlines so badly overlooked the possibilities in short hauls at low prices?

---

is a "real maniac," said Thomas J. Volz, vice president of marketing at Braniff Airlines. "But who can argue with his success?"[1]

Kelleher grew up in Haddon Heights, New Jersey, the son of a Campbell Soup Company executive. He graduated from Wesleyan University and New York University law school, then moved to San Antonio in 1961, where his father-in-law helped him set up a law firm. In 1968 he and a group of investors put up $560,000 to found Southwest; of this amount, Kelleher contributed $20,000.

In the early years he was the general counsel and a director of the fledgling enterprise. But in 1978 he was named chairman, despite having no managerial experience, and in 1981 he became CEO. His flamboyance soon made him the most visible aspect of the airline. He starred in most of its TV commercials. A rival airline, America West, charged in ads that Southwest passengers should be embarrassed to fly such a no-frills airline, whereupon Kelleher appeared in a TV spot with a bag over his head. He offered the bag

---

[1] Kevin Kelly, "Southwest Airlines: Flying High with 'Uncle Herb'," *Business Week* (July 3, 1989): 53.

to anyone ashamed to fly Southwest, suggesting it could be used to hold "all the money you'll save flying us."[2]

He knew many of his employees by name, and they called him "Uncle Herb" or "Herbie." He held weekly parties for employees at corporate head-quarters, and he encouraged such antics by his flight attendants as organizing trivia contests, delivering instructions in rap, and awarding prizes for the passengers with the largest holes in their socks. But such wackiness had a shrewd purpose: to generate a gung-ho spirit to boost productivity. "Herb's fun is infectious," said Kay Wallace, president of the Flight Attendants Union Local 556. "Everyone enjoys what they're doing and realizes they've got to make an extra effort."[3]

THE BEGINNINGS

Southwest was conceived in 1967, folklore tells us, on a napkin. Rollin King, a client of Kelleher, then a lawyer, had an idea for a low-fare, no-frills airline to fly between major Texas cities. He doodled a triangle on the napkin, labeling the points Dallas, Houston, and San Antonio.

The two tried to go ahead with their plans but were stymied for more than 3 years by litigation, battling Braniff, Texas International, and Continental over the right to fly. In 1971 Southwest won, and it went public in 1975. At that time it had four planes flying between the three cities. Lamar Muse was president and CEO from 1971 until he was fired by Southwest's board in 1978. Then the board of directors tapped Kelleher.

At first Southwest was in the throes of life-and-death low-fare skirmishes with its giant competitors. Kelleher liked to recount how he came home one day "beat, tired, and worn out. So I'm just kind of sagging around the house when my youngest daughter comes up and asks what's wrong. I tell her, `Well, Ruthie, it's these damned fare wars.' And she cuts me right off and says, 'Oh, Daddy, stop complaining. After all, you started 'em.'"[4]

For most small firms, competing on a price basis with much larger, well-endowed competitors is tantamount to disaster. The small firm simply cannot match the resources and staying power of such competitors. Yet Southwest somehow survived. Not only did it initiate the cut-throat price competition, but it achieved cost savings in its operation that the larger airlines could not. The question then became: How long would the big carriers be content to maintain their money-losing operations and match the low prices of Southwest? The big airlines eventually blinked.

---

[2]Kelly, "Flying High," 53.
[3]Richard Woodbury, "Prince of Midair," *Time* (Jan. 25, 1993): 55.
[4]Charles A. Jaffe, "Moving Fast by Standing Still," *Nation's Business* (Oct. 1991): 58.

In its early years, Southwest faced other legal battles. Take Dallas, and Love Field. The original airport, Love Field, is close to downtown Dallas, but it could not geographically expand at the very time when air traffic was increasing mightily. So a major new facility, Dallas/Fort Worth International, replaced it in 1974. This boasted state-of-the-art facilities and enough room for foreseeable demand, but it had one major drawback: It was 30 minutes further from downtown Dallas. Southwest was able to avoid a forced move to the new airport and to continue at Love. But in 1978 competitors pressured Congress to bar flights from Love Field to any-where outside Texas. Southwest was able to negotiate a compromise, now known as the Wright Amendment, that allowed flights from Love Field to the four states contiguous to Texas. In retrospect the Wright Amendment forced onto Southwest a key ingredient of its later success: the strategy of short flights.[5]

GROWTH

Southwest grew steadily but not spectacularly through the 1970s. It domi-nated the Texas market by appealing to passengers who valued price and fre-quent departures. Its one-way fare between Dallas and Houston, for example, was $59 in 1987 vs. $79 for unrestricted coach flights on other airlines.

In the 1980s Southwest's annual passenger traffic count tripled. At the end of 1989, its operating costs per revenue mile—the industry's standard measure of cost-effectiveness—was just under 10 cents, which was about 5 cents per mile below the industry average.[6] Although revenues and profits were rising steadily, especially compared with the other airlines, Kelleher took a conservative approach to expansion, financing it mostly from internal funds rather than taking on debt.

Perhaps the caution stemmed from an ill-fated acquisition in 1986. Kelleher bought a failing long-haul carrier, Muse Air Corporation, for $68 million and renamed it TransStar. (This carrier had been founded by Lamar Muse after he left Southwest.) But by 1987 TransStar was losing $2 million a month, and Kelleher shut down the operation.

By 1993 Southwest had spread to 34 cities in 15 states. It had 141 planes, and these each made 11 trips a day. It used only fuel-thrifty 737s and still concentrated on flying large numbers of passengers on high-frequency, one-hour hops at bargain fares (average $58). Southwest shunned the hub-and-spoke systems of its larger rivals and took its passengers directly from city

---

[5]Bridget O'Brian, "Southwest Airlines Is a Rare Air Carrier: It Still Makes Money," *Wall Street Journal* (Oct. 28, 1992): A7.

[6]Jaffe, "Moving Fast," 58.

to city, often to smaller satellite airfields rather than congested major metropolitan fields. With rock-bottom prices and no amenities, it quickly dominated most new markets it entered.

As an example of Southwest's impact on a new market, it came to Cleveland, Ohio, in February 1992, and by the end of the year was offering 11 daily flights. In 1992 Cleveland Hopkins Airport posted record passenger levels, up 9.74 percent from 1991. "A lot of the gain was traffic that Southwest Airlines generated," noted John Osmond, air trade development manager.[7]

In some markets Southwest found itself growing much faster than projected, as competitors either folded or else abandoned directly competing routes. For example, America West Airlines cut back service in Phoenix in order to conserve cash after a Chapter 11 bankruptcy filing. Of course, Southwest picked up the slack, as it did in Chicago when Midway Airlines folded in November 1992. And in California, Southwest's arrival led several large competitors to abandon the Los Angeles-San Francisco route, unable to meet Southwest's $59 one-way fare. Before Southwest's arrival, fares had been as high as $186 one way.[8]

Now cities that Southwest did not serve were petitioning for service. For example, Sacramento, California, sent two county commissioners, the president of the chamber of commerce, and the airport director to Dallas to petition for service. Kelleher consented a few months later. In 1991 the airline received 51 similar requests.[9]

A unique situation was developing. On many routes, Southwest's fares were so low they competed with buses, and even with private cars. By 1991 Kelleher did not even see other airlines as his principal competitors: "We're competing with the automobile, not the airlines. We're pricing ourselves against Ford, Chrysler, GM, Toyota, and Nissan. The traffic is already there, but it's on the ground. We take it off the highway and put it on the airplane."[10]

Following are several tables and graphs that depict various aspects of Southwest's growth and increasingly favorable competitive position. See Tables 16.1, 16.2, and 16.3, and Figure 16.1. Although Southwest's total revenues are still far less than those of the four major airlines in the industry (five if we count Continental, emerging from its second bankruptcy), its growth pattern indicates a major presence, and its profitability is second to none.

---

[7]"Passenger Flights Set Hopkins Record," *Cleveland Plain Dealer* (Jan. 30, 1993): 3D.
[8]O'Brian, "Rare Air Carrier," A7.
[9]O'Brian, "Rare Air Carrier," A7.
[10]Subrata N. Chakravarty, "Hit `Em Hardest with the Mostest," *Forbes* (Sept. 16, 1991): 49.

Table 16.1   Growth of Southwest Airlines; Various Operating Statistics, 1982–1991

Year	Operating Revenues (in $ thousands)	Net Income (in $ thousands)	Passengers Carried (in hundreds)	Passenger Load Factor
1991	$1,314	$26.9	22,670	61.1%
1990	1,187	47.1	19,831	60.7
1989	1,015	71.6	17,958	62.7
1988	880	58.0	14,877	57.7
1987	778	20.2	13,503	58.4
1986	769	50.0	13,638	58.8
1985	680	47.3	12,651	60.4
1984	535	49.7	10,698	58.5
1983	448	40.9	9,511	61.6
1982	331	34.0	7,966	61.6

Source: Company annual reports.
Commentary: Note the steady increase in revenues and in number of passengers carried. While the net income and load factor statistics show no appreciable improvement, these statistics still are in the vanguard of an industry that has suffered badly in recent years. See Table 16.2 for a comparison of revenues and income with the major airlines.

Table 16.2   Comparison of Southwest's Growth in Revenues and Net Income with Major Competitors, 1987–1991

	1991	1990	1989	1988	1987	% 5-year Gain
Operating Revenue Comparisons (in $ millions)						
American	$9,309	$9,203	$8,670	$7,548	$6,369	46.0
Delta	8,268	7,697	7,780	6,684	5,638	46.6
United	7,850	7,946	7,463	7,006	6,500	20.8
Northwest	4,330	4,298	3,944	3,395	3,328	30.1
Southwest	1,314	1,187	1,015	860	778	68.9
Net Income Comparisons (in $ millions)						
American	(253)	(40)	412	450	225	
Delta	(216)	(119)	467	286	201	
United	(175)	73	246	426	22	
Northwest	10	(27)	116	49	64	
Southwest	27	47	72	58	20	

Source: Company annual reports.
Commentary: Southwest's revenue gains over these 5 years outstripped those of its largest competitors. While the percentage gains in profitability are hardly useful because of the erratic nature of airline profits during these years, Southwest stands out starkly as the only airline to be profitable each year.

Table 16.3 Market Share Comparison of Southwest With Its Four Major Competitors, 1987–1991

	1991	1990	1989	1988	1987

Total Revenues:
  American, Delta,
  United, Northwest
	$29,757	$29,144	$27,857	$24,633	$21,835

Southwest Revenues:	1,314	1,187	1,015	860	778
Percent of Big Four	0.044	0.041	0.036	0.035	0.036
Increase in Southwest's market share, 1987—1991: 22%					

Source: Company annual reports.

Tapping California

The formidable competitive power of Southwest was perhaps never better epitomized than in its 1990 invasion of populous California. By 1992 it had become the second largest player, after United, with 23 percent of intrastate traffic. Southwest achieved this position by pushing fares down as much as 60 percent on some routes. The big carriers, which had tended to surrender the short-haul niche to Southwest in other markets, suddenly faced a real

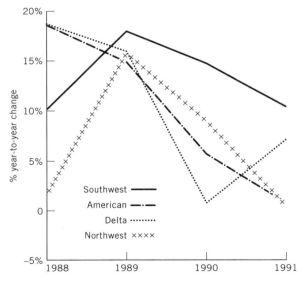

Figure 16.1. Year-to-year percentage changes in revenues, Southwest and its four major competitors, 1988–1991.

quandary in competing in this "Golden State." Now Southwest was being described as a "500 pound cockroach, too big to stamp out."[11]

The California market was indeed enticing. Some 8 million passengers each year fly among the five airports in metropolitan Los Angeles and the three in the San Francisco Bay area, making it the busiest corridor in the United States. It was also one of the pricier routes, as the low fares of AirCal and Pacific Southwest Airlines had been eliminated when these two airlines were acquired by American and US Air.

Southwest charged into this situation with its low fares and frequent flights. While airfares dropped, total air traffic soared 123 percent in the quarter Southwest entered the market. Competitors suffered: American lost nearly $80 million at its San Jose hub, and US Air still lost money even though it cut service drastically. United, the market leader, quit flying the San Diego-Sacramento and Ontario-Oakland routes where Southwest had rapidly built up service. The quandary of the major airlines was all the greater since this critical market fed traffic into the rest of their systems, especially the lucrative transcontinental and trans-Pacific routes. They could hardly abdicate California to Southwest. American, for one, considered creating its own no-frills shuttle for certain routes.[12] But the question remained: Could anyone stop Southwest, with its formula of lowest prices and lowest costs and frequent schedules? And, oh yes, good service and fun.

INGREDIENTS OF SUCCESS

Although Southwest's operation under Kelleher had a number of rather distinctive characteristics contributing to its success pattern and its seizing of a strategic window of opportunity, the key factors appear to be cost containment, employee commitment, and conservative growth.

Cost Containment

Southwest has been the lowest cost carrier in its markets. Although its larger competitors might try to match its cut-rate prices, they could not do so without incurring sizable losses. Nor did they seem able to trim their costs to match Southwest's. For example, in the first quarter of 1991, Southwest's operating costs per available seat mile (i.e., the number of seats multiplied by the distance flown) were 15 percent lower than America West's, 29 percent lower than Delta's, 32 percent lower than United's, and 39 percent lower than US Air's.[13]

---

[11] Wendy Zellner, "Striking Gold in the California Skies," *Business Week* (Mar. 30, 1992): 48.
[12] Zellner, "Striking Gold," 48.
[13] Chakravarty, "Hit 'Em Hardest," 50.

Many aspects of the operation contributed to these lower costs. With a single aircraft type, Boeing 737, for all its planes, costs of training, maintenance, and inventory were low. And since a plane earns revenues only when flying, Southwest was able to achieve a faster turnaround time on the ground than any other airline. Although competitors take upwards of an hour to load and unload passengers and then clean and service the planes, some 70 percent of Southwest's flights have a turnaround time of 15 minutes, and 10 percent have even pared the turnaround time to 10 minutes.

In areas of customer service, Southwest curbed costs as well. It offered peanuts and drinks, but no meals. Boarding passes were reusable plastic cards. Boarding time was minimal because there were no assigned seats. Southwest subscribed to no centralized reservation service. It did not even transfer baggage to other carriers; that was the passengers' responsibility. Admittedly, such customer service frugalities would be less acceptable on longer flights—and this helped to account for the difficulty competing airlines had in cutting their costs to match Southwest's. Still, if the price is right, many passengers might also opt for no frills on longer flights.

Employee Commitment

Kelleher was able to achieve an esprit de corps unmatched by other airlines despite the fact that Southwest employees were unionized. But there was no adversarial relationship with unions like Frank Lorenzo had at Eastern and Continental Airlines. Southwest was able to negotiate flexible work rules, with flight attendants and even pilots helping with plane cleanup. Employee productivity remained very high, permitting the airline to be leanly staffed. Kelleher resisted the inclination to hire extravagantly when times were good, necessitating layoffs during leaner times. This contributed to employee feelings of security and loyalty. And the low-key attitude and sense of fun that Kelleher engendered helped, perhaps more than anyone could have foreseen. Kelleher declared, "Fun is a stimulant to people. They enjoy their work more and work more productively."[14]

Conservative Growth Efforts

Not the least of the ingredients of success was Kelleher's conservative approach to growth. He resisted the temptation to expand vigorously—for example, to seek to fly to Europe or get into head-to-head competition with larger airlines with long-distance routes. Even in its geographical expansion, conservatism prevailed. The philosophy of expansion was to do so only when

[14]Chakravarty, "Hit 'Em Hardest," 50.

enough resources could be committed to go into a city with 10 to 12 flights a day, rather than just 1 or 2. Kelleher called this guerrilla warfare, concentrating efforts against stronger opponents in only a few areas, rather than dissipating strength by trying to compete everywhere.

Even with a conservative approach to expansion, the company showed vigorous but controlled growth. Its debt, at 49 percent of equity, was the lowest among U.S. carriers. Southwest also had the airline industry's highest Standard & Poor's credit rating, A minus.

POSTSCRIPT

In its May 2, 1994, edition, prestigious *Fortune* magazine devoted its cover and a feature article to Herb Kelleher and Southwest Airlines. It raised an intriguing question: "Is Herb Kelleher America's Best CEO?" It called him a "people-wise manager who wins where others can't." The operational effectiveness of Southwest continued to surpass all rivals: for example, in such productivity ratios as cost per available seat mile, passengers per employee, and employees per aircraft. Only Southwest remained consistently profitable among the big airlines.

Perversely, also in May 1994, despite the low costs, booming business, and steady profit growth, investors began bailing out of the company, and the stock dived almost 32 percent from its high in February. Analysts wondered whether big rivals, notably UAL and Continental, who were trying to emulate Southwest's low-fare style, were poised to become more aggressive. Another concern was possible negative affects of the company's being dropped from four big computer-reservations systems that U.S. travel agents use to book flights for clients. Southwest refuses to pay those services' booking fees, and some investors feared this might curb the growth. Still, Kelleher and Southwest, as we go to press, are moving merrily along.[15]

WHAT CAN BE LEARNED?

The power of low prices, and simplicity of operation. If a firm can maintain prices below those of its competitors and can do so profitably and without sacrificing quality of service, then it has a powerful advantage. Southwest was able to do this with its simplicity of operation. Competition on the basis of price is seldom used in most industries (although the airline industry has been an exception), primarily because competitors can quickly match prices

---

[15]Kenneth Labich, "Is Herb Kelleher America's Best CEO?" *Fortune* (May 2, 1994): 45-52; Bridget O'Brian, "Southwest Airlines Stock Is Hit by Downdraft As Some Investors Are Wary of Rival's Moves," *The Wall Street Journal* (May 24, 1994): C2.

with no lasting advantage to anyone. As profits are destroyed, only customers benefit, and then only in the short run. See the following issue box for a discussion of the controversy of competing on price, and the alternative.

ISSUE BOX

PRICE COMPETITION: SHOULD WE ATTEMPT IT?

The great limitation in using price as a competitive weapon is that competitors may retaliate and create a price war. It is not difficult to lower a price. It is not difficult to offer a stripped-down model to match a competitor's low price. Not only may no seller benefit from such a situation, but prices may even settle permanently at a lower level. As a result, most firms—except in new, rapidly growing, and technologically changing industries—find it best to compete on *nonprice* bases, rather than face a cut-throat pricing situation.

With nonprice competition, emphasis is placed instead on such factors as service, warranties, delivery, quality, and all possible efforts to obtain greater product differentiation. For example, a good reputation for quality and dependability is not easily and quickly matched by competitors.

The classic example of the impotence of price competition was the 1972 WEO, or "Where Economy Originates," campaign of A & P. Amid heavy advertising, A & P began lowering prices on 90 percent of the merchandise in its 4200 stores. This action resulted in vicious price wars that destroyed the profits of the entire supermarket industry in 1972. But A & P suffered the most: Its net loss for the year was $51.3 million, the worst in the company's modern history. Although it had a small gain in sales and in market share, the results were not lasting.[16]

Price wars usually are anathema to sellers, but customers benefit. On balance, do you see any disadvantages of price wars from the customers' viewpoint?

The durability of Southwest's cost control points out the true competitive importance of low prices. Customers love the lowest price producer, if quality, comfort, and service are not sacrificed too much. Although there was some sacrifice of service and amenities with Southwest, most customers found it acceptable because of the short-haul situation; and dependable and reasonable service was still maintained.

The power of a niche strategy. Directing marketing efforts toward a particular customer segment or niche can provide a powerful competitive advantage. This is especially true if no competitor is directly catering to this niche or is likely to do so with a concerted effort. Such an untapped niche then becomes a strategic window of opportunity.

[16]For more detail on the disastrous A & P price campaign, see Robert Hartley, *Marketing Mistakes*, 5th ed., (New York: Wiley, 1992), Chapter 11. Also relevant is Chapter 8 on the Yugo car.

Kelleher was quick to reveal the niche strategy of Southwest: When other airlines set up hub-and-spoke systems in which passengers are shunted to a few major hubs from which they are transferred to other planes going to their destination, "we wound up with a unique market niche: We are the world's only short-haul, high-frequency, low-fare, point-to-point carrier . . . we wound up with a market segment that is peculiarly ours, and everything about the airline has been adapted to serving that market segment in the most efficient and economical way possible."[17] See the following information box for a discussion of the criteria needed for a successful niche or segmentation strategy.

INFORMATION BOX

CRITERIA FOR SELECTING NICHES OR SEGMENTS

In deciding what specific niches to seek, these criteria should be considered:

1. *Identifiability.* Is the particular niche identifiable so that the persons who constitute it can be isolated and recognized? It was not difficult to identify the short-route travelers, and while their numbers may not have been readily estimated, this was soon to change as demand burgeoned for Southwest's short-haul services.
2. *Size.* The segment must be of sufficient size to be worth the efforts to tap. And again, the size factor proved to be significant: Southwest soon offered 83 flights daily between Dallas and Houston.
3. *Accessibility.* For a niche strategy to be practical, promotional media must be able to reach the segments without much wasted coverage. Southwest had little difficulty in reaching its target market through billboards and newspapers.
4. *Growth potential.* A niche is more attractive if it shows some growth characteristics. The growth potential of short-haul flyers proved to be considerably greater than for airline customers in general. Partly the growth reflected customers won from other higher cost and less convenient airlines. And some of the emerging growth reflected customers' willingness to give up their cars to take a flight that was almost as economical and certainly more comfortable.
5. *Absence of vulnerability to competition.* Competition, both present and potential, must certainly be considered in making specific niche decisions. By quickly becoming the low-cost operator in its early routes, and gradually expanding without diluting its cost advantage, Southwest became virtually unassailable in its niche. The bigger airlines with their greater

---

[17]Jaffe, "Moving Fast," 58.

> overhead and less flexible operations could not match Southwest prices without going deeply into the red. And the more Southwest became entrenched in its markets, the more difficult it was to pry it loose.
>
> Assume you are to give a lecture to your class on the desirability of a niche strategy, and you cite Southwest as a classic example. But suppose a classmate asks, "If a niche strategy is so great, why didn't the other airlines practice it?" How will you respond?

Southwest has been undeviating in its pursuit of its niche. Although others have tried to copy it, none have fully duplicated it. Southwest still remains the nation's only high-frequency, short-distance, low-fare airline. As an example of its strong position, Southwest accounts for more than two-thirds of the passengers flying within Texas, and Texas is the second largest market outside the West Coast. Now that Southwest has invaded California, some San Jose residents drive an hour north to board Southwest's Oakland flights, skipping the local airport where American has a hub. And in Georgia, so many people were bypassing Delta's huge hub in Atlanta and driving 150 miles to Birmingham, Alabama, to fly Southwest that an entrepreneur started a van service between the two airports.[18]

Unlike many firms, Southwest has not permitted success to dilute its niche strategy. It has not attempted to fly to Europe or to get into head-to-head competition with a larger airline on longer domestic flights. And it has not sacrificed growth potential in curbing such temptations: Its strategy still has many cities to embrace.

Seek dedicated employees. Stimulating employees to move beyond their individual concerns to a higher level of performance, a truly team approach, was by no means the least of Kelleher's accomplishments. Such an esprit de corps enabled planes to be turned around in 15 minutes instead of the hour or more of competitors; it brought a dedication to service far beyond what could ever have been expected of a bare bones, cut-price operation; it brought a contagious excitement to the job obvious to customers and employees alike.

The nurturing of such dedicated employees was not due solely to Kelleher's extroverted, zany, and down-home personality—although this certainly helped. So did a legendary ability to remember employee names. And company parties. And a sincere company and true interest in the employees. Flying in the face of conventional wisdom, which says an adversarial relationship between management and labor is inevitable with the presence of a union, Southwest achieved its great teamwork while being 90 percent unionized.

[18] O'Brian, "Rare Air Carrier," A7.

Whether such worker dedication can pass the test of time, and the test of increasing size, is uncertain. Kelleher himself was 62 in 1993, and his retirement looms. A successor will be a different personality. Yet there is a model for an organization growing to large size and still maintaining employee commitment. In a later case we will examine the leadership style of Sam Walton and the growth of Wal-Mart to become the largest retailer.

Part of the attainment of dedicated employees is a product of the firm itself, and how it is growing. A rapidly growing firm—especially when such growth starts from humble beginnings, with the firm as an underdog—promotes a contagious excitement. Opportunities and advancements depend on growth. And where employees can acquire stock in the company and see the value of their shares rising, potential financial rewards seem almost infinite. Success tends to create a momentum that generates continued success. Yet we know that eventually, with all organizations, growth slows and may even turn around: Witness, for example, IBM and Sears.

CONSIDER

Can you identify additional learning insights that could be applicable to other firms in other situations?

QUESTIONS

1. In what ways might airline customers be segmented? Which segments or niches would you consider to be Southwest's prime targets? Which segments probably would not be?
2. Do you think the employee dedication to Southwest will quickly fade when Kelleher leaves? Why or why not?
3. Discuss the pros and cons for expansion of Southwest beyond short hauls. Which arguments do you see as most compelling?
4. Evaluate the effectiveness of Southwest's unions.
5. On August 18, 1993, a fare war erupted. To initiate its new service between Cleveland and Baltimore, Southwest had announced a $49 fare (a sizable reduction from the then-standard rate of $300). Its rivals, Continental and US Air, retaliated. Before long the price was $19, not much more than the tank of gas it would take to drive between the two cities—and the airlines also supplied a free soft drink. Evaluate the implications of such a price war for the three airlines.
6. A price cut is the most easily matched marketing strategy, and it usually provides no lasting advantage to any competitor. Identify the circumstances when you see it as desirable to initiate a price cut and a potential price war.

7. Do you think it is likely that Southwest's position will continue to remain unassailable by competitors? Why or why not?

INVITATION TO ROLE PLAY

1. Herb Kelleher has just retired, and you are his successor. Unfortunately, your personality is far different from his: You are an introvert and far from flamboyant, and your memory for names is not good. What is your course of action to try to preserve the great employee dedication of the Kelleher era? How successful do you think you will be? Did the board make a mistake in hiring you?

2. Herb Kelleher has not retired. He is going to continue until 70, or later. Somehow, his appetite for growth has increased as he has grown older. He has charged you with developing plans for expanding into longer hauls, and maybe to South and Central America and even to Europe. Be as specific as you can in developing such expansion plans.

Kelleher has also asked for your evaluation of these plans. Be as persuasive as you can in presenting this evaluation.

INVITATION TO RESEARCH

What is the current situation with Southwest? What is its market share in the airline industry? Is it still maintaining a high growth rate? Has its stock continued to climb? Has it expanded beyond its short-haul strategy?

CHAPTER 17

GM's Saturn:
A New Auto Strategy

In many ways General Motors' Saturn subsidiary has been a sales and marketing success. It represents the first really effective effort by a U.S. automaker to emulate and even surpass Japanese cars, offering low prices, good looks, and surprising reliability. In addition, the Saturn has been the vanguard of enlightened customer service. Sales have exceeded expectations, as well as production capability, with customers waiting up to 2 months for their Saturn. In an advertising campaign in late 1992, Saturn pleaded with customers not to be discouraged and buy another brand—that a Saturn was worth the wait.

However, as of early 1993, the Saturn is at best a dubious success. Although the car was not expected to make money for several years after production started in November 1990, losses have been far higher than anticipated: more than $700 million in 1991.

How can any product possibly be considered even remotely a success with such a profit drain, despite the encouraging customer satisfaction and sales and the major challenge it presents to Japanese cars? And yet, potentially, Saturn could be the U.S. car industry's greatest success—if GM doesn't muff this window of opportunity.

PRELUDE

The beginnings of Saturn, its conception, go back to 1982. Originally, it represented an ambitious effort by General Motors to make small cars in the United States as cheaply and well as they could be made overseas. Roger

Smith, the CEO of GM at the time, called the $5 billion undertaking "the key to GM's long-term competitiveness."[1]

The project represented GM's attempt to rethink every aspect of auto making. It was hoped that production innovations could save $2,000 from the cost of building a subcompact car. Initial plans called for selling 400,000 units yearly.

So important was the project deemed to be in the total GM scheme of things that by 1985 Saturn had become a new GM subsidiary. A new factory was to built from scratch, and in the search for a new site, bids flooded in from dozens of states. GM finally chose a site near Spring Hill, Tennessee.

Hardly had work begun on the new factory in early 1986 than some company goals began changing. As new models of low-price imports began coming in from Korea and Yugoslavia, GM executives abandoned the idea of being cost-competitive with these. Now they began targeting the car for the middle of the import pack, where prices were several thousand dollars higher. As a result the car had grown larger, now positioned between cars like the Chevy Cavalier and the company's midsize cars such as the Oldsmobile Ciera. And sales estimates were downsized. A "first-phase" plant was opened with a capacity for 250,000 cars, with a second factory to be added only if sales were strong enough.

By early 1987 pessimists were predicting that the Saturn was doomed. Although production was at least several years away, already demand seemed to be slackening for small cars, and GM was experiencing difficulty with high-tech factories. The more optimistic rumors were that GM might try to save face by folding the separate Saturn subsidiary into the Chevrolet or Pontiac division.

INTRODUCTION

As the 1980s were drawing to a close, GM's share of the U.S. passenger-car market slumped to 33 percent, a loss of 11 points in only 5 years. At the same time, Japanese car makers had a 7-point gain in market share, to 26 percent. Consumer surveys were even bleaker: A study by J. D. Powers & Associates found that 42 percent of all new-car shoppers would not even consider a GM car.[2] Now Saturn began to assume a position of greater importance to GM. Its new fundamental goal was to sell 80 percent of its cars to drivers who otherwise would not have bought a GM car.

---

[1] William J. Hampton, "Will Saturn Ever Leave the Launchpad?" *Business Week* (Mar. 16, 1987): 107.

[2] James B. Treece, "Here Comes GM's Saturn," *Business Week* (April 9, 1990): 57.

Saturn's ascendancy on the eve of its production inauguration had the full support of GM chairman Roger Smith, although his term of office was soon to end. Smith saw the Saturn as having a bigger role than simply appealing to import buyers. He saw it as an example for the rest of GM as to how to reform its own ponderous and tradition-ridden culture. Indeed, Saturn had created an innovative blend of enlightened labor relations, participatory management, and new technology for the latest manufacturing operations. GM was especially interested in the manufacturing and labor breakthroughs that Saturn had initiated. Just as much so, but not to be recognized until a year or so later, was the great innovation in traditional passenger-car marketing and customer relations and servicing.

The company was now becoming so optimistic of Saturn's competitiveness that one marketing strategy under consideration was to have dealers place a Honda Civic, Toyota Corolla, and Accura Integra in the same showroom with a Saturn, and let customers make their own direct comparisons.

Admittedly, the final version of the Saturn was not the 60-mile-per-gallon, $6,000 subcompact as originally envisioned, but it was a gem nevertheless. Dealers were allowed to drive prototypes at GM's Mesa, Arizona, proving grounds, and they were enthusiastic about the car's power train and handling: "We went 100 miles per hour, and it was still going strong," said a Saturn dealer from St. Louis. "It was going through curves at 75 to 80 that imports couldn't."[3] Another dealer who also sold Hondas remarked that Saturn, besides having the quickness and nimbleness of a Honda, "doesn't have the vibrations that the current domestic models have."[4]

The first Saturns were ready for sale in November 1990. In that first month, 641 were sold. Sales more than doubled by January 1992, to 1,520. And the rush was on, limited only by the production capabilities of the single factory. Table 17.1 shows the growth in units sold from the beginning through July 1992. Table 17.2 shows comparative figures of the sales and market share of Saturn to other GM units and also to major Japanese competitors and the total car market for 1991 and 1992. Saturn's surge was awesome.

AFTER TWO YEARS

As demand outstripped supply, dealers were staring at empty lots. In July 1992 Saturn dealers sold 22,305 cars—an average of 115 apiece, twice the rate per dealer for the nearest competitor, Toyota.[5] Foreign rivals continued to flood the market with new models, but Saturn was meeting them head on. It had become the highest quality American-made brand, with as few defects

---

[3]Treece, "Here Comes GM's Saturn," 58.
[4]Treece, "Here Comes GM's Saturn," 58.
[5]David Woodruff, "Saturn," *Business Week* (Aug. 17, 1992): 86.

251

Table 17.1   Selected Monthly Sales, Saturn, November 1990–July 1992

Month	Units	Percent Increase
November 1990	641	
January 1991	1,520	137.1%
March 1991	3,302	117.7
May 1991	6,832	106.9
July 1991	8,538	25.0
November 1991	8,355	(2.1)
January 1992	10,757	28.7
March 1992	16,757	55.8
May 1992	18,031	7.6
July 1992	22,305	23.7

Source: David Woodruff, "Saturn: GM Finally Has a Real Winner, But Success Is Bringing a Fresh Batch of Problems," *Business Week* (Aug. 17, 1992): 86–87.
Commentary: Note the steady increase in monthly sales during this time period. Table 17.2 shows further statistics on Saturn's growth. A winner of major proportions for a U.S. automaker seemed to be emerging.

Table 17.2   Saturn Sales and Market Share Comparisons

	August 1991	August 1992	Year to Date 1991	Year to Date 1992
Retail Sales (units):				
Saturn	7,000	12,039	40,858	129,753
All GM Subcompacts	33,387	36,322	224,127	306,952
All Subcompacts	171,089	153,936	1,152,287	1,212,509
Total GM	221,547	198,172	2,012,599	1,992,835
Total Industry	690,442	644,808	5,601,704	5,584,494
Market Share:				
Saturn	1.0%	1.9%	0.7%	2.3%
All GM Subcompacts	4.8	5.6	4.0	5.5
Total Detroit Subcompacts	10.0	10.6	8.8	10.0
Total Toyota	5.0	4.3	4.0	4.2
Total Nissan	1.9	2.8	1.9	2.2
Total Honda	4.1	3.5	2.8	2.6
Total Japanese Nameplates	13.0	12.3	10.3	10.8
Total Subcompacts	24.8	23.9	20.6	21.7

Sources: Industry statistics.
Commentary: Note the substantial Saturn gains, both in sales and market share, from 1991 to 1992 against all other makes, domestic and foreign. Note in particular the market share gains against Japanese competitors: Toyota, Nissan, and Honda. The GM charge for Saturn to take away business from the Japanese imports appeared to be fully realized as 1992 drew to a close. And Saturn had yet to make a profit.

as Hondas and Nissans. In customer satisfaction ratings, according to a survey by J. D. Power & Associates, buyers rated the Saturn ahead of all American-made cars and most imports. Only Lexus and Infiniti—much higher priced cars—were ranked higher. (See Table 17.3.)

The success of Saturn, however, was causing some problems at GM headquarters. To bring plant capacities in line with the demand, GM would have to pump in more money at a time when the auto giant was facing serious financial problems. In 1991 its North American operations had a devastating $7.5 billion loss. Every dollar spent on Saturn meant that struggling divisions such as Chevrolet, which badly needed to update its outmoded models, would receive less. And at a time when GM was closing assembly plants to the anguished consternation of union workers and local governments, the arena was politically not conducive for a still-money-losing Saturn to receive funds to fully capitalize on its burgeoning customer demand.

A GM decision to delay any new investment would seriously jeopardize Saturn. At the end of July 1992, Saturn dealers had only a 10-day supply of cars on hand. This was one-sixth the normal stock. Dealers worried that customers would switch to competing brands because of unacceptable delays in servicing their orders, which could devastate Saturn's momentum and make it easy for the great GM bureaucracy to downplay an innovative but unprofitable new division.

Table 17.3 1992 Customer Satisfaction Ratings
(Score on J. D. Power's Survey of New-Car Buyers)

Lexus	179
Infiniti	167
Saturn	160
Acura	148
Mercedes-Benz	145
Toyota	140
Industry Average	129

Source: J. D. Power's Survey of New-Car Buyers, 1992, as reported by David Woodruff, "Saturn," *Business Week* (Aug. 17, 1992): 86-87; and Raymond Serafin and Cleveland Horton, "Automakers Focus on Service," *Advertising Age* (July 6, 1992): 3, 33.

Commentary: Nissan's Infiniti and Toyota's Lexus have established new industry benchmarks for coddling luxury-car buyers. Into that elite group, Saturn has surprisingly placed a close third, by redefining the standard for treatment of buyers of lower-priced mass-volume cars. This high rating is credited to Saturn's elimination of price haggling, a high commitment to quality control, and the trailblazing example of replacing 1800 cars after a coolant mix-up. Saturn's customer-satisfaction commitment is not lost on Chrysler: All Chrysler brands finished below industry averages, and Chrysler announced a $30 million massive training effort to improve the way its dealerships handle shoppers and owners.

Several options short of massive new plant investments were possible. GM chair Robert C. Stempel, who replaced Roger B. Smith, thought it possible to up the productivity at the single Spring Hill plant. Saturn President Richard G. LeFauve was rightly concerned about the dangers of pushing too hard for production at the expense of quality. During a visit by Stempel, after production goals had been increased along with the number of defects, line workers staged a slowdown, resulting in an easing of production goals. LeFauve saw a temporary solution in adding a third shift, which could boost capacity by 44 percent.[6]

Rather than add another plant, LeFauve proposed an additional $1 billion investment in Spring Hill, which would bring its capacity to 500,000 and enable the division to meet demand for new models. Increased production would permit expansion beyond the 195 original Saturn dealers so that all states could be covered.

Saturn executives worried how to keep their value-conscious buyers as the buyers grew older and wanted to upgrade to bigger cars with more comfort and features. Plans for larger cars and new models depended on further GM investment.

Stempel argued that present Saturn buyers should easily move up to existing GM brands that traditionally cater to older buyers, such as Oldsmobile, Buick, and Cadillac. Still, it was doubtful that Saturn buyers would readily fall into such a trade-up mode, given that most of them were former import buyers who would not have purchased a GM product other than a Saturn.

If GM top management could be convinced to expand Saturn, it was more likely that an older plant would be retooled, rather than a new one built from scratch, regardless of the technological advantages a new facility would offer. Rejuvenating an older plant would save several hundred million dollars and would be more palatable to unions and communities that had experienced the trauma of plant shutdowns. The following issue box discusses the decision problems in allocating scarce resources among competing claims.

The unique relations of Saturn with its auto workers will be described more fully in the next section. All workers were given a voice in management decisions, and 20 percent of their pay was linked to quality, productivity, and profitability. In late 1992, dissident union workers forced a vote on the teamwork-oriented labor contract that had been approved in November 1991 by a 72 percent margin. They claimed that this innovative contract ignored some seniority rights earned at other GM plants. On January 13, 1993, workers voted 2-to-1 to keep their teamwork-oriented labor contract, with the vote

[6]Woodruff, "Saturn," 88.

ISSUE BOX

HOW SHOULD WE PARCEL OUT INVESTMENT FUNDS?

By mid-1992, the GM executive suite was facing a dilemma of mean consequences. Record multi-billion-dollar losses had strapped the company financially. Yet perhaps never before had the demands for additional investment been so compelling. Saturn, although yet to turn a profit, was a bright star that needed substantial additional production facilities to fully tap its potential. But other divisions, ones dating to the beginnings of GM, needed substantial expenditures to either keep them competitive, or to bring them back from the brink. Chevrolet in particular needed funds:

This flagship division of GM two decades ago was selling one-fifth of all cars in the United States. Now its market share had fallen to only 12.1 percent. Accentuating the seriousness of Chevrolet's decline, it had long served as GM's entry-level division, the one whose customers often "graduated" to bigger, more expensive GM cars. Chevy dealers were convinced that the aging, hard-to-sell cars in their showrooms were the direct result of GM's generosity to Saturn.[7]

How should problems like this be resolved? Should the nascent star receive whatever it takes to fulfill its promise? Should scarce dollars be committed to resurrecting and sustaining deprived divisions? Should some sort of compromise be worked out, satisfying no one but creating the most equitable solution? Stake-holders in such allocation decisions are more than employees and managers; dealers, communities where plants are located, suppliers, even customers, have a stake.

How would you resolve this dilemma? Explain your rationale, and support it as persuasively as you can.

"reflecting strong endorsement of the partnership between union and management, which works hand in hand with Saturn's mission, philosophy, and values."[8]

INGREDIENTS OF SUCCESS

A New Labor-Management Climate

A large part of Saturn's success has been an enlightened labor-management relationship, one unique among U.S. carmakers in its sharing of responsibility, although a similar approach has been used by Japanese firms.

[7]Kathleen Kerwin, "Meanwhile, Chevy Is Sulking in the Garage," *Business Week* (Aug. 17, 1992): 90-91.
[8]"Saturn Workers Keep Contract," *Cleveland Plain Dealer* (Jan. 15, 1993): E1.

At first the Saturn plant was conceived as a high-tech operation with robots and automated guided vehicles. But GM's experiences in a joint venture with Toyota Motor Corporation in Fremont, California, suggested that a change in labor-management relations could be more important for productivity and quality.

LeFauve, the president of the new subsidiary, was convinced that factory-floor workers could make a difference, and he led the way for GM management and the United Auto Workers (UAW) to work closely together almost from the beginning. Saturn employees and managers ate in the same cafeterias. Under a "team concept," workers were split into groups of six to 15 and headed by a supervisor chosen jointly by workers and managers. Each team was responsible for meeting its own training and production goals. Workers started at a base pay equal to about 90 percent of the average pay at GM and other major U.S. automaker plants. Then they earned bonuses if specific production levels and quality targets were met.

In 1988 Saturn managers began visiting GM plants and UAW halls in search of workers. Recruiters sought current and laid-off workers willing to shed old habits and work as a team. The choice was not easy for some: They would have to quit their union locals and give up all seniority rights. And there would be no going back. Those who accepted the challenge developed a cultlike commitment.

Training was rigorous. New arrivals faced five days of "awareness training" to teach them how to work in teams and build consensus. Beyond that, workers received 100 to 750 hours of training that even included learning to read a balance sheet, since Saturn opened its books internally and wanted employees to know how much their operations were adding to the cost of a car.

Integration of Production

In contrast to other GM assembly plants, Spring Hill went beyond the usual paint shop and body and assembly plant. Its highly integrated facility includes a power-train factory that casts, machines, and assembles engines and transmissions. A plastic-molding plant and a shop for assembling the instrument panel and dash into a single unit are also on site. Saturn consequently does not have to rely on key components supplied by factories hundreds of miles away, thus saving on freight costs and shipping delays. Still, some glitches could occur, and a minor delay could shut down the whole operation, but these delays have become increasingly rare.[9]

[9]Woodruff, "Saturn," 89.

Quality Control

From the beginning, Saturn sought to emphasize quality and freedom from defects. If it was ever to have a chance with its target customers, buyers of imports, this was essential. The customer satisfaction ratings (see Table 17.3) confirmed that Saturn had indeed achieved this objective. And while many buyers of imports were skeptical of any American car at first, the durability of Saturn's reputation for quality was converting more and more of them back to an American car.

Buyers' complaints had been quite limited, but Saturn strove to correct those received. Early on there were two recalls: one for defective seats and another for corrosive engine coolant. Some early complaints were of insufficient headroom and noisy, vibrating engines. The company addressed these complaints quickly, lowering rear seats half an inch below the initial design, redesigning engine mounts, and adding more insulation under the hood. However, the company's handling of the necessary recalls epitomized a unique approach to customer relations and to the commitment to quality. The following information box details an almost unbelievable innovation in the treatment of recalls.

Most often credited for the high quality ratings was the revolutionary labor agreement. This agreement made partners of Saturn's blue-collar and white-collar workers and gave everyone the authority to solve quality problems, from phoning suppliers for corrective action to rearranging machinery to improve quality and productivity. Motivation was spurred by bonuses for meeting specific production levels and quality targets.

Worker comfort was considered in design of the final assembly line, the theory being that less strain on workers translates into fewer mistakes. Consequently, the whole facility was air conditioned. The floor of the assembly line was wood instead of concrete—a first in North America—thus making standing all day less tiresome. And the line itself was designed with the worker in mind: Car bodies moved on pallets that could be raised or lowered for the worker's ease, and workers rode with the body they were working on rather than walking to keep up with the body, as on other assembly lines.

Dealer Strategy

While the success of Saturn left many dealers with insufficient cars to even come close to meeting demand, still dealers had to be pleased when their monthly sales of 115 apiece in July 1992 were twice the rate per dealer of their nearest competitor, Toyota. Saturn had been slow in opening new dealerships, especially with demand outstripping production capability. With only 195 dealers by late 1992, these were virtually assured of no close

---

INFORMATION BOX

RECALL MAGIC IN FOSTERING QUALITY CREDIBILITY

Only a few months after production commenced for the Saturn, the company was forced to send out 1836 letters to customers, telling them that the car's radiator had been supplied with a faulty coolant and that the cars must be recalled. Such recalls are rather common in the industry, and car owners grudgingly put up with the inconvenience. But Saturn's recall was different. It offered to replace the cars, not just repair them. Consequently, regardless of odometer readings, each customer was supplied with a brand new Saturn, at no cost. One couple, unwilling to wait 3 weeks for Saturn to deliver a replica of their old car, chose a red model from the lot. It had a sunroof, unlike their old car, but they were given this $530 option for free. Saturn also paid for a rental car for the delay and even drove the couple to the rental company's lot.[10] Not surprising, Saturn's actions converted the recall into a major coup in customer relations and initiated the image—as no words alone could ever have—of an overwhelming commitment to quality and customer satisfaction.

In the process of handling the recall, Saturn broke other new ground. It publicly named Texaco as the supplier of the bad coolant. When Texaco learned that it would be identified in the Saturn recall, it rushed its explanation to customers: a freak accident, in which a special order of coolant contained too much sodium hydroxide, making it caustic and corrosive, especially for Saturn's aluminum engines. In light of the unfavorable publicity focused on the supplier, Texaco prepared to bear the costs associated with this mistake.

Thus, Saturn placed new responsibilities on its suppliers, that they provide parts meeting specifications without requiring Saturn inspectors to ensure quality. At risk was severe damage to a supplier's reputation.

Assess the pros and cons of such drastic handling of recalls in other situations and with other firms. On balance, can we as consumers expect such liberalization in any other recalls of the auto industry?

---

competition from other Saturn dealers. This strategy of maintaining fewer dealers flies in the face of traditional practice of having many dealerships in each market.

Initially most dealerships were on the east and west coasts, the heart of import demand. For example, in California's Santa Clara County, imports had more than 65 percent of the market. Many of the chosen dealers had also

---

[10]"Offers New Cars to Customers Whose Cars Were Recalled," *Business Week* (May 27, 1991): 38.

sold imports, because Saturn management believed they would know best how to appeal to such buyers.

The decision to concentrate initially on the coasts left some states without any dealerships. It also left the populous Midwest undercovered. The Midwest was the heart of the "Buy American" sentiments, however, and the area where GM was already strongest. It was believed that aggressive Saturn efforts here could cannibalize sales from other GM makes instead of stealing sales from foreign automakers.

Advertising

The company turned to San Francisco's Hal Riney & Partners for folksy, offbeat advertising. The target customer was similar to a target Honda Civic buyer: median age, 33; 68 percent female; 52 percent married; 60 percent with college degrees; 46 percent holding managerial or professional jobs; and with median household income over $40,000.[11] Ads focused on buyers' lifestyles, playing up product themes that baby boomers could easily relate to, such as safety, utility, and value. The approach did much to create an image for Saturn as an unusual car company. And the pricing practices further advanced this theme.

Innovation in Pricing and the Selling Process

Saturn initiated a new approach to pricing and the car-selling process that was a revolution in the auto industry. A variable price policy had long been traditional in this industry: A customer would attempt to drive the best bargain possible and in the process be in an adversarial contest with the car salesperson and his or her sales manager. Since the consumer lacked sufficient knowledge abut costs and markups, and often was uncomfortable and inexperienced with haggling, many car buyers disliked having to negotiate and were never sure if they were getting a reasonable deal.

Saturn cars carried no rebates, and they were priced at a set bottom price, with no haggling or negotiating needed or accepted. In late 1992 prices started at $9,195, even after an average 8 percent hike for 1993 models. Customers loved the change in automobile retailing. And they knew they were not paying more than a neighbor for the same car.

Other automakers began to emulate Saturn. Ford started selling its subcompact Escort models at one low price. Chrysler was testing the concept. Even Japanese companies were closely watching the acceptance of the inno-

[11] Larry Armstrong, "If It's Not Japanese, They Wouldn't Bother Kicking the Tires," *Business Week* (April 9, 1990): 61.

vation. Somehow, GM appeared slow to embrace the one-price policy elsewhere in the organization.

Ruling out haggling was only one part of the Saturn innovation in retailing. In formal courses in Spring Hill, managers and salespeople were instructed in low-pressure selling techniques. (The following box discusses the issue of high pressure versus soft sell.) The theme of the training was that pampering customers could create word-of-mouth advertising that would be particularly effective in such high-priced and even traumatic purchases as cars.

Combining a good product and top-notch service was bound to lead to happy Saturn customers. But good customer relations went even further. Both dealerships and Saturn headquarters followed up with customers to ascertain their satisfaction.

GM'S DILEMMA

Saturn's apparent success was not a particular cause for rejoicing at corporate headquarters in late 1992. Undoubtedly it would have been if the new venture were proving profitable, but several years and billions of dollars of new investment were expected to be necessary before Saturn turned the corner. Meanwhile, General Motors faced a serious cash crunch, all the more serious after a $7.5 billion loss from North American operations in 1991. At issue was how limited investment dollars should be allocated. (Refer back to a previous box for more discussion of this management dilemma.)

Once former chair Roger B. Smith, who conceived the Saturn project as a laboratory in which to reinvent his company, retired from GM, the firm's commitment may have cooled. Saturn has initiated some notable innovations in American car making, including labor relations changes such as intensive training programs, rewards for high customer satisfaction ratings, and joint responsibility with management. Its no-dicker, one-price policy was being emulated by other carmakers, but not by GM elsewhere in its organization. Its commitment to customer satisfaction became an actuality and not merely talk. And most of all, Saturn achieved—whether permanently or temporarily—quality levels deemed impossible by U.S. firms still bedeviled by defects and by an uncomplimentary image compared with foreign imports. So Saturn had much to offer its parent. It remains to be seen whether the ponderous-moving behemoth with its host of entrenched interests will be able to embrace enough of the Saturn innovations for a significant turnaround. It also remains to be seen at the time of this writing whether a myopic devotion to profits might doom the Saturn as a great experiment that failed.

ISSUE BOX

HIGH PRESSURE VERSUS SOFT SELL: WHICH IS MORE EFFECTIVE?

We can recognize a wide range of selling techniques, ranging from a laissez-faire approach, which we sometimes encounter in retail stores with bored clerks almost having to be forced to ring up the purchase, to such high-pressure techniques that unethical and illegal practices result. The continuum below reflects this range.

High Pressure	Medium Pressure	No Pressure	
deceptive tactics and false statements	strong selling efforts	soft sell	laissez-faire

What degree of pressure or lack of pressure is the most effective? To a considerable extent this depends on the audience of the sales presentation. If the prospect is a sophisticated and professional purchasing agent or buyer, obvious efforts to high pressure would be anathema. On the other hand, effective selling requires some pressure, even though this may be kept very subtle: the salesperson should be persuasive and at least ask for the order and encourage the prospect to make a decision. With a naive consumer, high pressure can be very effective, and there is the temptation to misuse it. Selling practices in the ghetto have often involved high pressure and dishonest tactics. With educated and sophisticated consumers, it is doubtful that strong high pressure makes for very effective selling.

Mayer and Greenberg, after seven years of field research, concluded that ego drive and empathy were the key ingredients in the most effective selling.[12] Ego drive makes the salesperson want and need to make the sale—it becomes a conquest and a powerful means of enhancing the ego. But empathy—the ability to feel as the other person does—must complement this. Otherwise, the salesperson will tend to bulldoze the way through to close a sale and thereby drive off many prospects. So we can conclude that some middle ground between no pressure and high pressure is best for most selling situations and with most prospects.

As a customer, have you experienced high pressure? What was your reaction? What conclusions can you draw about the effectiveness of high pressure?

[12]David Mayer and Herbert M. Greenberg, "What Makes a Good Salesman," *Harvard Business Review* (July-Aug. 1964): 119-25.

POSTSCRIPT

Officials announced on June 17, 1994 that Saturn operations would be profitable for the year. U.S. sales were expected to reach 270,000 units, up from just under 230,000 the year before. Donald Hudler, head of Saturn sales and marketing, estimated eventual sales of about 500,000 cars a year, with about 100,000 coming from overseas. To achieve this would require substantial investment in production and engineering as well as additional dealers.

Some analysts were skeptical of such projections without major product redesigns: the basic sedan, for example, has not changed appreciably since first introduced in 1990. But Saturn's small size and money-losing history hardly gives it the resources to finance significant model changes without major additional investment by GM. Saturn also faces increasing competition, even from GM with its new Chevrolet Cavalier.

Still, Saturn has the great customer appeal of superior dealer service and rigorous quality control; it continues to have the highest customer satisfaction ratings of any U.S. cars. But can such standards be sustained? Saturn stands at a crossroads in this latter half of 1994.[13]

WHAT CAN BE LEARNED?

A good reputation lingers, but it must be zealously safeguarded. Saturn gained a notable reputation for quality, unique among U.S. cars and one of the best among all cars. Such a reputation for being defect-free was an invaluable asset, both in keeping present customers who were likely to rebuy a Saturn (provided that appealing new models were forthcoming) and in attracting new customers by word-of-mouth publicity.

However, one of the ironies of a good reputation or public image is that it can quickly be destroyed. In the case of Saturn, if the company lapses a bit on its quality control—especially in pursuit of the profit demands of the parent—then the good reputation will be jeopardized. Then Saturn will reside with the other U.S. cars: just another domestic car unable to compete with the imports in workmanship and quality.

In large firms, politics and profit potential are not always compatible, perhaps to the detriment of the firm. Saturn, with its untapped and growing consumer demand, would seem worthy of substantial additional investment by GM. This may not fully come to pass, and corporate pressures may intensify to do more with less. GM now finds itself with limited financial resources and consequent allocation problems. Long entrenched divisions such as

[13]Neal Templin, "GM's Saturn Unit Expects a Profit, May Ask to Expand," *Wall Street Journal* (June 17, 1994): B5.

Chevrolet and Oldsmobile are competing with Saturn for needed funds. This intrafirm rivalry has not escaped the attention of the national business press, as noted in a preceding information box.

In the presence of long-established corporate power relations, Saturn, the upstart, may find itself thwarted by internal jealousies and entrenched interests.

Is there a moral here? Perhaps it is that huge organizations have profound difficulty in breaking from their traditional patterns (might we even call these ruts?). For some it may be impossible; for others, great adversity may sweep a new climate of change into a moribund organization.

Imitation is not a dirty word. Many organizations shun imitation; nothing else will do but to be innovators. Executive pride is often at stake. *Innovation* suggests leadership; *imitation* denotes a follower.

However, imitation has much to recommend it. Successful practices deserve to be imitated. Adopting such practices lessens risks from striking out on your own and often can hasten profitability.

Saturn represented innovation with General Motors. But most of the Saturn ideas were borrowed liberally from Japan. For example, just-in-time parts shipments were holding manufacturing costs down, but not without some danger of slowing the assembly line. Saturn workers were trying to eliminate bottlenecks and reduce costs, just as workers do at factories run by Toyota and Honda. Likewise, management and union relations were Japanese in style. The result became a commitment to quality unique among U.S. carmakers but imitative of Japanese imports.

Customer service is so much more than lip service. To most firms an expressed commitment to customer service falls in the same realm as apple pie, motherhood, and the flag—that is, it conveys a pious statement that no one could disagree with. But a solid commitment to customer service, as in the Saturn example, has immediate short-term profit consequences. To pamper customers, especially to the extraordinary extent of replacing the product—in the case of Saturn another new car—smacks of an unbelievable disavowal of profits. If defective products are out of control, such a practice can become an albatross. But the publicity of correcting company or supplier faults by going far beyond the expected or reasonable can pay dividends. It gives concrete evidence of the whole-hearted commitment of the firm to providing defect-free products, thus often garnering publicity that millions of dollars of advertising never could. It makes a major statement to employees and suppliers alike that deviations from quality standards cannot be tolerated. It shows that the company is willing to sacrifice its profitability in the quest for absolute quality standards. Nothing else could engender such a spirit of pride and responsibility.

CONSIDER

What additional learning insights do you see as emerging from the Saturn case?

QUESTIONS

1. Do you see GM management facing any problems if it tries to transplant the Saturn concepts to other divisions?
2. Do you fault top management for pressuring Saturn to turn a profit at this critical juncture of its growth? Why or why not?
3. What problems do you see for Saturn in maintaining its quality and customer relations? Is it likely that these can be resolved?
4. Evaluate the Saturn policy of relatively few dealers, each having a wide sales territory. What pros and cons do you see?
5. How do you personally feel about the haggling that is involved in most car purchases? Do you prefer a one-price policy?
6. "Saturn is experimenting with a `pie in the sky' marketing strategy. It is an abdication of reality." Evaluate this statement.

INVITATION TO ROLE PLAY

1. You are a staff assistant to GM CEO Roger Smith in the early 1980s. He has asked you to give a briefing to the executive committee on whether Saturn should be set up as a separate division or should be made part of Chevrolet. Prepare the briefing, listing as many pros and cons as you can for such a separate division, how you evaluate their importance, and finally, what your recommendation would be.
2. You are one of the biggest and most successful Chevy dealers, but now you are incensed at the investment dollars given Saturn at the expense of Chevrolet. What do you do? How effective do you think this action will be?

INVITATION TO RESEARCH

What is the present situation of Saturn, with regard to production and sales, consumer attitudes regarding satisfaction and quality, the labor force, and top management's commitment?

CHAPTER 18

Wal-Mart:
Now Retailing's Biggest

In March 1992 Sam Walton passed away after a 2-year battle with bone cancer. Perhaps the most admired businessman of his era, he had founded Wal-Mart Stores with the concept of discount stores in small towns and had brought it to the lofty stature of the biggest retailer in the United States—ahead of the decades-long leader, Sears, ahead of another great discount-store success, Kmart, and ahead of a charging J. C. Penney Company. And all this from rather humble beginnings.

THE EARLY YEARS OF SAM WALTON

Samuel Moore Walton was born in Kingfisher, Oklahoma, on March 29, 1917. He and his brother, James, born 3 years later, were reared in a family tradition of hard work and thrift. They grew up in Missouri in the depths of the Great Depression.

By the time Sam had entered the eighth grade in Shebina, Oklahoma, he was already exhibiting the character traits that would dominate his future life: quiet and soft-spoken, but a natural leader who became class president and captain of the football team. He even became the first Eagle Scout in Shebina's history.

At the University of Missouri, Sam excelled in academics and athletics. But he worked his way through college by delivering newspapers, working in a five-and-dime store, lifeguarding, and waiting tables at the University.

After graduating in 1940, Sam went with the J. C. Penney Company, and became a management trainee at the Des Moines, Iowa, store. There he applied his work ethic, competed to become Penney's most promising new man, and became imbued with the Penney philosophy of catering to smaller towns and having "associates" instead of employees or clerks. He also met J. C. Penney himself and was intrigued with his habit of strolling around stores and personally meeting and observing customers and salespeople. After 18 months, Walton left Penney to go into the U.S. Army. But what he learned in the Penney store in Des Moines, Iowa, was to shape his future ideas.

GROWTH OF WAL-MART

Sam Walton was discharged from the Army in August 1945. By chance he stumbled on an opportunity to buy the franchise of a Ben Franklin variety store in Newport, Arkansas, and he opened it a month later. The lease arrangement with the building's owner did not work out, so he eventually relocated in Bentonville, Arkansas, in 1950. During the 1950s and early 1960s, Walton increased the number of Ben Franklin franchises to 15. In the winter of 1962 he proposed at a Ben Franklin board meeting that the company should aggressively turn its efforts to discounting, citing the great potential of discount stores. The company refused to consider such an innovative idea, so Sam and his brother went ahead anyway and opened a Discount City in Rogers, Arkansas, in 1962; they opened a second store in Harrison, Arkansas, in 1964. The company was incorporated as Wal-Mart Stores on October 31, 1969. It became a publicly held company a year later. In 1970 Walton also opened his first distribution center and general office: a 72,000-square-foot complex in Bentonville, Arkansas. By 1972 Wal-Mart was listed on the New York Stock Exchange.

In 1976 Walton severed ties with Ben Franklin in order to concentrate on the expansion of Wal-Mart. His operations had extended to small towns in Arkansas, Missouri, Kansas, and Oklahoma.

The essence of Walton's management philosophy during these building years was that of an old-fashioned entrepreneur; Walton personally roamed through his own stores, as well as those of competitors, always looking for new ideas in mass-merchandising (i.e., maximizing sales at attractive prices).

But rather than confronting the major retailers—department stores, chains such as Penney's and Sears, and the strong discounters such as Kmart—he confined his efforts to the smaller cities, ones deemed to have insufficient market potential by the major retailers. He saw these towns as a strategic window of opportunity, untapped by competitors. (Review the Southwest Airline case for a similar seizing of a strategic window.)

Growth accelerated. By the end of 1975 there were 104 stores with nearly 6000 employees and annual sales of $236 million, which generated $6 million net profit. The next year the number of stores had increased to 125, employees to 7500, and sales to $340 million, with $11.5 million in profit.

Table 18.1 compares the growth of sales and number of stores of Wal-Mart and Kmart, its major competitor, from 1980 to 1990, the decade in which Wal-Mart forged ahead to become the biggest retailer. By the end of fiscal 1991, Wal-Mart had 1573 stores located in 35 states.

Some of these new stores were Wal-Mart Supercenters, considerably larger than the regular Wal-Marts, having a warehouse-style food outlet under the same roof as the discount store. While such food stores carried items comparable to products in a regular urban supermarket, the assortment and service were superior to most direct competitors in the smaller cities. And the key motivation for adding food stores to the general-merchandise discount store was the greater frequency of customer shopping: Customers shop weekly for groceries, and such patronage exposes them to the other merchandise in the discount store far more frequently than would otherwise be the case.

Wal-Mart by now was also opening another category of stores: Sam's Wholesale, also known as Sam's Clubs. First introduced in 1984, by 1991 there were 148. This wholesale club concept came about as regular discount stores seemed to be reaching saturation in some locations. The wholesale warehouse went a step further in discounting.

Table 18.1 Comparison of Growth in Sales and Number of Stores, Wal-Mart and Kmart, 1980–1990

	Kmart		Wal-Mart	
	Sales (in $ millions)	Number of Stores	Sales (in $ millions)	Number of Stores
1980	$14,204	1,772	$ 1,643	330
1981	16,527	2,055	2,445	491
1982	16,772	2,117	3,376	551
1983	18,597	2,160	4,667	642
1984	20,762	2,173	6,401	745
1985	22,035	2,332	8,451	859
1986	23,035	2,342	11,909	980
1987	25,627	2,273	15,959	1,114
1988	27,301	2,307	20,649	1,259
1989	29,533	2,361	25,810	1,402
1990	32,070	2,350	32,602	1,573

Source: Company annual reports.

Commentary: Several of these statistics are of particular interest. The comparison of the sales from 1980 to 1990 show the tremendous growth rate of Wal-Mart, starting at little more than 10 percent of Kmart sales figures to forge ahead by 1990. And Kmart was no slouch during this period.

Second, Wal-Mart achieved its leadership in total sales with almost 800 fewer stores than Kmart. This means that Wal-Mart's stores were achieving much higher sales volume than Kmart's. This is further borne out by the statistics in Table 18.3.

Sam's Club stores are large, ranging up to 135,000 square feet. Each store is a membership-only operation, with qualified members including businesses and those individuals who are members of certain groups, such as government employees and credit union members. Although the stores are huge, they carry less than 5 percent of the total variety of items carried by regular discount stores. Assortments are limited to fast-moving home goods and apparel, generally name brands, with prices 8 to 10 percent over cost, well under those of discount stores and department and specialty stores. The ability of these stores to compete, with their very low markups compared with other retailers, rested on the concept of turnover, discussed in the following box. Sam's Club provided the initial entry for Wal-Mart into the big metropolitan markets that it had avoided in most of its great growth.

In December 1987 Wal-Mart opened its newest merchandising concept, Hypermart USA, in Garland, Texas, a suburb of Dallas. The hypermart offers a combination of groceries and general merchandise in over 200,000 square feet of selling space. The stores also include a variety of fast-food and service shops, such as a beauty shop, shoe repair, and dry cleaners. Thus, it creates a mall-like atmosphere to achieve one-stop shopping.

In spite of optimistic beginnings, the hypermarket idea was not as successful as expected. A scaled-down version was the supercenter. Plans were suspended for building more hypermarkets in favor of the supercenter concept.

For a comparison of sales and profitability of Wal-Mart with Kmart, Sears, and Penney, see Table 18.2. Note that profitability comparisons include both operating profit as a percentage of sales and the more valid measure of profitability, the return on equity (i.e., the return on the money invested in the enterprise). From this table we see that the growth of Wal-Mart in sales and profitability compared with its nearest competitors is awesome. Table 18.3 shows another operational comparison, this time in the average sales per store for Wal-Mart and Kmart. And again, the comparison shows the great growth performance of Wal-Mart.

The Future

Sam Walton received the Medal of Freedom from President Bush on March 17, 1992. Unfortunately, he did not live long to enjoy this high honor bestowed on him (among many honors, such as Man of the Year, Horatio Alger Award in 1984, and "Retailer of the Decade," in 1989); he died of cancer nine days later, on March 26, 1992.

David Glass, 53 years old, assumed the role of president and chief executive officer. Glass was known for his hard-driving managerial style. He had gained his retail experience at a small supermarket chain in Springfield, Missouri, and had joined Wal-Mart as executive vice president for finance in

---

INFORMATION BOX

IMPORTANCE OF TURNOVER ON PROFITABILITY

Consider the following comparison of a department store operation and a similar size discount store for an example of the effect of higher turnover on profitability.

Department Store

Sales	$12,000,000
Net profit percent	5
Net profit dollars	$600,000
Stock turnover	4
Average stock 12,000,000 ÷ 4)[1]	$3,000,000
Return on investment (without considering investment in store and fixtures)	$\frac{600,000}{3,000,000} = 20\%$

A similar size discount store might have a turnover of 8, whereas net profit percentage might be only 3 percent:

Discount Store

Sales	$12,000,000
Net profit percent	3
Net profit dollars	$360,000
Stock turnover	8
Average stock (12,000,000 ÷ 8)	$1,500,000
Return on investment	$\frac{360,000}{1,500,000} = 24\%$

Thus, the conventional discount store can be more profitable than the comparable department store (as measured by the true measure of profitability, the return on investment), even though the net profit is less. Furthermore, the discount store not only has a lower investment in inventory to produce the same amount of sales, but also has less invested in store and fixtures.

Sam's Club stores carry this concept of lean inventory assortment and the concomitant high turnover to the furthest. Coupled with austere fixtures, the very low prices can still produce very attractive profits.

A supermarket also operates on a very high turnover. If a supermarket had the same sales as the preceding examples, but only 1 percent net profit with a turnover of 25, what would be its profitability? How does the supermarket attain such a higher turnover?

[1]To simplify this example, inventory investment is figured at retail price, rather than cost, which is the retailer's actual investment. However, the significance of increasing turnover is more easily seen here.

Table 18.2   Ten-Year Comparison of Gross Revenues, Percentage of Operating Margin, and Return on Equity Between Wal-Mart and Its Competitors

| | Wal-Mart | | | Kmart | | | Sears | | | J C Penney | | |
| | | % Operating | | | % Operating | | | % Operating | | | % Operating | |
Year	Gross Revenue	Profit Margin %	Equity Return %	Gross Revenue	Profit Margin %	Equity Return %	Gross Revenue	Profit Margin %	Equity Return %	Gross Revenue	Profit Margin %	Equity Return %
1981	$ 2,445.0	5.6	25.6	$16,527.0	2.2	9.0	$27,357	7.2	8.2	$11,860	7.5	13.2
1982	3,376.3	7.8	25.4	17,040.0	4.3	10.1	30,020	8.8	10.1	11,414	8.3	13.3
1983	4,666.9	8.3	26.6	18,878.9	6.0	16.7	35,883	9.7	14.4	12,078	8.7	13.1
1984	6,400.9	8.5	27.5	21,095.9	6.7	15.4	38,828	10.5	14.1	13,451	7.8	11.4
1985	8,451.5	7.2	25.6	22,420.0	6.2	14.4	40,715	9.5	11.5	13,747	7.7	9.8
1986	11,909.1	7.1	26.6	23,812.1	5.7	14.5	44,282	9.1	10.4	15,151	8.6	11.0
1987	15,959.3	6.8	27.8	25,626.6	5.8	15.7	48,439	8.5	12.1	15,747	9.1	14.6
1988	20,649.0	6.4	27.8	27,301.4	6.5	16.0	50,251	9.2	3.0	15,296	8.3	20.4
1989	25,810.7	6.5	27.1	29,532.7	5.8	6.5	53,794	9.2	10.6	16,405	9.2	18.4
1990	32,601.6	6.0	24.1	32,070.0	5.4	14.0	55,971	7.4	7.0	16,365	2.4	15.6

Note: Gross revenue $ in billions.
Source: Company annual reports.
Commentary: The comparison with major competitors shows Wal-Mart far exceeding its rivals in revenue growth. While the operating profit percentage exceeds Kmart for most years, Sears and Penney look better here. However, the true measure of profitability is return on equity. And here Wal-Mart shines: It indeed is a very profitable operation, while offering consumers attractive prices.

Table 18.3   Average Sales Per Store, Wal-Mart and Kmart, 1980–1990

	Kmart	Wal-Mart
1980	$ 8,015,801	$ 4,978,788
1981	8,042,338	4,979,633
1982	7,922,532	6,127,042
1983	8,609,722	7,269,470
1984	9,554,533	8,591,946
1985	9,448,970	9,838,184
1986	9,835,611	12,152,040
1987	11,274,527	14,325,852
1988	11,833,983	16,401,111
1989	12,508,682	18,409,415
1990	13,646,808	20,726,001

Source: Computed from Table 18.1.

Commentary: The great increase in sales per store for Wal-Mart is particularly noteworthy. In 1980 Wal-Mart's average store's sales was hardly one-half that of an average Kmart. By 1990 the average Wal-Mart store was generating more than 50 percent greater sales than an average Kmart.

1976. He had been named president and chief operating officer in 1984, while Sam Walton had kept the position of chief executive officer. About the transition of executives, Glass had said:

> There's no transition to make, because the principles and basic values he (Walton) used in founding this company were so sound and so universally accepted. . . . We'll be fine as long as we never lose our responsiveness to the customer.[2]

Whether a new generation can continue the successful growth efforts of Wal-Mart, now entering the tougher competitive environment of larger metropolitan areas, remains to be seen, but the prospects seem positive.

INGREDIENTS OF SUCCESS

Management Style and Employee Orientation

Sam Walton cultivated a management style that emphasized individual initiative and autonomy over close supervision. He constantly reminded employees that they were vital to the success of the company, that they were essentially "running their own business," that they were "associates" or "partners" in the business, rather than simply employees.

---

[2]Susan Caminiti, "What Ails Retailing," *Fortune* (Jan. 30, 1989): 61.

In such employee relations, he borrowed from James Cash Penney, the founder of the J. C. Penney Company, and his formulation of the "Penney Idea" in 1913. This Penney idea also stressed the desirability of constantly improving the human factor, of rewarding associates through participation in what the business produces, and of appraising every policy and action as to whether it squares with what is right and just.

Walton emphasized bottoms-up communication, thereby providing a free flow of ideas from throughout the company. For example, the "people greeter" concept (described in the following box) was implemented in 1983 as a result of a suggestion received from an employee in a store in Louisiana. This idea proved so successful that it has since been adopted by Kmart, some department stores, and even shopping malls.

Another example of listening to employees' ideas came when an assistant manager in an Alabama store ordered too many marshmallow sandwiches, or Moon Pies. The store manager told him to use his imagination to sell the excess. So John Love came up with an idea to create the first World Championship Moon Pie Eating Contest. It was held in the store's parking lot. The event was so successful that it became held every year, drawing spectators not only from the community but from all over Alabama as well as surrounding states.[3]

Wal-Mart has a profit-sharing plan, dating back to 1972, in which all associates share in a portion of the company's profits each year. As one celebrated example of the benefits of such profit sharing, Shirley Cox had worked as an office cashier earning $7.10 an hour. When she decided to retire after 24 years, the amount of her profit sharing in 1988 was $220,127.[4] In addition, associates may participate in the payroll stock purchase plan in which Wal-Mart contributes part of the cost.

The Sam Walton philosophy of business and management was to create a friendly, "down-home" family atmosphere in his stores. He described it as a "whistle while you work philosophy," one that, as he saw it, stressed the importance of having fun while working because you can work better if you enjoy yourself.[5] He was concerned about losing this attitude or atmosphere: "The bigger Wal-Mart gets, the more essential it is that we think small. Because that's exactly how we have become a huge corporation—by not acting like one."[6]

---

[3]Example described in Don Longo, "Associate Involvement Spurs Gains (Wal-Mart Employees Are Encouraged to Suggest Ideas for Promotions)," *Discount Store News* (Dec. 18, 1989): 83.

[4]Example cited in Vance H. Trimble, *Sam Walton: The Inside Story of America's Richest Man* (New York: Dutton, 1990), 233.

[5]Trimble, *Sam Walton*, 105.

[6]Trimble, *Sam Walton*, 104.

INFORMATION BOX

GREETERS

All customers entering Wal-Mart stores encounter a store employee assigned to welcome them, give advice on where to find things, and help with exchanges or refunds. These "greeters" also thank people exiting from the store, while unobtrusively observing any indications of shoplifting.

Staffing exits and entrances is not uncommon by retailers; what makes Wal-Mart's greeters unique is their friendliness and patience. Wal-Mart has found that retirees supplementing pensions usually make the best greeters and are most appreciated by customers. As noted earlier, the greeter idea originated as a suggestion from an employee (associate); Sam Walton liked the idea, and it became a companywide practice.

Do you personally like the idea of having a store employee greet you as you enter and thank you as you leave an establishment? On balance, do you think the greeter idea is a plus or a minus? Explain.

Another incentive is given to all employees in stores that manage to reduce shrinkage (that is, the loss of merchandise due to shoplifting, carelessness, and employee theft). Employees receive $200 each a year if shrinkage limits are met. This causes associates to become detectives by watching shoppers and each other. In 1989 Wal-Mart had a shrinkage rate of 1 percent of sales, below the industry average of 2 percent.[7]

A rather unusual way of making employees feel a vital part of the Wal-Mart operation is information sharing, which amplifies the idea that employees are associates of the business. Management shares the good news and the bad news about the company's performance. In each store, managers share operating statistics with employees, including profits, purchases, sales, and markdowns. Every person, from assistant managers to part-time clerks, sees this information on a regular basis. The result: Employees tend to think of Wal-Mart as truly their own company.

Part of the open and people-oriented management style fostered by Sam Walton is what he called MBWA, "Management by Walking Around." From store level to headquarters, managers are required to walk around the stores to stay familiar with what is going on, to talk to the associates, and to encourage them to share their ideas and concerns. Such interactions permit a personal touch usually lacking in large firms but so far still dominant as Wal-Mart grows large.

---

[7]Charles Bernstein, "How to Win Employee and Customer Friends," *Nation's Restaurant News* (Jan. 30, 1989): F3.

And how have unions fared in such an environment? Not surprisingly, they have had no success. Walton argued that in his "family environment," associates had better wages, benefits, and bonuses than any union could get for them. In addition, the bonuses and profit sharing were inducements far beyond the ability of a union to negotiate. As partners in a business operation, how could employees turn to a union?

State of the Art Technology

Sam Walton's decentralized management style led to a team approach to decision making. But this approach would have been difficult to achieve without a heavy commitment to supporting technology. A huge telecommunications system permits Wal-Mart executives to broadcast and communicate to store managers. In addition, home-office management teams, using the company's 11 turboprop planes, fly to various stores to assess their operations. Coming back to headquarters for Friday and Saturday meetings, they assess any problems and coordinate needed merchandise transfers among stores. Through the use of a six-channel satellite, messages can be broadcast to all stores, and a master computer tracks the company's complex distribution system.

Small Town Invasion Strategy

Adopting a strategy similar to that of the J. C. Penney Company of more than half a century before, Wal-Mart shunned big cities and directed its store openings to smaller towns, where competition consisted only of local merchants and small outlets of a few chains, such as Woolworth, Gamble, and Penney.

These merchants typically offered only limited assortments of merchandise, had no Sunday or evening hours, and charged substantially higher prices than would be found in the more competitive environments of larger cities. Other larger retailers, especially discounters, had shunned such small towns as not offering enough potential to support the high sales volume needed for the low-price strategy.

But Wal-Mart found potential in abundance in these small-town markets, as customers flocked from all the surrounding towns and rural areas for the variety of goods and the prices. (In the process of captivating small-town and rural consumers, Wal-Mart wreaked havoc on the existing small-town merchants. See the following information box for a discussion of the sociological impact of Wal-Mart on small-town merchants.) The company honed its skills in such small towns, isolated from aggressive competitors, and found enough business to become the world's largest retail enterprise. Then, flexing its muscles, it began moving confidently into the big cities,

---

INFORMATION BOX

IMPACT OF WAL-MART ON SMALL TOWNS

In most of its growth years, Wal-Mart pursued a policy of opening stores on the outskirts of small rural towns, usually with populations between 25,000 and 50,000. Attractive both in prices and assortment of goods, its stores often became beacons in drawing customers from miles around. Wal-Mart also was likely to be the biggest employer in the town, with 200 to 300 local hires.

But the dominating presence of Wal-Mart was a mixed blessing for many communities. Small-town merchants were often devastated and unable to compete. Downtowns in many of these small towns became decaying vestiges of what perhaps a few months previously had been prosperous centers. But consumers benefitted.

The tradeoffs and the controversy: Was rural America better or worse off with the arrival of Wal-Mart? On balance, most experts saw the economic development brought on by Wal-Mart as more than offsetting the business destruction it caused. But few could dispute the sociological trauma.[8]

What is your assessment of Wal-Mart's effect on a rural town? How might your assessment differ depending on your particular position or status in that community?

---

where competitors were as fearful of Wal-Mart as had been the thousands of small-town merchants.

Controlling Costs

Sam Walton was a stickler for holding costs to a minimum in the quest to offer customers the lowest prices. Cost control started with Wal-Mart vendors. Wal-Mart gained a reputation of being hard to please, of constantly pressuring its suppliers to give additional price breaks and cooperative advertising.[9] In further efforts to buy goods at the lowest possible prices, Wal-Mart attempted to bypass middlemen and sales reps and buy all goods direct from the manufacturer. In so doing, a factory presumably would save money on sales representatives' commissions of 2 to 6 percent of the purchase order and thus pass this savings on to Wal-Mart. Understandably, this aroused a heated controversy by groups representing sales reps.

---

[8]For more discussion of the impact of Wal-Mart, see Karen Blumenthal, "Arrival of Discounter Tears the Civic Fabric of Small Town Life," *Wall Street Journal* (Apr. 14,1987): 1 ff.; Hank Gilman, "Rural Retailing Chains Prosper by Combining Service, Sophistication," *Wall Street Journal* (July 2, 1984): 1 ff.

[9]Toni Apgar, "The Cash Machine," *Marketing and Media Decisions* (Mar. 1987): 82.

Wal-Mart was able to achieve great savings in distribution. Its sophisticated use of distribution centers and its own fleet of trucks enabled it to negotiate lower prices when buying in bulk directly from suppliers. More than three-fourths of the merchandise sold in a Wal-Mart store is processed through one of the company's 16 distribution centers. Each center serves 150 to 200 stores with daily delivery. For example, the distribution center in Cullman, Alabama, is situated on 28 acres with 1.2 million square feet. Some 1042 employees load 150 outbound Wal-Mart trailers a day and unload 180. On a heavy day, laser scanners will route 190,000 cases of goods on an 11-mile conveyor.[10]

Each warehouse uses the latest in optical scanning devices, automated materials-handling equipment, bar coding, and computerized inventory. With all of the stores using the previously discussed satellite network, messages quickly flash between stores, distribution centers, and corporate headquarters in Bentonville, Arkansas. Hand-held computers assist store employees in ordering merchandise. The result is a distribution system that provides stores with on-time delivery at the lowest possible cost. By using the most advanced technologies, Wal-Mart's distribution expenses are only 3 percent of total sales, which is about one-half that of most chains.[11]

Wal-Mart has previously been able to achieve great savings in advertising costs, compared with major competitors. While discount chains typically spend 2 to 3 percent of sales for advertising, Wal-Mart has been able to hold advertising to less than 1 percent of sales. Much of this difference reflects low media rates in most of its markets, the smaller towns. As Wal-Mart moves into larger metropolitan markets, the advertising cost advantage may diminish.

Finally, Wal-Mart's operating and administrative costs reflect a spartan operation that is rigidly enforced. A lean headquarters organization, and a minimum of staff assistants compared with most other retailers, completes the cost-control philosophy and reflects the frugal thinking of Sam Walton that dates back to his early days.

"Buy American" and Environmental Programs

As foreign manufacturers increasingly began taking market share away from American producers—and in the process, destroying some American jobs—sentiment began mounting for import restrictions to save jobs. And as the number of imports grew, so did the trade deficit, with consequences not fully understood by most persons but generally understood to be something very bad. However, the idea of restricting world trade is highly controversial; many experts question whether tariffs, quotas, and other restrictions are

---

[10]John Huey, "America's Most Successful Merchant," *Fortune* (Sept. 23, 1991): 54.
[11]*Facts About Wal-Mart Stores*, Company publication, Bentonville, Arkansas (n.d.), 4.

in the general best interest. Some say the best scenario is to induce American consumers to "buy American," or at least give preferential treatment to products produced in this country by American workers. Such a policy would eliminate import restrictions but enhance consumer support of American workers and factories.

In March 1985 Sam Walton became very concerned with what seemed to him to be a serious national situation. He sent a message to his buyers to find products that American manufacturers would soon have to stop producing because they couldn't compete with foreign imports. This was the beginning of Walton's "buy American" program, which had the long-range objective of strengthening the free enterprise system. The program was essentially a cooperative effort between retailers and domestic manufacturers to reestablish a competitive position of American-made goods in price and quality.

This program showcased the power of the huge retailer. Magic Chef, 3M, Farris Fashions, and many other manufacturers joined Walton's crusade, as Wal-Mart pledged to support domestic production for items ranging from film to microwave ovens to flannel shirts and other apparel.

Wal-Mart has been a leader in challenging manufacturers to improve their products and packaging in order to protect the environment. As a result, manufacturers have made great improvements in eliminating excessive packaging, converting to recyclable materials, and eliminating toxic inks and dyes.

The company participates in Earth Day events, with tree plantings, information booths, and videos to show customers how to improve their environment. It has also been active in fund-raising for local environmental groups, and in "adopt-a-highway" programs, in which store personnel volunteer at least one day every month to collect trash and clean up local highways and beaches.

UPDATE

As we move into the mid-1990s, Wal-Mart continues its merry climb. Sales in 1993 were $67.34 billion, and expectations were for $84 billion in 1994. Such expansion would come from 110 to 115 new Wal-Mart stores, 65 to 70 supercenter openings, and the transformation of 122 Canadian Woolco units to Wal-Marts. Plans for 1995 included vigorous expansion beyond North America into Brazil and Argentina.[12]

---

[12]Bob Ortega, "Wal-Mart Looks Beyond North America, Plans to Expand in Argentina, Brazil," The *Wall Street Journal* (June 6, 1994): A9.

WHAT CAN BE LEARNED?

Take good care of people. Sam Walton was concerned with two groups of people: his employees and his customers. By motivating, and even inspiring, his employees, he found that customers also could be well served. Somehow in the exigencies of business, especially big business, this emphasis on people tends to be pushed aside. Walton made caring for people common practice.

By listening to his employees, by involving them, by exhorting them, and by giving them a real share of the business—all the while stressing friendliness and concern for customers—Walton fostered a business climate almost unique in any large organization. In addition to providing customers with the friendliest of employees, his stores also offered honest values and great assortments. They catered to the concerns of many middle-income Americans for the environment and American jobs.

Go for the strategic window of opportunity. Strategic windows of opportunity sometimes come in strange guises. They always represent areas of overlooked or untapped potential business by existing firms. But in the formative and early growth years of Wal-Mart, no window could ever have seemed less promising than the one Sam Walton milked to perfection and to great growth. Small towns and cities in many parts of rural America were losing population and economic strength because of the decline in family farms and the accompanying infrastructure of small businesses. It was therefore not surprising that the major discount chains focused their growth efforts on large metropolitan areas. Although many small cities had Penney and Sears outlets, as well as such other chains as Woolworth, Gambles, and Coast to Coast stores, these were usually small stores, often old, marginal, and rather in the backstream of corporate consciousness. This retail environment was one of small stores with limited assortments of merchandise and relatively high prices.

In this environment Sam Walton seized his opportunity. He saw something that no other merchants had: that the limited total market potential meant a dearth of competition. He also saw that the potential was far greater than the population of the small town and its immediate surrounding population. Indeed, a large Wal-Mart store in a rather isolated rural community could draw customers from many miles away.

Do such windows of opportunity still exist today? You bet they do, for the entrepreneur with vision, an ability to look beyond the customary, and the courage to follow up on his or her vision.

A potent strategy can be the marriage of old-fashioned ideas and modern technology. Sam Walton embraced this strategy with more success than any other entrepreneur in modern business, and he made it work throughout his organization, despite its growth to great size. In the forefront of retailers in the use of communication technology and computerized distribution, he still was able to motivate his employees to offer friendly and helpful customer services to a degree that few large retailers have consistently been able to achieve.

Other firms can benefit from the example of Wal-Mart in cultivating home-spun friendliness with awesome technology, and competitors are trying to emulate the company. The particular difficulty that many are finding, however, is in achieving consistency.

Showing environmental concern can pay dividends. Today as perhaps never before, many persons are concerned about the environment. It seems high time that we have such concern, while much of the environment can still be salvaged and protected from the abuses of a modern industrial age. Given such sentiment, the firm that takes a leadership position for environmental protection stands to benefit from customer approval and positive media attention.

Another issue important to many Americans involves foreign inroads to the detriment of many U.S. manufacturers and jobs. Regardless of the great controversy over the desirability of free trade, many middle-class Americans have applauded the leadership of Wal-Mart in its widely publicized "buy American" policy.

What is the moral for other businesses? Be alert to the concerns of the public, and when possible, act on them to achieve a leadership role.

CONSIDER

Can you identify additional learning insights that could be applicable to other firms in other situations?

QUESTIONS

1. How might you attempt to compete with Wal-Mart if you were
   a. a small hardware merchant?
   b. a small clothing store for men?
   c. a Woolworth store?
2. Do you think Wal-Mart is vulnerable today? If so, in what way? If not, do you see any limits to its growth?
3. Why do you think the hypermarket idea failed to meet expectations? Was Wal-Mart too quick to table expansion plans for its hypermarkets?
4. What weaknesses do you see Wal-Mart as having now or potentially, and what would you advise to help overcome them?

5. Wal-Mart is now entering urban areas. What new challenges does this present? Will Wal-Mart need to change? Can "the Wal-Mart way" work only in rural areas?

6. Can discounting go on forever? What are the limits to growth by price competition?

7. Discuss Wal-Mart's business practices (especially in regard to unions, invasion of small towns, and supplier relations) in terms of the ethical ramifications for the industry and for society. Should students be encouraged to emulate these practices?

INVITATION TO ROLE PLAY

1. Assume the role of a top executive of Kmart. You have seen Wal-Mart's phenomenal growth to the point that it now is the biggest retailer, surpassing Kmart in size. Admittedly most of this growth has come in smaller communities where you were not a presence. Now Wal-Mart is invading your turf. How do you counter this competitive thrust of the world's most successful retailer? Be as specific as you can. (If Kmart and Wal-Mart stores are both in your community, you may want to visit and analyze the strengths and weaknesses of both.)

2. You are the principal adviser to David Glass, who has replaced Sam Walton as chief executive. What advice do you give for continuing the successful growth pattern now that the charismatic founder is no longer there to inspire the organization? Be as specific as you can, and make assumptions if needed, but spell them out.

INVITATION TO RESEARCH

Has Wal-Mart faltered since Sam Walton's death? Are there any ominous signs on the horizon?

PART V

ENTREPRENEURIAL ADVENTURES

CHAPTER 19

Parma Pierogies: Latent Promise

Mary Poldruhi may well be the best-known entrepreneur in Cleveland, Ohio. Even President Clinton knows her. While on the campaign trail in Cleveland in August 1992, he, his wife Hillary, and the Gores stopped in to have lunch at her year-old restaurant. This, of course, brought national exposure by the press. It also led to Mary's invitation to Washington for an inaugural luncheon, "Faces of Hope," a unique celebration of ordinary citizens who faced and conquered hardships. Clinton had drawn the guest list from thousands of persons he met during his cross-country campaign. Those invited for the inauguration had stories that touched him in a more personal way: "There are people here today who've succeeded against all odds," Clinton told his guests. "There's a young woman here today who opened a restaurant, when no bank would give her money. She just got on the telephone and called everybody with a Polish surname, said she wanted to open a Polish restaurant. Finally, she found enough people to bankroll her."

MARY POLDRUHI

Born into a big, traditional, ethnic family in Cleveland, Ohio, Poldruhi is the oldest of eight children. Because of her father's opinion that "girls don't have to go to college, just be secretaries, get married, and have babies," she worked as a secretary at Ohio Bell Telephone Company. She was promoted to customer service official and then advertising consultant for the Yellow Pages. Finding no challenge in these jobs, she left Ohio Bell to acquire a real estate license. But she dreamed of being an entrepreneur, and a Polish restaurant seemed a natural business opportunity. Working in real estate gave her the flexible hours she needed to pursue her dream.

"Everybody has that American dream to start their own company. You start from nothing with a lot of energy. I feel if you are committed to it and do a lot of hard work, you can succeed." At 33 years old, Poldruhi is a dynamo. "I am thinking global. The sky's the limit. Every city in the country has ethnics. I think we will be the next hottest fast food chain in the country." Well, perhaps it is a little soon to think about beating up on McDonald's, but Central European food could fill a unique marketing niche.

Articles about Poldruhi and her restaurant have appeared in *Time*, *Cleveland Magazine*, *Restaurant Hospitality*, and *Tempo* and in such newspapers as the *Wall Street Journal*, the *Cleveland Plain Dealer*, and a number of smaller suburban newspapers. Poldruhi was honored as "Woman-of-Achievement of 1993" by the National Association for Women in Careers.

Poldruhi's ingenuity was hardly better evidenced than in her initial fund raising, which the president referred to. At first she had tried to get seed money from banks, but those she contacted either refused or made unacceptable demands as loan conditions. Showing a nascent flair for promotion and media relations, she wrote to two local TV celebrities, explaining her project and her plight and soliciting their interest and, hopefully, their public support. She must have been very compelling and persuasive, for they joined her endeavor. Next, she began looking in the Yellow Pages for people who might have money to invest, such as doctors, dentists, and lawyers. Since her business idea was for an ethnic restaurant, Poldruhi thought the best way to segment the market for investors would be to seek out only those who might have an ethnic heritage, as evidenced by names ending in "-ski." She made cold calls mostly by telephone and raised $240,000 from 80 investors. In a quote that appeared in *Time* magazine, Poldruhi said, "I would have called every "-ski" in the United States and Poland if I had to."[1] Her persistence, confidence, and focus raise an interesting question: Is there an entrepreneurial personality? See the following box.

THE RESTAURANT

Poldruhi named her restaurant Parma Pierogies—Parma being the name of the Cleveland suburb—and she gave it the motif of a pink flamingo in white socks. (Pink flamingos still grace some yards in Parma.) The menu is for the most part ethnic and, naturally, features pierogies. These pierogies are offered boiled or deep-fried and come stuffed with such traditional fillings as potato and cheddar as well as innovative ones like spinach and mozzarella, all topped

[1] Thomas McCarroll, "Starting Over," *Time* (Jan. 6, 1992): 63.

ISSUE BOX

IS THERE AN ENTREPRENEURIAL PERSONALITY?

The issue of whether certain persons have the right personality traits for self-employment and others do not and should not even consider it is akin to the enduring controversy of the leadership personality and even the sales personality: Are certain persons, because of their innate personality traits, bound to be leaders or to be great salespeople?

Most experts today disagree with the idea that leaders, and great salespeople, are born, not made. Diverse personalities have found success in leadership and in sales. But still the belief persists among some that the great ones were naturals.

How about entrepreneurship? Psychologists have designed tests to determine if a person has the right aptitude, but the tests' validity is suspect. Still, we can identify certain traits that may make some persons more successful in working for themselves. Most of this identification comes from the beliefs and actions of already successful entrepreneurs.

The true entrepreneur is a doer, not a dreamer. A lot of people have ideas, but few are determined to do something about them now, and few have the courage to give up the security of a regular paycheck to do it. Persistence, great self-confidence, an ability to disregard disappointments and rejections and keep trying—these are often mentioned by entrepreneurs. And some people just cannot stand working for someone else.

Mary Poldruhi most likely would have been successful outside of entrepreneurship. The qualities that make for successful entrepreneurs should work well in other endeavors. But her dream of entrepreneurship was irrepressible.

Do you think you have what it takes to be an entrepreneur? Why or why not?

---

with butter and onions. Some call them Polish ravioli. The moderately priced menu is rounded out with other ethnic specialties such as potato pancakes and a selection of fruit-filled dessert pierogies. Poldruhi has also reluctantly offered the popular kielbasa, although this violates her conception of healthy food.

Mary Poldruhi likes to emphasize the healthiness of pierogies. They are high in carbohydrates, and each contains only one gram of fat. They have considerably fewer calories than most other fast foods, as the menu prominently notes:

PIEROGIES ARE GOOD FOR YOU!

1/2 Dozen even with 1 oz. real butter and 1 oz. real sour cream is only about 500 calories! A "big burger" and fries is 1200 calories!

Prices are modest. A half-dozen pierogies with the toppings and salad cost only $4.99, and there is no tipping.

A VISIT

The first Parma Pierogies is located in a one-story building on the corner of a street with heavy local traffic. It shares the building with a bakery. The parking lot is small, having a capacity for about 10 cars. Her neighbors are mostly small commercial establishments, but all other fast food restaurants are at least a quarter-mile away.

Upon entering the premises, one is conscious of a predominance of pink and green colors and of soft music. The menu is on the wall and easily visible as you enter. Along another wall are articles and photographs highlighting the history of this restaurant, including pictures of celebrities. The eating area is small, accommodating 16 tables, with a maximum capacity of 64 people. The feeling is one of casual comfort.

Customers give the cashier their order and receive a drink, straw, napkin, and a disposable fork and knife on a tray with the number of the order. They pay, take the tray, and find a seat, and employees bring the order to the table in a few minutes. Those who order coffee can expect free refills from an attentive waitress.

The restaurant is open seven days a week. During weekdays and Sundays, Mary Poldruhi has three to four servers; on the busy weekends she needs a few more employees. Overall, she has about 20 employees. Some 60 percent of the business comes from people dining in the restaurant: the rest comes from carry-out. Customers come from all over metropolitan Cleveland, and some even from as far away as Columbus, Ohio, 150 miles distant. In her one establishment, Mary sells 12,000 pierogies a week.

One of her concerns—one shared by most fast-food restaurants—is the turnover of employees. Most are part-time; the few full-time employees are housewives whose hours are limited to daytime. Students are the major source of part-time employees, but many prospectives would rather babysit on weekends, because it is easier work. Consequently, Poldruhi has to rely more than she would like on unskilled workers, and she has problems finding sufficient time to fully train them. She has also employed handicapped workers.

THE FUTURE

Mary Poldruhi is eager to expand. The 12,000-pierogies-a-week business convinces her that there is good potential for more restaurants with the same format. Are such growth ideas merely idle dreams, or do they represent a realistic probability? Several factors need to be considered.

First, does the ethnic food idea have staying power? Are pierogies a menu item that customers will order time after time? After two years of successful operation, the answer seems to be *yes*: repeat business has been strong.

Second, does the menu have broad appeal, or is it limited to a narrow consumer sector? The restaurant features Central European ethnic food, and many large cities in the north and northeast have sizable ethnic populations. These groups should be as attracted to the Parma Pierogies concept as the people of Cleveland.

Third, can the customer base be expanded? That is, are non-ethnics likely to be attracted to such a menu? Mary Poldruhi believes this is very much the case, and she notes that her restaurant is already appealing to many different consumers. Furthermore, she sees the health food idea as having great potential in a nation becoming more and more concerned about healthy living and health foods.

Fourth, is she likely to acquire the capital to expand fairly rapidly, or is this such a limiting factor that competitors may easily wedge into the market as they see the food concept becoming popularized? Financing may not be all that big a problem, for several reasons, as we will discuss next. The possibilities for obtaining venture capital and growth money outside of normal banking channels should be encouraging for many other small entrepreneurs. But some banks are more receptive to new entrepreneurial ideas and well-thought-out business plans than others.

Mary is already thinking about going public—that is, selling stock to investors. Once a business achieves fair success, with a good track record and a promising future, a public offering of stock is likely to be eagerly subscribed to by investors wanting in on the ground floor. This is even more likely when the business is somewhat unique from existing businesses, as Mary Poldruhi's is. Given her talent for gaining publicity, Poldruhi should be as successful in selling stock as she was in initially getting celebrities and 80 investors to back her.

The use of franchising offers the possibility for rapid expansion. See the following box for a discussion of franchising.

Mary Poldruhi already has a list of 2000 potential franchisees from coast to coast, and she faces the possibility of a real business breakthrough. Additional expansion in metropolitan Cleveland is the first step, a sort of "testing of the waters." The ethnic compositions of Chicago, Detroit, and Pittsburgh are very similar to Cleveland's, making those cities reasonable expansion candidates. Interestingly, Mary Poldruhi sees great potential in non-Central European markets such as Los Angeles, "where we can play up the health aspect. Healthy food and good service are the wave of the future, and this concept fits right in there."[2]

---

[2]"Five for the Future," *Restaurant Hospitality* (Dec. 1993): 80.

INFORMATION BOX

FRANCHISING

Franchising is a contractual arrangement in which the franchisor extends to independent franchisees the right to conduct a certain kind of business according to a particular format. While the franchising arrangement may involve a product, a more common type of franchise today provides a service rather than a product. The major contribution of the franchisor is a carefully developed, promoted, and controlled operation. Franchise operations depend on similar physical facilities and external signs to identify their far-flung outlets. Important to a franchise are prescribed standards and procedures to ensure uniform offerings and service.

A firm realizes two major advantages in expanding through franchised outlets rather than company-owned units. First, expansion can be very rapid, since the franchisees put up some or most of the money. Almost the only limit to growth is the need to screen applicants, to find suitable sites for new outlets, and to develop the managerial controls necessary to ensure consistency of performance. Second, people normally operate their own outlets more conscientiously because they are entrepreneurs with a personal stake, not hired managers.

The potential franchisee or licensee finds that the major advantage over other means of self-employment lies in the lower risk of business failure or, to say it positively, a greater chance of success. By going with an established franchisor, an entrepreneur will have a business that has proven customer acceptance and recognition. The franchisee can also benefit from well-developed managerial and promotional techniques and from the group buying power that is afforded.

One of the controversies between franchisors and franchisees is how rigid should be the controls and standards of operation. These range from the very strict policies of McDonald's to the much looser ones of many of the small franchise operations. As a prospective franchisee, which would you favor, and why?

WHAT CAN BE LEARNED?

Mary Poldruhi's accomplishments lead us to several rather significant insights for entrepreneurs. While individuals and situations differ, the latent promise of Parma Pierogies has considerable transferability to other persons and situations.

If at all possible, seek to differentiate. Such an admonition applies to all business, not merely to entrepreneurs. But it is more important to the latter simply because they are trying to wrest a place in the market with a new enterprise. If resources are limited—as they are with most small businesses—an attractive difference from existing competitors may be the crucial ingredient.

The pierogi, with its Central European flair and its healthy food connotation, offers an interesting change from the hamburger, chicken, taco, and pizza menus of the major fast-food restaurants. The market for pierogies is many times less than that for hamburgers, but this fact is offset by the absence of competition. The existence of a niche suggests that aggressive growth efforts, even in such a limited market, could bring great success. And Mary Poldruhi does not even accept the idea that the market may be limited: "healthy foods . . . are the wave of the future."

Good publicity can jet-start an entrepreneurial effort. Poldruhi excelled in gaining publicity for her nascent enterprise, even to the unbelievable extent of gaining the patronage of the president of the United States and being singled out as an outstanding example of entrepreneurship. She zealously cultivated all efforts at publicity, spending little for advertising as a result. Early on she was able to enlist the interest and support of local television celebrities, and the ingenuity of her fund-raising was a natural for media attention. But Mary Poldruhi enhanced her media exposure, not by blatantly seeking it out, but rather by being cooperative and appreciative of any reporters or researchers who had an interest.

Publicity can be a powerful tool for any business if it is carefully crafted, being neither too overt and self-seeking nor too secretive and proprietary. In particular, the media are attracted to a good story.

The franchising format offers great opportunities, but also lurking dangers. Franchising is significantly different from other types of business operations. Rapid growth is possible through franchising—far more rapid than the growth a firm can achieve on its own, even with substantial resources. Because somebody else is putting up most or all of the capital for an outlet, the major requirements for expansion are finding and wooing sufficient investors/licensees and locating attractive sites for additional units. Both requirements can be met carelessly in the quest for wild expansion or carefully for controlled expansion.

In franchising a few poor operations can hurt the other outlets because all operate under the same format and logo. This is similar to the situation of any chain operation (a few stores can hurt the image of the rest of the chain), but a franchise system is composed of independent entrepreneurs who tend to be less controllable than the hired managers of a chain.

The rapid growth made possible through a franchise system can be its downfall. Because growth in the number of units can occur easily and quickly, it is tempting to rush headlong into opening more units to meet the demand of prospective licensees and receive the up-front licensing fee. Emphasis on growth often means that existing operations are ignored. As a consequence, they are undercontrolled, and emerging problems do not receive adequate attention. Screening of people and locations tends to become superficial. Eventually, the bubble may burst, and the franchisor may be faced with the realization that many outlets are marginal and need to be closed. It remains to be seen whether Mary Poldruhi will be prudent in her quest for expansion or succumb to the very real temptation to be reckless.

Tight controls are particularly needed in franchise operations. All firms, but especially franchise chains, need to maintain tight controls over widespread outlets in order to be sufficiently informed about emerging problems and opportunities, to optimize use of resources, and to protect a desired image and standard of performance.

Establishing a control process requires three basic steps:

1. Standards of performance must be set and communicated to those persons involved.
2. Performance should be checked against these standards.
3. Deviations from expected performance usually require corrective action.

As a franchise enterprise grows, such controls become all the more important. For Mary Poldruhi, formal controls will be less important with a handful of outlets than with 20 or more.

When standards are specifically designated and communicated to those responsible for adhering to them, the next step of the control process can be imposed: measuring performance against the standards. Performance is best measured when outside auditors, inspectors, or district and home-office executives visit the premises unannounced, perhaps with a checklist in hand, and grade actual against expected performance. All aspects of the operation should be checked—from the grease content of the french fries to the soap supply in the restrooms.

After deviations from the standards are identified and their importance assessed, measures should be taken to correct the situation. Although franchise operations involve independent owners, the franchisor still has authority to impose sanctions on unacceptable performance. Such sanctions typically consist of warnings, probation, and finally, if performance still does not meet standards, removal of the franchise. Will Mary Poldruhi be tough enough to do this? In expanding a new enterprise, owners may be tempted to be soft in order to avoid alienating desired franchisees. In the long run, this can be most unwise.

CONSIDER

Do you see any other learning insights coming from this adventure in entrepreneurship?

QUESTIONS

1. Do you think Mary Poldruhi's expansion dreams are realistic? Why or why not?
2. What do you think of Parma Pierogies's motif of a pink flamingo with white socks?
3. The high turnover of employees makes for uneven service. Do you have any constructive ideas for improving this?
4. Does the menu of Parma Pierogies appeal to you? What, if anything, would you like to see added?
5. Mary Poldruhi is actively involved in the day-to-day operation of her business. Do you see any potential problems as she expands geographically?

INVITATION TO ROLE PLAY

Mary Poldruhi has hired you as a marketing expert to guide her growth beyond metropolitan Cleveland. What marketing strategy plans can you offer? Be as specific as possible, and defend your ideas.

INVITATION TO RESEARCH

Investigate the current situation with Parma Pierogies. Has expansion taken place? Has the business been taken public? How successful does it appear to be?

CHAPTER 20

Potpourri of Entrepreneurial Adventures

CLEVELAND ANTIQUARIAN BOOKS

William Chrisant is a slender, soft-spoken man. He graduated from Akron University with a degree in ancient history. However, it did not take him long to realize that his major did little to help him get a job.

His future career course was formed when he went to a book auction. He had $50 to spend. Old books were packed in cartons, and customers bid on the cartons. Most of the authors Bill Chrisant had never heard of, but the books were old, some were first editions, and some were even signed by the authors, so he thought they must have some value to someone. The bidding started low and did not get much higher; he was able to buy three cartons at an average price of $13. One carton was filled with science fiction books, and not long after Bill lugged the books home he heard of a dealer in Michigan who might be interested in old science fiction titles. Bill made his first sale for $400.

He opened an antiquarian bookstore in Akron, Ohio, and stayed there for 16 years. He remembers the buyer from Los Angeles who paid $20,000 for books. It was the largest amount ever spent by a single customer in his store. Patricia Barrett was one of his customers in Akron. She owned a shop selling oriental rugs and read everything he had on oriental rugs. She and her husband, a psychologist, often spent $1000 a month on books for their library.

THE MOVE TO CLEVELAND

In 1993 Bill closed his Akron store and moved to Cleveland's East Side. "People here are cultured, well-educated, and wealthy," he said. "I think it's promising for my business." He found a streetfront location in a commercial neighborhood of antique dealers and small shops, which seemed most compatible with his type of store. The major drawback was that the premises required considerable customizing to be suitable, and Bill spent almost $60,000 doing so. The landlord graciously gave him 3 months' rent free.

Unfortunately, in less than a year Bill realized that the store was not big enough for his 20,000 and growing number of books. Furthermore, foot traffic was nonexistent in the evening as all the stores, except for a few restaurants, were closed. He believed that for a store of this type the "friends of books" like to gather in the evening, have a cup of coffee and enjoy the "wonderful mix of old books" in a "gorgeous atmosphere." He found another location about eight blocks away in a bustling neighborhood center having half a dozen restaurants, some with sidewalk cafes; four movie theaters; and green space for walkers and entertainment. The clincher for the decision to move was that the space available was three times the size of his present store.

So, the $60,000 initial investment in store premises, as well as his time and effort in the remodeling, turned out to be of only short-term value.

THE MARKETING STRATEGY

The Product

Most antique book dealers specialize in only a few subjects, but Chrisant has a large inventory of books with diverse topics. "Most of my antique books are illustrated with photos, paintings or drawings," he said. "I've lots of books on arts, antiques, and some on history. You can find in my store Chaucer's works from 1561 for $6000 and a novel by Ernest Hemingway for $6." He believes in emphasizing quality more than quantity. "I think it's better to have 10 good books than 1000 ordinary ones, because these 10 will be a better investment." He maintains that the price of antique books is rising more rapidly than that of gold. "People who have money and like books realize that they can buy a good book and make a good investment at the same time."

Chrisant seeks books that have some quality that makes them collectible or scarce. In this quest he is an eager buyer of old books; in fact, since he opened in Cleveland he has bought more books than he has sold. His inventory grows ever larger—hence the sudden realization that the store he so painstakingly renovated in 1993 is now, in less than a year, hardly big enough.

Pricing

After more than 16 years in the business, Bill Chrisant has a rather good intuitive "feel" for the value of a book and what price he is likely to get for it. For less expensive books he will try to double his cost; for the more expensive ones he may test the waters at several times the cost. On those occasions when he thinks he has bought a real jewel at an attractive price, he may mark it up at many times his cost. The expensive books, of course, sell infrequently. In order to attract passersby into the store, he has a table of $3 used books.

Chrisant maintains a firm policy of no haggling or negotiating on prices. If a customer will not accept the price marked, he invites them to pick out a less expensive book. The one exception to this rigid one-price policy is his policy toward book dealers, who sometimes have come from considerable distance in search of a specific book requested by a customer. He gives legitimate dealers a 10 percent discount.

Promotion

Chrisant is concerned about his promotional efforts. Part of his concern is due to the great peaks and valleys of his business. Some days he does not record a single sale; other times he needs several part-time salespeople. His annual sales are close to $250,000.

Generally, once a month he places small ads in suburban newspapers, since he believes most of his customers come from the eastern suburbs. He will begin using some direct mail promotional flyers, especially after he makes his change of location. He intends to have one—and if it goes well, more—open house at his new store, so he has been diligently recording customers' names and addresses and has a mailing list now in the hundreds.

Customers

Who buys antique books, some of them expensive? Usually these are rather affluent, often professional, people who collect old books, sometimes for investment purposes, perhaps more often simply to adorn a bookshelf or bookcase. Many potential buyers are looking for books limited to a certain subject, such as Napoleonic history, primitive art, or native folklore. Some buyers have no intent to become book collectors, but in browsing find something of interest. This may start them on the path of antique book collecting.

ANALYSIS

This small store has found a marketing niche. Although other stores sell old books in northeastern Ohio, none has the breadth of inventory of Cleveland Antiquarian Books. Rather, they stick with only a few specialized topical areas. A knowledgeable book buyer observed: "One couldn't find another bookstore like this in the whole area. I saw a few similar places in New York and in Chicago, but not in northern Ohio."

Of some question regarding this unique niche is how large it really is—despite the "hundreds" of names and addresses that Bill has accumulated. Undoubtedly some of these represent old customers from his Akron store, and while some of these may venture the 50 miles to Cleveland, most, not so dedicated to collecting, probably will not. Other names are surely casual stoppers-in, who bought something on impulse but are unlikely to provide much repeat business.

The profitability of the business is very questionable, despite the $250,000 annual revenue. Chrisant lives very frugally, over the store. Most of what he earns he plows back into buying more books; this is almost an obsession for him. He admits that his net profit is very low, but he had given little thought to the fact that return on investment is the true measure of profitability. For example, to obtain the $250,000 in sales, he has about that amount tied up in his inventory of books. See the following box for a discussion of return on investment.

SOUTHERN MOTEL

Ray and Dorothy Cummings had an important decision to ponder. In early 1993 Dorothy had inherited an old motel in a small Georgia town just off I-95, the main north/south route to Florida from the northeast. The motel was seemingly on its last legs. Whether it could be resurrected into a viable enterprise was uncertain. If Ray and Dorothy Cummings were to actively operate this family albatross, they would have to move from Atlanta. Somehow, this did not trouble either one: They were tired of the big city and had no strong ties and commitments there. But could they make a go of this aged motel?

BACKGROUND

Southern Motel got its start as a tourist camp in the late 1920s. At that time it was the only tourist camp or motel in the town, and one of the first such operations in that part of the state. However, the town's location on the main highway leading to the east coast of Florida looked promising for such an enterprise. Furthermore, the town was a central marketplace for the tobacco, cotton, and truck farmers of the surrounding area, and a considerable number of buyers and sellers for the farm trade and various tobacco auctions gave further potential.

Dorothy's grandparents used billboard advertising heavily, and business increased satisfactorily. They added new units as well as a gas station and a restaurant, thereby enabling patrons to satisfy all their needs at one stop.

INFORMATION BOX

THE GREAT IMPORTANCE OF RETURN ON INVESTMENT

The true measure of the profitability of any enterprise is the return on investment (ROI)—that is, the interest, dividends, or profits we get for the money invested. This is the case whether the money is in a money market fund paying 3 percent or in a business where it may realize much more.

To demonstrate the key importance of ROI and, for the retailer, how this relates to the investment in inventory, let us consider the two following scenarios: A depicts Bill Chrisant's present situation; B shows what his ROI would be if he could hold his book inventory in check:

	A	B
Sales	$250,000	$250,000
Investment in store fixtures and decor	60,000	60,000
Net profit percent of sales	4%	4%
Net profit dollars	10,000	10,000
Investment in books at retail	250,000	125,000
Estimated cost of books inventory	125,000	62,500
Return on investment:	$\dfrac{10,000}{185,000} = 5\%$	$\dfrac{10,000}{122,500} = 8\%$
net profit $s divided by (inventory cost + investment in fixtures)		

Discussion: In example A, which approximates Chrisant's present position because of his high investment in inventory and initial fixtures, ROI is 5 percent, not much more than Chrisant could get putting this money into money market funds. If he could halve his book inventory, he would increase his ROI to 8 percent. Actually, many retailers are able to keep their inventory investment to no more than one-fourth of sales.

Do you think Bill's sales would suffer much if he reduced his inventory investment by one-half? Why or why not?

However, the Great Depression and the end of the Florida land boom adversely affected business, with tourism coming to a virtual standstill. The camp survived due to the sporadic use by those attending the tobacco auctions and other agricultural market activities.

World War II brought an upsurge of business, not from tourists, due to gasoline rationing, but from an air force base in the proximity. The camp, now called a motel, provided housing for the construction workers at the base and later for the families of those stationed there. With the ending of the war, tourist trade accentuated, and the family constructed more units. Several new motels were built in the town, but competition did not seem a serious problem. The Korean war and increased activity at the base benefited the entire business community.

By the beginning of 1980, Southern had been a profitable operation for almost 60 years. But the situation was worsening. Three major problems threatened the viability of the whole enterprise:

1. The interstate highway bypassed the town, thereby reducing the number of travelers and the exposure of the motel to through traffic.
2. The motel business itself had become heavily saturated as major motel chains and franchise operations, such as Holiday Inn and Ramada, opened nearby. These motels offered modern decor and other amenities such as television, air conditioning, swimming pools, atmosphere restaurants, and—very important—reservation service. The latter, for a motel chain, was a powerful influence in keeping tourist patronage within the chain: Many travelers find the convenience of having a night's lodging ensured at a destination a day's journey away much to be preferred over the need to "shop" for a motel at the end of a long, tiring day on the highway.
3. Southern Motel was also encountering problems with its gas station and restaurant operations. Both of these had been operated by lessees for a number of years. The lessees, however, had permitted the physical facilities to deteriorate, management and service was a continuing problem, and in light of increased competition, neither the gas station nor the restaurant was any longer profitable.

THE PRESENT SITUATION

The overbuilding of motel/hotel facilities all over the United States in the late 1980s had been particularly hard on older, marginal operations. The restaurant and gas station operations had been abandoned. And the motel proper, some 70 rooms, had fallen into an acute state of disrepair. The last years of Dorothy's father, who owned and operated the motel, had not been a time for reinvesting and aggressive management.

Just down the road a half mile are a 140-room Holiday Inn and a 90-room Ramada, original motels from the 1970s and early 1980s, but refurbished about 1990. Three miles up the interstate at the next exit is a 4-year-old Days Inn, with some 60 rooms, offering prices 20 percent less than Holiday Inn and Ramada and not far different from Southern's.

The interstate highway bypassing the town had in recent years become more and more busy, practically year round now. The natural attractions of Florida, the great draw of Disney World and Cape Kennedy, and many other attractions made Florida by the 1980s practically a mecca. And most of the travelers stopped for rest and lodging somewhere on the route. This, of course, brought considerable business to the town. But it also intensified the competition around Southern Motel, to its severe detriment.

Ray Cummings winced as he looked over the operating reports of the last several years. Occupancy averaged only about 20 percent, and some nights barely 10 percent. While expenses were lessened with the abandonment of the gas station and restaurant, the low occupancy put the enterprise in the red many weeks. What made the situation of more concern to Ray was that the trend of occupancy was ever downward: Things were steadily getting worse.

To be really competitive in terms of facilities would require a major investment in rebuilding and modernizing. He mused about this, and rue-fully had to admit to himself that such an investment could not even ensure that the competitive problem would be solved, since these chain motels had engendered brand loyalty on a national scale and heavily promoted their reservation service (whereby, free of charge, one motel would contact an-other at the subsequent destination for availability of rooms and placement of reservations).

In defense against the chain motels, some independent motel operators were joining motel associations, such as Quality Inns, Days Inns, Best Western, and a number of others. These permitted the member firms to ben-efit from joint advertising expenditures, a recognized national or regional sign and motif, a uniform and carefully maintained reputation for quality and service, some interaction with other motel operators and their problems and solutions, as well as certain managerial and accounting aids. And, not least, they had the reservation services.

However, to join such an association would also require a considerable investment in remodeling an older motel and bringing it up to the standards required for membership. And joining would still not give Southern Motel any distinct advantage over its present competitors and would certainly add to the cost burden to be met before any profits would be forthcoming: not only fran-chise and association costs, but the fixed expense due to the financing of the new construction needed. This would require a higher occupancy rate to break even.

OPTIONS

The basic question remained: Could an older motel compete and survive in today's arena of big business and sophisticated technology? It seemed to Ray Cummings that he and his wife faced three options with Southern Motel.

The first option would be to try to join a motel association. Ray's inves-tigations indicated that he would need $1 to $1.5 million dollars to bring

Southern up to standards for acceptance in an association. Assuming that Ray could find such financing, he would still be left with hefty interest overhead. And while occupancy would certainly be improved, he wondered if it would be enough to compensate for the debt burden.

The second option would be to simply continue as is. The steadily declining occupancy rate dissuaded Ray from this alternative. Should he and his wife waste their next few years on a doomed enterprise? He wondered at this point how they might get out from under this white elephant. They could hardly abandon it completely; there would still be property taxes to pay and liability insurance. And the city council was not overjoyed at the prospect of an abandoned, derelict motel on the outskirts of town. To convert the complex to some other use could solve the problem. The logical changeover would be to apartments or to a nursing home, but the economics of the town hardly supported the first possibility, and elderly people of the town and surrounding community were reasonably taken care of with existing facilities.

A few days before, Dorothy Cummings had suggested another possibility. "What if we try to do something in between upgrading to association standards and continuing the way we are," she had said. "Instead of coming up with a million or so, if this is even possible, could we do enough refurbishing for $50,000 or maybe $100,000 at the most—new carpeting, drapes, new TVs, painting, maybe some new mattresses—to make this more attractive?"

He remembered telling her that this still wouldn't solve the problem of getting into a reservation network. And without that, he didn't see how the occupancy rate could be improved. But a germ of an idea had kept gnawing at him since this conversation. He began toying with some figures. See the following box.

Ray pondered the decision. Could they possibly raise the occupancy rate high enough to make this a viable undertaking? "Let's give it a try," Dorothy said.

ANALYSIS

In examining this not-uncommon dilemma of a small enterprise trying to compete with big firms having far more resources, we need to consider several questions. We will try to answer them in the context of this small enterprise.

1. Can we as a small firm find any unique strengths against the larger competitors?
2. If so, how can we best capitalize on them?
3. What types of customers can we best cater to?

INFORMATION BOX

BREAKEVEN ANALYSIS—REVISITED

The breakeven point was discussed in Chapter 9. As you may recall, the general formula is

$$\text{Breakeven} = \frac{\text{Total fixed costs}}{\text{Contribution to overhead}}$$

In shuffling through the records, Ray saw that presently with expenses held down to almost minimum customer service, the business could barely be in the black at about a 20 percent occupancy; when occupancy fell below this, as it often did, then the motel lost money. He then calculated the breakeven point for his 70 rooms based on a $30 room rate as about $420 per night $12,600 per month, and $151,200 for the year. This did not include any compensation for Ray and Dorothy. If they did some moderate refurbishing, and committed another $5,000 for advertising or promotion and perhaps better customer service, then the breakeven point would rise. And Ray thought he ought to add $20,000 for some compensation for himself and Dorothy. Checking with a bank, he found he could get a $75,000 loan at 10 percent with a 3-year payback. This would increase their overhead $25,000 for the payback on principal plus $7,500 interest per year. The new breakeven number of rentals per year would be

$$\text{BE} = \frac{\$151,200 + \$32,500 + \$5,000 + \$20,000}{\$30}$$

$$= 6,957 \text{ room rentals per year at } \$30 \text{ each}$$
$$\text{or } \frac{6,957}{360} = \text{about 20 rentals per night.}$$
$$\text{This is an occupancy rate of } \frac{20}{70} = 25.6\%$$
$$\text{to breakeven.}$$

If the room rate for Southern were reduced to $22 in an effort to maximize its competitive pricing advantage, how would this affect the occupancy rate needed to breakeven? Do you think such a low price would be highly effective? Why or why not?

At first examination, a small entrepreneur with an aging facility may see no competitive strengths. Yet, there often are some. In situations like Southern Motel, these strengths may even be substantial. For example, the single greatest strength that Southern can offer against the likes of Holiday Inn, Ramada, and Days Inn is its breakeven point. With the major facilities paid for years before, even with moderate refurbishing the breakeven point of Southern is likely to be several times lower than that of its competitors, who may well be facing room occupancy breakevens of 75 percent and higher. This has several major consequences for our small firm, all positive. First, it can offer prices significantly lower than its competitors' and still do well. And second, it can be profitable with a much lower occupancy rate.

Of course, the advantage of our small firm must be capitalized on. It needs to communicate to would-be customers that it has clean and comfortable facilities at real economy prices. And this poses some creative challenges as to how to advertise this message.

Given its price advantage over competitors, Southern needs to determine who its prime target customers are, the ones who are most interested in low prices. Are these customers likely to be business travelers? Except for a few who have no expense accounts, most of these will opt for the Holiday Inn or Ramada. But other travelers, such as families with children and senior citizens traveling to and from Florida, should be a prime market segment. The challenge is to reach these people. But it can be done.

WHAT CAN BE LEARNED?

Is a unique niche always desirable? Cleveland Antiquarian Books has a unique niche. But is it really that attractive for a would-be entrepreneur? To be considered is whether the target niche is likely to be big enough to support an operation and provide sufficient potential. While Antiquarian Books' sales of a quarter million dollars seem reasonably satisfactory for a startup business, in reality it may not be if the potential for antique books is little larger. The investment needed to achieve such sales reduces the return on investment and makes the whole enterprise only marginally profitable without growth possibilities. Hopefully, the potential will be expanded as more customers are shown the advantages in investment appreciation and pride of ownership of such books.

A major advantage of a small, unique niche is that it should be reasonably free from major competitors who see it as not worth their effort. The tradeoff of such competitive insulation, however, is often a diminished potential and growth opportunity.

Return on investment is more important than net profit dollars. The true measure of profitability is the return on investment. If a small enterprise will yield no better return than it can get from investing in mutual funds or savings accounts, why go to all the effort—unless there is good long-term potential? For retailers the major investment usually is inventory. Some businesses can operate with very lean inventories (as we saw in the Wal-Mart case) and thus produce very good returns on investment. For the small entrepreneur, the temptation, as it was for Bill Chrisant, is to pour more and more money into merchandise. While this may be attractive to some customers who want the greatest variety to choose from (with other customers, a great variety becomes only confusing), it devastates the return on investment.

Older small firms can have a significant advantage over newer, bigger competitors. The breakeven analysis highlights the powerful advantage of small firms that have paid off most or all of their building investment. They can compete on a price basis and be profitable at a far lower sales volume than newer competitors can. They can seek out unique identities and customer niches. For the small entrepreneur with an aging store or shopping center who is inclined to give up when a larger competitor comes on the scene, a better course of action may be to carefully assess the competitive strengths and draw up strategies to maximize them. The lower breakeven point, the possibility of lower prices, and the much lower sales volume needed to cover overhead often makes such businesses surprisingly viable.

A small firm often has opportunity for promotional creativity. Ray and Dorothy Cummings determined to get the word out that their motel offered cleanliness and hospitality at attractive prices. They recognized that they had to promote themselves; they had no association to help with reservations. Accordingly, they used billboards where possible for miles in either direction. They passed out fliers to gas stations for 100 miles up and down the interstate, offering attendants a commission for any tourists they could direct their way. They solicited names and addresses of friends of their guests and used a mailing campaign with considerable effectiveness. They found that friendliness and careful catering to their customers' needs was a great asset and necessity in their business. Since many of their customers were repeats, it was even more important to ensure their satisfaction.

Bill Chrisant is groping for ways to promote his antique bookstore. He thinks he has found it in diligently building a mailing list of customers and planning one or more open houses. Perhaps additional ideas can still be found.

A challenge for any small firm is how best to promote, given that advertising funds necessarily are limited. But this often can be done in nontraditional and creative ways. Beware going head to head in promotional strategy with bigger competitors.

CONSIDER

Can you think of other learning insights coming from these small entrepreneurial cases?

QUESTIONS

1. Do you think a highly specialized bookstore, such as a store for antique books, can compete against the superstores for books? Why or why not?
2. Can you think of any other creative promotional strategies for Cleveland Antiquarian Books?
3. Critique the rigid one-price policy Bill Chrisant created for his bookstore.
4. How optimistic are you about the survival of Southern Motel? Support your position.
5. How desirable is it for Southern Motel to cater to truckers?
6. Evaluate the desirability for Southern to seek an affiliation with AAA. Would it be worth an additional $500,000 investment for renovating? Why or why not?
7. Do you agree with Ray and Dorothy Cummings's decision regarding Southern Motel? Why or why not?

ROLE PLAY

1. You are Dorothy Cummings. You desperately need to come up with new promotional ideas for your motel, especially since you have decided not to seek an affiliation with a motel association. What other promotional ideas can you think of besides the ones mentioned in the case? Be as creative as you can.
2. How will you attempt to maximize customer service and hospitality in your motel? What special touches will you consider? How much might these add to your overhead?
3. You have been offered first option to purchase the Antiquarian Bookstore at what seems like a most reasonable price. Given that the financing would be no problem, will you consider this opportunity? Why or why not? If you will consider such a venture, what changes do you think should be made?

CHAPTER 21

OfficeMax:
Promise Fulfilled

For success and sheer drama, few business stories . . . rival that of OfficeMax, a Cleveland-based chain of office-supply superstores. Beginning with little more than a blank sheet of paper, OfficeMax founders Michael Feuer and Robert Hurwitz built—in five years' time—a 300-store retail operation with 1993 sales estimated at $1.5 billion. OfficeMax's official business plan—backed by the real estate and financial clout of majority shareholder Kmart Corp.—calls for a total of 500 stores by 1997, with annual sales of $2.5 billion or more.[1]

THE START

OfficeMax officially began on April Fools' Day, April 1, 1988. The most precious asset at the time was a blank sheet of paper. But the concept, laid out that day on paper, was simple: Create an exciting office products superstore that featured breadth and depth of merchandise, present it in a contemporary manner with professional, friendly service, and then offer prices 30 to 70 percent less than those of more traditional office supply retailers.

Michael Feuer and his partner had recognized a flaw—a strategic window of opportunity—in the existing system for marketing office products,

---

[1] John R. Brandt, "Taking It to the Max," *Corporate Cleveland* (Sept. 1993): 17. To date, little has been written about the success of OfficeMax. Occasional news briefs have mentioned a store opening or acquisition, but until the Brandt article in which Michael Feuer, the founder, detailed the OfficeMax history, nothing had really reached the business press. However, much of the material and the quotes have come from speeches that Feuer has made to various business and graduate business school classes.

and they resolved to "milk it," if they could convince enough investors to give them the resources they needed. The traditional channel of distribution for this merchandise was from manufacturers to wholesalers or distributors and finally to stationers, who were usually small retailers. This rather lengthy channel imposed markups at each stage of the distribution and resulted in relatively high prices for the end user. Feuer saw this as an archaic marketing method, akin to the "old-time mom-and-pop groceries on every corner," which was eventually replaced by more efficient and much lower-priced supermarkets. Newer processes bypassed the wholesalers and distributors and went directly to manufacturers. While Feuer was not unique in recognizing the flawed method of distribution for this product category, he was certainly in the forefront.

Feuer had started with Fabri-Centers of America, now a 600-store chain, 17 years before. He quickly rose through the ranks, but by age 42 was bored. He likes to describe himself in those days as suffering from the Frank Sinatra syndrome—"I wanted to do it my way." And he got tired of what he called *CYB*, "covering your backside," which he saw most executives spending too much of their time trying to do, at the expense of total effectiveness. If he had his own business he could escape these drains on career satisfaction and constraints on his potential. However, he likes to repudiate the common notion of the true entrepreneur as one who has enormous self-confidence, enough to give up the security of the paycheck and go off on his or her own. "I'm not a true entrepreneur because I suffer acutely from what I call 'F of F,' the fear of failure."

In his pursuit of entrepreneurship, Feuer turned down a number of big-money corporate jobs and the perks that go with them. He felt an overwhelming urge to be his own man, to succeed or fail on his own terms. He soon realized, however, the reality of starting a small business from scratch and the contrast with what might have been if he had chosen the corporate option.

Feuer and his partner Robert Hurwitz (who is no longer active in the firm on a full-time basis) were able to mass $3 million from 50 investors, some friends and family members as well as a number of doctors and lawyers. The two partners did not use any debt financing, nor did they seek venture capitalists. They shunned these most common sources of capital, not wanting to give up some control of their enterprise; neither did they want to answer to skeptics and defend every major decision. However, for many promising small businesses, the use of venture capital can provide needed startup funds difficult to obtain otherwise. See the following box for more discussion of venture capitalists and their role in fostering small enterprises.

While Feuer and Hurwitz recognized what seemed an attractive market opportunity, they were not the only ones to do so. In May 1988 an industry trade paper listed all the embryonic firms in the emerging office products

INFORMATION BOX

VENTURE CAPITALISTS: AID TO ENTREPRENEURS

The biggest roadblock to self-employment is financing. Banks tend to be unreceptive to funding unproven new ventures, especially for someone without a track record. Given that most would-be entrepreneurs have limited resources from which to draw, where are they to get the financing needed?

We saw in Chapter 19 how Mary Poldruhi did it, by persuading people with Polish names to buy a share of her forthcoming Polish restaurant. And Feuer and Hurwitz bypassed conventional sources of financing by finding 50 willing investors. For many other would-be entrepreneurs, venture capitalists may be the answer.

Venture capitalists are wealthy individuals (or firms) looking for extraordinary returns for their investments. At the same time, they are willing to accept substantial risks. Backing nascent entrepreneurs in speculative undertakings can be the route to a far greater return on investment than possible otherwise—provided that the venture capitalist chooses wisely who to stake. This decision is much easier after a fledgling enterprise has a promising start. Then venture capitalists may stand in line for a piece of the action. But until then, the entrepreneur may struggle to get seed money.

How do these sources of funding choose among the many business ideas brought to them? "They look at the people, not the ideas," says Arthur Rock, one of the foremost venture capitalists. "Nearly every mistake I've made has been because I picked the wrong people, not the wrong idea."[2]

For a would-be entrepreneur seeking venture capital, then, the most important step may be in selling yourself, in addition to your idea. Intellectual honesty is sometimes mentioned by venture capitalists as a necessary ingredient. This may be defined as a willingness to face facts rigorously and not be deluded by rosy dreams and unrealistic expectations.

Those who win the early support of venture capitalists will likely have to give away a good piece of the action. Should the enterprise prove successful, the venture capitalist will expect to share in the success. Indeed, the funds provided by a venture capitalist may be crucial to even starting, or they may mean the difference in being adequately funded or so poorly funded that failure is almost inevitable.

Selling a definitive business plan to a prospective venture capitalist is usually a requirement for such financing. In the process, of course, you are selling yourself. You may want to do this exercise: Choose a new business idea, develop an initial business plan, and attempt to persuasively present it to a would-be investor.

[2]John Merwin, "Have You Got What It Takes?" *Forbes* (Aug. 3, 1981): 61.

superstore industry. OfficeMax rated number 14 on a list of 15. "We would have been dead last, but another company had started a week later than we did, although neither one of us had any stores."[3]

Feuer and Hurwitz established headquarters offices in a tiny 500-square-foot brick warehouse. It had little heat or air conditioning. The company owned only a few pieces of office furniture, a coffee-maker, and a copy machine, but no fax. The restroom had to be unisex since there was only space for one toilet. They had recruited seven people who were only half-jokingly told that they needed to have small appetites because there was little money to pay them. But Feuer promised that they would share in the financial success of the company, and for these seven their faith and hope for the future was enough. Feuer likes to tell the story of how he reinterviewed a candidate for a vice-president's position who had turned him down in 1988. Had he accepted the job then he would have been a multimillionaire by 1993.

THE FIRST YEAR

Even with $3 million of seed money from the 50 investors, OfficeMax had limited resources for what it proposed to do. A major problem now was to convince manufacturers to do business with this upstart firm in Cleveland. Most manufacturers were satisfied with the existing distribution channels and were reluctant to grant credit to a revolutionary newcomer with hardly a store to its name.

The key to winning the support of these manufacturers lay in convincing them that OfficeMax had such a promising future that it could offer them far more business potential than they would ever have with their present distributors—that OfficeMax would soon be a 30-, 50-, even 300-store chain in a few years. "We explained to them that it was in *their* best interest to help us today—to guarantee a place with us tomorrow."

To make its message credible, OfficeMax needed to create an image of stability and of a firm poised to jump. To help convey this image, Feuer convinced a major Cleveland bank to grant the company an unsecured line of credit. There was only one condition: OfficeMax had to promise that it would never use it. But this impressive-looking line of credit, bespeaking the faith that a major bank seemingly had in the embryonic firm, brought respect from manufacturers. Then OfficeMax even went so far as to ask them for unheard-of terms of sale—such as 60, 90, even 120 days with a discount.

Xerox was somehow persuaded to grant a year's payment delay for purchases. Many other manufacturers also accepted the outlandish requests.

[3]Brandt, "Taking It to the Max," 19.

The bold promise of growth was realized, and many manufacturers 5 years later found OfficeMax to be their best customer. OfficeMax became so important at Xerox that the account is now handled by a divisional president and chief financial officer.

The first store was opened July 5, 1988, 3 months after the enterprise itself was started. This was an amazingly short time to fine-tune the concept, find a site, remodel as needed, and merchandise and staff the store. Feuer explains that the firm urgently needed some cash to survive, hence the desperate efforts to bring the first unit on line. In addition to providing needed cash flow, the first store had to confirm the viability and promise of the superstore concept to investors and suppliers alike.

This the first store quickly did. Customers eagerly embraced the great variety yet lowest prices of the superstore, more commonly known today as a category killer store for office products. (See the following box for more discussion of category killer stores.) The only publicity had been a newspaper story 2 days before. Yet, the store racked up $6400 in sales that first day. (Today, this flagship store achieves six-figure sales every week.)

In the next 90 days, stores two and three were opened, also in metropolitan Cleveland. The fourth store opened in Detroit, not far from the executive offices of Kmart, destined a few years later to become a majority shareholder. Within 6 months the company was breaking even before corporate expenses.

As Feuer describes his work schedule in those early days, he typically was in the corporate office from 7:00 AM to 7:00 PM, stopping at his home just long enough to change into nondescript clothing before going to the first store, where he could inconspicuously observe the shopping activity and talk to customers, asking them what they liked and didn't like about the store. He likes to recount how he would even follow customers who left without buying anything out to the parking lot to ask them why OfficeMax did not meet their needs.

Following the example of Feuer, from its inception the company has had a strong commitment to its customers. For example, OfficeMax accepted collect calls from customers. Any complaints had to be resolved in less than 24 hours, complete with an apology from OfficeMax. The company's objective was to build loyalty. "We're not embarrassed to say that we were wrong—and the customer was right."

As the company began making a small profit, Feuer's worst nightmare was that the accounting had been "screwed up," and that OfficeMax was on the verge of bankruptcy without realizing it. With this tormenting thought, he went back to the existing shareholders after 6 months to raise additional capital. The early success of the enterprise enabled them to raise the per-share price 75 percent over the original placement.

INFORMATION BOX

CATEGORY KILLER STORES

A category killer store is the ultimate in specialty stores. It carries a limited number of product categories, but offers a tremendous choice within those categories. Category killers get their name from the marketing strategy of carrying such a large amount of merchandise at such good prices that they destroy the competition.

The first category killer was Toys "R" Us, started in the late 1950s. It offered such a great assortment of toys at everyday low prices that most department stores had to abandon their toy departments and concede the market to the category killers. Sportmart, a Chicago-based sporting-goods chain, offers customers a choice of 70 models of sleeping bags, 265 styles of socks, and 15,000 fishing lures. The huge category killer bookstores of Borders and Barnes and Noble offer some 100,000 book titles. The pioneer category killer in office supplies was probably Staples, founded in 1985; Office Depot was founded a year later. And OfficeMax entered the market in 1988.

Do you think the category killer superstores could result in overkill, in that they offer customers too much variety? Do you see any negative implications for a bookstore offering 100,000 different titles?

By the end of the first full year, OfficeMax had 6 stores operational in Ohio and Michigan, with total sales of $13 million. The stores were profitable due to undeviating cost-consciousness.

GROWTH CONTINUES

By early 1990, 2 years into the operation, OfficeMax had 17 stores in operation. Unexpectedly, Montgomery Ward proposed a merger between OfficeMax and Office World, a similar operation that Ward had funded along with a number of venture capitalists. Office World had been started with what seemed to OfficeMax executives as almost a king's ransom. But it proceeded to lose $10 million in a very short time. In the negotiations, OfficeMax was in the power position, and it acquired Office World and its seven Chicago locations on rather attractive terms: Its major concession was to relinquish 2 of its 10 board seats to Montgomery Ward and the venture capitalists, but it acquired along with the stores several million dollars in badly needed cash.

By the summer of 1990, OfficeMax had about $25 million in cash, with 30 stores in operation. It raised another $8 million in a third private placement, at a share price 600 percent higher than the original investors had paid just two years before. Corporate offices were now moved into a building with space for both men's and women's restrooms.

Feuer began an aggressive new expansion program, calling for opening 20 additional stores. Competition was heating up in this new superstore industry, and several competitors had gone public to raise funds for more rapid expansion. Several others had gone bankrupt.

The Kmart Connection

The biggest threat facing OfficeMax now came from news that Kmart was poised to roll out its new Office Square superstore chain, which would be a direct threat to OfficeMax. With all the resources of Kmart—financial, managerial, and real estate expertise and influence—Feuer and company saw themselves being crushed and driven into Lake Erie. Feuer consoled himself that being left penniless would at least be character building.

Mostly as a defensive strategy, Feuer sought to open talks with Kmart. Kmart top executives proved to be receptive, and in November 1990 an agreement was negotiated in which Kmart made an investment of about $40 million in return for a 22 percent equity stake in OfficeMax. As part of the agreement, the feared Office Square became a possession of OfficeMax, and Kmart received one seat on the OfficeMax board.

Now the expansion program could begin accelerating, with Kmart's full cooperation and support. So good was the rapport that within 10 months of the initial transaction, discussions were started concerning a broader business relationship with Kmart.

As the original goals of the business were being realized, it was perhaps time to cash in some of the chips, Michael Feuer thought. Two options seemed appropriate for the original investors: (1) go public, or (2) structure a new deal with Kmart. The company decided to go with Kmart. Kmart agreed to buy out all of the shareholders, with the exception of 50 percent of the shares of Feuer and partner Hurwitz, for a total market capitalization of about $215 million. This was up from zero just 42 months earlier. What made the deal particularly attractive was the fact that while 92 percent of OfficeMax was sold to a well-heeled parent, it could still retain total autonomy.

By the end of 1993, OfficeMax had about 325 stores from coast to coast. The typical store was 23,000 square feet and had 6000 items. Faster growth now could be achieved by acquisitions. And in 18 months, OfficeMax made two major acquisitions: the 46-store Office Warehouse chain and the 105-store BizMart chain. It would record about $1.5 billion in sales in 1993 and should achieve $2 billion in 1994. The official business plan called for 500 stores in operation by 1997 and annual sales in excess of $2.5 billion, and these projections looked conservative. Figures 21.1 and 21.2 show the growth in sales and in number of stores from 1988 through 1993.

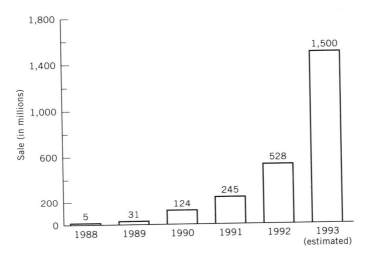

In 1988, OfficeMax projected 1993 sales of less than $100 million; actual 1993 sales will likely be 15 times larger.

Figure 21.1.

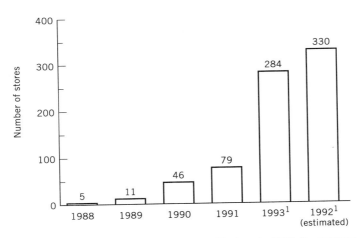

OfficeMax's 1988 business plan called for 50 stores by 1993: the company should end the year with nearly seven times that number.

[1] Includes BizMart stores.
[2] Net of estimated 10 closings.

Figure 21.2.

THE FUTURE

With newfound national scope and financial clout, the future of OfficeMax seemed heady. The target market appeared ripe for expanding beyond small- and medium-sized businesses to large firms. Institutions such as school boards and universities were also targets, and the low prices of OfficeMax were a powerful inducement. A new program was established for next-day delivery of office supplies, based on calls to telephone centers with toll-free lines. And the international arena beckoned powerfully, with stores planned for Mexico and Europe.

Meantime, in its quest for additional monies to provide a badly needed facelift for its stores, Kmart was considering selling a 25 percent share of OfficeMax and some of its other subsidiaries to raise a needed $3 billion in cash. A future as a public company rather than a subsidiary of Kmart could be in the cards. The following box discusses the prescription for great wealth in going public.

ANALYSIS

Here we see an outstanding entrepreneurial success. The growth rate in only a few years rivals the best we have seen. In the same year that OfficeMax was started, 685,095 other new businesses formed in the United States, but more than half of these eventually failed. Of the survivors only a small percent will ever achieve a value over $50 million. Only a handful will ever reach $200 million. What makes OfficeMax so uniquely successful?

It was not that it had identified a great idea and nurtured it exclusively. While OfficeMax launched on to a business opportunity arising from the archaic distribution structure of the office-supplies industry, it was far from unique in this identification. Indeed, the concept of category killer stores was in the ascendancy for all kinds of different retail goods. Why did OfficeMax succeed brilliantly and most of its competitors fail or succumb to a precarious existence?

Much of the success seems to accrue from the efforts of the principal founder, Michael Feuer. His vision was to retain control of the nascent enterprise by shunning venture capitalists and debt financing. While the money initially raised, $3 million, would seem adequate for most ventures, for a category killer chain it was barely sufficient. But severe austerity with the promise of great rewards in the future satisfied both employees and suppliers. This required optimism and an enthusiastic selling job by Feuer. And it also required a trusting relationship with investors, employees, and suppliers.

Great attention to details—dedication to customer service, to cost containment to the point of austerity, to the myriad of details needed for open-

---

INFORMATION BOX

THE PRESCRIPTION FOR GREAT WEALTH FOR ENTREPRENEURS

An entrepreneur often has much to gain by going public with an enterprise after a few years if it shows early success and a promising future. The entrepreneur keeps a portion of the stock and offers the rest to the public. With an attractive new venture, the offering price may be high enough to make the entrepreneur an instant multimillionaire.

Take Office Depot, for example. This is the largest office supply superstore chain in North America, although it is not that much bigger than OfficeMax. It is listed on the New York Stock Exchange, and its 94,143,455 shares of common stock sell for about $39 a share, giving a total market value of about $3.7 billion. If OfficeMax went public and had a similar relative market value, and if Feuer and Hurwitz held 8 percent of the total capitalization, they would be worth about $296 million, or almost $150 million apiece.

What rationale do you see for Feuer's decision to structure a new deal with Kmart rather than go public? Do you agree with his rationale?

---

ing stores with adequate employees and merchandise in severe deadline situations—all these were part of the success package.

Building on the growth without losing sight of the austerity heritage was perhaps even more important as the enterprise grew from a few stores to 20, 50, and more.

Of particular interest for any growing enterprise is the opportunity to make attractive acquisitions of former competitors who have fallen into desperate straits. The successful firm is in a position to quickly build on the bones of former competitors who could not make it.

WHAT CAN BE LEARNED?

Successful entrepreneurship is not easy. Not many who opt for business for themselves expect this to be an easy road, a comfortable and lazy lifestyle. Yet the work ethic of successful entrepreneurs can be awesome, even for those prepared for long hours and worries in the night. Michael Feuer customarily puts in 12- to 18-hour days between working at corporate headquarters and keeping in close touch with stores and customers and suppliers. He admits to waking up at 3 AM to stare at the ceiling while wondering if he made the right decision. And he feels a responsibility to his employees, no longer just the seven original ones whose jobs depended on his decisions: By the end of 1993 he admitted to having more than 19,000 reasons to worry in the night.

Would he be less successful with a more moderate work ethic? Perhaps, or perhaps not. But the personal stake in a growing business is a powerful drive for many entrepreneurs to become workaholics even to the point of sacrificing other aspects of their lives, including family.

There is power in a growth image, even if it is only an illusion. In perhaps one of the most crucial moves taken, in the early and most vulnerable months of the embryonic enterprise, Feuer and his people were able to sell both bankers and manufacturers on the great growth prospects for the company, that "we would rapidly become a 20-, 50-, or even 300-store chain. We explained that it was in *their* best interest to help us today—to guarantee a place with us tomorrow."

What makes a strong growth company so attractive to investors, creditors, suppliers, and employees? Part of the attractiveness certainly is that everyone likes to be associated with a winner. The greatest appeal of growth companies is their economic promise. This embraces investors, of course, because their investment grows with the business. Creditors and suppliers see more and more business coming their way as the company grows ever larger. And employees see great career opportunities continually opening up in a rapidly growing organization.

Perhaps in creating the image of OfficeMax as a company on the threshold of great growth, Feuer was simply very persuasive. But perhaps many of the people he talked with were so eager to be convinced and to be offered the opportunity to get in on the ground floor of what might be the stuff of dreams that they would accept even grandiose conjecture.

Go the extra miles in customer relations. It is easy for an organization to proclaim its dedication to customer service and good customer relations. Too often, however, it is only lip service, pious pronouncements without real substance. OfficeMax went far beyond lip service. Feuer and his executives, at least in the early years, sought close contact with customers in stores, even to the point of following them to the parking lot to see what might have been lacking in the merchandise or service that discouraged a purchase. The company accepts collect calls from customers, who might have problems or complaints or special needs. A promise of satisfaction of all complaints within 24 hours, the guiding "How can we make you happy?" question in all customer dealings, and a readiness to apologize attest to a customer commitment beyond the ordinary. With few exceptions, all businesses depend on customer loyalty and repeat business for their success. Perhaps in office products, where many customers are businesses, customer loyalty is all the more important. But it is easy to delude yourself and an organization that the loss of any single customer is not all that important, and that the firm must guard against being taken advantage of by unreasonable customers. Where should a firm, particularly a retailer, draw the line? Can any retailer be too liberal in handling customer complaints?

Again, the power of "lean and mean." In several earlier cases we have noted the problems of bloated bureaucracies and many management layers. We examined several highly successful firms, notably Southwest Airlines and Wal-Mart, that followed a policy of flat organizational levels and of continued frugality despite increasing size. The temptation with great growth is to let down the barriers and open the spending spigots. OfficeMax is resisting this urge and, as a result, is profitable where many of its superstore competitors have not been.

Again, dedicated employees can give a powerful advantage. As with Southwest Airlines, and also Wal-Mart, OfficeMax was able to stimulate its employees to move beyond individual concerns to a higher level of performance, a true team approach. This dedication, and the vague promise of future great expectations, brought employees to OfficeMax for very low wages, some turning down much higher paying jobs for the dream that might or might not come to pass. The dedication of these employees made possible opening the first store from scratch barely 3 months after the company was founded, with other stores quickly following.

The hope for great growth, a trusted leader, and an organization geared to a team effort seem to be most compatible in producing dedicated employees. One suspects there is also a close relationship in lean and mean organizations, where limited bureaucracy and management levels bring ease of communication.

CONSIDER

Can you identify other learning insights coming from this case?

QUESTIONS

1. In the hiring process, how would you identify candidates who are most likely to become dedicated employees?
2. Can a firm be too liberal in handling customer complaints?
3. The two office supply superstore chains closest to OfficeMax in size and growth are Office Depot, mostly located in the west and south, and Staples, predominantly in Florida and the northeast. OfficeMax, on the other hand, has stores coast to coast. Is OfficeMax being sufficiently prudent in spreading itself so widely at this time?
4. Do you think Feuer was being entirely ethical when he sold manufacturers on the desirability of doing business with OfficeMax in the very early days of the company? Why or why not?

5. Do you see any limitations to the future of category killer stores?
6. Can you think of some types of merchandise where category killer stores are unlikely to be successful?
7. Feuer puts in 12- to 18-hour days regularly. Do you think he would have been as successful with less of a work ethic? Why or why not?
8. Do a SWOT analysis (see Chapter 16) for OfficeMax. What do you conclude as far as future prospects?

ROLE PLAY

1. You own a small office supply store. Business has been steady and sufficient for a good living for you and your family up to now. Now an OfficeMax has opened less than a mile away. Discuss how you possibly can compete against such a superstore when you cannot come close to matching the variety of goods or the prices.
2. You are the assistant to Feuer. He wants you to draw up plans for targeting large institutions and businesses. Be as specific as you can be, making assumptions where needed, and persuasively support your recommendations.

INVITATION TO RESEARCH

What is the situation with OfficeMax today? Are there any dangers on the horizon? Does the stock market still value the stock of Office Depot and Staples with high price-earnings ratios?

PART VI

The Impact of
Ethical and
Social Pressures

CHAPTER 22

Dow Corning and Silicone Breast Implants: Product Safety on the Line

On February 10, 1992, Dow Corning Corporation replaced its top executive, John S. Ludington. The same day, it released hundreds of internal memos and other documents that revealed the company had received complaints for decades of medical problems associated with its silicone breast implants.

Was the released data so incriminating that it would bring down the company? Should silicone implants have been taken off the market years before? Was the company guilty of deception, fraud, cover-up, and disregard for human life and welfare? Was it a despicable corporate citizen? Or was Dow Corning as innocent a victim as some of its customers, caught up in the disclosure of an unsafe product years after this product was thought to have been a blessing to thousands of women? Judge for yourself as the picture unfolds. And note the hazards engendered by product safety issues in a litigious environment.

ATTEMPTING TO STEM THE EVER-MOUNTING CRISIS

The man selected to replace Ludington on February 10 was Keith R. McKennon, 58 years old, executive vice president responsible for research and development, manufacturing, and engineering at Dow Chemical.

McKennon had a reputation as a negotiator and peacemaker, and this, the *Wall Street Journal* speculated, might signal a more conciliatory attitude by the company. The fact that McKennon had struggled with lymph cancer seven years before might give him special rapport with implant patients who were concerned about their health. In the past, McKennon had dealt effectively and diplomatically with a major safety issue: Dow Chemical's

Agent Orange defoliant, which was used during the Vietnam War. He had also handled another crisis situation effectively, this one concerning Dow's drug for morning sickness during pregnancy, Bendectin. The drug was the subject of numerous health and safety lawsuits. McKennon's experience in dealing publicly and internally with these problems uniquely qualified him, so the company thought, in coping with one of its biggest crises: the silicone breast implant.

To his credit, McKennon took several quick actions, as well as actions costly to the firm. These included paying the medical costs of women who wanted to have their breast implants surgically removed but could not afford to do so. (The price for removing breast implants typically ranges from $4500 to $6500.) He also proposed sitting down with the Food and Drug Administration (FDA), its advisory panel, the physicians on both sides of the controversy, and the women involved, all toward seeking a consensus about new research that needed to be done (at company expense).[1]

PRELUDE

On January 6, 1992, FDA Commissioner Dr. David A. Kessler ordered a 45-day moratorium on the sale and use of silicone gel implants. He urged manufacturers to stop marketing the devices and surgeons to stop inserting them. Other countries, such as Spain and Australia, quickly followed, whereas Canada, Britain, and France reviewed their policies.

A horde of lawyers eagerly waited in the wings. An estimated 1 to 2 million women in the United States alone had received breast implants over the last 30 years. If the implants could be proven sufficiently dangerous, the potential liability suits could run in the billions of dollars.

Instances of medical problems with the implants had been surfacing, and lawsuits were increasing. For example, soon after Karen Reid felt something pop in one of her implanted breasts, she developed immunological problems and noticed nodules popping up on her arms and legs. Convinced that the source of her problems was silicone that had leaked from a ruptured breast implant, she sued for millions in damages from the manufacturer, Dow Corning Corporation.[2]

Kali Korn was diagnosed with scleroderma a decade after she had had silicone implants inserted for cosmetic reasons. In scleroderma the skin thickens and stiffens and there is a buildup of fibrous tissue in the lungs and other organs. Doctors removed the implants, and her condition improved.[3]

---

[1] Thomas M. Burton and Joan E. Rigdon, "Management Shake-Up at Dow Corning Signals a More Conciliatory Attitude," *Wall Street Journal* (Feb. 12, 1992): A3.

[2] Example from John Carey, "I'm Frightened for My Life," *Business Week* (Jan. 20, 1992): 32.

[3] Example from "A Strike Against Silicone," *Time* (Jan. 20, 1992): 40.

Mariann Hopkins claimed that her 1976 implants ruptured and damaged her immune system. The trial resulted in a $7.34 million jury award against Dow Corning.[4] Internal company documents that were rather incriminating surfaced during the Hopkins trial.

Acting on pressures resulting from these cases, as well as from revelations of internal company memos expressing early concern about the implants, the FDA imposed the moratorium until further evaluation of the possible link between silicone gel and immune system diseases could be made.

HISTORY OF BREAST IMPLANTS

In the early 1960s, Dow Corning and several other firms began marketing silicone-filled breast implants. Although most women opted for this operation for cosmetic purposes, about 20 percent did so after the travail of a mastectomy. Such implants became the third most popular form of cosmetic surgery, after nose and liposuction operations.

Breast implants were not regulated by the FDA until 1976. They were already on the market when Congress for the first time empowered the agency to regulate medical devices, which included implants. This was largely due to the Dalkon Shield catastrophe, which motivated the May 28, 1976, Medical Device Amendments.

Concerns about the safety of such implants began increasing by 1990, triggered, as we have seen, by a series of lawsuits and some multimillion-dollar awards for women claiming that the implants deteriorated and the silicone leached throughout their bodies, causing serious health problems. Thus, uneasiness had been surfacing before the January 1992 moratorium.

In April 1991 the FDA told implant manufacturers to prove scientifically that their products were safe. In November 1991 the FDA advisory panel judged that the data the manufacturers submitted were insufficient to demonstrate safety, but decided to leave the implants on the market because of what it called a "public health need" for the devices. This permission, of course, was revoked with the moratorium, which called for a review of new information that had come to light in the recent product-liability suits against Dow Corning.

An investigation by *Business Week* some months earlier had uncovered evidence that the industry had been aware for at least a decade of animal studies linking implants to cancer and other illnesses.[5] But these studies, which suggested some risks for humans, were not publicized until the more recent court cases.

---

[4]Example from Tim Smart, "This Man Sounded the Silicone Alarm—in 1976," *Business Week* (Jan. 27, 1992): 34.

[5]Tim Smart, "Breast Implants: What Did the Industry Know, and When," *Business Week* (June 10, 1991): 94.

A Whistleblower

Thomas D. Talcott had been a Dow Corning materials engineer for 24 years. In 1976, he quit his job in a dispute over the safety of the implants. He had helped develop the silicone gel that the company earlier used to fill implants. When Dow switched to a more liquid gel designed to make the implants softer, Talcott believed the thinner gel could migrate through the body, causing harm, and he wanted no part of that. After leaving Dow Corning, he worked for two other implant makers, then started his own materials-consulting business.

Talcott's warnings were unheeded, and his quitting Dow Corning in protest went ignored—until 1991. Then he testified as an expert witness in the California lawsuit brought by Mariann Hopkins, and was instrumental in her $7.34 million jury award against Dow Corning. "The manufacturers and surgeons have been performing experimental surgery on humans," he told a congressional panel in December 1991.[6] He obtained a list of confidential documents, which he circulated to the head of the FDA's advisory panel, top FDA officials, and Congress. This was a factor in the FDA's decision to impose a 45-day moratorium on the sale of implants.

Dow Corning attempted to refute Talcott's allegations in a January 13 press conference. Company officials restated their contention that breast implants were safe, and they dismissed the memos as part of the normal give-and-take of scientific debate. The next day, however, the company halted implant production.

Company officials further questioned Talcott's objectivity and integrity, noting that he earned $400 an hour for his expert testimony. He "left as a disgruntled employee. You've got to question to some degree his motive," said Dan Hayes, president of Dow Corning's breast implant subsidiary.[7]

The Company, Dow Corning

Dow Corning was incorporated in Michigan in 1943 by Corning Glass Works and Dow Chemical Company. It is owned equally by these two major corporations. Dow Corning is principally engaged in the development, production, and sale of silicone and related products. Corporate offices and principal R & D facilities are in Midland, Michigan.

Although far smaller than its parents, Dow Corning is still of considerable size. Sales in 1990 were $1.7 billion, with a net income of $171 million. As of December 31, 1990, there were approximately 8000 employees. Al-

[6]Smart, "Breast Implants," 94.
[7]Smart, "This Man Sounded the Silicone Alarm," 34.

though the company was a leading manufacturer of implants, this business represented less than 1 percent of the company's product line and had had five years of financial losses. Robert Rylee, Dow Corning's health care general manager, said that the company had been staying in the implant business because the medical profession and "millions of women [have been] counting on us."[8]

The Role of Lawsuits

Although the FDA vacillated on declaring a moratorium on implants until January 1992, earlier lawsuits were critical and damaging to the company. In 1984 a San Francisco federal court jury concluded that the company had committed fraud in marketing its implants as safe, and awarded Maria Stern $1.5 million in punitive damages. United States District Judge Marilyn Hall Patel wrote that the company's own studies "cast considerable doubt on the safety of the product," doubt which was not disclosed to patients, and she said that the jury could conclude that Dow's actions "were highly reprehensible."[9]

In 1985 after the Stern case, Dow Corning included a package insert with the product, warning of the possibility of immune-system sensitivity and other medical problems should the implant rupture. This was apparently intended to blunt subsequent legal contentions that the company had not adequately disclosed potential risks.

But in 1987, Dow Corning discounted the immune-system problem, maintaining that silicone of improved purity was now being used.

Following the settlement of the Hopkins case in 1991 (in which whistle-blower Talcott was the key plaintiff witness), hundreds of women began filing suits, alleging that their implants had deteriorated and caused serious medical problems. Some lawyers began comparing the legal possibilities to the multibillion-dollar litigation over the Dalkon Shield.

Dow Corning and the other implant makers still downplayed the legal dangers, pointing out that the awarded damages were not very high in the majority of cases, since health problems were relatively modest. But Ralph Nader's Public Citizens Health Research Group now joined the battle, and trial lawyers began organizing to coordinate attacks. Pressure was mounting for full disclosure of all documents relating to the silicone implants, and Dow Corning capitulated on February 10, 1992.

[8]"Dow Corning Makes Changes in Top Posts," *Wall Street Journal* (Feb. 11, 1992): A4.
[9]Smart, "Breast Implants," 98.

Although the newly released company documents did not disclose cancer and immune-system problems, they did show a long history of complaints, leaky implants, production problems, and concern for public relations. Listing the complaints received required nearly 20 pages of computer printouts. Most complaints involved rupture of the implant, but there were also reports of leakage, discoloration, bubbles, sterilization, infection, optical nerve atrophy, and tumors.

SHIFTING FDA POSITION

Although the early Dow Corning studies with rats showed the presence of malignant tumors in up to 80 percent of the test animals, the figures were so high that the review panel considered the research suspect and inconclusive. Another Dow study 10 years later found that tumors could be induced in rats when foreign agents, such as silicone, were put in them. But FDA officials, who again reviewed the research, concluded that the rat studies provided no proof that humans would be similarly affected.

The FDA also vacillated on banning the sale of an implant made by Bristol-Myers. A link was apparently found between the foam used to coat the device and a cancer-causing agent, 2-toluene diamine (TDA). The foam was primarily used in automobile air and oil filters, and one could question its use in breast implants. Indeed, in the 1970s, the FDA banned TDA's use in hair dyes because of increased risk of birth defects. Bristol-Myers withdrew its implant following FDA disapproval. But on April 17, 1991, the FDA seemed to reverse itself, playing down the cancer risk in public pronouncements.

Many, including lawmakers, were wondering why the FDA had not acted more forcefully regarding an apparently unsafe product. On April 26, 1991, Representative Ted Weiss (D-NY), chairman of a subcommittee studying the implant issue, criticized the agency for moving so slowly: "FDA documents indicate that for more than 10 years, FDA scientists have expressed concerns about the safety of silicone breast implants that were frequently ignored by FDA officials."[10] The agency offered the excuse of having higher priority matters to deal with.

Now, with pressure mounting steadily for action by the FDA, the moratorium was issued.

Explanation for FDA Vacillation

Several factors appear to have contributed to the FDA's foot-dragging:

[10]Smart, "Breast Implants," 95.

1. The health dangers were not as well defined and severe as those in such cases as the Dalkon Shield. One could wonder whether the still rather few cases where problems arose (one out of several million operations) were not blown out of proportion by trial lawyers and some activists.
2. The FDA's advisory panels—made up of medical experts upon whom the FDA relies—may not have been completely unbiased and objective. For example, 2 years after the 1976 law gave the FDA jurisdiction over medical devices, its advisory panel recommended that implants be so classified that manufacturers could sell them without having to prove they were safe. This advisory panel was heavily staffed with plastic surgeons. And plastic surgeons are the medical specialty most heavily involved in implant surgery, to the tune of some $450 million a year in medical fees.
3. The FDA does not have the personnel or the budget to do all the research needed for approval of a new drug or medical device. Therefore, although it scrutinizes the results of industry research, it has to trust the accuracy, objectivity, and full disclosure of the pharmaceutical manufacturers.

The Power of the FDA

A curious and unhappy anomaly exists with respect to the FDA: It is entrusted with ensuring the safety of all medical drugs and devices in the United States, but it is rather a toothless watchdog. Unlike most other federal agencies, it lacks the legal clout to subpoena a company's internal records if a problem is suspected. Nor has it been able to use emergency powers to pull a dangerous drug from the market.

Pressure is building to increase the FDA's scrutiny of medical drugs and devices. In particular, some are advocating postapproval monitoring. Such surveillance would expand the evaluation from a few hundred or thousand clinical trials over a relatively short period of time to many thousands and even millions over a lengthy time period. Thus, long-term side effects and risks could be uncovered that never could be under normal procedures.

Damned If You Do and Damned If You Don't

The implant controversy accentuates a familiar dilemma for the FDA. On the one hand, the FDA is pressured by lawyers, aggrieved victims, activists, and some legislators to ban a drug or a medical device for being unsafe and putting users at risk. On the other hand, sizable numbers of people are willing to accept some risk in the quest for improved health, longevity, or simply for cosmetic beauty reasons, such as a bigger bust. Who do you please?

The answer is that you cannot please everyone, you cannot avoid criticism, you can always be second-guessed, and, worst, you can have your objectivity questioned. Such is the unenviable position of Dr. Kessler and the FDA.

On February 7, 1992, the *Wall Street Journal* reported that a group of concerned women and doctors together sued the FDA, alleging that its moratorium on silicone breast implants was illegal and unconstitutional.[11] "The FDA has torn loose from its legal moorings and spread fear and panic among women, with no scientific basis," Stanley Brand, an attorney for the group, asserted at a news conference. Pulling silicone implants off the market would "constitute a major tragedy for hundreds of thousands of women who would benefit from them," said one of the plaintiffs, John Woods, a plastic surgeon at the Mayo Clinic. The suit also argued that silicone is widely used in testicular implants, pacemakers, heart valves, needles, and syringes, none of which had been banned by the FDA.

Further criticism was leveled that a senior aide to Dr. Kessler was biased against implants because her husband was a senior attorney for the Public Citizen Litigation Group and its director, Sidney Wolfe, a leading critic of silicone implants.

IN DEFENSE OF THE INDUSTRY

Were Dow Corning and the other implant makers guilty of deception, greed, and callousness to product safety and public health? (An article in *Time* broadened the scope of the question: "Can Drug Firms be Trusted?")[12] Is the trusting relationship between the medical-products industry and the FDA being violated?

Dr. Kenneth Kaitin of the Center for the Study of Drug Development at Tufts University observed: "If a drug has to be pulled from the market, it's very bad for public relations, financially and in every possible way. It just doesn't make sense that they [manufacturers] would intentionally conceal real problems."[13]

With the controversy heating up, Dow Corning initially released 90 corporate documents requested by the FDA. Robert Rylee expressed his concerns about such publicity: "In fact we are doing nothing more than fanning the flames created by contingency-fee lawyers who base their cases against manufacturers not on what the scientific evidence shows, but on 15-year-old memos that state one person's opinion about what research should have been done."[14] (See the following box concerning possible excesses of litigation.)

[11] Bruce Ingersoll, "FDA's Moratorium on Breast Implants Prompts a Lawsuit," *Wall Street Journal* (Feb. 7, 1992): B5A.

[12] Christine Gorman, "Can Drug Firms Be Trusted?" *Time* (Feb. 10, 1992): 42–46.

[13] Gorman, "Can Drug Firms Be Trusted?" 43.

[14] "Fanning the Flames," *Forbes* (Feb. 17, 1992): 30.

Other Proponents of Breast Implants

Through early 1992, about 3500 women had complained to the FDA that their implants caused pain, infection, and hardness. Many of these women said that migrating gel from ruptured implants had caused autoimmune diseases, arthritis, and scleroderma, a skin-tightening disease. Implants can also delay detection of breast cancer. But the proportion of women having problems with their implants was still relatively small.

Not the least of the voices raised in favor of silicone implants were those of many women. On the night of February 7, 1992, the prime-time TV program "20/20" questioned a number of models about their use of implants. Overwhelmingly, they responded that such breast enhancers were not only desirable but necessary to earn a living. The general consensus was that the implants resulted in increased assignments, with income tripling or quadrupling. Without hesitation, these women stated that they would accept any slight risk in order to meet the modern standards of beauty and thereby safeguard their economic livelihood. They said that if such implants were banned in this country they would have no choice but to go to Mexico or other foreign countries to have the operation performed.

Virginia Postrel, editor of *Reason* magazine, has argued that many products in common use by women carry some health risks—for example, both the Pill and tampons (which, unlike breast implants, have been definitely linked with fatalities caused by Toxic Shock Syndrome). Postrel condemned the notion that "political appointees in Washington will decree what's necessary and what's better, with help from puritanical pressure groups."[15]

INFORMATION BOX

IS LITIGATION GETTING OUT OF HAND?

The publicity about the dangers of silicone implants represented a bonanza for many trial lawyers. As of February 1992, more than 1000 lawsuits had already had been filed on behalf of women who claimed they were harmed by the devices. With the February 10 release of more Dow Corning documents, it became obvious that many more suits would be filed. In what seemed on the verge of becoming a feeding frenzy, some lawyers had

- Set up toll-free telephone numbers to encourage more litigation.
- Advertised in newspapers, on billboards, and on TV with the themes, "We can help" and "Learn the facts and your rights about breast implants."[16]

---

[15] Virginia I. Postrel, "Is This An FDA Right?" *Cleveland Plain Dealer* (Feb. 1, 1992): 5C.
[16] Michael D. Lemonick, "Lawyers to the Rescue," *Time* (Feb. 1992): 46.

• Held conventions to discuss strategies in breast-implant suits.

In its February 17, 1992, issue, *Forbes* magazine reported on the skyrocket-ing cost of tort suits in the United States.[17] The rewards for lawyers can be huge in such suits. Lawyers usually work on contingency fees for such damage suits, whereby no fee is charged if the suits fail but 30 percent or more of any proceeds (which may run into the millions) are charged if the actions are successful.

On the other hand, legal action and its threat can be a powerful deterrent to reckless or uncaring corporate actions. For the person who has been harmed, it provides a needed recourse. Sometimes deficiencies of regulatory agencies can be uncovered and corrected.

The problem seems one of degree—that is, too many lawyers promoting as much business as they can. Abusive practices can creep into such as frivolous lawsuits, including the use of expert witnesses, sometimes called "hired guns," who do not always have the right qualifications but are experienced in impress-ing jurors and ignoring the benefits of drugs and medical devices while attacking problems in what may be a small percentage of cases.

Vice President Dan Quayle had pushed for tort reform. Among his propos-als were banning contingency fees for expert witnesses, curbing punitive dam-ages (whereby the defendant is assessed a "punishment" beyond the amount of the plaintiff's injury and suffering), and adopting the English Rule, whereby losers pay the winners' court costs, thus discouraging frivolous suits.

On balance, what do you see as the pro and con arguments for contingency suits? Do you think they should be banned?

As the debate heated up, a powerful media and lobbying campaign sur-faced in late 1991. The nation's plastic surgeons and implant makers flooded Congress and the media with their side of the story: women's satisfaction with their implants. In October 1991, 400 women, accompanied by their plas-tic surgeons, flew to Washington to lobby members of Congress. A massive letter-writing campaign resulted in thousands of letters to Representative Ted Weiss (D-NY), who had pushed to have implants investigated, and Senator Edward Kennedy, chairman of the Senate Labor and Human Re-sources Committee. The FDA received an unprecedented 20,000 letters in support of implants.

To encourage the organized protest, the plastic surgeons' society (the American Society of Plastic and Reconstructive Surgeons) accumulated a $1.3 million fund for lobbying. At stake were hundreds of millions of dollars a year that its members charged for implant surgery.

So we have the two sides arrayed in strong opposition: women sup-ported by trial lawyers and professional activists versus women allied with

---

[17]Leslie Spencer, "The Tort Tax," *Forbes* (Feb. 17, 1992): 40–42.

their plastic surgeons and implant makers. Women may have justification for siding with either position (if they have had complications, they are against implants; if they have not, they tend to be strongly positive), but their supporters can hardly be cast as objective and unbiased. (See the following box for a discussion of the issue of right of choice.)

LATER DEVELOPMENTS

Late in February 1992, the FDA's advisory panel, after a three-day marathon of hearings, voted unanimously *not* to ban implants. Dr. Elizabeth Connell, an Emory University professor and chair of the panel, explained: "We don't feel a clear cause and effect relationship has been established."[18] At the same time, in a confusing obfuscation, the panel recommended sharply limiting breast implants while conducting far-reaching clinical trials. Women with mastectomies would get preference, but all women receiving implants from now on would essentially be guinea pigs, with their results closely monitored. Presumably, the bureaucracy would determine how many women would get future implants, and under what circumstances they would get them—not a very satisfactory resolution of this issue.

Although women were left in a position of great uncertainty regarding the risks of future implants, manufacturers were in a worse quandary. The advisory panel had said there was no proven risk, but manufacturers knew they faced millions of dollars in litigation suits. There were rumors that Dow Corning was earnestly seeking to get out of the implant business.

As of March 1992, despite 30 years of use, knowledge about breast implant safety was still shockingly sparse. No one knew for sure how many women had had implants: Estimates ranged from 1 to 2 million. There were no statistics on how many implants had ruptured, or how many were leaking, or even what the health significance was of stray silicone in the body. Confusion prevailed.

In early March 1992, responding to the heat arising from its hesitant stance regarding the breast implants, the FDA announced that, under the provisions of the 1976 Medical Device Amendments, it would begin scrutinizing more than 100 untested medical devices that were put into use before 1976. Included were implants for the testes, shoulders, and knees; electrical brain stimulators; balloons that open arteries; and lens implants for the eye. Signaling a new stance, agency officials noted that while these devices had been in use for 15 years or more, reports about adverse reactions had been sparse, and thus health problems might have gone unreported and unstudied heretofore.[19]

[18]"FDA Does and Doesn't," *Wall Street Journal* (Feb. 24, 1992): A14.
[19]Philip V. Hilts, "FDA Wants Safety Data from All Implant Makers," *Cleveland Plain Dealer* (Mar. 5, 1992): 11F.

INFORMATION BOX

SHOULD GOVERNMENT TAKE AWAY A PERSON'S RIGHT OF CHOICE?

In this case we have seen women vehemently taking sides in the issue of risk-versus-choice. How far should a government agency go in dictating whether or not we can use a certain product? How much must we be protected from our darker leanings, without infringing on our right of choice?

With the Dalkon Shield, there was no question about the appropriateness of banning a notoriously unsafe product. Such is not the case with silicone implants. These have significant benefits, some of them merely cosmetic, but verging on the essential for those needing reconstructive surgery. The use of implants for cosmetic reasons can provide powerful psychological benefits. So we have a gray area indeed.

An extension of this controversy concerns the right of government to dictate how we should protect ourselves. Safety helmets for cyclists have been made mandatory in many states; so have seat belts and children's car seats. Are such statutes intruding on our right of choice? How about government going a step further and banning dangerous sports, such as bungee jumping, hang gliding, mountain climbing, even sandlot football? There is the massive issue of abortion and a woman's right of choice. How much do we need to be protected from the more reckless aspects of our nature, or what some would see as a violation of the natural law?

Like so many issues, the judgment is rather one of degree. We need protection from some extreme risk-embracing—for example, dueling, Russian roulette, playing "chicken" on the highway. These can hardly be tolerated. But should not women have a choice to have a breast enhancement operation, as long as they know the risks involved and are willing to accept them?

How do you feel about the government taking away some of your freedom of choice? How far do you think the hand of government should extend to protect us from ourselves?

On March 19, 1992, Dow Corning announced that it was pulling out of the implant business, and would give women up to $1200 each to help pay for having its implants surgically removed.

ANALYSIS

Was Dow Corning a villain? You have seen the evidence.

This issue is still evolving as we go to press, and we cannot assess it as thoroughly as we would like with the benefit of hindsight. Still, certain reasoned judgments are possible.

As with many issues and controversies, the matter is not clearcut, but some shade of gray. The villain is not entirely a villain, but has some redeeming qualities. Other protagonists are right in some respects, but not in others.

Dow Corning was reluctant to reveal memoranda and other documents of questionable or recriminating nature. It undoubtedly suppressed information from the general public and the press, although it appears that the FDA was apprised of some of this data, if not of all the internal memos.

Dow Corning wanted to convey the best image for the implants as possible. Accordingly, it did not release the full scope of complaints. Many people would not see this as the actions of a responsive firm. And yet, the problems did not seem to be serious or widespread (as was the case with the Dalkon Shield). Although Dow Corning executives were concerned, they reasoned that the implants resulted in far more good than harm.

Dow Corning was certainly concerned with its public image, the negative impact that full revelations of certain product leakages and harmful consequences would have brought. It had hoped to prevent public relations problems—but was eventually unable to—by not disclosing the full extent of the complaints of physicians and their patients. This can hardly be condoned. The company was guilty of withholding incriminating evidence. But the company was earnestly striving to correct the problem, which seemed to emanate from quality control lapses. Is Dow Corning therefore a monster?

Perhaps the main issue rests on the judgment of whether the problems outweighed the benefits—in other words, the risk/reward ratio. For many thousands of women, the ratio would seem favorable. For those suffering the severe trauma of mastectomies, the breast implants represented a return to a normal lifestyle; for other women, breast enhancements could provide a psychological boost; for models, actresses, and others in the limelight, they could provide strong economic and professional advantages—despite the risk of some medical problems.

So, does the good outweigh the bad? You be the judge. Although Dow Corning was guilty of some cover-up—and is paying for this in damage suits—was it calloused and uncaring? At least under the new regime of Keith McKennon, company policies seem to have shifted to a more conciliatory and responsive attitude.

Nevertheless, the dire consequences to the company and to some of its customers represent a major marketing blunder, which perhaps should have been handled better. (See the following box, which asks whether management must assume the worst scenario.)

POSTSCRIPT

On April 25, 1994, newspapers revealed that chemical companies and other manufacturers of materials used to make heart valves, artificial blood ves-

---

INFORMATION BOX

MUST MANAGEMENT ASSUME THE WORST SCENARIO?

Does ignorance of future dire consequences relieve a firm of much of its blame? The contentious segment of the general public—lawyers as well as politicians eager to mollify their constituents—sees a "no mercy" scenario: The corporation is guilty despite ignorance of any wrongdoing, or any danger, at the time. But is this the most equitable viewpoint?

We live in a complex world. And our products are increasingly more complex technologically; some products, such as drugs, asbestos, and cigarettes, may well have long-term consequences far beyond our ability to predict. Was not this the case with the silicone breast implants?

In today's environment, firms are unable to escape the long-term negative consequences of their products. The litigious environment will not permit this, however ignorant the firm may have been. Ethically, the blame has to be more muted for a firm that could not see any dire consequences, despite reasonable prudence. But does the very fact of not knowing really excuse a company? Should not management consider the worst-case scenario before introducing a product with some potential for problems? Whether we consider this issue ethically or not, the fact remains that in a firm's own self-interest today, it certainly should examine and assume a worst-case scenario. Otherwise, its very viability may be at stake.

Discuss the implications arising from firms reluctant to introduce many new products because of possible long-term product safety problems. Do you see any practical resolution for this issue?

---

sels, and other implants had been quietly warning medical equipment companies that they intended to cut off deliveries because of fears of lawsuits. Such major firms as Du Pont and Dow are dropping the medical business in response to the high risk of lawsuits filed against implant makers by consumers who say they have been injured by defective products. Physicians are concerned that some life-saving implants may no longer be available and that the development of new devices will be devastated.[20]

WHAT CAN BE LEARNED?

A firm today must zealously guard against product liability suits. Any responsible executive now has to recognize that product liability suits can bankrupt a firm. The business arena has become more risky, more fraught with peril for the unwary or the naively unconcerned. Consequently, any firm needs careful and objective testing of any product that might even

---

[20]For example, "Shadow of Lawsuits Threatens Supply of Life-Saving Implants," *Cleveland Plain Dealer* (April 25, 1994): 1A.

remotely affect customer health and safety—and this must be undertaken even if product introduction is delayed and competitive entry encouraged.

In particular, long-term dangerous side effects of drugs and medical devices can seldom be predicted with absolute certainty. Initial tests prior to approval for distribution may guarantee minimal short-term risks, but research of only a few years cannot possibly ensure there will be no long-term problems. Hence, the manufacturer faces risks of unknown, even monumental, degree. In one year alone, 1991, Upjohn's sleeping pill, Halcion, was linked with paranoia and agitation; Eli Lilly's antidepressant, Prozac, was linked with extreme agitation; and Hoffmann-La Roche's liquid anesthetic, Versed, was linked with deaths due to breathing and heart problems. Further, Pfizer's Bjork-Shiley heart valve was blamed for more than 300 deaths due to valve fractures and weak welds, and Bolar's Dyazide high-blood-pressure pill was found to be defective.

Can we as a society expect no risks? Probably not. But we should be able to expect the risks to be minimal and to occur in a very low percentage of total usage. Otherwise, the testing and approval process is seriously flawed. For the firm, the risk/reward ratio should favor putting the product on the market. If longer or more intensive testing is needed to improve the risk/reward ratio, then this should be undertaken. It is misguided indeed to rush a product to market to reap a large payoff, only to learn later of serious health and safety problems.

Suspicions and complaints about product safety must be thoroughly investigated. We should learn from this case that immediate and thorough investigation of any suspicions or complaints must be undertaken—regardless of the confidence that management may have in the product or of the glowing recommendations of persons whose objectivity could be suspect. To procrastinate or ignore complaints poses risks that should be unacceptable.

Unbiased judgment and objectivity are hard to find in issues involving business firms, special interest groups, lawyers, and regulatory bodies. Despite the desirability of evaluating issues soberly and objectively, this is often not done. In this case, we saw the lines being drawn between manufacturers, tort lawyers, and certain activist groups, with women themselves strongly divided on the issue.

And the hapless FDA was in the middle, pressured by both sides. Not to be overlooked among the players is a press eager to sensationalize, quick to criticize, and often just as biased as the other players.

In such a stew of conflicting and competing interests, how are justice and fair decisions ever to come about? Alas, that is the great challenge of our socioethical framework. Executives should recognize the reality of unfair and biased confrontation.

Strong support by some users of a product may not be enough in the presence of strong opposition by other factions to the same product. Dow Corning faced strong controversy with its silicone implants, and it eventually fled the field. Charges and countercharges between the company and opposing groups can damage a company's reputation. Although the product may have considerable support, this may not be sufficient to save it. Such a hostile environment for doing business is uncomfortable at best, and fraught with legal peril at worst. Often the easier course of action is to withdraw the product.

If a courageous management attempts to ride out the storm and combat the detractors while embracing the supporters, then public relations must be well honed. In particular, the company should seek good rapport with reporters and other media representatives through honesty and full disclosure. Executives who may be interviewed on camera should be well trained and coached in this important role of company spokesperson.

A coverup of negative research findings will seldom remain unrevealed. Why are firms so reluctant to reveal negatives about their product(s), especially when such involve health and safety? The common rationale is that the limitations or dangers have not been proven to the company's satisfaction, and the products therefore are presumed safe. But company documents have a way of turning up in legal proceedings, which may brand a firm as calloused and deceptive. Would it not be better for all concerned—the company, its customers, and physicians alike—if any possible health risks were readily, objectively, and dispassionately revealed?

CONSIDER

Can you identify other learning insights from this case?

QUESTIONS

1. Do you think the FDA's January 6, 1992, moratorium on implants should have been imposed? Should it have been imposed sooner? If so, when?
2. Do you think the whistleblower, Thomas Talcott, was justified in his actions? Why or why not?
3. Should Dow Corning be banned from producing any more implants as a punishment for its lack of candor and full disclosure of implant problems? Defend your position.
4. From the perspective of trial lawyers and plastic surgeons, what are the pro and con arguments for banning implants? Which side's position is more compelling?

5. How can a firm guarantee complete product safety?
6. "In essence, Dow Corning exploited women's bodies for profit." Discuss.
7. "A firm has to take some risks with new product introductions. Not to do so means leaving the arena to your competitors." Discuss.

INVITATION TO ROLE PLAY

1. You are the public relations director of Dow Corning in early 1980. Information has surfaced about continuing problems with your implants. What do you advise the CEO to do? Be as specific as you can, and defend your recommendations.
2. Defend as persuasively as possible Dow Corning's decision to withhold most of the incriminating data for years. Also defend the company's decision to continue manufacturing silicone breast implants.
3. Taking the position of David Kessler, the FDA commissioner, defend your long procrastination in banning these breast implants.

INVITATION TO RESEARCH

What is the current situation regarding Dow Corning? Regarding implants?

CHAPTER 23

Cigarette Controversies

Cigarettes are among the world's most profitable consumer products. A cigarette "costs a penny to make, sell it for a dollar, it's addictive, and there's fantastic brand loyalty," said takeover specialist Warren Buffett as he unsuccessfully sought to take over RJR Nabisco, the tobacco conglomerate.[1] Perhaps because of its profitability, the morality of the business has long been suspect.

EARLY SOCIAL PRESSURES AGAINST CIGARETTES

Almost from the beginning, tobacco has faced social disfavor from certain sectors of the population, notably medical and religious groups, as well as others who espoused particular moral beliefs. Cigarettes were being referred to as "coffin nails" even before the Civil War. A group of educators, doctors, and the famous showman P. T. Barnum formed an alliance to fight the nicotine habit. Later, Horace Greeley, publisher of the *New York Tribune*, condemned tobacco. School children were exhorted to join the Anti-Cigarette League with a pledge to abstain. Some businesses refused to hire men and boys who smoked.

Antismoking legislation was also passed by some states. Some banned the use of cigarettes by any person under 16 years of age. Some legislation prohibited the use of coupons in cigarette packages; a 1901 New Hampshire law even went to the extreme of declaring it illegal to make or sell any form of cigarette. In New York women were absolutely forbidden to smoke in

---

[1] "The Tobacco Trade: The Search for El Dorado," *Economist* (May 16, 1992): 21.

public. By 1910 only in Wyoming and Louisiana had no antismoking legislation passed by either state or local bodies.

World War I brought a major change in attitudes toward smoking. The cigarette fitted perfectly the needs of fighting men for an easy-to-carry and easy-to-use short reprieve from the rigors of military life. The public was encouraged by no less than John J. Pershing, commanding general of the armies, to send cigarettes to soldiers, most of whom were ardent cigarette smokers when they returned home.

The increased tempo of life that came with the congestion and strains of urban life favored the short smoke of cigarettes over the more leisurely smokes of cigars and pipes. This trend was further accentuated by the shift of population from rural to urban. The voices of the social reformers were drowned out by the stampede to cigarette smoking in the late 1920s by all sectors of society. The development of mass communication advertising media—at first radio, then TV—expanded the love affair for cigarettes by most elements of society. World War II provided even more impetus for a societal addiction.

Later Societal Pressures

By the 1960s negative publicity was again surfacing about cigarettes. The surgeon general issued a report on January 11, 1964, stating that cigarette smoking was injurious to health and shortened life. Subsequent studies began to provide overwhelming evidence of the dangers of cigarette smoking, despite contrary claims by the tobacco industry. The Federal Trade Commission on June 22, 1964, issued a trade regulation order that all cigarette labeling and advertising must carry a health warning. That same year Congress passed the Federal Cigarette Labeling and Advertising Act reaffirming the regulation of the FTC and the required statement: "Warning: The Surgeon General Has Determined That Cigarette Smoking Is Dangerous to Your Health."

Then, as of January, 2, 1971, cigarette commercials were banned from TV and radio. At that time it was thought that the $250 million spent annually by the industry for TV and radio commercials could never be completely rechanneled, with the result that tobacco usage would decline without such potent advertising stimulation.

This hope was quickly dispelled. Advertising expenditures for 1971, the first year of the ban, had practically all been rechanneled into other media.[2]

[2]"Where the Cigarette Men Go After the TV Ban," *Business Week* (Nov. 21, 1970): 64–69; "Cigarette Makers Do Great Without TV," *Business Week* (May 29, 1971): 56–57; and "Where Cigarette Makers Spend Ad Dollars Now," *Business Week* (Dec. 25, 1971): 56–57.

Gradually over the next two decades, growing publicity about the health consequences of cigarette smoking coincided with an emerging social concern with health and fitness. As a result, cigarette consumption in the United States dropped substantially, and smoking was banned from domestic air flights and many buildings as even second-hand smoke was considered harmful by medical experts.

CONTROVERSIAL STRATEGIES IN TODAY'S SHRINKING MARKET

Faced with a steadily declining market in the United States, the tobacco industry has responded with a proliferation of brands: More than 300 brands were created, boasting such features as being longer, slimmer, cheaper, flavored, microfiltered, pastel colored, and even striped. One of these was an R. J. Reynolds brand called Uptown.

The Controversy over Uptown

Uptown was packaged in a showy black-and-gold box and was a menthol blend. R. J. Reynolds designed the product to appeal to a particular market segment, much as the other new brands had been designed.

Because cigarette consumption had fallen in the United States, tobacco companies were increasingly directing their efforts to specific groups, such as women, Hispanics, and blacks. Blacks in particular seemed a fruitful target market: 39 percent of black males smoke, while 30.5 percent of white males do.[3] Using careful research and design, everything about Uptown— even the name—was tailored to the tastes of black consumers. It was, indeed, the first cigarette aimed specifically at African-American smokers. Alas, this was the rub.

A storm of protests quickly ensued. Critics maintained that the marketing of Uptown represented a cold-blooded targeting of blacks, who already suffered a lung cancer rate 58 percent higher than whites. The protests even reached the office of Louis Sullivan, the Secretary of Health and Human Services. He quickly sided with the critics: "Uptown's message is more disease, more suffering and more death for a group already bearing more than its share of smoking-related illness and mortality."[4] He called for an "all-out effort to resist the attempts of tobacco merchants to earn profits at the expense of the health and well-being of our poor and minority citizens."[5]

[3]Michael Quinn, "Don't Aim That Pack at Us," *Time* (Jan. 29, 1990): 60.
[4]Quinn, "Don't Aim That Pack," 60.
[5]Ben Wildavasky, "Tilting at Billboards," *New Republic* (Aug. 20, 1990): 19.

Given the virulence of the protests, R. J. Reynolds abandoned its plans to test market the cigarettes in Philadelphia. It decried the negative attention being focused on the brand by a few zealots and angrily compared the acceptability of a retailer designing a line of clothing for blacks with the outcry accompanying the same marketing strategy for a cigarette.

On March 16, 1990, the *Chicago Tribune* announced that R. J. Reynolds Tobacco Company had stated it was not likely to pursue the controversial marketing of Uptown. But the company defended its marketing efforts.[6] The critics had won.

A Similar Controversy: Dakota

Another new cigarette brand, also targeted to a specific group, found itself beset with controversy. This was Dakota, aimed at "virile females."[7] Critics of tobacco's relationship with lung cancer and heart disease were quick to attack this as a blatant appeal to women.

Another group was especially upset. In some American Indian native languages, *Dakota* means friend. Yet, to a group that already had high rates of smoking addiction, such a brand name seemed a betrayal.

Controversies over Tobacco Company Sponsorships

As a result of the 1971 ban on the use of TV and radio cigarette commercials, the tobacco companies desperately sought other media in which to place their hundreds of millions of advertising dollars. They were fairly successful in doing so, but by the early 1990s serious questions were being raised about their use of certain of these media.

Great criticisms and aggressive actions taken against billboards promoting cigarettes and alcohol in black communities already have been seen. Advertising support of black media by tobacco companies was also coming under fire. Yet, such support for many years existed in a vacuum, with few other major firms and industries supporting advertising in black media.

Now, tobacco company support for minority organizations also began to be questioned. The National Association of Black Journalists turned down a $40,000 Philip Morris donation: "we couldn't take money from an organization deliberately targeting minority populations with a substance that clearly causes cancer," said the group's president, Thomas Morgan. "We simply became more aggressive in our fund-raising so we could do

---

[6]Janet Cawley, "Target Marketing Lights Smoky Fire," *Chicago Tribune* (Mar. 16, 1990): 1.
[7]Paul Cotton, "Tobacco Foes Attack Ads that Target Women, Minorities, Teens and the Poor," *Journal of the American Medical Association* (Sept. 26, 1990): 1505.

without it."[8] But for many small minority publications, such resistance was not an option: They would have simply folded without the advertising dollars furnished by tobacco companies.

Women's organizations also are beholden to support from the tobacco industry, which has liberally provided money to such groups at a time when other sources were virtually nonexistent. As a major example of such support, Virginia Slims brought women's tennis into prominence at a time when no one else would. And this raises another major controversy, discussed in the following box.

The Old Joe Camel Controversy

In 1988 R. J. Reynolds Tobacco Company stumbled upon a promotional theme for its slumping Camel brand. Using a sunglass-clad, bulbous-nosed cartoon camel that it called Joe, a $75-million-a-year advertising campaign was instituted. The company featured Joe in an array of macho gear, and it targeted the campaign to appeal to younger male smokers who had been deserting the Camel brand in droves.

The campaign was an outstanding success. In only 3 years, Camel's share of sales among the 18- to 24-year age group almost doubled, from 4.4 percent to 7.9 percent.

But the appeal of Old Joe went far beyond the target age group. It was too potent. It was found to be highly effective in reaching young people, especially children under 13. Children were enamored with the camel character. Six-year-olds in the United States even recognized Joe Camel at a rate nearly equal to their recognition of Mickey Mouse.[9]

According to a study published in the *Journal of the American Medical Association*, teenagers are far better able than adults to identify the Camel logo. Children as young as three could even identify the cartoon character with cigarettes. Of even more concern, Camel's share of the market of underage children who smoke is nearly 33 percent, up from less than a percentage point before the Old Joe campaign. See Table 23.1 for the results of the survey.

THE PROTESTS EXPAND

Uptown

Critics of Uptown initially focused attention on its billboard advertising in ghetto neighborhoods. They soon expanded their protests beyond a single

---

[8]Cotton, "Tobacco Foes Attack Ads," 1506.
[9]Judann Dagnoli, 'JAMA' Lights New Fire Under Camel's Ads," *Advertising Age* (Dec. 16, 1991): 3, 32.

ISSUE BOX

TOBACCO COMPANY SPONSORSHIP OF ATHLETIC EVENTS

Is it right to allow tobacco companies to sponsor certain athletic events? What seems like a simple and uncontroversial question becomes far more complex when we consider the sponsorship of tennis tournaments such as Virginia Slims. There is no longer any doubt that cigarette smoking causes serious damage to heart and lungs. Yet, tennis requires top physical fitness and aerobic capacity.

Although the sponsorship of such athletic events came about as the industry sought alternative media after being banned from TV and radio, their sponsorship has particular advantages from the industry's perspective. It creates the false association of cigarette smoking with vitality and good health, and it directly targets women. Essentially, the company is taking advantage of the inadequate funding of women's sports by making itself a strong presence in this sector.

So we have an unhealthy product—as almost all experts but the tobacco industry stoutly maintain—sponsoring a prestigious athletic event for women that would probably never be able to exist without such funding. Do we refuse to accept this sponsorship? Do we ban all cigarette promotions that appear to have some tie-in with health and fitness? Does the evil outweigh the good?

You are a militant feminist leader with strong convictions that women's athletic events should be promoted more strongly. The major source of funding for tennis and golf tournaments has been the tobacco industry, with no alternative sponsors likely in the near future. Discuss your position regarding the acceptability of tobacco company sponsorships. What is your position on this controversy? Present your rationale as persuasively as you can.

---

cigarette brand to cigarettes in general and to alcohol as well and began whitewashing offending billboards. Their only recourse, they argued, was to use civil disobedience to attract attention to their cause. Although maintaining that they had nothing against billboards in general, protestors

Table 23.1 Survey Results of Knowledge and Attitudes Regarding Camel's Old Joe Advertisements

	Students	Adults
Have seen Old Joe	97.7%	72.2%
Know the product	97.5	67.0
Think ads look cool	58.0	39.9
Like Joe as friend	35.0	14.4
Smokers who identify Camel as favorite brand	33.0	8.7

Source: Data from the *Journal of the American Medical Assn.,* as presented in Walecia Konrad, "I'd Toddle a Mile for a Camel," *Business Week* (Dec. 23, 1991): 34. The results are based on a survey of 1055 students, ages 12 to 19 years, and 345 adults, aged 21 to 87 years.

demanded more educational themes as well as such wholesome products as orange juice for these billboards in ghetto neighborhoods.

Dr. Harold Freeman, director of surgery at Harlem Hospital, is coauthor of a study that found that men in Harlem have a lower life expectancy than men in Bangladesh, at least partly because of alcohol and tobacco use. Speaking to an audience at Harlem's Abyssinian Baptist Church, Dr. Freeman asked, "Is it ethical, is it moral, to sell cigarettes and alcohol specifically to a community that is dying at a much higher rate than others?"[10] And with this, the church's pastor, Rev. Calvin O. Butts III, led his flock out of the church and throughout the city, painting signs with black paint to denote their Afrocentric perspective.

The agitation against billboards was by no means limited to Harlem. For example, in Dallas, County Commissioner John Wiley Price led a group that whitewashed 25 billboards, resulting in arrests and misdemeanor charges. And Chicago priest Michael Pfleger was also arrested for allegedly painting billboards and throwing paint at a billboard company employee.

Antismoking and antibillboard activists were having a field day. California launched a $28.6 million antismoking campaign using money from cigarette taxes. Similarly, the Office of Substance Abuse Policy began a nationwide 7000-billboard campaign targeting drug and alcohol abuse.

Business began heeding the mounting pressure. In June 1990 the Outdoor Advertising Association of America, representing 80 percent of billboard companies, announced a new policy encouraging its members to keep billboard ads for products that are illegal for minors at least 500 feet from schools, as well as from places of worship and hospitals. The association also recommended voluntary limits on the number of billboards that advertise cigarettes and alcohol in any given area, such as minority neighborhoods. Gannet Outdoor, the largest billboard company in North America, began putting decals on billboards near schools and churches indicating that no alcohol or tobacco ads were to be posted there.

Assessment of the Controversy of Targeting Minorities. Was R. J. Reynolds Company the ogre that some critics depicted it as? Or were the critics self-seeking extremists more interested in publicity and crying wolf when the wolf was really rather toothless?

Without question, inner-city blacks have shown higher rates of tobacco and alcohol use than their suburban contemporaries; along with this, they have higher incidences of the accompanying health problems. And despite a few weak company disclaimers, there can be little doubt that tobacco firms

---

[10]Dagnoli, 'JAMA' Lights New Fire," 3, 32.

thought they had developed a new and effective market targeting strategy. The dispute hinges on this:

> Are certain minority groups—such as blacks and women—particularly susceptible to marketing blandishments so that they need to be protected from potentially unsafe products?

While the proponents of controls argue that certain groups, such as young blacks, need such protection, others see that as indicative of paternalism. Even some black leaders decry the billboard whitewashing and the contentious preachings of certain ministers. To Adolph Hauntz, president of the Dallas Merchants and Concessionaires Association, whitewashing signs "treats blacks as if we are a stupid bunch of people that are overly influenced by billboards." And NAACP Executive Director Benjamin Hooks makes the same point, condemning billboard whitewashing for "saying that white people have enough sense to read the signs and disregard them and black people don't."[11] Certainly, tempting people is hardly the same as oppressing them. After all, no one has to buy cigarettes and alcohol.

Butts, Sullivan, and others countered that comments such as those of Hooks simply reflected the tobacco and alcohol industries' success in muting criticisms of their minority targeting policies by their large donations to such groups as the NAACP, the United Negro College Fund, and the National Urban League.

Regardless of the pro and con arguments concerning the susceptibility of inner-city youth to advertisements for unhealthy products, there is more validity to the contentions of susceptibility when we consider the vulnerability of children to the attractive and sophisticated models found in most of these commercials.

Finally, if local, state, or federal legislation is enacted to ban certain products from being promoted on billboards, as was done with radio and TV advertising two decades ago, where should the line be drawn? Should promotions in ghetto neighborhoods be banned for products that are economically extravagant, such as expensive athletic shoes? Or should promotions be banned for high-cholesterol foods that might cause high blood pressure? Or for high-powered "muscle" cars?

Joe Camel

Not surprisingly, a storm of criticism ensued after the American Medical Association's disclosure of the study that found that Joe Camel appealed far

---

[11] Wildavasky, "Tilting at Billboards," 20.

more to children than to adults. Health advocates demanded that the Federal Trade Commission ban the ads. Surgeon General Antonia Novella took the unprecedented step of asking RJR to cancel its campaign voluntarily. Even *Advertising Age* published an editorial entitled "Old Joe Must Go."[12] The basis for the concern, of course, was that the popular ads might encourage underage children to start smoking.

RJR refused to yield. It denied that the ads are effective with children: "Just because children can identify our logo doesn't mean they will use the product."[13] Defensively, Reynolds moved to counter the bad press. It distributed pamphlets and bumper stickers and put up billboards discouraging kids from smoking. And it stoutly maintained its right to freedom of speech.

Assessment of the Old Joe Controversy. Some advertising people believed RJR's stubbornness was badly misguided: "RJR . . . is taking a huge chance. By placing Old Joe as a freedom-of-speech issue instead of an unintentional marketing overshoot, the conglomerate risks goading Congress into bans and restrictions on all tobacco advertising. Lawmakers might, for instance, look more favorably on legislation just introduced . . . which would shift responsibility for tobacco products to the Food and Drug Administration [which] could regulate the tobacco industry into oblivion."[14]

Old Joe was a marketing success beyond all management expectation. But in a time of increasingly critical attention by society, should any firm in a sensitive industry hold itself aloof from a groundswell of denunciations? Are some bumper stickers and billboards with messages to discourage kids from smoking likely to be more than token and impotent efforts, given the popularity of a cartoon character that commands virtually as much recognition and affection as Mickey Mouse?

Then this thought may be raised (while we hesitate to denigrate any firm): Could it be that targeting the young is a long-range strategy for gaining future smokers? See the following box for identification of more cigarette issues.

TARGETING FOREIGN MARKETS

With increasing restraints on cigarette advertising in the United States and the steadily diminishing per capita consumption of cigarettes, it is not sur-

---

[12] "Old Joe Must Go," *Advertising Age* (Jan. 13, 1992).

[13] "Old Joe Must Go."

[14] Craig Stoltz, "RJR Appears Intent on Sticking with Old Joe to the Bitter End," *Adweek Eastern Edition* (Mar. 23, 1992): 18.

ISSUE BOX

CIGARETTES AND SMOKING

The controversies concerning cigarettes go beyond those detailed in this chapter.

- Should smoking be restricted to the workplace? In restaurants? In airplanes?
- What about some firms' decision to bar employees from smoking even when they are not at work?
- Should the tobacco industry pay for employee suits concerning their "right to smoke"?
- Should nonsmokers be protected against passive smoke?
- In general, are the rights of smokers being violated?

Discuss, and even debate, these questions and any other smoking issues you come up with.

---

prising that the industry began focusing greater attention on foreign markets. Unfortunately for cigarette makers, criticisms and restraints did not long remain subdued in these markets, either.

At least as early as 1984, the Royal College of Physicians in the United Kingdom harshly denounced tobacco usage, stating that smoking killed 100,000 people a year in the United Kingdom and resulted in 50 million lost working days a year.[15] But the Royal College particularly condemned the lack of availability of low-tar cigarettes, "which are practically unknown in the Third World. The incidence of lung cancer among men in the Natal Bantustan in South Africa has increased 600 percent in the last 11 years. Developed countries bear a heavy responsibility for the worldwide epidemic of smoking."[16]

By 1990 the *New York Times* was reporting strong criticisms by women's groups and health organizations in India over attempts to promote Ms, a new cigarette brand aimed at upwardly mobile Indian women. Billboards and print ads for the products showed strong, happy Indian women in Western-style clothes and affluent settings. Opposition groups condemned the "evil message that cigarette smoking is part of a healthy and logical way of feminine life."[17]

[15]"Developing Countries: Governments Should Take Action Against Cigarettes Before Too Many People Acquire the Potentially Lethal Habit," *New Scientist* (Dec. 1, 1983): 42.
[16]"Developing Countries," 42.
[17]"Women in Delhi Angered by Smoking Pitch," *New York Times* (National Edition), (Mar. 18, 1990): 11.

Despite intense lobbying by the tobacco industry, two European community (EC) directives on tobacco advertising were proposed by the European Commission in 1989. The first, barring television advertisements, was readily accepted by EC governments and went into effect in October 1991. The second directive would ban press and poster advertising, and was backed by the European Parliament. The second measure awaiting passage would ban tobacco advertising in "any form of communication, printed, written, oral, by radio and television broadcast and cinema." Even logos on cigarette lighters and matches would be forbidden. The tobacco industry, which claimed there was no link between tobacco publicity and the 430,000 deaths a year in Europe from smoking-related diseases, not surprisingly was frantic at this possible outcome.[18] But John Major, prime minister of Great Britain, opposed the measure, and a minority of countries were likely to block it temporarily. (However, bans on print ads for tobacco are already in force in such EC countries as France, Italy, and Portugal.)

With Western Europe's mounting inhospitality to the industry, U.S. tobacco firms today are eagerly pushing into Asia, Africa, Eastern Europe and the former Soviet Union. These markets are big—$90 billion a year—and the local cigarette makers appear highly vulnerable to the slick and aggressive efforts of U.S. firms. For example, Marlboro's cowboy is even more widely known in most of Asia than in the United States. As a result, Philip Morris can get its message across simply by playing the brand's theme song or flashing a single image of the cowboy.[19]

For years, Western companies were kept out of these lucrative markets by governments eager to preserve state tobacco monopolies or anticapitalist ideologies. But these barriers have crumbled, especially in Eastern Europe. Tobacco companies have been invited into enormous new markets such as the former Soviet Union, where "cigarette famines" have long existed. Now Philip Morris is shipping billions of cigarettes to Russia.

Countries in the expanding sales area have few marketing or health-labeling controls. In Hungary, for example, Marlboro cigarettes are even handed out to young fans at pop music concerts.[20]

In Asia protectionist tariffs and import bans had to be cracked before these markets could be entered by foreign tobacco firms. The United States was successful in using Section 301 of its 1974 Trade Act to threaten retaliatory tariffs on the exports of such countries as Japan, South Korea, Taiwan, and Thailand if their markets were not opened to U.S. tobacco firms.

---

[18] "EP Backs Ban on Tobacco Advertising," *Europe 2000* (Mar. 1992): R41.

[19] Mike Levin, "U.S. Tobacco Firms Push Eagerly into Asian Market," *Marketing News* (Jan. 21, 1991): 2.

[20] "The Tobacco Trade: The Search for El Dorado," *Economist* (May 16, 1992): 23.

Tobacco-state representatives in Congress have been strong influences in such pressures, and they were successful in opening up these markets. By 1992 cigarette advertising on television in Japan—it is not allowed in the United States—had soared from fortieth to second place in air time since 1987 and even appears during children's shows. Smoking has greatly increased among women, who were largely ignored before the Western firms arrived but are now prime targets. Tobacco companies found good market potential among women in such Asian areas as Hong Kong, where fewer than 5 percent of women smoke. Philip Morris is tapping this market with its Virginia Slims, a feminine brand famous for its slogan, "You've come a long way, baby."[21]

Assessment of the Overseas Push by U.S. Tobacco Firms. A firm seems entitled to make all the profit it can make. If certain markets are drying up or are being severely constrained, should not a firm have the right to seek other markets aggressively? This is what the tobacco companies are doing.

The issue is clouded because cigarette smoking is generally conceded to be hazardous to health. But it is not immediately so, and by no means certainly so. As long as many people are willing to take the risk, how can the tobacco makers and growers and advertisers and retailers be so negatively judged?

When sophisticated and aggressive promotional efforts are directed at developing countries, where consumers are more easily swayed and far more vulnerable to promotional blandishments, does our perception of what is ethical and what is undesirable conduct change? Should it?

POSTSCRIPT

As we go to press, the social criticisms of the tobacco industry are increasing, as are the governmental threats. On March 25, 1994, a few days after a new $1.25 per pack cigarette tax cleared a House subcommittee, FDA Commissioner David A. Kessler asked Congress for guidance on regulating tobacco as a controlled substance like drugs. The same morning, the Labor Department proposed a virtual ban on smoking in the nation's 6 million private workplaces. The state of Vermont and more than 500 communities, including Los Angeles and San Francisco, have already restricted smoking in malls, restaurants, and other public places. Amid all this, ABC's "Day One" program charged tobacco companies with rigging nicotine levels to hook new smokers.

[21]"The Tobacco Trade," 24.

The industry is fighting back with heavy lobbying. The industry claims that new regulations would take away people's "right to make individual choices." Philip Morris filed a headline-grabbing $10 billion libel suit against ABC. R. J. Reynolds Tobacco Company is increasingly defending its Joe Camel. It boosted spending on Joe Camel ads in 1993 to $37.5 million for the first 11 months of the year, 63 percent more than its budget for all of 1992.

The tobacco industry still has one great strength: plenty of money. For example, industry leaders Reynolds and Philip Morris had a domestic cash flow of $4 billion in 1993. Such funds can go a long way in buying time, both in the courts and in the battle over public policy.[22]

WHAT CAN BE LEARNED?

Public perception of unethical conduct seems to be ever expanding. Formerly, deceptive practices or unsafe products were the most commonly condemned examples of misconduct. But as we have seen in these last few cases, such no longer holds true. The ethical arena for a firm is no longer finite and predictable. It is a lurking quicksand for the unwary or the unconcerned. Consequently, the need for vigilance is greater, and more attention and sensitivity must be accorded a diverse and changing environment.

Effective marketing strategies may need to be reconsidered in today's changing social milieu. Strategies honed in the past may no longer be appropriate; they may be vulnerable to public protests, boycotts, negative publicity, even governmental pressure and regulation. How is a firm to cope with this changing environment?

The answer would seem to lie in increased sensitivity, especially concerning relations with minorities, whether of race, sex, or age. A new brand or a new marketing strategy should be carefully assessed for its acceptability and freedom from potential criticism, before widespread introduction. Even then, surprises may come. And stoutly maintaining a strategy in the face of mounting opposition may not be the best course of action, for the firm or its industry. Sometimes this assessment may necessitate scrapping a successful product or brand or advertising campaign.

[22]Maria Mallory, "Is the Smoking Lamp Going Out for Good?" *Business Week* (April 11, 1994): 30–31; John Carey, "It's Time for Regulators to Stop Blowing Smoke," *Business Week* (Mar. 14, 1994): 34; Maria Mallory, "That's One Angry Camel," *Business Week* (Mar. 7, 1994): 94–95; Junda Woo, "Tobacco Firms Face Greater Health Liability," *Wall Street Journal* (May 3, 1994): A3, A4.

Unacceptable actions in one environment may no longer be transferred to another without risk. Cigarette firms, finding the U.S. market hostile to aggressive promotions, naturally turned their efforts to more hospitable market segments and countries. Not many years ago, such efforts would have been not only effective but would have activated very little critical attention or publicity. Now, a firm may find only a short-term advantage in targeting another market for products and practices criticized at home. Criticism tends to become contagious, even though oceans may separate markets. A firm may no longer be insulated from adverse publicity and possible punitive regulations when it attempts to move aggressively into minority segments and foreign markets.

Does a vocal minority in its aggressive efforts to promote its own self-interest represent acceptable behavior? In a pluralistic society, many minorities are openly encouraged to present their positions. The issue becomes one of degree: What level of critical behavior is acceptable? Is whitewashing or destroying billboards acceptable behavior? Is firebombing the stores of opportunistic shopowners of different ethnic origins acceptable? Where do we draw the line? Unfortunately, there is no common ground for society's approval; inconsistencies abound. For example, society generally views burning stores to be unacceptable. But whitewashing offending billboards seems to be acceptable. Where should the line be drawn, and who is to be the judge: a firebrand preacher, a government agency, the police department, the courts?

Is it ethically right for a firm to vigorously promote a product that is seen by almost everyone except its own industry as unsafe and even deadly? This issue gets to the heart of the whole matter of tobacco production and marketing. Generally considered by all health experts as dangerous and in the long term, life threatening, tobacco is still protected by powerful governmental interests, even if the industry is no longer pampered.

The tobacco industry stubbornly refuses to admit the health charges, citing its own research to the contrary. And the industry is huge, with many stakeholders: tobacco growers, processors, retailers, tax collectors, and influential people in the halls of government.

Not the least of the proponents for the industry are the users themselves—even though this is a declining number every year in this country. The health dangers can be discounted as being both far in the future and affecting only a minority of users. "And never me!"

The morality? It is easy for the stakeholders to rationalize that any bad consequences are uncertain at best, that the good outweighs any bad possibilities. But somehow, some of us are left with the sneaky feeling that maybe, just maybe, the profit motive is deemed stronger than any possible dire consequences to society.

CONSIDER

Can you think of other learning insights or ethical issues?

QUESTIONS

1. Do you have any problems with the idea of militant ministers leading their followers to whitewash offensive billboards? If not, is tearing down such billboards acceptable? Please discuss as objectively as possible.
2. Do you consider the proof adequate that cigarettes pose a substantial health threat and should be banned or tightly constrained? If you accept this position, should tobacco growers be allowed to continue growing such "unsafe" harvests?
3. Is there really any difference in the targeting of minority markets by brewers and the liquor industry and the obvious targeting by certain tobacco brands?
4. Playing the devil's advocate (one who argues an opposing point for the sake of argument), what arguments would you put forth that the cigarette manufacturers should be permitted complete freedom in targeting developing countries?
5. How do you assess the relative merits of the tangible financial contributions that the tobacco industry has made to various minority groups and media, and the negative health consequences of smoking?
6. What is the ethical difference between promoting cigarettes and promoting fatty, cholesterol-laden foods?
7. Are the rights of nonsmokers being too highly emphasized? Do smokers have any rights?
8. Do you actually think Joe Camel leads youngsters to become smokers when they become older? Why or why not?

INVITATION TO ROLE PLAY

1. You are the public relations spokesperson for a major cigarette maker. How do you defend your company's aggressive marketing practices in developing countries?

2. You are a young black woman who uses Uptown cigarettes and likes them. At a church outing your minister denounces Uptown and the company that makes them. Describe how you might respond to such a tirade against your favorite brand.

INVITATION TO RESEARCH

1. Has the hubbub over minority targeting by cigarette companies subsided?
2. Is the popularity of Joe Camel waning today?
3. What is the most current situation regarding overseas incursions by U.S. tobacco companies?
4. Have any fresh criticisms arisen for the tobacco industry?

CHAPTER 24

Conclusions: What Can Be Learned?

In considering mistakes, we should note three things: (1) even the most successful organizations make mistakes but survive as long as they can maintain a good "batting average," (2) making mistakes can be an effective teaching tool, thereby enabling a firm to avoid similar errors, and (3) firms can bounce back from adversity—they can turn around.

We can make a number of generalizations from companies' mistakes and successes. Of course we need to recognize that marketing is a discipline that does not lend itself to laws or axioms. Examples of exceptions to every principle or generalization can be found. However, the business executive does well to heed the following insights. For the most part, they are based on specific corporate and entrepreneurial experiences and are transferable to other situations and other times.

INSIGHTS REGARDING OVERALL ENTERPRISE PERSPECTIVES

The Importance of Public Image

The impact, for good or bad, of an organization's public image was a common thread through a number of cases (for example, the cases in Part I: Food Lion, United Way, and Perrier). But public image certainly played a big role, positively or negatively, in many other cases, such as Harley Davidson, Southwest Airlines, Wal-Mart, and the tobacco industry.

Food Lion showed how bad publicity can destroy, at least temporarily and maybe for much longer, the growth of a company. Coupled with a militant and hostile union that would not let the publicity die, the fallacy of cutting corners to enhance profitability turned out to be misguided indeed. The not-for-profit organization United Way was brought to its knees by revelations about the excesses of its long-time chief executive, William Aramony. Donations dwindled and local chapters withheld funds from the national organization as the reputation of the largest charitable organization was sullied. The frantic efforts of Perrier to protect its image of purity when quality control problems surfaced perhaps exacerbated the situation. The market share it lost during the episode was never to be regained. As for the tobacco industry, it seems to be forever putting its foot in its mouth in its undeviating quest to maximize profits at any cost.

Harley Davidson, the cycle maker, shows an image turnaround of monumental proportions. For decades the image of the black-jacketed motorcyclist was in the pits; but in the 1980s this turned around to become even a status symbol. Harley executives helped develop the new mystique, and then exploited it.

We saw some successes in enhancing an image and capitalizing on a positive image. For example, Saturn, Wal-Mart, and Southwest Airlines were able to nurture positive public images that enhanced their growth. And Mary Poldruhi of Parma Pierogies showed an innate talent in building a public image, even catching the attention and support of President Clinton.

The importance of a firm's public image is undeniable, yet some continue to disregard it and either act in ways detrimental to image or else ignore the constraints and opportunities that a reputation affords.

The Power of the Media. We have seen or suspected the power of the media in a number of cases. Coca-Cola, Food Lion, United Way, Perrier, IBM, Dow Corning, and the tobacco industry are obvious examples. This power is often used critically—to hurt a firm's public image. The media can fan a problem or exacerbate an embarrassing or imprudent action. In particular, this media focus can trigger the herd instinct, in which increasing numbers of people join in protests and public criticism.

We can make five key generalizations regarding image and its relationship with the media:

1. It is important to maintain a stable, clear-cut image and undeviating objectives.
2. It is very difficult and time-consuming to upgrade an image.
3. An episode of poor quality has a lasting stigma.
4. A good image can be quickly lost if a firm relaxes in an environment of aggressive competition.
5. Well-known firms, and particularly not-for-profit firms depending on voluntary contributions, are especially vulnerable to critical public scrutiny and must be prudent in safeguarding their reputation.

The Need for a Growth Orientation—But Not Reckless Growth

The opposite of a growth commitment is a status quo mindset, one uninterested in expansion and the problems and work involved. In its early years, Harley Davidson was content with the status quo, and as we saw, this eventually, albeit slowly, changed. Yet even now with favorable public attitudes toward its big motorcycles, the company is choosing a slow growth production policy and only partially satisfying demand. One wonders whether the image of the Harley will sufficiently protect it from major competitive inroads.

In other cases firms had strong growth commitments but somehow let competitiveness slip and fell back, sometimes after decades of market dominance. IBM and Sears readily come to mind here, as does Borden. Now they face downsizing, selling off some of their businesses, to concentrate on the core.

In general, how tenable is a low-growth or no-growth philosophy? Although at first glance it seems workable, such a policy sows the seeds of its own destruction. Almost four decades ago the following lesson was pointed out:

> Vitality is required even for survival; but vitality is difficult to maintain without growth, at least in the American business climate. The vitality of a firm depends on the vigor and ambition of its members. The prospect of growth is one of the principal means by which a firm can attract able and vigorous recruits.[1]

Consequently, if a firm is obviously not growth-minded, its ability to attract able people diminishes. Customers see a growing firm as reliable, eager to please, and constantly improving. Suppliers and creditors tend to give preferential treatment to a growing firm because they hope to retain it as a customer when it reaches large size. We saw an extreme example of this in one entrepreneurial case, OfficeMax.

An emphasis on growth can be carried too far. Somehow the growth must be kept within the abilities of the firm to handle it. Several examples, such as Microsoft, Wal-Mart, and Southwest Airlines, showed how firms can grow rapidly without losing control. But we have the bungled growth efforts of Maytag's Hoover Division in the United Kingdom and of Osborne Computer to warn us that good financial judgment must not be sacrificed to the siren call of growth.

We can make seven generalizations about the most desirable growth perspectives:

1. Growth targets should not exceed the abilities of the organization to assimilate, control, and provide sufficient managerial and financial resources. Growth at any cost—especially at the expense of profits

[1] Wroe Alderson, *Marketing Behavior and Executive Action* (Homewood, IL: Irwin, 1957), 59.

and financial stability—must be shunned. In particular, tight controls over inventories and expenses should be established, and performance should be monitored promptly and completely.

2. The most prudent approach to growth is to keep the organization and operation as simple and uniform as possible, to be flexible in case sales do not meet expectations, and to keep the break-even point as low as possible, especially for new and untried ventures.

3. Concentrating maximum efforts on the expansion opportunity is like an army exploiting a breakthrough. The concentration strategy—such as that of Southwest Airlines—usually wins out over more timid competitors who diffuse efforts and resources. But such concentration is more risky than spreading efforts.

4. Rapidly expanding markets pose dangers from both too conservative and overly optimistic sales forecasts. The latter may overextend resources and jeopardize viability should demand contract; the former opens the door to more aggressive competitors. There is no definite answer to this dilemma, but the firm should be aware of the risks and the rewards of both extremes.

5. A strategy emphasizing rapid growth should not neglect other aspects of the operation. For example, older stores should not be ignored in the quest to open new outlets. Basic merchandising principles, such as inventory control and new merchandise planning, should not be violated. Otherwise, the sales coming from expansion are built on a shaky foundation, growth is not assimilated, and the seeming strength and success is only an illusion.

6. Decentralized management is more compatible with rapid growth than a centralized organization since it puts less strain on home office executives. However, delegation of decision making to field executives must be accompanied by well-defined standards and controls and executed by high-caliber field personnel. Otherwise, the Maytag Hoover fiasco may be repeated.

7. In the quest for rapid growth, the integrity of the product and the reputation of the firm must not be sacrificed. This should be a major consideration when customers' health and safety may be jeopardized. Today the risk of providing poor-quality or unsafe products and services may threaten the very viability of the firm, as we saw with Food Lion, Perrier, and Dow Corning.

Strategic Windows of Opportunity

Four of the great successes we examined resulted from finding and exploiting strategic windows of opportunity. Microsoft's software breakthroughs and its continuing innovative aggressiveness led it to far surpass once-mighty IBM in stock market valuation and profits. Wal-Mart became the nation's largest retailer by giving small-town consumers a variety of goods at the lowest prices, despite the conventional thinking that small towns offered no opportunities. Wal-Mart further exploited its strategic window by developing efficiencies unmatched by other retailers and still providing friendly service. Southwest Airlines found its opportunity by being so cost effective that it could offer cut-rate yet highly dependable short-haul service no other airline could match. And OfficeMax, one of the early category killer chains for office goods, outmatched other chain competitors by being more efficient.

We can make several generalizations regarding opportunities and the finding of strategic windows:

1. Opportunities often exist when a traditional way of doing business has prevailed in the industry for a long time.
2. Opportunities often exist when there are gaps in serving customers' needs by existing firms.
3. Innovations are not limited to products but can involve services as well as such things as method of distribution.
4. For industries with rapidly changing technologies—usually new industries—heavy research and development expenditures are usually required if a firm is to avoid falling behind its competitors. But heavy R & D expenditures do not guarantee being in the vanguard, as shown by the tribulations of IBM despite its huge expenditures.

The Power of Judicious Imitation

Some firms are reluctant to copy successful practices of their competitors; they want to be leaders, not followers. But successful practices or innovations may need to be copied in order for a company to survive. And sometimes the imitator outdoes the innovator. Success can lie in doing the ordinary better than competitors can.

GM's Saturn achieved its initial success by imitating many of the successful practices of its Japanese competitors. Iacocca did the same with Chrysler. And Nike outdid Adidas by imitating the Adidas marketing strategy. We can make this generalization:

> It makes sense for a company to identify the characteristics of successful competitors (and even similar but noncompeting firms) that contributed to their success, and then adopt these characteristics if they are compatible with the imitator's resources. Let someone else do the experimenting and risk taking. The imitator faces some risk in waiting too long, but it usually is far less than the risk that the innovator is taking.

The Need for Prudent Crisis Management

Crises are unexpected happenings that pose threats, ranging from moderate to catastrophic, to the organization's well-being. A number of cases involved crises: for example, Food Lion, United Way, Perrier, Maytag, Osborne, Dow Corning, even Euro Disney. Most handled their crises reasonably well, such as Food Lion, United Way, Dow Corning, and Euro Disney, although we can question how the firms allowed the problems to happen in the first place. However, Perrier, Maytag, and Osborne either overreacted or else failed badly in salvaging the situation.

Most crises can be minimized if a company takes precautions, is alert to changing conditions, has contingency plans, and practices risk avoidance. For example, it is prudent to prohibit key executives from traveling on the same air flight; it is prudent to insure key executives so that their incapacity will not endanger the organization; and it is prudent to set up contingency plans for a strike, an equipment failure, plant shutdown, unexpected economic conditions, or a serious lawsuit. Some risks can be covered by insurance; others need good planning in a calm atmosphere. The mettle of any organization may be severely tested by an unexpected crisis. Such crises need not cause the demise of the company, however, if alternatives are weighed and actions taken only after due deliberation.

Crises may necessitate some changes in the organization and the way of doing business. Firms should avoid making hasty or disruptive changes or, the other extreme, making too few changes too late. The middle ground is usually best. Advanced planning can help a company minimize trauma and enact effective solutions.

Vulnerability to Competition

Competitive advantage can be short-lived, success does not guarantee continued success, and innovators as well as long-dominant firms can be overtaken and surpassed. Perhaps a worst-case scenario is that of Perrier: leaving a market wide open for competitors. With Harley Davidson, IBM, Sears, Adidas, and even United Way, we saw the three C's syndrome of complacency, conservatism, and conceit that often blankets the mindset of leading organizations in their industry. We suggest that a constructive attitude of never underestimating competitors can be fostered by several policies:

- Bringing fresh blood into the organization for new ideas and different perspectives
- Establishing a strong and continuing commitment to customer service and satisfaction

- Periodically conducting a corporate self-analysis designed to detect weaknesses as well as opportunities in their early stages
- Continually monitoring the environment and being alert to any changes

We will discuss environmental monitoring, or sensors, in a later section. For now let us emphasize that the environment is dynamic, sometimes with subtle and hardly recognizable changes. To operate in this environment, an established firm must constantly be on guard to protect its position.

Management by Exception. With diverse and far-flung operations, it becomes difficult to closely supervise all aspects. Successful managers therefore focus their attention on performances that deviate significantly from the expected at *strategic control points*. Subordinates can handle ordinary operations and less significant deviations. Thereby the manager is not overburdened with details.

Management by exception failed, however, with Maytag and its overseas Hoover division. The flaw lay in failing to monitor faulty promotional plans. By the time results were coming in, it was too late.

The Deadly Parallel. As an enterprise becomes larger, a particularly effective organizational structure is to establish operating units of comparable characteristics. Sales, expenses, and profits can then be readily compared, identifying both strong and weak performances so that appropriate action can be taken. Besides providing control and performance evaluation, this *deadly parallel* fosters intrafirm competition, and this can stimulate best efforts.

For the deadly parallel to be used effectively, the operating units must be as equal as possible in sales potential. This is not difficult to achieve with retail units, since departments and stores can be divided into various sales volume categories—often designated as A, B, and C stores—and operating results of stores within the same volume category can be compared. While the deadly parallel is particularly effective for chain-store organizations, it can also be used with sales territories and certain other operating units where sales and applicable expenses and ratios can be directly measured and compared with similar units.

Environmental Monitoring. A firm must be alert to changes in the business environment: changes in customer preferences and needs, in competition, in the economy, and even in international events such as nationalism in Canada, OPEC machinations, changes in Eastern Europe and South Africa, and advances in Japanese productivity and quality control. IBM, Sears, and Harley Davidson failed to detect and act upon significant changes in their industries. Borden misjudged the dynamics of its industry.

How can a firm remain alert to subtle and insidious or more obvious changes? A firm must have *sensors* constantly monitoring the environment.

The sensor may be a marketing or economic research department, but in many instances such a formal organizational entity is not really necessary to provide primary monitoring. Executive alertness is essential. Most changes do not occur suddenly and without warning. Feedback from customers, sales representatives, and suppliers; news of the latest relevant material and projections in business journals; and even simple observations of what is happening in stores, advertising, pricing, and new technologies can provide information about the environment and how it is changing. Unfortunately, some executives overlook or disregard important changing environmental factors that presage impact on their present and future business.

Lean and Mean. A new climate is sweeping our country's major corporations. In one sense it is good: It enhances their competitiveness. But it can be destructive. Wal-Mart, Microsoft, and Southwest Airlines have been in the forefront of the lean-and-mean movement. This movement also has led to the entrepreneurial success of OfficeMax. These firms developed flat organizations with few management layers, thus keeping overhead low, improving communication, involving employees in greater self-management, and fostering innovative-mindedness. Iacocca in the early 1980s was able to make Chrysler the lowest cost domestic automaker. However, illustrative of how difficult it is to keep costs under control, rising overhead forced Iacocca to institute another cost-cutting crusade in the late 1980s.

In contrast, we saw the organizational bloat of such behemoths as IBM, Sears, and Borden, with their many management levels, entrenched bureaucracies, and massive overhead. A virtual cause-and-effect relationship exists between the proportion of total overhead committed to administration/staff and the ability to cope with change and innovate. It is like trying to maneuver a huge ship: Bureaucratic weight slows the response time.

The problem with the lemming-like pursuit of the lean-and-mean structure is knowing how far to downsize without cutting into bone and muscle and becoming counterproductive. As thousands of managers and staff specialists and college graduates can attest, the loss of jobs and the destruction of career paths has been traumatic both for the economy and for society.

Resistance to Change. People as well as organizations are naturally reluctant to embrace change. Change is disruptive; it destroys accepted ways of doing things and muddles familiar authority and responsibility patterns. It makes people uneasy because their routines are disrupted and their interpersonal relationships with subordinates, coworkers, and superiors are modified. Previously important positions may be downgraded or even eliminated, and people who view themselves as highly competent in a particular job may be forced to assume unfamiliar duties amid the fear that they cannot master the new assignments. When the change involves wholesale terminations in a major downsizing, as with IBM, Sears, Borden, Chrysler, and Euro Disney, the resistance and fear of change can become so great that personnel efficiency is seriously jeopardized.

Normal resistance to change can be combatted by good communication with participants about forthcoming change. Without such communication, rumors and fears assume monumental proportions. Acceptance of change is facilitated if employees are involved as fully as possible in planning the changes, if their participation is solicited and welcomed, and if assurance can be given that positions will not be impaired, only changed. Gradual rather than abrupt changes also make a transition smoother.

In the final analysis, however, making needed changes and embracing different opportunities should not be delayed or canceled because of possible negative repercussions on the organization. If change is desirable in order to be competitive, as it usually is with long-established bureaucratic organizations, then it should be initiated. Individuals and organizations can adapt to change—it just takes some time.

Following are generalizations regarding vulnerability to competition:

1. Initial market advantage tends to be rather quickly countered by competitors.
2. Countering by competitors is more likely to occur when an innovation is involved than when the advantage involves more commonplace effective management and marketing techniques, such as superb customer service.
3. An easy-entry industry is particularly vulnerable to new and aggressive competition, especially if the market is expanding. In new industries, severe price competition usually will weed out the marginal firms.
4. Long-dominant firms tend to be vulnerable to upstart competitors because of their complacency, conservatism, and even conceit. They frequently are resistant to change and myopic about the environment.
5. Carefully monitoring performance at strategic control points and comparing similar operating units and their trends in various performance categories can help a company detect weakening positions that need corrective action before competitors intrude.
6. In expanding markets it is a delusion to judge performance by increases in sales rather than by market share; an increase in sales may hide a deteriorating competitive situation.
7. A no-growth policy or a temporary absence from the marketplace, even if fully justified by extraordinary circumstances, invites massive competitive inroads.

SPECIFIC MARKETING STRATEGY INSIGHTS

Strengths and Limitations of Advertising

We can gain several insights regarding the power and effectiveness of advertising, but we face some unanswered questions and contradictions. At the time of the case, Coca-Cola was spending $100 million more for advertising than Pepsi, and all the while was losing market share. Such performance casts doubts about the power of advertising.

However, the right theme can bring success. The Pepsi Generation and the Pepsi Challenge promotions are models of effective advertising. Maytag Hoover's promotional campaign certainly created great attention and interest, misguided though the plan was. The advertising of Perrier and Evian succeeded in promoting products of questionable value. And how can we forget the success of the Joe Camel theme, despite public protests?

Planning and budgeting advertising present some problems. Certain advertisements and campaigns are more effective than others. Other campaigns with higher budgets fall short of expectations. Therein lies the great challenge of advertising. One never knows for sure how much should be spent to get the job done, to reach the planned objectives of perhaps increasing sales by a certain percentage or possibly gaining market share. However, despite the inability to measure directly the effectiveness of advertising, it is the brave—or foolhardy—executive who decides to stand pat in the face of aggressive promotions by competitors.

We draw these conclusions:

> There is no guaranteed correlation between expenditures for advertising and sales success. However, advertising can be effective in generating initial trial. If the other elements of the marketing strategy are relatively attractive, customers can be won.

Limitations of Marketing Research

Marketing research is usually touted as the key to better decision making and the mark of sophisticated professional management. It is commonly thought that the more money spent for marketing research, the less chance for a bad decision. But heavy use of marketing research does not guarantee the best decision, as we saw with Coca-Cola.

At best, marketing research increases the "batting average" of correct decisions—maybe only by a little, sometimes by quite a bit. To be effective, research must be current and unbiased. Marketplace attitudes can change radically if months elapse between the research and the product introduction. And the several million dollars in taste-test research for Coca-Cola hardly reassure us about the validity of even current marketing research.

Admittedly, results of taste tests are difficult to rely on, simply because of the subjective nature of taste preferences. Still, the Coca-Cola research did not even uncover the latent and powerful loyalty toward tradition, and it gave a false "go" signal for the new flavor.

We do not imply that marketing research has little value. Most flawed studies would have been invaluable with better design and planning. And one wonders whether better market research would not have enabled Disney to structure its pricing and other strategies more realistically to the market conditions facing its Euro Disney project.

Surprisingly, we see that many successful new ventures initially used little formal research. Microsoft, Southwest Airlines, and Wal-Mart relied on entrepreneurial hunch rather than sophisticated research. As did Michael Feuer of OfficeMax. Why have we not seen more extensive use of marketing research for new ventures? Consider the following major reasons:

1. Most of the founding entrepreneurs did not have marketing backgrounds and therefore were not familiar and confident with such research.

2. Available tools and techniques are not always appropriate to handle some problems and opportunities. There may be too many variables to ascertain their full impact, and some of these will be intangible and impossible to measure. Much research consists of collecting past and present data that, although helpful in predicting a stable future, are of little help in charting revolutionary new ventures. If the risks are higher without marketing research, these are often offset by the potential for great rewards.

The Importance of Price As an Offensive Weapon

We generally think of price promotion as the most aggressive marketing strategy and the one most desirable from the point of view of society. We have seen two notable marketing successes that geared their major strategy on lower prices than competitors: Southwest Airlines and Wal-Mart. We saw another case where high prices were a real detriment in meeting performance goals: Euro Disney.

The major disadvantage of low prices as an offensive weapon is that other firms in the industry are almost forced to meet the price-cutter's prices—such a marketing strategy is easy to match. Consequently, prices for an entire industry fall; no firm may have any particular advantage, and all suffer the effects of diminished profits. Thus, in many situations competitive advantage is seldom won by price-cutting. But the exceptions to this generally believed statement are, again, Southwest Airlines, Wal-Mart, and OfficeMax. Because of their greater operating efficiencies and lower overhead cost structure, these firms realize good profits while most of their competitors do not even attempt to meet their prices.

In general, other marketing strategies are more successful for most firms—strategies such as better quality, better product and brand image, better service, and improved warranties. All are aspects of nonprice rather than price competition.

At the same time, we have to recognize that in new industries, which are characterized by rapid technological changes and production efficiencies, severe price competition can be expected—and is even necessary to weed out the host of marginal operations that hoped to cash in on a rapidly growing market. However, as Osborne learned, even a substantial position in such an industry does not protect a firm from price competition that can jeopardize its very viability.

ETHICAL CONSIDERATIONS

We have examined Dow Corning's exposure to the silicone breast implant controversy as well as several recent examples of public criticisms toward the tobacco industry. While we cannot delve very deeply into social and ethical issues, several insights are worth noting:[2]

1. A firm can no longer disavow itself from the possibility of critical ethical appraisal. Activist groups will publicize alleged misdeeds long before governmental regulators will. Legal actions may follow.
2. Public protests may take a colorful path, with marches, picketing, billboard whitewashing, and the like, and may enlist public and media support for their criticisms.

Should a firm attempt to resist or to defend itself? No! The bad press, the confrontation, and the effect on public image are hardly worth such a confrontation. The better course of action is to back down as quietly as possible, repugnant though such an action may be to a management convinced of the reasonableness of its position.

GENERAL INSIGHTS

The Impact of One Person

In many of the cases, one person had a powerful impact on the organization. Sam Walton of Wal-Mart is perhaps the most outstanding example. The accomplishments of Lee Iacocca are well known, both with the Mustang and

[2]For much more depth of coverage, see R. F. Hartley, *Business Ethics* (New York: Wiley, 1993).

with the resurrection of Chrysler. Bill Gates, the youthful founder of Microsoft and America's richest man, is perhaps just as well known. The cover and feature article of *Fortune* magazine, May 2, 1994, highlighted Herb Kelleher, the CEO of Southwest Airlines: "Is Herb Kelleher America's Best CEO?"[3] Less well known, but truly an entrepreneur to be emulated, is Michael Feuer of OfficeMax.

One person can also have a negative impact on an organization. William Aramony almost destroyed United Way by his high living and arrogance. Less well known is Adam Osborne, the flamboyant founder of Osborne Computer, who propelled his firm to $100 million in sales in only 18 months, only to sit helpless as it collapsed into bankruptcy a few months later. The impact of one person, for good or ill, is one of the recurring marvels of history, whether business history or world history.

Prevalence of Opportunities for Entrepreneurship Today

Despite the maturing of our economy and the growing size and power of many firms in many industries, abundant opportunity for entrepreneurship still exists today. Such opportunity is present not only for the change-maker or innovator, but even for the person who seeks only to do things a little better than existing, and complacent, competition.

Thousands of entrepreneurial successes are unheralded, although dozens have been widely publicized. While we dealt specifically with new business ventures in Part V, other cases are not so many years away from their births: Microsoft, Wal-Mart, and Southwest Airlines. Opportunities are there for the dedicated. Venture capital to support promising new businesses has increased to more than $1 billion a year. New stock issues and new company formations are booming. But, as we saw with Mary Poldruhi and her Parma Pierogies and Michael Feuer of OfficeMax, some entrepreneurs have successfully bypassed traditional sources of financing.

We explored the great competitive advantage that some older small firms have owing to much lower breakeven points than newer competitors. But in the adventures of entrepreneurship, some owners still leave themselves vulnerable by permitting inventories and accounts receivable to get out of hand, and eventually succumb to cash flow problems. So, entrepreneurship is not for everyone. The great venture capitalists look at the person, not the idea. Typically they distribute their seed money to resourceful people who are courageous enough to give up security for the unknown consequences of their embryonic ventures, who have great self-confidence, and who demonstrate a tremendous will to win.

[3] Kenneth Labich, "Is Herb Kelleher America's Best CEO?" *Fortune* (May 2, 1994): 44–52.

CONCLUSION

We learn from mistakes and from successes, although every marketing problem seems cast in a unique setting. One author has likened marketing strategy to military strategy:

> Strategies which are flexible rather than static embrace optimum use and offer the greatest number of alternative objectives. A good commander knows that he cannot control his environment to suit a prescribed strategy. Natural phenomena pose their own restraints to strategic planning, whether physical, geographic, regional, or psychological and sociological.[4]

He later adds:

> Planning leadership recognizes the unpleasant fact that, despite every effort, the war may be lost. Therefore, the aim is to retain the maximum number of facilities and the basic organization. Indicators of a deteriorating and unsalvageable total situation are, therefore, mandatory.... No possible combination of strategies and tactics, no mobilization of resources ... can supply a magic formula which guarantees victory; it is possible only to increase the probability of victory.[5]

Thus, we can pull two concepts from military strategy to help guide marketing strategy: the desirability of flexibility in an unknown or changing environment and the idea that a basic core should be maintained in crisis. The first suggests that the firm should be prepared for adjustments in strategy as conditions warrant. The second suggests that there is a basic core of a firm's business that should be unchanging; it should be the final bastion to fall back on for regrouping if necessary. Harley Davidson stolidly maintained its core position, even though it let expansion opportunities slither away. Sears and IBM have solid cores that they should be able to maintain and from which they can mount new attacks. Chrysler in its dark days almost lost its core position, but Iacocca was just able to pull it through, with the help of a federal loan guarantee.

In regard to the basic core of a firm, every viable firm has some distinctive function or "ecological niche" in the business environment:

> Every business firm occupies a position which is in some respects unique. Its location, the product it sells, its operating methods, or the customers it serves tend to set it off in some degree from every other firm. Each firm competes by making the most of its individuality and its special character.[6]

Woe to the firm that loses its ecological niche.

---

[4]Myron S. Heidingsfield, *Changing Patterns in Marketing* (Boston: Allyn & Bacon, 1968), 11.
[5]Heidingsfield, *Changing Patterns*, 11.
[6]Alderson, *Marketing Behavior*, 101.

QUESTIONS

1. Design a program aimed at mistake avoidance. Be as specific, as creative, and as complete as possible.
2. Would you advise a firm to be an imitator or an innovator? Why?
3. "There is no such thing as a sustainable competitive advantage." Discuss.
4. How would you build controls into an organization to ensure that similar mistakes do not happen in the future?
5. Array as many pros and cons of entrepreneurship as you can. Which do you see as most compelling?
6. Do you agree with the thought expressed in this chapter that a firm confronted with strong criticism should abandon the product or the way of doing business? Why or why not?
7. We have suggested that the learning insights discussed in this chapter and elsewhere in the book are transferable to other firms and other times. Do you agree with this? Why or why not?

INVITATION TO ROLE PLAY

Your firm has had a history of reacting rather than anticipating changes in the industry. As the staff assistant to the CEO, you have been assigned the responsibility of developing adequate sensors of the marketplace. How will you go about developing such sensors?